The Cilappatikāram
of Iḷaṅkō Aṭikaḷ

Translations from the Asian Classics

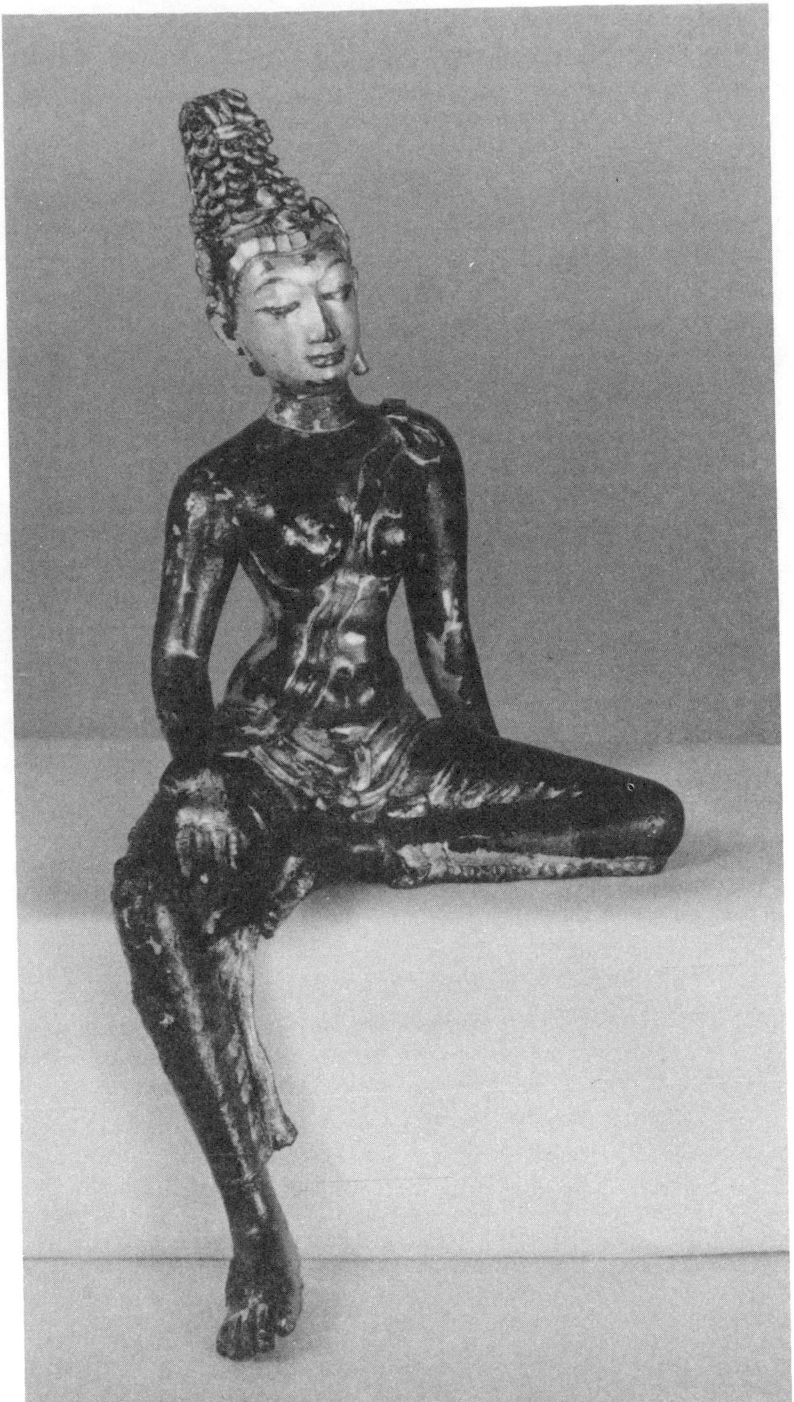

The Cilappatikāram of Iḷaṅkō Aṭikaḷ

An Epic of South India

Translated,
with an Introduction and Postscript, by
R. Parthasarathy

Columbia University Press

New York

Columbia University Press wishes to express its appreciation of assistance given by the Pushkin Fund in the publication of this translation.

Akanāṉūṟu 110 from *Poets of the Tamil Anthologies: Ancient Poems of Love and War,* translated by George L. Hart, Princeton Library of Asian Translations (Princeton, N.J.: Princeton University Press, 1979), and *Kuṟuntokai* 131 from *The Interior Landscape: Love Poems from a Classical Tamil Anthology,* translated by A. K. Ramanujan (Bloomington: Indiana University Press, 1967) are reprinted by permission.

Columbia University Press
New York Oxford

Library of Congress Cataloging-in-Publication Data

Iḷaṅkōvaṭikaḷ.
[Cilappatikāram. English].
The Cilappatikāram of Iḷaṅkō Aṭikaḷ: an epic of South India / translated, with an introduction and postscript, by R. Parthasarathy.
p. cm. — (Translations from the Asian classics)
Translation of: Cilappatikāram.
Includes bibliographical references and index.
ISBN 0–231–07848–X
1. Iḷaṅkōvaṭikaḷ. Cilappatikāram. 2. Epic poetry, Tamil—Translations into English. 3. Epic poetry, English—Translations from Tamil. 4. Epic poetry, Tamil—Translations into English—History and criticism. 5. Epic poetry, English—Translations from Tamil—History and criticism. I. Parthasarathy, R. II. Title. III. Series.
PL4758.9.I4C538513 1992
894′.81111—dc20 92–14647
CIP

Casebound editions of Columbia University Press books are Smyth-sewn and printed on permanent and durable acid-free paper.

Printed in the United States of America

c 10 9 8 7 6 5 4 3 2 1

For

My Mother and Father

Translations from the Asian Classics

Contents

The Book of Maturai

The Book of Vañci

Illustrations and Map

The Pronunciation of Tamil

VOWELS

TRANSLITERATION	SOUND INITIAL	MEDIAL	FINAL	EXAMPLE
a	*a* as in **ago**	*u* as in **cut**	*e* as in **the**	aruḷ, pakkam, cila
ā	*ho* as in **honest**	*a* as in **palm**	*ah* as in **shah**	āciriyar, pāl, nilā
i	*i* as in **is**	*i* as in **ship**	*ey* as in **valley** (British English)	ilai, kōyil, kucci
ī	*ea* as in **easy**	*i* as in **police**	*i* as in **be**	īram, taṇṇīr, tī
u	*u* as in **umlaut**	*u* as in **bull**	*o* as in **to**	uppu, tiruku, teru
ū	*oo* as in **ooze**	*u* as in **rude**	*u* as in **flu**	ūr, nūl, pū
e	*a* as in **any**	*e* as in **bed**		ellai, mey
ē	*a* as in **ace**	*ei* as in **vein**	*é* as in **café**	ēṭu, tēr, mēlē
ai	*ais* as in **aisle**	*ui* as in **guide**	*y* as in **try**	aintu, paiyaṉ, kai
o	*e* as in **entente** (Br. English)	*ou* as in **cough** (Br. English)	*os* as in **gros** (French)	oru, noṭi
ō	*o* as in **old**	*o* as in **note**	*oe* as in **toe**	ōcai, pōla, etō
au	*ou* as in **ounce**	*ou* as in **loud**	*ow* as in **cow**	auvai, vauvāl, nau

CONSONANTS

	VELAR	PALATAL	RETROFLEX	ALVEOLAR	DENTAL	BILABIAL
STOP	k	c	ṭ		t	p
NASAL	ṅ	ñ	ṇ	ṉ	n	m
LATERAL			ḷ	l, r		
			ḻ	ṟ		
SEMI-VOWEL		y				v

TRANSLITERATION	SOUND	EXAMPLE
VELAR		
k	(a) *k* as in **sky**	kaṭavuḷ
	(b) *h* as in **home** in the final or penultimate syllable	akam, Kaṇṇaki, Pukār *Cilappatikāram*
	(c) *g* as in **peg** after ṅ, ṇ, or ṉ	Iḷaṅkō, Ceṅkuṭṭuvaṉ kaṇkaḷ, tiṉkiṟēṉ
ṅ	*ng* as in **song**	aṇaṅku, Araṅkam
PALATAL		
c	(a) *s* as in **yes**	*Cilappatikāram* Cēral, Vaikāci
	(b) *ch* as in **bench** after c, ṭ, or ṟ	taccāṉ, kāṭci, payiṟci
	(c) *j* as in **jump** after ñ	Vañci, Neṭuñceḻiyaṉ
	(d) represents Sanskrit loanwords with the sibilants /ś, ṣ, s/	cirāvakaṉ (śrāvaka) Caṇmukaṉ (Ṣaṇmukha) Caracuvati (Sarasvatī)
ñ	*ny* as in **canyon**	aṟiñaṉ, ñāyiṟu
y	*y* as in **yard**	uyir
RETROFLEX		
ṭ	(a) *d* as in **red**	māṭu, aṭikaḷ, Pāṇṭiya
	(b) doubled ṭṭ is pronounced *tt* as in **letter**	pāṭṭu
ṇ	no corresponding sound in English	āṇṭu, maṇam
ḷ	no corresponding sound in English	makaḷ, puḷḷi
ḻ	no corresponding sound in English	Tamiḻ, Cōḻa
ALVEOLAR		
ṉ	*n* as in **man**	iṟaivaṉ, kāṉal
l	*l* as in **pale**	vayal, cōlai
r (flapped)	*r* as in **cry**	marapu, kuravai
ṟ (trilled)	(a) *r* as in **borrow**	puṟam, aṟivu
	(b) when ṟ follows ṉ, ṉṟ is pronounced *ndr* as in **kindred**	maṉṟam, kaṉṟu
	(c) doubled ṟṟ is pronounced *tr* as in **metro**	Koṟṟavai, nāṟṟam
	(d) maram, "tree," and maṟam, "victory" are homophones, that is, they sound the same, but are different in meaning	
DENTAL		
t	(a) *th* as in **cloth**	tuṇi
	(b) *th* as in **other** between vowels and after n	kātai, viruntu
n	(a) *n* as in **name**	nākku
	(b) the dental n and the alveolar ṉ are often interchanged in writing	canniyāci or caṉṉiyāci

BILABIAL		
p	(a) *p* as in **epic**	pacu
	(b) doubled pp is pronounced *pp* as in **pepper**	paṭippu
	(c) *b* as in **above** after m or ṉ	rompa, nōṉpu
m	*m* as in **mother**	mayil, tāmarai
v	*v* as in **verse**	vācakam

Other aspects of Tamil pronunciation are discussed in the postscript in the section on "Translating the *Cilappatikāram.*"

Preface

The Sanskrit epics, the *Mahābhārata* and the *Rāmāyaṇa,* have dominated the study of the epic traditions of India to the exclusion of poems in the eloquent vernaculars. I hope this translation of the *Cilappatikāram,* a Tamil epic from South India, will set right the imbalance by drawing the attention of readers to, and by making accessible to them, the nearest approach to a great epic that India has produced in a language other than Sanskrit. It is the first translation into modern English verse, and it attempts to discuss the poetics of the Tamil epic based on a study of the *Cilappatikāram* and of such discussions of the issues as are available in Tamil. My aim is a modest one; to offer a translation of the *Cilappatikāram* that will be a pleasure to read as a poem, and to open a window through which to view the work by reconstructing the theoretical issues involved.

The *Cilappatikāram* first appeared in print in 1892. It was published by an unknown Tamil pandit of the Government College at Kumpakōṇam: U. Vē. Cāminātaiyar. This translation in English, published by Columbia University Press to mark the one hundredth anniversary of that notable event, honors the memory of an unusual man to whom Tamils everywhere are indebted for the restoration of their classical literature.

The *Cilappatikāram* is the quintessential Tamil poem that in the words of the poet Subramania Bharati "rends the hearts" (*"neñcai aḷḷum cilappatikāram"*) of all Tamils. This is one reason why it has possessed their imagination for more than fifteen hundred years as a staple in both its oral and its written traditions, crossing generic boundaries, to be retold in verse, prose, fiction, drama, and film.

This translation was completed at the University of Texas at Austin, and what I owe my mentors on that campus—Thomas M. Cable, Betty Sue Flowers, Winfred P. Lehmann, Christopher Middleton, Américo Paredes, and Raja Rao—is immeasurable. Their counsel and encouragement supported me in a difficult undertaking. They meticulously read every draft, testing the lines over and over again on their ears. Their sensitive criticism has enhanced the quality of the translation.

A. K. Ramanujan has, over the years, encouraged my attempt to translate the *Cilappatikāram.* His fine translations from the Tamil "broke new wood," and led us to the "time for carving." I have benefited from the encouragement and challenges of George L. Hart who has recently made us the gift of Kampaṉ in English. Columbia University Press could not have found two more distinguished readers than they.

Both the translation and the study have greatly profited from the discussions in the NEH Institute on Masterworks of Asian Literature in Comparative Perspective at Columbia University, New York, 1987–89, conducted with great distinction by Barbara Stoler Miller, to whom and to A. K. Ramanujan I am grateful for bringing this work to the attention of Jennifer Crewe, senior executive editor, and of Anne McCoy, managing editor, of Columbia University Press. Their patience with me in the preparation of the press copy has been exemplary. John Miles Foley and Walter J. Ong introduced me to the world of oral traditions in the NEH Summer Seminar on "The Oral Tradition in Literature" at the University of Missouri, Columbia, 1987. I thank them for their unstinting support.

At Skidmore College, my three chairs, Phyllis A. Roth, now dean of the faculty, Terence E. Diggory, and Susan A. Kress, together with David J. Burrows, the associate dean, and Ralph A. Ciancio, a former chair, have been extremely supportive of my efforts to open up the canon to include the study of Asian literature in translation. Robert Boyers, Charlotte M. Goodman, Regina M. Janes, Murray J. Levith, Thomas S. Lewis, and Philip J. West, my colleagues in the English Department, were generous with their comments and suggestions. The introduction and postscript benefited from Diggory's painstaking revision, which helped to put them in sharp focus. Barry N. Goldensohn helped me to fine-tune the poem. By looking at it with a poet's eye, he saved me from many embarrassing slips of the tongue.

For their help, always ungrudgingly offered, I thank Merry Burlingham of the South Asia Collection, Mark Rosenberg of the Collection Deposit Library, and Susan Roeckle of the Inter-Library Loan Service of the Perry-Castañeda Library of the University of Texas at Austin, and Marilyn Sheffer and Shirley Webb of the Lucy Scribner Library of Skidmore College.

This work would not have been completed but for the support of my wife Shobhan, and sons Gautam and Arjun. They sustained in me, day after day, the belief that it was worth doing.

R. Parthasarathy
Saratoga Springs, New York
August 20, 1992

INDIA IN THE 5TH c. C.E.

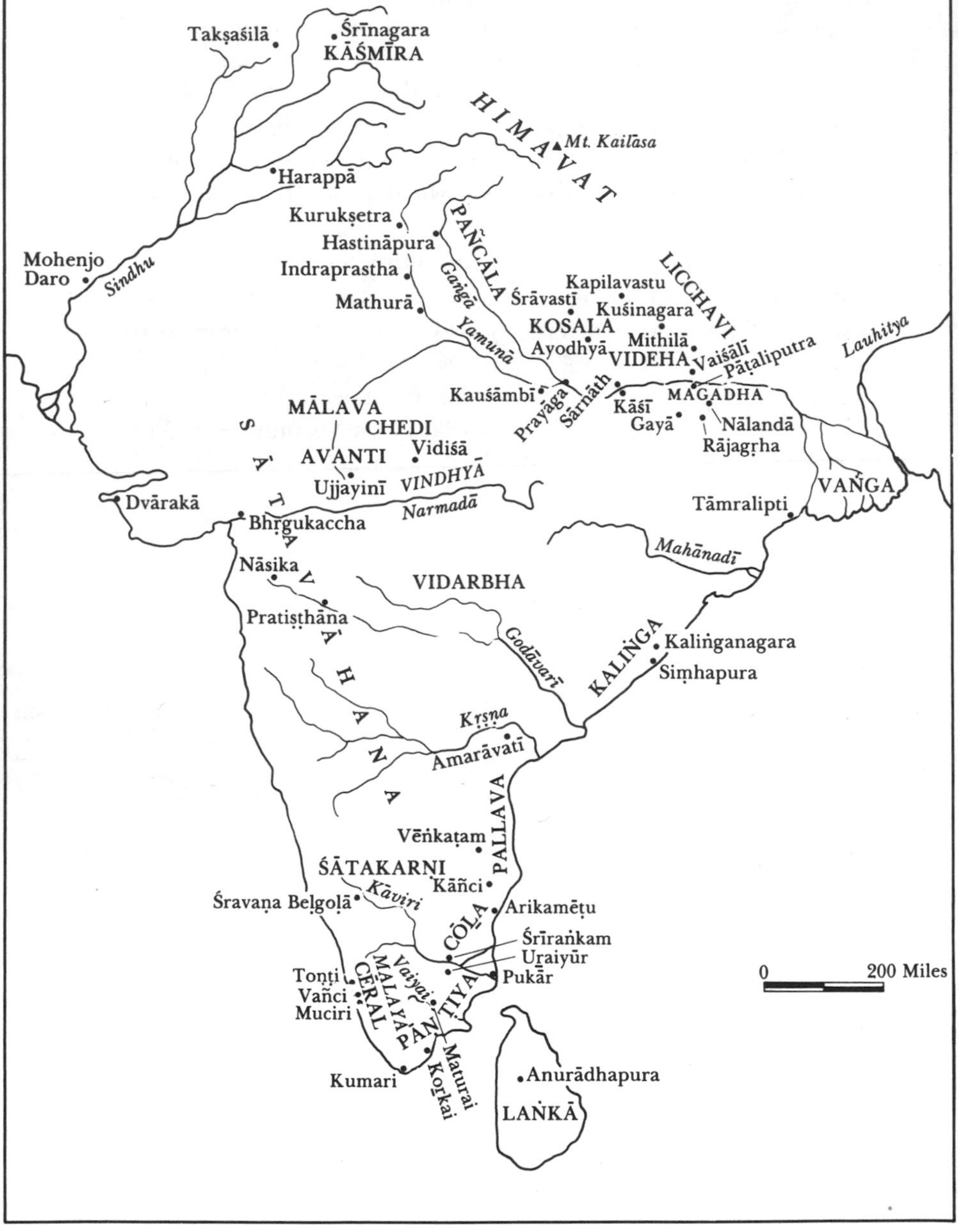

Introduction

A title often encourages readers to ask what kind of poem the work is, and what expectations they should bring to it. In his biography of Dante, for instance, Boccaccio made explicit the poet's intention when he added the epithet *"divina"* to the title *Commedia.* The poem, the *Cilappatikāram,* likewise quite explicitly signals its intention. It tells the story (Ta. *atikāram* < Skt. *adhikāraḥ*) of the events centered around an anklet (Ta. *cilappu, cilampu*). Since the anklet is one of the insignia of the goddess Pattiṉi, the title establishes the sacred character of the story: the heroine Kaṇṇaki's apotheosis into the goddess.

For nearly two thousand years, the Tamil country in southern India has had a distinct culture of its own. Early Tamil literature speaks of the country as bounded by the Vēṅkaṭam Hills (Tiruppati) in the north, by the ocean in the east and west, and by the Kumari Hill (Cape Comorin) in the south. It consisted of the three Tamil kingdoms of the Cōḻa, the Pāṇṭiya, and the Cēral. Two Greek works, *The Periplus of the Erythraean Sea* (1st c. C.E.) and Ptolemy's *Geography* (2d c. C.E.), mention the flourishing Roman trade with southern India, which the Tamil kings encouraged. Poets from Kapilar (2d c. C.E.) to Subramania Bharati (1882–1921) have sung the praise of the Tamil country. Iḷaṅkō is no exception. The *Cilappatikāram* speaks for all Tamils as no other work of Tamil literature does: it presents them with an expansive vision of the Tamil imperium, and at the same time embodies a concern for spiritual knowledge represented by Kaṇṇaki's apotheosis. No other work has endeared itself more to the Tamils than the unhappy tale of Kōvalaṉ and Kaṇṇaki.

The *Cilappatikāram* is one of the literary masterpieces of the world: it is to the Tamils what the *Iliad* is to the Greeks—the story of their civilization. Anyone interested in comparative religion will find it especially useful since it abounds in Jaina, Buddhist, and Hindu traditions. It spells out the problems that humanity has been wrestling with for a long time: love, war, the inevitability of death, evil, and God's justice. It unequivocally admonishes us to "Seek the best help to reach heaven" (30.196–97), since life is unstable, and we cannot escape from our fate. Iḷaṅkō is, after all, a Jaina monk who renounces the world, and his perspective on the events in the epic strongly reflects his own spiritual bias. Epics from *Gilgamesh* (c. 2000 B.C.E.) onwards have reflected on these problems.

The Story

Pukār (the Khaberis of Ptolemy), a flourishing seaport and the Cōḻa capital at the time of the story, is in a festive mood as it celebrates the wedding of Kōvalaṉ and Kaṇṇaki who belong to two of its prominent families. After their marriage, the couple live together happily for some years. Kaṇṇaki excels in keeping house, and Kōvalaṉ dotes on her.

Mātavi, a courtesan, is honored by the Cōḻa king in recognition of her talent as a dancer. He presents her with a garland and one thousand and eight pieces of gold. Mātavi puts the garland up for sale through her maid Vacantamālai, who announces that her mistress will welcome the buyer as her husband. On hearing this, Kōvalaṉ buys the garland. He leaves Kaṇṇaki and moves in with Mātavi. Abandoned by Kōvalaṉ, Kaṇṇaki is heartbroken.

It is spring, and Pukār celebrates the festival of Indra, the king of the gods. People throng the seashore to take part in the revels. Kōvalaṉ and Mātavi join the revelers and set up a pavilion on the seashore. Mātavi takes her lute out and puts it in Kōvalaṉ's hands, and he sings one song after another about a lovely woman who hurts her lover. Mātavi hastily assumes that

Kōvalaṉ is no longer interested in her. She takes the lute from him and sings about a woman betrayed in love. Kōvalaṉ too thinks that she is in love with someone else and leaves her at once. Mātavi returns home with an empty heart. She writes Kōvalaṉ a touching letter to coax him back. But he refuses the letter sent through her maid. In Kōvalaṉ's view, Mātavi's love for him was nothing but an elaborate masquerade. After all, he tells Vacantamālai, Mātavi is only a dancing girl, and he should have known better. Unsuccessful in persuading him to return, Mātavi quietly endures the agony of his loss.

Meanwhile, Kaṇṇaki has a terrible dream in which she learns of some misfortune striking Kōvalaṉ. Soon Kōvalaṉ arrives and confesses his indiscretion. Together they decide to leave for Maturai, the Pāṇṭiya capital, to recoup their fortune with a pair of Kaṇṇaki's anklets, since Kōvalaṉ had squandered all he had on Mātavi. Early next morning, unbeknownst to their parents, they leave Pukār. On the way, they are joined by Kavunti, a Jaina ascetic, with whom they travel to Uṟaiyūr. The three journey south through the bleak forests separating the Cōḻa and Pāṇṭiya kingdoms. Kōvalaṉ and his two companions arrive on the banks of the Vaiyai overlooking the towers of Maturai. He leaves Kaṇṇaki in Kavunti's care and slips unnoticed into Maturai past the Yavana guards to take in the sights of the city. When he returns to the grove where Kavunti is, the brahman Māṭalaṉ informs him of the birth of Maṇimēkalai, his daughter by Mātavi. Kōvalaṉ tells the brahman of his dream in Pukār in which he saw himself riding a horned buffalo, the mount of Yama, the king of the dead. Thinking that misfortune might strike him there, Kōvalaṉ explains, he left for Maturai immediately. Kavunti entrusts Kaṇṇaki to the care of the herdswoman Mātari. Both Kōvalaṉ and Kaṇṇaki follow her to the herdspeople's quarters, while Kavunti remains behind in the grove outside the city.

Kaṇṇaki, with the help of Mātari's daughter Aiyai, prepares food and serves it to Kōvalaṉ. A deeply troubled Kōvalaṉ, once again, despises himself for the troubles he has brought on Kaṇṇaki and their parents, and confesses that he hadn't kept to the straight and narrow path. Kaṇṇaki, for the first and only time, reproaches him and speaks her heart out about the pain his indiscretion has caused her. After a tearful farewell, he leaves for the marketplace with one of her anklets, which he hopes to sell and put aside as capital. As he walks out, a humped bull appears before him, but he does not notice it. It is a bad omen. He sees the royal goldsmith and approaches him to estimate the price of the anklet. The goldsmith examines it and asks Kōvalaṉ to wait near his hut. The goldsmith hurries to the palace and reports to the king that he has caught the thief who had stolen the queen's anklet. The king is on his way to pacify the queen following a quarrel with her. He orders his guards to execute Kōvalaṉ and recover the anklet, thus bypassing the law and doing away with a trial in his anxiety to be reconciled to the queen. The king's guards follow the goldsmith to his hut. Struck by Kōvalaṉ's innocence, they hesitate to kill him. But the goldsmith lectures to them on the skill and cunning of thieves. Just then, one of the guards cuts Kōvalaṉ down with his sword. The goldsmith feels relieved that his crime will now remain a secret, for of course it is he who has stolen the queen's anklet.

Mātari notices inauspicious omens in the herdspeople's quarters, and suspects that some evil is about to happen. To ward off any calamity, she arranges for a round dance enacting incidents from the life of the god Kṛṣṇa to be performed in his praise. When the dance is over, Mātari walks down to the river Vaiyai to bathe. There she hears about Kōvalaṉ's murder, but does not have the heart to tell Kaṇṇaki. Instead, a stranger breaks the news to Kaṇṇaki that Kōvalaṉ has been killed by the king's guards on a charge of theft. Kaṇṇaki is beside herself with grief, and denounces the Pāṇṭiya king Neṭuñceḻiyaṉ. The people of Maturai condemn their king for his injustice. Kaṇṇaki finds her husband in a pool of blood and embraces him. It appears to her that he rises on his feet, wipes the tears from her eyes, and ascends to heaven, telling her to live in peace.

Kaṇṇaki rushes to the palace to demand an explanation from the king. The queen sees inauspicious omens in a dream and is telling the king about them when Kaṇṇaki's cry rends the air insisting on an audience with him. Anklet in hand, she charges the king with the murder of her husband. The king defends himself saying that it was his duty to kill a thief. Kaṇṇaki then breaks open her anklet and gems leap out proving Kōvalaṉ's innocence since the queen's anklet only contains pearls. Kaṇṇaki proves Kōvalaṉ's innocence; the king acknowledges his guilt and dies; the queen follows him. In a rage, Kaṇṇaki walks out of the palace. She curses Maturai, wrenches her left breast off her body, and hurls it over the city, which instantly goes up in flames. The tutelary deity of Maturai appears before Kaṇṇaki and consoles her. She tells her that Kōvalaṉ, in a former birth, was known as Bharata. While he was in the service of King Vasu, he mistook one Caṅkamaṉ, a merchant, for a spy and beheaded him. Distraught beyond words, Caṅkamaṉ's wife Nīli cursed Bharata as she jumped off a cliff. The deity tells Kaṇṇaki that in fourteen days she will join her husband in heaven. Kaṇṇaki then leaves Maturai and travels west till she arrives at Neṭuvēl Hill in the Cēral country from where she ascends to heaven in Indra's chariot.

The hill dwellers witness Kaṇṇaki's ascension. They meet the Cēral king Ceṅkuṭṭuvaṉ camping on the banks of the Periyār and report to him what they had seen. The poet Cāttaṉ is also there, and he relates to the king the unhappy tale of the events that had occurred in Maturai. Queen Iḷaṅkō Vēṇmāḷ tells the king that Kaṇṇaki should be worshiped as a goddess. Ceṅkuṭṭuvaṉ decides to install a memorial stone for Kaṇṇaki taken from the Himālaya and inscribed with her image. He prepares to march to northern India to obtain the stone and also vows to subdue the Ārya rulers who had spoken with contempt about the Tamil kings. He defeats them in a pitched battle. He engraves the image of Kaṇṇaki as the goddess Pattiṉi on the stone brought from the Himālaya and has it lustrated in the river Gaṅgā. The brahman Māṭalaṉ arrives at the king's camp, and informs him that both Kavunti and Mātari have taken their lives to atone for their failure to protect Kaṇṇaki, and that Mātavi has entered a Buddhist nunnery and taken the holy vows. Ceṅkuṭṭuvaṉ then returns home to his capital Vañci. He installs the image of Pattiṉi in a temple, dedicates it, and orders the daily worship of the goddess. On the advice of Māṭalaṉ, he performs the *rājasūya,* "the royal sacrifice," as a mark of his undisputed sovereignty and establishes himself as the universal emperor of the Tamil country. He endows the temple of Pattiṉi and offers worship with a host of kings, including Gajabāhu of Laṅkā. The goddess herself blesses the occasion.

The Form and Theme

The *Cilappatikāram* is a poem that consists in the original Tamil of 5,730 lines, composed in the *akaval* meter probably in the fifth century C.E.[1] This meter is also called the *āciriyam,* "the master's meter," and is the predominant meter of epic poetry. Each line has four feet, except the penultimate one which has only three feet. The shortened penultimate line indicates the approaching end of a canto. Two other meters are also used in the poem: the *kali* and *veṇpā.* There are a few passages of prose; one of them runs to fifty-six lines. They are the earliest examples of prose in Tamil literature.[2] The poem is divided into three books (*kāṇṭams*), and each book is, in turn, divided into cantos (*kātais*).[3] The books are named after the capitals of the three Tamil kingdoms (the Cōḻa, Pāṇṭiya, and Cēral) that constitute the poem's setting. "The Book of Pukār" comprises nine cantos; "The Book of Maturai," eleven cantos; and "The Book of Vañci," five cantos. The cantos range in length from 53 to 272 lines. In addition to the cantos, there are five song cycles that function as a chorus to comment on the events of the narrative: "The Love Songs of the Seaside Grove," "The Song and Dance of the Hunters," "The Round Dance of the Herdswomen," "The Round Dance of the Hill Dwellers," and "The Benediction." The song cycles follow the conventions of classical Tamil poetry.

The three books represent the three distinct phases through which the narrative moves—the erotic, the mythic, and the heroic. The erotic (*akam*) and the heroic (*puṟam*) are the traditional categories of Tamil discourse. The poet enlarges and deepens its resonance by adding a mythic (*purāṇam*) dimension to it. Love in its all its aspects is explored in "The Book of Pukār" using the conventions of Tamil erotic poetry. "The Book of Maturai" retells the myth of Kaṇṇaki's apotheosis into the goddess Pattiṉi (*Pattiṉikkaṭavuḷ*). The heroic aspects of kingship are the subject of "The Book of Vañci." Here again the poet follows the conventions of Tamil heroic poetry. Kaṇṇaki's exemplary life as a chaste wife impacts on all the three phases of the narrative and makes it structurally coherent.

The Author: Iḷaṅkō Aṭikaḷ

Tamil tradition ascribes the composition of the *Cilappatikāram* to Iḷaṅkō Aṭikaḷ (The Venerable Ascetic Prince), the younger brother of the Cēral king, Ceṅkuṭṭuvaṉ (2d c. c.e.). However, there is no mention of Iḷaṅkō in Paraṇar's praise-poem on Ceṅkuṭṭuvaṉ in the *Patiṟṟuppattu* (The Ten Tens, 2d–3d c. c.e.), an anthology of panegyrics on the Cēral kings and used by historians such as K. A. Nilakanta Sastri to reconstruct Tamil history.[4] There is also no mention of Iḷaṅkō in the poem itself. His name appears only in the *patikam,* "prologue," which scholars are of the opinion is a later interpolation. U. Vē. Cāminātaiyar, the poem's first editor, identifies the "I" in "I also went in" (30.167)[5] with Iḷaṅkō Aṭikaḷ.[6]

Canto 30 recounts the tradition that Iḷaṅkō renounced his home and the world on hearing the royal astrologer's prediction that he, and not his elder brother Ceṅkuṭṭuvaṉ, would succeed his father Imayavarampaṉ Neṭuñcēralātaṉ as the Cēral king (169–78). Iḷaṅkō then leaves the palace, and enters a Jaina monastery on the outskirts of Vañci. There he takes the holy vows, thus renouncing temporal authority in favor of the spiritual. It is somewhat exceptional in the Indian tradition for a renouncer (*saṃnyāsin*) to have composed a secular classic such as the *Cilappatikāram,* which is totally unlike a religious one such as the *Rāmāyaṇa* (200 b.c.e.–200 c.e.).

Except for such traditions that have gathered around the poet, there is nothing else we know about him. Even his name is unknown. Gananath Obeyesekere questions Iḷaṅkō's kinship with Ceṅkuṭṭuvaṉ, and considers it "a late interpolation."[7] Since Ceṅkuṭṭuvaṉ's recognition of the cult of the goddess Pattiṉi gave it legitimacy, and institutionalized its status, it is in keeping with the conventions of early Indian literature to ascribe the composition of the poem to a prince of the royal house of the Cērals. This ensures an appropriate pedigree for the poem. Like Homer, Iḷaṅkō was possibly a redactor who took the story of Kōvalaṉ and Kaṇṇaki from the oral tradition and put it into writing.

That the eponymous author was perhaps a Jaina there is little doubt, for Jaina ideas crisscross the poem like a golden thread. Kavunti Aṭikaḷ, a Jaina nun and Kōvalaṉ's spiritual guide through the forests separating the Cōḻa and Pāṇṭiya kingdoms, is an eloquent and persuasive apologist for Jainism. The plot of the poem, again, is firmly tethered to the Jaina doctrine of karma, which we shall discuss in the postscript.

The Epic World

The *Cilappatikāram* shares few epic features with its Indo-European cousins, the *Mahābhārata* (400 B.C.E.–400 C.E.) and the *Iliad* (725–675 B.C.E.). In the Sanskrit and Greek epics, the action is centered around events in the courts of kings and culminates in a great war. The action in the Tamil epic is focused on events in the life of two ordinary people from the influential merchant class that rose to prominence in the centuries following the end of the Mauryan empire, events that ultimately bring the protagonists into conflict with the Pāṇṭiya king. War, therefore, is not central to the Tamil epic as it is to the Sanskrit and Greek. This is understandable. Given its Jaina bias, the Tamil epic is informed throughout by the idea of nonviolence, as the nun Kavunti never fails to emphasize. The *Mahābhārata* and the *Iliad,* on the other hand, revel in violence. An explanation can, perhaps, be sought in the historical experience of the peoples themselves: the Indo-Europeans were nomadic herdspeople, whereas the Dravidians were tillers and settled in their way of life.

In the *Mahābhārata* and the *Iliad,* the protagonists Yudhiṣṭhira and Achilles are male; the protagonist Kaṇṇaki, in the *Cilappatikāram,* is a female. This feature alone is significant enough for us to propose that the *Cilappatikāram* stands in a subversive relationship to the *Mahābhārata.* By making a woman the protagonist, Iḷaṅkō rewrites the epic tradition by subverting its essentially androcentric bias. He displaces the semidivine warrior, and the heroic ethos that surrounds him, with a mortal woman who is transformed into a divinity. Iḷaṅkō's work is unmistakably revisionary. It does not imitate the Sanskrit epic, prestigious though that is. It builds upon forms indigenous to Tamil, which it perfects. As a female protagonist, Kaṇṇaki disrupts the epic structure and calls its presuppositions into question. In her grief, she becomes a woman out of control and therefore dangerous. Viewed in this light, "The Book of Vañci" is probably an elaborate rite of propitiation to appease the wrath of Kaṇṇaki and to invoke her blessing as the goddess Pattiṉi. By foregrounding Kaṇṇaki, rather than any one of the three Tamil kings as would be normal in an epic, Iḷaṅkō shows his preference for the mythic and to a lesser extent the erotic over the heroic aspects of the poem.

The hero in the Indo-European epic is usually semidivine. Yudhiṣṭhira's father is Dharma, the god of justice, and his mother Kuntī is a Yādava princess. Achilles' mother is the nereid Thetis, and his father is Peleus, king of Thessaly. In the Tamil epic, the protagonist is invariably human. Kaṇṇaki is born into a noble merchant family of Pukār, but changes into a goddess in the course of the epic. The *Cilappatikāram,* therefore, represents a bold departure from the epic tradition as we understand it. While society in the *Mahābhārata* is organized on the basis of caste (*varṇa*), the *Cilappatikāram* depicts a pattern of social organization indigenous to the Tamils. The organization follows the traditional division of the Tamil country into its four regions (hill, forest, farmland, seashore, and wasteland) and the occupations of the people associated with them.

In spite of these obvious differences, there are however some resemblances between the *Cilappatikāram* and other epics. The function of the epic was originally, as Albert Lord reminds us, magical and ritual.[8] It was performed to ward off evil. Only when the function became obscured or was forgotten, did the epic come to be looked upon as entertainment. Both the *Mahābhārata* and the *Rāmāyaṇa* are revered as sacred poetry even today. The *Mahābhārata* has its ritual underpinning: it is considered the fifth Veda. The *Rāmāyaṇa* is recited as incantation and ritual and performed as entertainment on the festival of Rāma, the Rāmanavamī, in Caitra (March–April). The hexameter in the *Iliad* once had, as Jan de Vries points out, an apotropaic effect.[9] The meter was the vehicle of Apollo's oracle in Delphi. The apotheosis of Kaṇṇaki into the goddess Pattiṉi confirms the sacred character of the *Cilappatikāram.*

The Indian epics are sacred texts exemplifying and promoting the four great ends of humans—duty, wealth, desire, and liberation—through the characters as they evolve in the course of the story. The poet, protagonist, and audience participate equally in the regeneration of the human spirit. The poet is never primarily an entertainer, but essentially a guide who offers enlightenment beyond the local social and political knowledge. This vision ultimately shapes the generic characteristics recognizable in every epic poem. The epic attempts to narrate this regeneration dramatically in terms of a sequence of onset, conflict, reversal, and denouement. Events are carefully selected as emblems of spiritual dilemmas. The action is circular in that the protagonists find their way back to themselves after a series of humiliations and ascend to an enlightenment beyond time.

We do not know if the *Iliad* was at any time a sacred text for the Greeks. Simone Weil eloquently reminds us that it is only in the Gospels, and not so much in the *Iliad* or Attic tragedy, that the Greek genius "makes itself felt . . . by the fact of commanding us to seek to the exclusion of every other good 'the kingdom of God and his righteousness'."[10] Only for one triumphant moment does the *Iliad* veer towards the supreme grace of the Gospels: the love of one's enemies that overcomes the fury to avenge the death of a son, or of a friend.

> But when they had put aside their desire for eating and drinking,
> Priam, son of Dardanos, gazed upon Achilles, wondering
> at his size and beauty, or he seemed like an outright vision
> of the gods. Achilles in turn gazed on Dardanian Priam
> and wondered, as he saw his brave looks and listened to him talking.
> But when they had taken their fill of gazing one on the other . . . .
> *Iliad* XXIV.628–33[11]

Thus the Indian and Greek worldviews are fundamentally different. Faced with the inevitability of death, the Indian mind turns to metaphysical reflection while the Greek mind engages itself with life more fully and urgently. This difference is reflected in their epics. Consistent with the four ends of humans, the protagonists in the Indian epics are urged to renounce this world as unreal and to seek enlightenment. The protagonists in the Greek epics, on the other hand, cherish life and enjoy it to the utmost. While Homer lies embalmed in a book and is the special preserve of scholars, the daily life of the Hindus continues to resonate with the uplifting stories from their epics.

The Heroine: Kaṇṇaki

The epic world is dominated by patriarchy whose sexual fears it reflects. Patriarchy regards female sexuality as a threat to its power and attempts to contain it. Repressed for centuries by patriarchy, women were forced into silence while struggling to use a discourse that was inadequate to express reality fully. Women's voices have gone unheard, for historically they were excluded from participating in the cultural dialogue that shapes reality. In order to recover their voice, Claudine Herrmann urges women to be *voleuses de langue,* thieves of language, female Prometheuses.[12] The myth of Philomela is a classic statement of this theme: patriarchy reduces Philomela to the impotence of silence and she subverts it.

Abandoned by Kōvalaṉ, Kaṇṇaki silently puts up with indignity and grief. Under patriarchy, any other response by a faithful wife would be unacceptable. When Kōvalaṉ is executed, she is outraged: she finds her voice and severely censures the king. Her voice renders him speechless, and he collapses before her. In this confrontation between king and commoner, it is the king who is humbled and made to eat his words. Denied love, Kaṇṇaki turns into an outlaw: she has no father, husband, or son to live for, and under patriarchy a woman does not live for herself alone. Kaṇṇaki ritually unsexes herself. First, she breaks the anklet in the king's presence to establish her husband's innocence. A symbol of Kaṇṇaki, the anklet is in metonymic relation to her, and functions as an extension of her personality. She turns this ornament into a terrible instrument of vengeance against the king for his unjust execution of her husband. The anklet becomes a noose around the king's neck, and Kaṇṇaki in turn becomes his executioner.

As a symbol, the anklet is encrusted with resonances. In folklore, it is considered to be an effective symbol of protection against evil spirits. This probably derives from the symbolic value of the circle. Thus, an apotropaic effect is often attributed to it. Taking a person's anklet signifies robbing that person of connections, strength, and dignity. This is also true of the marriage pendant, the girdle, and the sacred thread. The investiture with the sacred thread is an essential part of spiritual consecration. In the Bible, the angels are thought to be girded as a sign of both their strength and their control over their sexual energy. Losing or breaking the girdle or anklet signifies calamity.

The fall of Maturai begins with the royal goldsmith's theft of the queen's anklet. Kōvalaṉ arrives in Maturai to dispose of Kaṇṇaki's anklet at this critical juncture—an inauspicious omen in itself. His meeting with the goldsmith is described in one telling image: "He was/ Like Yama's messenger" (16.119–20). To save his own neck, the unscrupulous goldsmith accuses Kōvalaṉ of the theft before the king, and Kōvalaṉ is instantly put to death on the king's orders.

Kaṇṇaki's breaking of her anklet in the presence of the king is perhaps the most inauspicious omen of all. It is an acknowledgment of the end of her married life. She releases her sexual energy that had so far been contained by the anklets on her person. The anklet, a symbol of her stern chastity, turns into an instrument of vengeance.[13] It also functions as a metonymy for her sexual organ. Breaking it signifies castration. With her husband dead, she has no use for sex. This is further reinforced when she wrenches her breast, an embodiment of sexual power, off her body and hurls it at the towers of Maturai. Āṇṭāḷ (9th c. C.E.) has this incident in mind when she says that her breasts are on fire, and that the fire can only be put out when her breasts are hurled at Kṛṣṇa:[14]

> He didn't ask for me. And it didn't trouble him
> I was melting inside, devastated. Brazen-faced
> that he is, he robs and plunders. These breasts
> of mine—it was pointless their gaping at him—
> I'll pluck them to their very roots,
> and fling them at his chest to put out their flames.
> *Nācciyār-tirumoḻi* 13.8[15]

I know of no occasion in any literature where a woman turns her breast into a fiery torch and burns down an entire city. Marlowe's Helen is, perhaps, the closest example:

> Was this the face that Launcht a thousand ships,
> And burnt the toplesse Towers of Ilium?
> *Dr. Faustus* V.i.1768–69[16]

Only the Amazons (< Gk. *a* – without + *mazos* breast), that race of female warriors who repeatedly battled the Greeks of mythology, removed a breast to facilitate throwing the spear or drawing the bow.

Finally, Kaṇṇaki ceremoniously snaps her golden bracelets in the temple of Koṟṟavai, the goddess of war and victory, on the outskirts of Maturai and confirms her status as a widow and outlaw. It is ironic that the goldsmith's theft of the queen's anklet parallels Kōvalaṉ's disposal of Kaṇṇaki's. Both actions are fraught with ominous implications for their owners: both Kaṇṇaki and the queen become widows; the queen dies from the shock, and Kaṇṇaki is changed into a goddess. The "anklet," as one of the two terms in the title *Cilappatikāram,* thus attests to Kaṇṇaki's importance as the heroine.

"The epic hero," observes Lawrence Lipking, "tends to define himself by leaving a woman behind."[17] The roster of abandoned women in epics includes Ariadne, Penelope, Dido, Aṃbā, Sītā, and Kaṇṇaki. Throughout history, patriarchy has oppressed women and excluded them from the centers of power. A few, however, resisted the oppression and freely spoke their minds. During Odysseus' absence from Ithaca, his wife Penelope remains faithful to him despite importunate suitors whom she puts off by weaving and unweaving a shroud for her father-in-law Laertes. In Wallace Stevens's poem, Penelope's intense meditation recreates Odysseus' return as she waits for her actual husband to come home and be reunited with her:

> His arms would be her necklace
> And her belt, the final fortune of their desire.
> "The World as Meditation"[18]

It is precisely this "final fortune" that Kaṇṇaki is denied. When Kōvalaṉ is killed, she forfeits both her anklet, and, what is even more precious, the "necklace" of his arms. A widow, she becomes empty (one of the etyma for "widow" is the Skt. *vindhate,* "it becomes empty") on the death of her husband. From an angel in the house, she is metamorphosed into an avenging Fury outside the law. It is as an outlaw that Kaṇṇaki challenges and subverts the authority of the king:

> Till the wrath that burns in me
> Is appeased, I will not hold my husband
> In my arms. I will confront the evil king
> And demand an answer (19.91–94).

The Pāṇṭiya king reels under the blow of her curse, and openly admits the error in his judgment:

> Am I a king? I listened to the words of a goldsmith!
> I alone am the thief! Through my error
> I have failed to protect the people
> Of the southern kingdom. Let my life crumble in the dust
> (20.89–92).

Neṭuñceḻiyaṉ atones for his failure to administer justice and dies of shock. Kaṇṇaki vindicates her husband's innocence. Her wrath is not appeased, however, till Maturai itself is reduced to ashes for its complicity in the murder. Such is the power of abandoned women: they are the scourge of patriarchy. Kaṇṇaki represents the ancient Tamil belief in a divine mechanism of retributive justice to those whom human law fails to protect. Her action is necessary to the orderly operation of society. Hélène Cixous reminds us:

> Women must write through their bodies. . . . For when the Phallic period comes to an end, women will have been either annihilated or borne up to the highest and most violent incandescence. Muffled throughout their history, they have lived . . . in silences, in aphonic revolts.[19]

Kaṇṇaki undergoes precisely such an "incandescence" when she hurls her severed breast on Maturai. By her unprecedented action, she is, in fact, inscribing her curse, writing it as a lasting record, stamping it on the face of Maturai. So effective is her curse that a fire soon engulfs the city and burns it down. Nowhere in literature that I am aware of is the power of a woman's body—a body that has, throughout history, been possessed, exploited, and abused by patriarchy—so fiercely depicted. Abandoned women such as Kaṇṇaki have the power to strike terror in the hearts of men and are therefore dreaded.

In Tamil folklore, it is an inauspicious omen to see a woman with her hair untied and disheveled. A classical Tamil poem speaks of a bard who is on his way to meet the king, his patron. He sees a woman with her hair undone approach him, and his thoughts at once turn to the king. Fearing for the king's life, he prays for his safety, but on his arrival he learns that the king is dead.[20] Widows are expected to leave their hair untied or to have it removed altogether. Widowed by her husband's death, Kaṇṇaki with her hair in disarray storms into the king's presence to demand an explanation. Iḷaṅkō transforms her at this moment into a force of nature:

> "I am a sinner," cried an onlooker.
> Tears pour from her blue-lotus eyes. Her hand
> Clasps a single anklet. Lifeless her body.
> Like a forest, her dark hair spread about her.
> The Pāṇṭiyan saw her, and died of terror
> (20.102–106).

Wild, disheveled hair, sometimes interlaced with snakes, refers to fearsome deities such as the Gorgon Medusa who had the power to turn into stone anyone who looked at her. Kaṇṇaki exercised a similar power over the king: he "saw her, and died of terror." When Kōvalaṉ was alive, she wore her hair in "five, fragrant plaits," one of the traditional coiffures of a married woman.

The comparison of a woman's disheveled hair to a forest is in itself unusual. As a symbol, the forest is enveloped in complex associations. It is connected with the symbolism of the female principle or of the Mother Goddess. All forms of life thrive uncontrolled in the forest. Since the female principle is associated with the unconscious, the forest is also a symbol of the unconscious. Forests generally are outside the pale of human settlements, and therefore represent the opposite of order and control. Iḷaṅkō suggests that Kaṇṇaki has removed herself from the human community to become an uncontrollable force of nature. We can see here the beginning of Kaṇṇaki's transformation into a deity.

Notes

1. No objective evidence in the form of archaeological or epigraphical records has survived on the basis of which to establish the dates. All dates are, therefore, only conjectural. In dating the texts, I have followed Zvelebil, *Tamil Literature* (1975).

2. See Asher, *Some Landmarks in the History of Tamil Prose,* p. 6.

3. Only twenty-two of the thirty cantos are called *kātai,* "story;" the other eight cantos are called by different names: one is a *maṅkaḷavāḻttuppāṭal,* "a song that praises or blesses," especially at the beginning or end of a poem; three are *vari,* a kind of folksong that may be combined with dance; two are *kuravai,* a round dance with song; and two are *mālai,* "a garland or wreath" of verses.

4. See Nilakanta Sastri, *A History of South India,* pp. 115–45.

5. The citations refer to the translation, and are indicated in the introduction and postscript parenthetically by canto and line numbers as here, or by canto and song numbers as 7:11–14.

6. *Cilappatikāram* of Iḷaṅkō Aṭikaḷ, ed. with the *Arumpatavurai* and Aṭiyārkkunallār's commentary by U. Vē. Cāminātaiyar, 8th printing (Madras: Śrī Tiyākarāca vilāca veḷiyīṭu, 1968), p. 586.

7. Obeyesekere, *The Cult of the Goddess Pattini,* p. 372.

8. Lord, *The Singer of Tales,* p. 67.

9. de Vries, *Heroic Song and Heroic Legend,* p. 9.

10. Weil, "The *Iliad,* Poem of Might," p. 260.

11. Lattimore, trans., *The Iliad of Homer,* pp. 491–92.

12. Quoted in Ostriker, *Stealing the Language,* pp. 210–11.

13. See Zvelebil's comments on the symbolism of the anklet in *The Smile of Murugan,* pp. 182–83.

14. Hardy, *Viraha-bhakti,* p. 425, fn. 34.

15. *Nālāyirativiyappirapantam* [The Four Thousand Divine Compositions], ed. Aṇṇaṅkarācāriyar. The translations from the Tamil and Sanskrit are mine, unless otherwise indicated.

16. Marlowe, *Dr. Faustus,* p. 220.

17. Lipking, *Abandoned Women and Poetic Tradition,* p. xvi.

18. Stevens, "The World as Meditation," p. 521.

19. Cixous, "The Laugh of the Medusa," p. 290.

20. *Puṟanāṉūṟu* 260.

The Cilappatikāram of Iḷaṅkō Aṭikaḷ

An Epic of South India

Prologue

"A chaste woman with only one breast
Stood in the thick shade of the kino
Tree, incandescent in its golden flowers.
Indra, lord of the immortals, with kindred gods
Came down, revealed her loving husband to her,
And before our very eyes led her to heaven.
It passed our belief. Be pleased to know this."

So reported the Kuṟavas from the Red Mountains
As they crowded round Ceṅkuṭṭuvaṉ,
The Cēral king, and brother of Iḷaṅkō,
Who had renounced the throne
To be a monk in the cloister at the East Gate.
With him was Cāttaṉ, poet of exquisite Tamil,
Who then spoke:
"I know what happened.
In Pukār, fabled city of the Cōḻa king
Wreathed in ātti flowers, lived
A merchant, Kōvalaṉ. Enamored with a dancing girl,
Mātavi, expert in her art, he ran through
His entire fortune. With his wife Kaṇṇaki,
He traveled to Maturai, Pāṇṭiya city
Acclaimed in song, to sell her echoing anklet.
There, on a street in the marketplace, Kōvalaṉ
Showed it to a goldsmith who exclaimed:
'No one, except the chief queen, is fit
To wear this anklet. Stay right here.'
At once, he informed the Pāṇṭiya king:

Lines 1–25

'I saw the queen's anklet, filled
With gems, in a stranger's hand. There's your thief.'
At that moment, Kōvalaṉ's karma came
Full circle. The king, wreathed in margosa,
Unthinking, ordered his faithful guards:
'Kill that thief. Recover the anklet.'

"Thus Kōvalaṉ died. His wife, now homeless,
Collapsed in a heap of tears. But her chastity
Became the king's scourge. Wrenching off
One of her breasts, the pearls still embedded
In it, she flung it at the towering city
Of Maturai, and burned it to ashes.
This is the Pattiṉi praised by all."

Iḷaṅkō then asked: "You said his karma
Was fulfilled. What was his karma?"

Cāttaṉ then replied:
"Listen, holy one!
One night, in the ancient city
Of Maturai of immaculate fame, I was resting
In the silver hall of the meeting place
In the temple of our lord Śiva, his matted hair
Adorned with the laburnum. It was then I saw
The guardian deity of Maturai appear
Before the awesome Pattiṉi, overcome with sorrow,
And speak to her: 'Woman, from whose breast
Sprung flames of wrath, the karma
Of your past lives has ended.

Lines 25–45

You and your husband, in an earlier life,
Were cursed by the wife of the merchant Caṅkamaṉ
From Ciṅkapuram of immortal fame. O woman,
Lovely in your thick, flowing hair,
In fourteen days from now, you will once again
See your husband, radiant in his divine,
Not human, form.' These prophetic words
I heard are indeed true."
Iḷaṅkō then spoke:

"We shall compose a poem, with songs,
To explain these truths: even kings, if they break
The law, have their necks wrung by dharma;
Great men everywhere commend
Pattiṉi of renowned fame; and karma ever
Manifests itself, and is fulfilled. We shall call the poem
The *Cilappatikāram,* the epic of the anklet,
Since the anklet brings these truths to light."
And Cāttaṉ begged of him:
"Be gracious enough,
Revered one, to write it yourself,
Since it relates to all the three kings."

In response to Cāttaṉ's solemn petition,
Iḷaṅkō Aṭikaḷ of illustrious fame
Composed a poem with songs, blended with prose,
In thirty cantos, each titled as follows:
The song of praise; the setting up of a home
By the parents; the recognition, by the king,
Of Mātavi's first performance; in praise

Lines 45–66

Of the evening; the celebration in the city of the festival
Of Indra; bathing in the sea; the love
Songs of the seaside grove, thick
With flowers; the pain of Mātavi's separation,
Inflamed by the coming of spring; the nature
Of the ominous dream; questions about country scenes;
The scenes of the forest; the song and dance
Of the hunters; Kaṇṇaki, her hair adorned with flowers,
Waiting on the outskirts of the city; the sights
Of the city resonant with the sound of drums;
The refuge offered to the lovely Kaṇṇaki;
The scene of the murder; the round dance of the herdswomen;
The wreath of sorrow as news of the fire
Spreads; the quaking of the city at midday
As Kaṇṇaki goes round it; her demand for justice
Before the king of peerless fame; the crown
Of wrath; the great fire; the explanation
Offered by the guardian deity of Maturai;
The round dance of the hill dwellers, their hair adorned
With flowers dripping honey; the choice
Of a stone; removing it; the lustration;
The dedication of the memorial stone; the benediction;
And the granting of a favor by the goddess.
The poem, composed by Iḷaṅkō, to explain
The ends of humans, Cāttaṉ, the grain dealer of Maturai,
Heard. This prologue speaks of its beginning.

Lines 66–90

The Book of Pukār

Canto 1
The Song of Praise

Let us praise the Moon. Like the cool, white parasol
Of the Cōḻa king, his garland heavy
With pollen, he blesses this good earth.
Let us praise the Sun. Like the proclamations
Of the lord of the Kāviri, he travels
Ever around Meru crowned with gold.
Let us praise the Rain. Like the Cōḻa king,
His kingdom shut in by the roaring sea,
He pours out abundantly his bounty from above.
Let us praise Pukār, this glorious city,
The fame of its royal seat of kings
Spread over the whole earth clasped
By the swelling waters.
Far-famed and inimitable
Is the city of Pukār, known for its ancient families
Undisturbed since time immemorial.
Like the Potiyil or Himālaya, it too remains
As constant as the great men who adorn it.
Thus speak the wise ones who have heard
And known everything. In fame Pukār rivals
Heaven itself, blinds the Serpentworld in pleasures.
Here lived Mānāykaṉ, heir to a noble family,
Generous as the rainclouds. A perfect branch
Of his tree, a shining creeper of gold,
Was his daughter Kaṇṇaki, who was twelve years
Old, and loved by Kōvalaṉ. She was blessed
With virtues. So women adored and praised her:

Lines 1–29

"She is Lakṣmī herself, goddess
Of peerless beauty that rose from the lotus,
And chaste as the immaculate Arundhatī."

And here also lived Mācāttuvāṉ, a man
Of immense wealth. Even the ruler
Of that great kingdom looked up to him as the chief
Among the noble families of his realm.
He was Kubera himself who gave away his wealth
To the needy. The fame of his son Kōvalaṉ,
Only sixteen years old, had already shrunk
The earth. Over and over again, in voices
Seasoned by music, with faces luminous
As the moon, women confided among themselves:
"He is the god of love himself,
The incomparable Murukaṉ." For it was love
That made them speak thus of the handsome Kōvalaṉ.

Their noble parents longed to see them
Take, on a favorable day, the marriage vows.
They rejoiced in the thought, and dispatched all over
The town girls resplendent in jewels
And mounted on elephants, to proclaim the news
Of their wedding. On the day the nomadic Moon
Drew near Rohiṇī, drums resounded;
Conches, as usual, boomed. White parasols
Were held aloft, as in a royal procession.
The bridal pendant was taken around the town.

In the pavilion itself, the canopy of blue silk

Lines 29–50

Was inlaid with pearls. Burnished with gems
And diamonds were the pillars, their tops pendent
With festoons. Around the ceremonial fire, walked
Kōvalaṉ observing the holy rites
The venerable priest solemnized.
Thus Kōvalaṉ
Married the fair Kaṇṇaki, spotless
As the bright star Arundhatī. The eyes
That beheld this sight were indeed fortunate.
Young girls offered perfumes
And flowers. Others, a little older,
Looked sidelong as they chatted and sang
Among themselves. High-breasted women,
With serpentine hair, carried incense,
Sandalwood paste, and scented powders.
Matrons, with gentle smiles, went round
With lamps, vessels, and pots brimful
With shoots of sprouted pālikai. All resembled
Golden vines, their disheveled hair
Plaited with flowers. With a rain of petals
They blessed the couple:
"Your arms forever knotted
In embrace, inseparable in love may you
Remain, and unblemished be your life."

Then to the auspicious nuptial bed
They led Kaṇṇaki, the Arundhatī
Of this gentle earth, and chanting withdrew:

"May the tiger-emblem, inscribed on the brow

Lines 50–65

Of the Himālaya, dwell on its golden crest
Forever. May Cempiyaṉ, of the spear fierce
In the great battle, whirl his ever-victorious wheel."

Lines 65–68

Canto 2
The Setting up of a Home

Great and renowned kings envied
The immense wealth of the seafaring merchants
Of the opulent city of Pukār. Ships
And caravans from foreign lands poured
In abundance rare objects and diverse
Merchandise. Its treasure would be untouched
Though the entire world, bound by the roaring seas,
Crowd into the city. The lotus-eyed Kaṇṇaki
And her loving husband were fortunate: they
Were highborn, and like their fathers heirs to untold
Riches. In this, Pukār resembled Uttarakuru
Where great austerities were performed.

Maya himself designed the jewel-legged
Couch that graced the upper floor
Of Mācāttuvāṉ's spacious mansion. As they
Abandoned themselves to love, the south wind
With a swarm of bees, at the opportune moment,
Entered through the lattice windows
Decorated with a fourfold chaplet of pearls
Strung together in a row. The wind was heavy
With the fragrance of red and purple water lilies;
Blue lotuses in flower; half-opened lotuses
Thick with humming drones;
And other flowers that blossomed in the fields:
The fragrant screw pine, its white petals
In bloom; and in the champak arbor, swirls of mātavi,

Lines 1–18

Drained of their nectar by bees who plunged
Into the lush hair of the bright-faced girl.

They walked up to the open terrace of the mansion
Where, under a full moon, Kāma, the god
Of love, sat in splendor with his arrow
Of sweet flowers. Bees gorged themselves
On the fresh blossoms that strewed their bed.
On Kaṇṇaki's broad shoulders
Kōvalaṉ drew a sugarcane and the fabled creeper
Of gold. Such was the scene as if the sun
And moon had together bathed the entire world,
Clasped by the sea, in their light. He wore
A wreath of jasmines in bloom: their white petals,
Opened by bees, was a broad expanse
Of moonlight. Hers was a garland
Of shimmering red and purple water lilies
In flower. As they embraced, their wreaths
Became entangled. His passions still unspent,
Kōvalaṉ looked into the radiant face
Of Kaṇṇaki and spoke his mind to her:
"Praised
By the gods is Śiva. In his knotted hair glows
The crescent moon which freely did he part with
When it became your forehead, dear Kaṇṇaki.
Wasn't the Moon born with you?
And Kāma, the shadowy god of love,
Pledged his lofty sugarcane bow
To you when it became your two dark eyebrows.
For isn't it an old custom that foes,

Lines 19–45

Routed in war, surrender their arms
On the battlefield? Indra bestowed on you
His divine thunderbolt that secures the immortal gods,
When it became your waist. Weren't you created
Long before ambrosia? With six-faced Murukaṉ
I have no cause for quarrel. He has blessed you
With his straight and fiery lance that turned
Into two dark glowing eyes on your face.
How he rejoices to see me thus writhe in pain!

"Eclipsed by your beauty, the bejeweled peacock
With its resplendent black feathers hides itself
In the fresh woods. Helpless before your elegant step,
My girl of the bright forehead, the swan
Vanishes into a field of limpid waters
Thick with lotuses. A blend of the pipe,
Lute and nectar is your sweet voice
That the young green parrots despair of.
Speechless, they love to perch forever,
My girl of graceful steps, on the lily of your hand.
Adorned in your flawless bridal pendant,
Of what use are your maids and ornaments,
My girl with fragrant blossoms in her hair?
Of what use, again, is the splendid wreath
Of flowers, when a handful of petals
Is enough to set off your black hair?
Of what use, I ask, is the unguent of musk
When common frankincense is good enough
To perfume your hair? Flourishes of sandalwood paste
Embellish your faultless breasts.

Lines 45–69

Why burden them with a string of pearls?
Are they out of their minds to heap ornaments
On you thus, forcing your bright face
To break out in a sweat and bend in pain
Your slender waist? My girl of the dark flowing hair,
You are pure gold, a pearl
From the right-spiraled shell, fragrance beyond praise,
Choice sugarcane, honey, a picture
Beyond my reach, life-giving nectar itself.
Noble daughter of a prince among merchants!
Over and over again, shall I swear you are an emerald
Not mined from the hills, nectar
Not cast up from the ocean, a melody
Not plucked from any lute?"

And on and on in so many words
He thus sang her praises. Wreathed
In fair garlands bursting with flowers,
In the intoxication of love they passed their days.

On such a day, the venerable woman,
Kōvalaṉ's mother, thoughtfully set up Kaṇṇaki
Of the rich flowing hair in a home
Of her own, with faithful servants and treasures
Of all sorts, that she may honor her kinsmen,
Ascetics, and guests in a manner befitting
The householder's life, and thus see for herself
Her fame spread far and near.
Some years passed. And beyond all praise
Was Kaṇṇaki's name renowned for making a home.

Lines 70–90

ENVOI

Like snakes coupled in the heat of passion,
Or Kāma and Rati smothered in each
Other's arms, so Kōvalaṉ and Kaṇṇaki
Lived in happiness past speaking,
Spent themselves in every pleasure, thinking:
"We live on earth but a few days."

Lines 91–94

Canto 3
The First Performance

Agastya of the divine Potiyil had once
Cursed Indra's son Jayanta, and Urvaśī.
That curse he graciously revoked
As Urvaśī displayed her talent for the dance
On the stage. And from that exalted line
Of heavenly nymphs was Mātavi descended.
A woman of flawless birth, of broad shoulders,
And curly hair, spilling pollen, she was
Noted for her style of great distinction.
For seven years she studied dancing,
Singing, and the art of enhancing her beauty—
Every one of them perfectly. At twelve, she wished
To perform before the king of heroic anklets.

An expert in the traditions of the dance, her tutor
Knew well the rules of the folk and classical styles.
He paired different types of dances
With the figures of song. He was adept
In the traditional modes of the eleven mythic dances,
With their appropriate songs and resounding drums,
In mime, singing, rhythm, and beat.
He was familiar too with gestures made
With one hand or both hands, and with hand poses
For mime and the dance. He distinguished
Between the one- and two-handed poses,
Never confused the pure with the expressive,
Or the kuravai with the vari dance.

Lines 1–25

He played well, her music teacher, the lute
And flute, following the beat. He had
A good voice, and from the drums even teased a low note
Or two. All these sounds he harmonized
With the dance: for the vari and āṭal, he played
The appropriate music. He knew well all the fine
Nuances of the impeccable tēcikam music.
Guided by the exact conventions of the texts,
He classified and elaborated upon the different types
Of dances, and songs that consort with them,
In the true spirit of their composers.

For his skill in Tamil the poet of exquisite song
Was renowned everywhere in the Tamil country,
Bound by the roaring sea. An expert
On the theater, he knew its two sections,
The vēttiyal and potuviyal, knew the melody
Improvised by the music teacher. Guided
By the exact conventions of the texts,
And aware of the faulty phrases of his rivals,
He was resolute to avoid them in his own work.

Her drummer was skilled in every type of dance,
In musical notes, singing, Tamil
Ways of speaking, melody, rhythm,
Modes of beating time, and the use
Of words of diverse origins. He was conscious
Of flaws in a performance. Playing, he would combine
Single beats, allow time for double beats
To be heard, and blend them with the flute, lute,

Lines 26–55

And voice. With his fingertips he would subdue
The drum, so other instruments are heard. At times
Drown them in the thunder of the barrel drum.

Her flutist was versed in the traditional lore.
He knew the way hard and soft consonants
Were mellowed to ravish the ear. He knew
Four kinds of trills, and listened with attention
To the first and fifth notes, and with ease
Chimed in with the sound of the timbal,
Kept time with the drummer. Progressing
By fifths, he tuned the ragas on the lute,
Closely followed the singer, improvised
On what he heard, and forestalled what was to come.
He showed his knowledge of melodies
By playing note by note so that each
Sound was heard without a flaw.

Her lute player was a wizard. To establish
The seven scales within the pattern
Of fourteen notes, he half plucked the low first
And the high seventh to tune the third.
The sixth he produced by the remaining half
Of the elegant and robust seventh which now vanished
Into the third. As the sixth faded, the third
Dissolved with it. Likewise, the rest of the notes
Melted into the others. He played on all
The fourteen strings, from the low fourth
To the high third, and sounded the cempālai
In the new tradition. In order, the scales

Lines 56–82

Would arise: the paṭumalai from the third, cevvaḻi
From the second, arum from the first, kōṭi
From the seventh, viḷari from the sixth, and mēṟcem
From the fifth. It is thus they were combined.
The notes of the lute got lower in pitch
From the left to the right. With the flute, they got lower
From the right to the left. An expert lute
Player can harmonize the low, high
And median notes to ravish the ear.

With care a site was chosen, and the quality
Of the soil inspected, following what learned
Men had prescribed, for constructing a stage.
To measure the stage, the texts recommended
A bamboo rod—the distance of a span
Between the two joints, and twenty-four thumbs
Long—from the sacred hills. The stage
Was eight rods long, seven deep,
And one high. It had two grand doors,
Conveniently located. Four rods was the distance
Between the crossbeams and the platform.
Images of demigods, placed above the stage,
Were worshiped and praised. Bright lamps
Glowed at the four corners so that the pillars
Cast no shadows. The stage curtain,
The curtain between the pillars to the right,
And the overhanging drop curtain were all drawn
By cords. And from the painted canopy flowed
Strings of rare pearls, wreaths and garlands
Of flowers. Such was the unusual workmanship

Lines 82–113

Of the stage. The handle of a splendid white parasol,
Taken in battle from illustrious kings,
Was the sacred rod, its middle done up
With a plate of the purest cāmpūnata gold,
Its joints inset with the nine gems
In a pattern. An emblem of Indra's son,
Jayanta, it was offered worship in the palace
Of the Cōḻa king who protects with his white parasol.
On the auspicious day when a dancer had to use
The rod, she washed it with holy waters
Collected in a golden pot, and later wreathed it
With a garland. And with a blessing, it was offered
To the royal elephant with a frontlet of gold ornaments.
In unison with other instruments, the drum
Resounded. The king appeared with his five groups
Of advisors, walked round the chariot, and gave
The rod to the court poet seated in it.
In a procession, they went round the town,
Entered the theater, and installed the rod.

Strictly in order the musicians took
Their seats. Her right foot Mātavi placed
Forward, and stepped on the stage. Reached
The pillar on the right, stood by it as required
By custom. And near the pillar on the left clustered
Other dancers likewise following an old custom.
So that virtue might flourish and evil vanish,
Two kinds of song were sung in turn.
At the end of the benediction all the musical instruments
Were sounded in unison. The lute followed

Lines 113–139

The flute; the barrel drum was tuned to the lute;
And the pot drum followed the barrel drum.
In unison with the pot drum resounded
The left-hand drum. Instruments tuned to it
Played in harmony. Two strokes made
One beat. And eleven beats were invariably counted
Following established practice. After the performance
Of the introductory dance, the auspicious song
In the pālai mode was sung with improvisations
Without straining its lofty measure.
Mātavi knew well the four impeccable parts
Of a song: she measured out three and ended
With one, and completed them with five beats.
Later, she danced to the vāram songs. Performed
The classical dance, and her skill fused
The five-beat mode of the folk and classical styles
Into one style. A golden vine
It was that danced, for her performance
Showed she knew well the text on dancing.

From the king, who protects, she received a garland
Of leaves and flowers, and one thousand and eight pieces
Of gold, the customary gift to dancers
That held the sacred rod and performed
For the first time. This garland Mātavi
Put in the hands of her doe-eyed maid,
A hunchback, asked her to wait in the street
Where the elite of the town walked about, and offer it
For sale, thus:
"A thousand and eight pieces

Lines 139–164

Of the most excellent gold is this garland worth.
Who buys the garland becomes the husband
Of our vinelike girl."
Kōvalaṉ bought the garland—
Mātavi with wide, lotus eyes. With the hunchback,
He entered Mātavi's residence: came
Under her spell the instant he took her in his arms.
He forgot himself, and wished never to part from her,
Forgot his own blameless and noble wife, and home.

ENVOI

The gold-bangled Mātavi of Pūmpukār caused
Her fame to spread over the earth. On the stage
She showed by word of mouth her talent
Concerning numbers, letters, the five types
Of literary Tamil, the four melodic patterns,
And the eleven kinds of dance that followed them.

Lines 164–179

Canto 4
In Praise of the Evening

"I don't see my sovereign lord, who disperses
His sprawling rays over the entire world
And rules with his one, unique disk.
The handsome prince, the Moon, who with his soft
Radiance lights up the heavens, O where
Is he?"
So cried in grief Queen Earth,
Deprived of her husband, the Sun,
But regal still in her robes of the billowing sea.
Pale were her four faces, the directions.
Red like flowers her eyes, and running over
With tears of dew. Her whole body trembled.
Like a petty chieftain who occupies and wastes
With the help of rebels the land of a king,
With an invincible army, when he's abroad
So that his taxpaying subjects are forced to place
Their hands on their heads and lament, so Evening
Stormed fertile, old Pukār
To the sorrow of chaste wives, alone
And parted from their husbands, and the joy of women
Embracing their lovers. With their flutes, cowherds
Spun the raga of parting. Humming
Bees drained the jasmine. From unopened
Buds the gentle south wind
Pushed the six-footed bees, and emptied
The perfume into the street. Women with radiant
Bangles lit their glowing lamps.

Lines 1–20

In spite of their youth the Pāṇṭiyas, ever glorious
In war, fought back hostile kings.
Likewise, the fair crescent Moon appeared
In the sky and routed the irritable chieftain,
Evening. His greatness unshorn, the silver
Moon, emperor of the sky's fish, the stars,
Dispersed his milky rays.
In the bedroom,
Mātavi's couch was sown with homegrown
Mullai petals, musk jasmine
And other flowers. Undone was her red,
Coral girdle that blazed over her mound
Of love, and the fine garment unwound
From her waist. Then to the open, moonlit terrace
She stepped on, and with a heart bursting
With passion drowned herself in Kōvalaṉ,
Or feigned a quarrel with him, stopping
Only to spruce herself up now and again.
Besides Mātavi, others with lotus eyes
Having spent themselves in lovemaking, were blissfully
Asleep on the chest of their lovers, cooled
By the south wind. Earlier, they had put out
The incense made of the white resin
From the western hills and the black agar
From the eastern. With the paste of sandalwood found
In the southern mountains, they had anointed
Themselves by rubbing it on the round, flat stone
Of unusual luster found in the northern mountains.
They wore fresh garlands of leaves
And flowers, plaited with the tender stalks

Lines 21–41

Of the red lotus, bright flowers
With pollen on them, the irresistible blue lotus,
The water lily and strings of big pearls.
Their large beds of flowers were smeared
With bright pollen laced with fine powders.

Kaṇṇaki was heartbroken. No anklets sounded
On her small, graceful feet. No girdle
Blazed over her mound of love wound
In a soft, white garment. No vermilion
Rouge was painted on her breasts. Except
For her bridal pendant, she wished for no ornament.
In the absence of earrings, her ears seemed
Pendulous and elongated. Her radiant moonlike face
Was not beaded with sweat, nor did kohl accent
Her wide fishlike eyes. Her forehead,
Bright as coral, was without the tilaka,
And the smile that revealed to Kōvalaṉ her pearly
Teeth had vanished. No oil lit up
Her thick, dark hair.
Parted from their lovers,
Women sighed like bellows puffing
And blowing in a forge. From bedrooms used
In summer they withdrew to occupy,
In autumn, rooms with narrow windows.
They were sad they couldn't embellish
Their fair breasts with sandalwood paste
From the Potiyil or with strings of pearls. They were
Sad they couldn't sink into couches
Of tempting flowers picked from pots

Lines 41–65

Of blue lotuses and cool, red water lilies,
Or sleep in peace on spacious beds
Made of the soft down shed
By the swan while mating with its loved one.
In a lovers' quarrel with their husbands,
Calm of mind, they rolled their eyes
From the tips of their noses to the lobes of their ears.
They were now sunk in despair. Red
With weeping, their bold, wide eyes drooped.
They let fall, in their loneliness, tears of woe.

The lake of sweet waters seemed a woman.
The swan's elegant gait, her walk.
The redolent water lilies dripping honey,
Her fragrance. The lotus, her red lips.
The cool, black sand, her thick hair.
To the nōtiṟam raga of bees singing
With the voice of poets, the lake opened
Her eyes of radiant blue lotuses.
The clamor of birds echoed like the sound
Of drums. The shrill conch-shell call
Of the spotted rooster of bright plumage
Sounded time and again. All these awakened
From its sleep the city of Pukār, spread out
Like the sea, as night receded with the coming
Of dawn. While no one slept a wink
Between midnight and early morning, the city
Itself became renowned for the close watch
Kept on it by the roving prince
With the victorious banner of fish, arrows

Lines 65–84

Of scented flowers and sugarcane bow.

ENVOI

The Moon at night helps flowers to blossom.
A native of the heavens, he offers
Cool shade to those who honor him, glowing
Heat to others. Like the white parasol
Of the Cōḻa king who protects, he appeared
Benign to Mātavi, ominous to lonely Kaṇṇaki.

Lines 84–88

Canto 5
The Celebration in the City of the Festival of Indra

The billowing sea, her robes. The hills,
Her breasts. The broad rivers, her garlands.
The clouds, her shock of hair. This vast
And boundless Earth seemed a woman.
On top of the Utaiya Hill the Sun
Rose, pulled down the veil of darkness
By splashing his bright rays to light up
This resplendent world. On open terraces,
On treasure houses with ornaments, on mansions
With airholes like the eyes of deer, he shone.
Near the harbor, the passerby was stopped dead
By the homes of Yavanas whose profits never shrunk.
On the edge of the burnished waters lived
And mingled as one traders from distant
Lands, come for goods carried
By ships. With paints, scented powders,
Cool sandalwood paste, flowers,
Incense and fragrant perfumes, hawkers
Went round the city streets.
One saw the fine work of making
Cloth from silk, fur, and cotton
In the weavers' quarter. Silk, coral,
Sandalwood, agar, flawless pearls,
Gems, gold, and an endless profusion
Of rare ornaments were piled high
In the commodious streets. Heaped separately

Lines 1–21

Were grains in the street of the grain merchants,
As also a variety of provisions distinct from one
Another. Pedlars of pastry, appam;
Women hawking wine; fishermen
Offering fish for sale; vendors
Of white salt; sellers of betel
Leaves; perfumers; butchers flogging
Different kinds of meat; oilmongers;
Overcrowded shops packed with food;
Braziers; coppersmiths; painters; sculptors;
Goldsmiths; jewelers; tailors; cobblers;
A host of artisans making various
Flawless objects with cloth and pith;
The homes of great musicians, expert
In the traditions of music, who could display
Impeccable skill on the flute and lute by sounding
The first seven notes; and other workers
Who excelled in the small crafts—
All had their homes in the suburbs of the city.
In the city itself stood the Kingsway,
The flagged car street, the market square,
The boulevard where merchant princes dwelt
In tall mansions, the brahman homes,
The houses of landed families and their tenant
Farmers, of physicians, astrologers, and those employed
In other tasks, the broad street
Of the homes of those who with skill bored
Holes into bright gems, and those who polished
Ornate conches. In separate houses
Lived charioteers, bards, panegyrists,

Lines 21–48

Astronomers, handsome dancers, harlots,
Actresses, flower-and-betel girls,
Maidservants, professional musicians,
Drummers of various sorts, and jesters.

Surrounding the fort were the spacious houses
Of cavalrymen with swift horses, riders
Of male elephants, drivers of lofty chariots,
Fierce-looking soldiers. Celebrated in song
Was this part of town and well known
For the great and renowned men who lived
There. Like a battlefield, where two great
Kings meet, was the open ground
Between the two halves of the city. The dense
Trees as pillars, shops sprang up
As a permanent marketplace with its untiring clamor
Of buyers and sellers.
On the day in Caitra
When the moon drew near the star
Cittirai, elderly women offered
As sacrifice pulses, sesame balls,
Boiled rice laced with suet,
Flowers, incense, and wine at the altar
In front of the entrance to the temple of the guardian
Deity, come there at the command of Indra,
King of the gods, to remove the evil
That might strike King Mucukuntaṉ
Of the victorious spear. Possessed by the spirit,
They performed the tuṇaṅkai and kuravai
Dances, and chanting aloud a prayer

Lines 49–70

Withdrew:
"May the king of this great land
Sustaining his kingdom be rid of hunger,
Disease, and enmity. May he be blessed
Abundantly with rain and prosperity."

The heroic warriors living on the outskirts
And the valiant men with armies outdid
Each other in reaching the sacrificial altar
First, and spoke out:
"May the evil that might strike
Our mighty king be removed. May the valor
Of those offering themselves as sacrifice
Know no bounds."
Stone-throwing slingers,
Those who hurled a rain of spears,
Flesh clinging to their shields of dark hide,
Beat their shoulders and roared
As in a victorious battle. On the holy, sacrificial
Altar, they placed their dark heads
With ruddy eyes that struck terror
And burned those who looked at them, praying:
"May the victorious king achieve success."
Then, like the roar of thunder, the voice
Of the guardian deity who will feast on the sacrificial
Offering of life sounded, with the drums
In concert, and she was appeased by the perfect sacrifice.

In the Tamil country of two frontiers,
Tirumāvaḷavaṉ, spoiling for a fight, despaired

Lines 70–90

He had no foes to wrestle with.
On an auspicious day he had taken out his sword,
Royal parasol, and war drum, praying: "May I,
On this earth, run into foes worthy
Of my broad shoulders," and to the north,
As the sacred direction, he marched. One day,
Thinking: "May my wish, full of firm resolve,
Not be thwarted. This fierce mountain
Obstructs my progress as a foe,"
He engraved his tiger-emblem on the nape
Of the Himālaya's neck where dwell the gods,
And giving up his northern march returned.
The king of the great Vajra country, bounded
By the vast waters, offered him as tribute
A pearl canopy. His onetime foe,
The king of Magadha, veteran in swordplay,
Offered him an audience chamber. And the king
Of Avanti was pleased to offer him a tall,
Finely wrought arch for his gateway.
Made of gold and gems, even to craftsmen
Of exquisite skill their art was a secret.
Maya himself created these and gave them
To the ancestors of these three kings, who excelled
In offering help to banish sorrow.
Put together, they formed a majestic
Temple-porch praised by great men.

Further, on the open waterfront were piles
Of merchandise, marked with their amount, weight
And the names of the newcomers. It had

Lines 90–112

No gate, no strong protective bolt,
And watching over it, no guards. Should thieves
Remove them, the spirit of the waterfront
Would make them tremble within themselves
And go round it, the pain of the burden
On their heads, and stop them from leaving.

If hunchbacks, dwarfs, the mute and deaf,
And lepers bathed in the pond and went round it,
They would become free of their deformities,
And their appearance would regain glowing color.
Those who turned mad, enticed into taking
Drugs, those afflicted by palsy by imbibing
Poison, those bitten by the sharp fangs
Of fire-breathing serpents, and those possessed
By ghosts with bulging eyes would end
Their suffering if they went round the tall, luminous
Stone that stood in the open square
And offered it worship.
"Their hands
I will bind with a rope, and beat
And devour those who behave unnaturally
Under the subterfuge of penance, unfaithful women
Who hide their evil, lascivious ministers
Who covet others' wives, false witnesses
And slanderers,"
thus spoke in a rough voice,
Loud enough to be heard for four leagues,
The goblin of the crossroads. Whenever swerved
The king's scepter, and preference was shown

Lines 112–136

In court by favoring one side
Against the rule of law, the statue that graced
The public square would never open
Its mouth but weep and let fall symbolic tears.
In these five places were offered precious
Sacrifices praised by wise men
Who knew their mystery.
The redolent drum
Of the temple of Indra's thunderbolt was raised
On the nape of the girdled elephant's neck,
And carried to the luminous temple, where stood
The young, white king of elephants.
This proclaimed the beginning and end of the festival.
Pulled aloft in the sky was the tall sacred flag
Which graced the temple of the wishing tree.
Set with emeralds and diamonds were pials
Of fine gold with round coral pillars
On all the porches of the stately mansions.
The wide entrances shone with ornamental
Fish-shaped hangings in the form of an arch
Painted with sacred objects, inlaid
With a row of bright pearls and rings
That adorn an elephant's tusk. The streets
Overflowed with flawless pitchers of pure gold,
Brimful with water, bright pālikai pots,
Lamps in the shape of women, golden pennants,
Pure yaktail fans and fragrant pastes.

Gathered in that place were the five great groups
Of the king's councilors, the eight great sets

Lines 136–157

Of courtiers, princes, sons of noble merchants,
Swift horsemen, elephant riders
And charioteers with fast horses,
Who proclaimed the undisputed sovereignty
Of their ruler in that excellent town Pukār,
Praying: "May our renowned king be victorious."
On their heads, one thousand and eight kings bore
Golden pots brimful with cool, holy water
Perfumed by the pollen abounding in the bathing ghats
Of the Kāviri, supporter of life in this wide world,
And caused the idol of the king of the gods
To lustrate in that excellent water to the wonder
Of heaven and earth. In the temple of the great lord,
Śiva, who was unborn; in the temple
Of the six-faced lord, Murukaṉ, of the red spear
Of radiant beauty; in the temple of Balarāma
With complexion like the white conch shell;
In the temple of the blue-hued Viṣṇu;
In the temple of Indra of the white parasol
And the wreath of pearls, were performed, on one side,
Sacrificial rites as ordained by the four Vedas
Born of the unerring word of Brahmā,
Ripe with vast wisdom. On another side,
The festivals of the four orders of the gods
And eighteen demigods and various other deities
Were scrupulously observed, keeping their differences
In mind. Inside the city were Jaina temples
And their holy ashrams; in the suburbs,
Their sacred charitable houses. In another place,
Public reciters performed their task.

Lines 158–181

Somewhere else excelled the grace of the ruler
With flagged chariots for removing the manacles
Of kings who didn't join forces with him. Elsewhere
The untold music rose, rare and excellent,
Of dancers, flutists, skilled players
Weaving melodies on the lute, and bards
Reciting poems. The drums in every lane
And street of that vast city glowing
With the joys of the festival resounded nonstop.

Not separated from her lover, Mātavi
Was charming in a pair of crescent earrings.
Laden with the perfume of the mātavi flower,
Homegrown mullai, jasmine, mayilai,
The potted blue lotus, and the red water lily
Encircled by bees, and splendid in a closely braided
Garland, the breeze from the Potiyil swept through
The city with highpitched bees and the early summer's
Gentle rays, like Kōvalaṉ roving about
With sweet-voiced bards and playboys. It exulted
In love's unending joy; took pleasure
In the garden thick with the odor of buds;
Entered into the fresh bouquet of forest blossoms
In the marketplace; scattered to the winds the incense
And the ever-wet sandalwood paste; and forever
Eavesdropped on lovers' playful talk and laughter.

Quipped one playboy:
"Afraid of the serpent
Rāhu, his foe, has the Moon who roams

Lines 182–207

The bright sky fled, and in your person
Reappeared bearing a black cloud
As your hair, the small hare as the parting,
And drawing two great minnows on his face
As your eyes, the kumiḻ flower between, as your nose?"
Teased another:
"Are you a flash of lightning
Brought up by Kāma, the fish-bannered one,
Come down to look for his body by drinking up
The precious drops of nectar that from the moist lips
Of the Moon fell on this wide earth?"
Exclaimed a third:
"Has the sweet lotus
Searching for its companion, the goddess Lakṣmī,
Disguised itself as two large, dark blue lotuses
One on each side of the kumiḻ flower?
Or, has it bloomed again into the fiery, red silk-cotton
And jasmine to proclaim that Lakṣmī has entered
This prosperous city so that the king of this vast world
May be blessed with abundant wealth?"
Said another:
"Is widemouthed Yama,
Devourer of untold lives, afraid
To oppose the king of the upright scepter,
His manhood bartered without giving up
His unusual work for the smiling face
Of a woman robed in modesty and prattling
Soft words like the notes of a lute?"

Like a great legion of the bodiless one, Kāma,

Lines 207–224

The women to the rakes gave battle and won,
Opposed and prevented them from fleeing. They rubbed
All over their chests the flourishes of sandalwood
Paste painted on their breasts. The marks
Still fresh on them, these broad-shouldered husbands
Entered their homes, clasped their sulking wives
Feigning displeasure, but chaste as Arundhatī,
And discreetly made love to them. Like sapphire
On the bright faces of women, their blue-lotus eyes
That had turned reddish failed to clear up
Even at the sight of guests who quailed helplessly
And observed: "In this vast world who can
Come up with a remedy to cure this?" Common
Were such scenes of love during the festive days.
Like the water lily that trembles when the sweet pollen
Within it comes apart and oozes honey,
So throbbed Kaṇṇaki's dark left eye
And Mātavi's red right one, shedding
Tears of sorrow and joy for the thoughts
Each had smothered within herself on the day
Of the festival of Indra, king of the gods.

Lines 225–240

Canto 6
Bathing in the Sea

In a garden, bursting with flowers dripping
Honey, in the vast and illustrious city
Of Cedi on the silver-peaked Mount Kailāsa,
A hero of the demigods, Vidyādharas, observed
With his girlfriend of wide, dark, fishlike eyes
The feast of Kāma, the god of love.
He told her:
"In the south is a prosperous city,
Pukār, and this is the day when the festival
Of Indra will be celebrated there. Hosts of swift-moving
Demons were overcome by King Mucukuntaṉ
Of heroic anklets who had kept watch
With the strength of a tiger over Indra's city.
Against him they let fly their arrows, filled his mind
With confusion. Then Indra ordered a powerful deity
To appear to dispel the violence that might befall
Mucukuntaṉ of the perfect spear. We will see
The place where the deity consumes the sacrifice
Offered to her to mark the event. We will see
The five grand assembly halls famed
For their majestic splendor, given by Indra,
And on the good earth put up by the king's ancestor
Who kept watch over Amarāvatī. The perfect music
Of Nārada's lute, and the vāram song
Of the dancing girls filled to the brim the ears
Of thousand-eyed Indra. Since Indra desired

Lines 1–22

Urvaśī as she danced before him, the lute was deprived
Of its power. A curse was laid upon her: 'Let her remain
On the earth.' In her line was Mātavi born,
Her mound of love a hooded cobra.
We shall see her dance, my girl of red lips
And waist slender as an hourglass drum!"

He showed her the far-peaked Himālaya, the Gaṅgā
Swollen with water, the city of Ujjayinī,
The Vindhyā forests,, the Vēṅkaṭam hills,
The land of the Kāviri encumbered with crops,
And reached Pukār, its parks bursting with flowers.
He showed her the city and, as custom required,
Worshiped Indra, and saw the joyous festival
In that ancient and fertile city.

"You will hear the hymns to Viṣṇu, the four songs
To the deities of the four castes, and the prayer
To the Moon that crawls in the sky for the welfare of all.
All these you will see: Śiva's dance of destruction,
Umā keeping time on one side, on the burning ground
Where Kālī danced following the beat,
And without violating tradition, when the big
Fire-tipped arrow obeyed his command
To burn down, at the wish of the gods,
The three cities of the demons; the great white dance
Śiva performed for the four-faced Brahmā
Standing before his chariot; the elephant dance
Of the dark one, Kṛṣṇa, after cutting short
The treachery of Kaṃsa, and the wrestler's dance

Lines 22–49

After slaying the demon Bāṇa; the drum dance
Of Murukaṉ on the ocean's stage after killing
The demon Sūra who had opposed him;
The umbrella dance of Murukaṉ when he lowered
His parasol before the demons who dropped their weapons
In dismay; the pot dance of Viṣṇu
Who measured the vast world after walking
The streets of Bāṇa's great city;
The eunuch dance of Kāma after giving up
His male form for a woman's costume;
The dance of Durgā on stilts on finding
The wicked deeds of the demons consumed
With intolerable anger; the dance of the statue
Performed by Lakṣmī, goddess of fortune,
When the demons in their fierce warlike attire
Surrendered; and the dance of Indra's consort
In the field near the north gate of Cō.
You will clearly see these eleven dances
With their appropriate songs, each performed
With its costumes and gestures, in erect and bent postures,
According to the glorious conventions of its art.
This is Mātavi descended from the line of the Mātavi
I had spoken of when we were in the garden rich
With the pollen of flowers."
Rejoicing at the prospect,
Thus spoke the highly illustrious Vidyādhara.

The festival of Indra also ended, with its dances,
Masquerades, and revels. The gods had come down
In disguise to witness them. To please Kōvalaṉ,

Lines 49–75

Sulking from a lover's quarrel, Mātavi
Rubbed her fragrant, black hair
With perfumed oil made of ten astringent lotions,
Five spices and thirty-two varieties
Of herbs soaked in fresh water.
She dried her hair, soft as flowers,
In incense fumes, anointed each plait
With the cool paste of the musk deer.
She adorned her small, elegant feet,
Reddened by rubbing lac, by putting
On her fine, slender toes choice rings,
And on her legs suitable ornaments like ankle-rings,
Tinkling anklets, plain anklets,
Strings of tiny bells and hollow anklets.
Her rounded thighs she covered with ornaments,
And around her waist fastened a girdle
Of thirty-two strands of large pearls
Worn over a fine, blue cloth
Sparkling with flowers. Armlets studded
With pure gems and radiant bracelets
Clasped her upper arms. Round her smooth wrists,
She wore ornamental bracelets set
With gems on the top and diamonds all round,
Bangles of pure gold, circlets
Of nine gems, conch bangles
And bangles of coral. To conceal
Her small, lotus-red fingers, she wore
On them a ring bent in the shape
Of an open-mouthed scabbard fish, a brilliant ring
Of red, shining gems, and a curved ring

Lines 76–98

Sparkling with emeralds and diamonds
Her lovely, delicate neck glowed
With a gold necklace, a thin chain,
A well-made ornamental cord and a garland.
She covered as well the small nape of her neck
With a fine string of pure, ornamental gems
Held by a clasp. In her soft, lovely ears
She wore a pair of earrings in which sapphires
Were placed in a circle in between diamonds.
She adorned her thick, dark, lovely
Hair with suitable head-ornaments,
Such as the cītēvi, right-spiraled shell
From the vast waters, toyyakam, and pullakam.
Mātavi then gave Kōvalan̲ the joys
Of love and of lovers' quarrel, and languished
In her pleasurable bedroom.
It was the night of the full moon
In that awesome, old city. Folks
Rushed toward the sea for water sports
In the seaside grove bursting with flowers.
Eager to see them was Mātavi who begged
Kōvalan̲ to go with her.
From lotuses in ponds
Birds cried out. Cocks sounded the hour of dawn.
Śukra blazed, melting the thick darkness.
On his garlanded chest Kōvalan̲ wore
Precious jewels. A prodigal cloud,
He mounted his mule, while doe-eyed Mātavi
Climbed into her horse-drawn chariot. They passed
Through the market street, crowded with mansions

Lines 99–122

That stored ten million bales of costly merchandise.
Radiant lamps were lit and some of them
Were decked with flowers. Courtesans,
Resplendent in their ornaments, scattered flowers,
Hariali grass, and paddy. Truly Lakṣmī
Dwelt in this street, on whose two sides
Folks wandered to and fro. Kōvalaṉ and Mātavi
Entered the main thoroughfare of the city
That prospered from the wealth of the ocean, and reached
The row of streets near the sea. In the lane
Where grains were heaped like unending waves,
The lofty banners seemed to proclaim:
"In this expanse of white sand is the wealth
Brought in ships by men who have voyaged
From their native lands to live here."

The place was bright with the lamps of the vendors
Of dyes, sandalwood, flowers, perfumes,
And varieties of sweets; with the elegant lamps
Of skilled goldsmiths; with the lamps of the pedlars
Of pastry seated in a row; with the lamps,
Placed on black, wide-mouthed earthern pots,
Of the pedlars of appam; with the lamps from shops
Where women offered things for sale;
With the lamps here and there of fishmongers selling
Fish; with the beacons lit up to guide ships
On the edge of the burnished waters; with the lamps
Of fishing boats from which fishermen cast
Their nets; with the undying lamps of foreigners
Speaking strange tongues; and with the lamps

Lines 123–144

Of guards watching over piles of merchandise.
Beyond reckoning was the light shed by all the lamps
Burning together. The seaside grove with its hedges
Of screw pine appeared more ravishing
Than the farmland with its redolent lotus petals
In the expanse of lapping waters. The prospect
Was such that even a seed of white mustard
Could be seen on the fine sands that resembled
A heap of flour. Slender as a creeper,
Mātavi arrived there to sport with her companions.
In a cove in the windswept grove were row
Upon row of boats overburdened with a profusion
Of fresh produce from the hills and seas.

Gathered in one corner of the seashore
Were young princes and their retinue, sons
Of noble merchants, and various clusters
Of women, and dancing girls and singing girls
In curtained pavilions. Their colorful garments
And babble of voices, on the occasion of the festival
Admirably observed, resembled the clamor
On the first day of the festivities when King Karikālan̠,
Whose great fame reached the heavens,
Celebrated the coming of the freshes in the Kāviri.
It became one with the wild tumult of the people
From all the four castes gathered
On the strip of land where the mighty river
Kāviri floods the seashore. Soft
As a flower, wide-eyed Mātavi then took
The good lute with perfect strings

Lines 145–172

From the hands of Vacantamālai, tired from standing.
With Kōvalaṉ, she ensconced herself on a white-legged couch
With a canopy screened off by painted tapestries.
It was placed on the freshly spread sand
In the shade of a laurel tree in an open space
Fenced in by the flowering screw pine
That wiped off the odor of fish from the sea.

ENVOI

Bees, the color of sapphire, sleep
In the evening shut inside the white petals
Of the flowering screw pine on the seashore.
To suck the hardy nectar and pollen,
They rise in the morning, like the chariot
Of the fiery-rayed Sun of radiant color.

Lines 173–178

Canto 7
The Love Songs of the Seaside Grove

PREFACE

1

Mātavi took the lute out from its picturesque covering and bowed to it. She held it in her hands. Its graceful body, painted with flowers, looked like a lovely bride with wide eyes lined with kohl. Its resonator, angle, turning pegs, and strings were faultless. She played the lute in eight different modes as advised by the texts: plucking the first and fifth notes and tuning their octaves, creasing the strings to indicate the mode, listening to the exact pitch of each note, observing the duration of rests, elaborating a melody with care, adopting the meter to the rhythm, playing delightfully, and improvising the style of expression.

Like a swarm of humming bees, her soft fingers, delicate as the red lotus and ringed with emeralds, hovered on the strings and flawlessly improvised ragas. She tested on her ears the eight kinds of plucking techniques classified by musicians: plucking with the index finger, plucking the string with up-and-down strokes, thrumming, changing from one string to the next, plucking with the pressure of fingers, rubbing the string to test the tone, sweeping the strings, and exquisite arpeggios.

She put the lute in Kōvalaṉ's outstretched hands, and said: "I shall not command. What is the beat I should follow?" To the delight of Mātavi's heart, he too began to sing a song to the Kāviri as well as other songs connected with the seaside grove.

HE SPEAKS TO THE RIVER

2

The king's wreathed, white parasol is a moon.
If he extends his scepter
And weds Kaṅkai,
Never sulk. O Kāvēri, may you live forever!

If he weds Kaṅkai,
Never sulk, you with fish eyes!
Patience is the highest virtue of young women.
So I've learnt. O Kāvēri, may you live forever!

3

Unfading wreaths has the king on his white parasol.
If he extends his upright scepter
And weds Kaṉṉi,
Never sulk. O Kāvēri, may you live forever!
If he weds Kaṉṉi,
Never sulk, you with fish eyes!
Patience is the highest virtue of unfading women.
So I've learnt. O Kāvēri, may you live forever!

4

The sound of plowmen, the sound of sluices,
The sound of breaking waters, the sound of revelers
Rejoicing over the first freshes—to their growing clamor
You flowed. O Kāvēri, may you live forever!
To the sound of revelers and their growing clamor
You continued to flow. In praising you
As the king's plenty, warriors refused to hold
Their tongues. O Kāvēri, may you live forever!

HER FRIEND SPEAKS TO HIM

5

To our girl with wide eyes like blue lotuses
They showed the sea god again and again,
But failed to keep their rich promises.
How can we know, sir,
Naive as we are, they aren't virtuous?

In Pukār, our town,
Seeing bright, spiraled conches and pearls,
The bud of the water lily opens
Taking them for the moon with outspread rays
And a cluster of stars.

6

In the seaside grove on the backwater,
They waylaid us from behind
As lovers bearing gifts in their hands.
How can we know, sir,
They will turn into strangers
And leave us standing to beg of them?
In Pukār, our town,
A whirling bee can't tell a woman's eyes
From a pair of blue flowers
Opening in the moon's reflection in the water.

7

Conches with echoing lips,
Tossed about by the huge, swirling waves,
Swept and hurled on the shore,
Plow over and wreck the sand houses, sir,
Made by the girls on the wrinkled sand.
In Pukār, our town,
Upset, they shred their garlands with soft fingers,
And fling the blue lotuses to scatter the conches.
Passersby in the evening see the flowers,
Take them for blinking eyes, and stop.

HIS FRIEND SPEAKS TO HIM

8

Shed by the heavy, flowering laurel,
A cloud of pollen covers the seaside grove,
Hides the whisper of furrows in the sand
Of trailing right-spiraled conches browsing
On the shore. Only her soft breasts,
It seems, flushed with beauty spots,
Will end the heartache caused
By her bright, full-moon face
And wide, fish eyes
That no flood of medicine can heal.

HE REPLIES TO HIS FRIEND

9

In the seaside grove thick with the odor of flowers
A girl keeps watch over fat, dried fish,
And pretends to drive the hovering birds away.
She holds a fetid cassia in her hand.
Round it hum and whirl a swarm of bees.
I didn't know she was a goddess.
Had I known, I wouldn't have gone there.

10

I didn't know the cruel god of death
Lives in the seaside grove of swirling waters
In the seductive form of a girl with wide eyes
Shaped like fatal spears. Flower in hand,
She keeps watch over fish dried for sale
In the frontyard of huts where fishermen dry their nets.
Had I known, I wouldn't have gone there.

HE SPEAKS TO HER
when he meets her alone

11

Is it the moon you see in this face,
Perfected by copying the fish, bow,
And black cloud, and by the work of Kāma?
Is it the moon you see that feared
The serpent of the vast and wonderful heavens,
And came to live in this small village
Of men with fishing boats?

12

Is it the cruel god of death
You see in these eyes like bloody spears
That flit from one side to the other
To the sound of conches flung upon the shore?
Is it the cruel god of death
You see in the graceful form of this young girl
Who came to reside in this small village
Of men who live by the sea?

13

This girl you see, driving the birds away
From the white, dried fish that smell, confuses
And troubles those who look at her. Is she a goddess?
Is it a goddess you see who took
The form of a girl, hair braided
In five, smooth plaits, and lives
In the cool seaside grove,
Wild with the goatsfoot creeper?

HE SPEAKS
his friend within earshot

14

Fragrant blossoms lavished by the grove,
The fresh smell of the expansive sand,
Her sweet, flawless speech,
Her fine, young, swelling breasts,
Her face like the full moon,
Her arched brows a pair of bows,
Her lightning waist beyond copying—
These are the things that trouble me.

15

The swirling waves lavished by the shore,
The seaside covered with fine sand,
Fragrant blossoms giving off perfume,
The shore with the thick grove,
Her curly hair giving off perfume,
Her face, bright like the moon,
Her two eyes a pair of minnows—
These are the things that trouble me.

16

The shore where conches grow,
The grove with its wafting odors,
Fragrant blossoms with unopened petals,
The path she treads alone,
Her teeth like tender, sprouting shoots,
Her face like the full moon,
Her two youthful breasts—
These are the things that trouble me.

HE SPEAKS
in pain

17

Your elder brothers live by going to sea and taking lives.
Will you also live by entering my body and taking my life?
Writhing under the weight of your hot breasts
That your taut bodice is unable to support,
Your waist grows thin. See that you don't lose it!

18

Your father takes lives with his cold-eyed net.
Will you also take my life with the net of your wide eyes?
Under the weight of your breasts, graced with a string of pearls,
Your narrow waist, like lightning among storm clouds,
Shrivels and grows thin. See that you don't lose it!

19

Your elder brothers take lives with their swift boats.
Will you also take my life with your arched brows?
You take pride in not thinking about others' woes.
Under the weight of your breasts, your narrow, slender waist
Grows weak. See that you don't lose it!

HE SPEAKS
to his heart

20

Holding a coral pestle in her hand,
She of the red eyes pounds the white pearls,
Pounds the white pearls, she of the red eyes
That are not dark lilies. Cruel, cruel are they.

21

Like a swan strutting in the shade of a laurel tree
Washed by the reeking waters, walks she of the red eyes.
Like a swan strutting, walks she of the red eyes
Of unspeakable cruelty. The eyes of death, of death.

22

Holding honey-tongued violets in her hand,
She of the red eyes drives the birds away from the drying fish,
Drives the birds away from the drying fish, she of the red eyes
That are not bright spears. Fierce, fierce are they.

HE SPEAKS TO A PASSERBY

23

Don't meet her, lovely swan! Don't meet her.
Your walk is unlike hers.
Don't meet her, lovely swan! Don't meet her.
Your walk is unlike hers.
She roams about inflaming the world, bound
By the waters of the swirling waves.
Don't follow her, lovely swan! Don't follow her.
Your walk is unlike hers.

INTERLUDE

24

Mātavi, with wide doe eyes, listened
To Kōvalaṉ's song of the seaside grove,
And thought: "There's a hint of another woman:
He's turned his back on me."
Though sulking, she pretended to enjoy
Meeting him. She took the lute from him,
And as if taking interest in another man, began

To play a song of the seaside grove. Varuṇa,
The god of the seashore, wondered at her skill.
Hearing her sweet voice accompanying the lute,
Folks all over the vast world rejoiced.

SHE SPEAKS TO THE RIVER

25

Covering yourself with a garment of beautiful flowers
Around which bees cluster and sing, you walked
With dark, fish eyes, open and rolling.
O Kāvēri, may you live forever!
With dark, fish eyes, open and rolling,
You flowed to the brim because unbent
Was your husband's perfect spear.
So I've learnt. O Kāvēri, may you live forever!

26

Your exciting garlands swung near as you flowed.
Peacocks danced and, following them,
Koels sang in the grove bursting with flowers.
O Kāvēri, may you live forever!
Your exciting garlands swung near as you flowed
To the brim, for you have seen
The power of his fierce spear.
So I've learnt. O Kāvēri, may you live forever!

27

May his fertile land that you raise,
As a mother raises her child, live forever,
Never stopping to heap great favors
For years on end. O Kāvēri, may you live forever!
Your flow never stops heaping

Great favors because of the grace of the king
Of the solar line who bears the wheel
And protects life. O Kāvēri, may you live forever!

HER FRIEND SPEAKS TO HIM

28

Like the god of love, sir, you come
Everyday. "Buy these pearls," you say.
Unlike the lovely teeth in her coral mouth
And her face radiant as the moon are they.
In Pukār, our town,
The roaring sea, like a trader, deals
In sparkling white pearls for wreaths of flowers
From the seaside grove heavy with fragrance.

29

Bangles on the glowing forearms of the women
Of the hardy fishermen's village by the sea
Reveal, by slipping, those who made love
In secret. How can we know
This, sir, naive as we are?
In Pukār, our town,
The white lily with a humming bee inside
Blossoms seeing a swan perched on a branch,
Burdened with the flowers of the tall laurel tree,
Thinking it to be the full moon among the stars.

30

In our seaside village the abuse of wine,
That ruins those who drink it, is no secret.
You cause this lasting sickness,
Without any cure, to our women.

How can we know this, sir?
In Pukār, our town,
Waves pull down our sand houses. And women,
Tears welling up from spearlike eyes,
Long wounds fresh on moon-faces,
Scoop sand by the handful to fill the sea.

HER FRIEND SPEAKS

31

He saw the spotted crab pair
With its mate. He also saw me in the seaside grove
Thick with a cluster of flowers.
I don't understand the nature of this head fisherman
Of the roaring waves. He lost his senses
And left us without a word, O girl
Of the curly hair braided in five plaits!

SHE SPEAKS

in pain

32

Has he left without thinking of us, taking with him
His kindness and his horse-drawn chariot?
Having forsaken us, let him leave.
O goatsfoot creepers with soft clusters of flowers!
O swans! We won't forget him who's forgotten us.

33

You won't grieve as my eyes do, weeping
On this evening of great sorrow. You will sleep.
Sweet, honey-tongued, blue lily!
Do you see in your dreams
That hard-hearted man coming to the seaside grove?

34

O sea with clear waters! You washed out
All the furrows made by the wheels
Of his chariot drawn by horses swift as birds.
What can I do?
O sea with clear waters? You washed out
All the furrows. You don't realize
You have joined hands with our foes here.
What can I do?

35

O sea with rolling waters, you washed out
The furrows made by the wheels
Of my dear lover's big, sturdy chariot!
O swan, playing in love! O cool grove
Of flowers! O wet, cool shore!
You didn't tell him: "This isn't right."

36

You have spread over and erased the furrows
Made by the wheels of my dear lover's big, sturdy chariot!
O waters of the sea, may you live forever!
You have spread over and erased the furrows
Made by the wheels of my dear lover's big, sturdy chariot!
Our love has ended though you pretend it hasn't.
O waters of the sea, may you live forever!

HER FRIEND SPEAKS TO HER

37

Lord of the sea, your waves roll
As far as the fields of golden paddy,
Sparkling with fine pearl ornaments

And wearing a bright coral girdle.
Fresh wounds made in the grove,
Thick with laurel flowers, by the young god
With a fish on his banner cover her beyond recognition.
If her mother sees, what can I do?

38

Lord of the sea, your waves open
Their lips of beautiful, red coral
And teeth of pearls, and roll as far as the frontyard
Of huts where fishermen dry their nets.
This girl has the color of the yellow flower
Of the sponge gourd that blossoms in the rains.
If her mother prays to the god and learns
Who inflicted this cruelty, what can I do?

39

Lord of the sea, your waves take pity,
Enter the seaside grove that is a park,
And spread the odor of the heap of faded flowers
To remove the stench of fish. The experience
Of many troubles doesn't help in knowing
For certain this one disease. Alone,
This girl is racked by anxiety. If her mother
Learns of this rare disease,
And worries and despairs, what can I do?

SHE SPEAKS TO HER FRIEND

40

It is early night. The sun, the maker
Of light, has vanished. Loneliness is hard
To get rid of: the eyes overflow with tears.
Girl with flowering blossoms in her hair!

Does this oppressive evening, that burst in
Spitting fire and making my bangles slip,
Show up in the land of the one who is gone?

41

The sun has vanished. Dark night
Has fallen. Eyes lined with kohl,
Like opening flowers, shed tears
Of sorrow. Girl with a face like the full moon!
Does this oppressive evening, that burst in
Consuming the sun and throwing up the moon,
Show up in the land of the one who is gone?

42

The song of the birds has ceased. The sun,
The maker of the day, has vanished. Wide eyes
Shed tears in great pain
That won't stop. Girl with thick, flowering blossoms
In your hair! Does this oppressive evening,
That burst into my life violently,
Show up in the land of the one who is gone?

HER FRIEND SPEAKS TO HER

43

Someone came through the backwater to the fence
Of screw pine, wrecked our games
And went away. That man, who wrecked our games
And went away, won't quit my loving heart.

44

Someone came through the backwater to the fence
Of the seaside grove, stood before us and said:

"Bestow your favors on me." That man who stood
Before us and said: "Bestow your favors
On me," won't forget our deerlike looks.

45

Someone saw a swan playing with its mate,
And stood watching us yesterday. That man,
Who stood watching us yesterday, won't leave us
Like the golden beauty spots on our breasts.

SHE SPEAKS TO THE CRANE

46

Don't come here, crane! Don't come to our seaside grove.
Don't come here, crane! Don't come to our seaside grove.
You won't tell the lord of the sea,
With the breaking waves, of my great pain.
Don't come here, crane! Don't come to our seaside grove.

INTERLUDE

47

Thus sang Mātavi of excellent ornaments.
With her soft fingers, like the petals of the glory lily,
She played the sweet-versed cevvaḻi raga
In which the third note coincided with the first.
Guided by the exact conventions of the texts,
She began playing a new raga.

SHE SPEAKS TO THE EVENING

48

When the fishermen sang the sweet viḷari raga,
The fifth note blending with the third,
Evening, you stayed with me. Charmed

By the fifth note blending with the third,
You stayed with me. Ruthless at plunder,
Take my life. O evening, may you live forever!

49

In the shade of the fine, gracious words
Spoken out of love by those who have parted,
They stood and wept. O evening you have laid waste
Their lives! How are you related to the enemy king
Besieging, from outside, the king within his fortress?
Likewise, O evening, you lay waste my life!

50

My pain grows. The sun, the maker of the day,
Drops and fades. Evening, who makes me swoon,
You have come to shut the eyes of the world.
If you are the twilight, and the sun my husband,
The world is truly ruined.
O evening, may you live forever!

HER FRIEND SPEAKS
he within earshot

51

"This evening, that makes us swoon, inflicts
Pain on us spread by its fire. We didn't imagine
It would trouble us thus. His kind words we took
For a pledge. Please bear with his false promises
Made in the seaside grove redolent of flowers."
God of the endless sea! We pray to your lotus feet.

POSTFACE

52

Hearing this, Kōvalan̲ thought: "I sang the song of the seaside grove. A hypocrite, she put together a pack of specious lies, and sang with someone else in mind." His karma now appeared, and found an excuse in the music of the lute. He took his caressing hands off her whose face was a full moon, and said: "Time here has indeed flown. Let us go." However, she didn't get up right away. Kōvalan̲ left at once with his attendants.

After he had gone, Mātavi put down the noise of her boisterous maids in the grove where flowers scatter pollen. She climbed into her horse-drawn chariot with an empty heart, and without her lover entered her home alone with a prayer:

"May Cempiyan̲ of the flaming sword
And elephant with a faceplate, make the kings
Of this vast world bow their heads to him.
May his wreathed, white parasol
Enclose within it the Cakravāla Mountains."

Canto 8
The Coming of Spring

Māraṉ, the king of great renown,
Sat on the throne and ruled, with his jovial friend
Spring, the fertile Tamil land
Scored by cool waters, and bounded
By the Vēṅkaṭam hills in the north and the Kumari sea
In the south, with towering Maturai,
Glorious Uṟantai, bustling Vañci
And Pukār with its roaring waters as its capitals.
Rising from the lush Potiyil hills
Of the illustrious sage Agastya, the herald
South wind breathed the coming of spring.
"Host of the triumphant fish-bannered prince!
Put on your flawless robes," trilled
The koel from a grove thick with creepers.
As Kāma's trumpeter, he sounded his command.

Mātavi, her wide eyes like dark flowers,
Returned alone from her lovers' quarrel
With Kōvalaṉ in the seaside grove, where the flowers
Opened their petals, near the arena of the water sports.
She pined for him, and climbed up to the room
Used in the spring at one end
Of the lofty, upper floor almost touching the sky.
Adorned with splendid ornaments, the portals
Of her breasts, flushed with kumkum, she brightened up
With pearls from the southern sea and sandalwood paste
From the southern hills. These choice, flawless offerings

Lines 1–21

She made as a fit tribute to spring.
Sitting up gracefully in the lotus posture,
One of nine, she took up the perfect lute
In her hands and sang a sweet song.
Entranced, she played it on the lute.
Bending the thumb of her right hand
And touching the neck with four fingers,
She gripped the screw-pins with the four fingers
Of her left hand, and played the cempakai,
Ārppu, kūṭam, and atirvu, having learned
To remove, in order, the dissonance. The series
Of fourteen notes she based on impeccable tradition,
Beginning with the fourth and ending with the third.
She looked for a hint of the notes made
By the second, fifth, sixth and third,
And fourth strings, and played the first note
On the fifth string. Besides, following tradition,
She plucked the fifth and seventh strings,
Beginning and ending with the fourth note
As well as beginning and ending with the first note.
Strictly observing the three levels of pitch,
She performed well the four types of ragas,
Akanilai, puṟanilai, arukiyal, and perukiyal,
And began the tiṟam raga which arose from them.
The flowering creeper, Mātavi, was beside herself
When she played the puṟanilai raga.

Won over by his sorrows of flowering blossoms,
Kāma all by himself brought under his rule
The entire world with his unique scepter.

Lines 22–52

In every corner of the earth he was
Adored and honored without exception,
And she wished Kōvalaṉ to hear the royal word
Of his coming. She took up a garland made
By tying together the champak, mātavi, gamboge,
Malabar jasmine, cuscus roots,
And the tender petals of the beautiful red lily,
And picked from its middle, plaited with flowering buds,
The white, bent petals of the ripe screw pine.
Taking in her hand as stylus the firm bud
Of a jasmine near it, she dipped it in a thick paste
Of red lac and wrote:
"Spring has come,
The young crown prince, who unites
All creatures with their loved ones.
Even the opulent moon is not impartial:
He burst in with the bitterness of parting that comes
With the evening. It is an old truth
That Kāma should take their sweet lives
By striking them with his arrows of fragrant blossoms
Whether they are people who spent a few hours
In love or people who parted and forgot
Their lovers. Do understand this."
All
The sixty-four arts that she practised deserted her,
Including the singing of ragas and tiṟams by the tongue
That slanders. Like the petals of a flower coming apart,
Her skills were choked by her solitary passion.
She spoke repeatedly in her innocent prattle and wrote.
That evening, redolent of memories, she was pale

Lines 53–67

As she called out to Vacantamālai:
"Come here.
Speak to Kōvalaṉ about all the ripe thoughts
Written on this garland of pure flowers,
And bring him here."
Accepting the garland,
She of the wide, spear eyes, flushed
With red streaks, spoke to Kōvalaṉ
In the street of the grain merchants.
Kōvalaṉ then replied:
"The girl in love performed
The dance of the meeting eyes, with kumkum
On her forehead, curly hair, small black bows
For eyebrows, the kumiḻ flower for the nose,
And lips the color of the scarlet kovvai fruit.
The often-seen dance the dark, wide-eyed girl
Performed, who came when I said, 'Come,' and went
When I said, 'Go,' with a bright moonlike face
Writhing in pain under the burden of her cloud
Of hair. Her eyes with seductive charm moved about
And wandered like minnows, and her handsome smile
Revealed teeth of bright pearls when she opened
Her coral mouth filled with sweetness.
On seeing me alone, she performed
The masquerade dance in the costume of her girlfriend,
With wide eyes, fatal as spears. She saw
My deprivation, caused by a mind full of troubles,
And pitied me with the coming of evening,
Who put to flight the parrot's sweet talk, the gait
Of the foolish swan, and the grace of the spry peacock.

Lines 68–87

She was of passionate looks and slender
Waist that can bear no ornaments,
And performed the minor dance of indifference
Outside my house to the tinkling of anklets
And the knock of the girdle. Though she saw
My deprivation, it seemed not to have changed her nature.
With a radiant forehead she appeared before me
And performed the dance of the offended, with a garland,
Flowing hair, locks brightened with petals,
A string of pearls, and large breasts
Hurting her lightning waist. Her young friend
Gave her my reply, and hearing the sullen words
Of my deep love for her, wrested their true meaning.
Languid in appearance and with soft, lovely hair,
She danced as if parting from me because of her sullenness.
When repeatedly thinking of her great sorrow,
She pined for me at the time I lived apart
From her, and talked about it to many of my relations,
As she performed the dance of taking counsel.
Her hair adorned with flowers opened
By bees, she was beside herself in the evening
When she spoke about her sorrow to every passerby
As she performed the dance of revelation.
Swooning time and again before them as they lifted
Her up, she concluded with the dance of raising.
My girl adorned with choice ornaments!
All these dances added luster to her
Of the fine bracelet, for she is only a dancing girl."

Vacantamālai was hurt and grief-stricken at heart

Lines 88–113

At Kōvalaṉ's refusal to accept the letter
Written on the fine petals of the screw pine
By Mātavi, adorned with choice ornaments,
Her lovely face brightened up with precious jewels.
Quickly she returned to Mātavi wreathed
In a garland of flowering petals and informed her.

"O girl adorned with fair ornaments!
If he doesn't come this evening,"
spoke Mātavi
Of the wide eyes, lovely like flowers,
"We shall surely see him in the morning."

With an empty heart she lay down alone
On the couch spread with flowers
Without her eyelids coming together in sleep.

ENVOI

The red lotus blooms, the sprouts of sweet mango
Blow, the brilliant aśoka opens its petals
When spring comes with its pageant of flowers.
O, what will now become of the mind of the girl
With eyes bright like sharp spears?

"You that quarreled with your lovers, it is the command
Of the Formless One that you love one another,"
Sang the koels. "You that grieved over her song
Of the seaside grove, see the letter on the soft flowers
Written by her who loved you in the long springtime!"

Lines 113–126

Canto 9
The Nature of the Dream

It is evening: the sun had vanished. Women
With vinelike waists scattered fiery buds
Of jasmine about to blossom and grains of paddy
All over their homes. They lit their jeweled
Lamps, and dressed themselves for the night.

One day, long ago, Mālati fed the child
Of her husband's second wife with milk.
The child choked with the milk and died.
Mālati wept:
"My husband, the brahman,
And his second wife will put the blame
On me, and will not listen to the truth."

Taking the child in her arms, she entered
The temple of the wishing tree of the immortals,
The temple of the white elephant, the temple
Of the beautiful white god, the temple
Of the sun, lord of the meridian, who comes
From the spot where the day breaks, the temple
Of the guardian deity of Pukār, the temple
Of the spear god, the temple of Indra's thunderbolt,
The temple of Mācāttaṉ who lives on the outskirts
Of the town, the temple of the Nirgranthas,
And the temple of the moon, and prayed: "O gods!
Cure me of my trouble." She then reached
The temple of Pācaṇṭa Cāttaṉ, prostrated before

Lines 1–15

The deity, and awaited his grace. Before her appeared
A young vinelike girl, as if reproaching others
By her beauty, who said:
"O faultless woman!
To those who haven't done penance, God
Won't grant a favor. This isn't a false utterance;
It's a true saying. Give me the body
Of the dead child you have in your hands."

She snatched it from her hands, and walked
In the thick darkness to the cremation grounds.
The goblin Iṭākiṉi, who devours the bodies
Buried there, took the child and put it
In her stomach. Before her who screamed and wept
Like a peacock at the roar of thunder appeared
The god Cāttaṉ and said:
"Mother!
Don't weep. Look at the living child
Before you."
Then, as that child, he approached
The shade of a grove thick with koels.
Without any suspicion, that woman took
The shadowy child, clasped it to her stomach,
And put it back in the arms of its mother.
Later, that holy brahman child grew
Into a boy and gained deep knowledge
Of the Vedas pregnant with meaning. When his parents
Died, he settled all disputes among their relations
And performed the funeral rites due to his father

Lines 16–32

And mother. One Tēvanti became his wife.
Having lived with her for some time, he told her:
"May your flowerlike eyes, lined with kohl,
Bear this light," and went to her. He revealed
His eternal youthfulness, and said: "Come
To my temple," and left.
She of impeccable speech
Who worshiped daily at his temple offered
This excuse:
"My wedded husband has left me
Saying that he will go and bathe
In all the sacred ghats. You will make him return
Here, and restore him to me."
Knowing
That the good woman Kaṇṇaki of perfect fame
Had cause for grief, and thinking of it
With a sorrowful heart, Tēvanti worshiped
The god by offering hariali grass,
Flowers of the wool plant and grains
Of paddy. She went to Kaṇṇaki with the prayer:
"May your husband return to you!"
But Kaṇṇaki replied:
"Even if he returns to me,
My heart will still ache because of a dream
In which he held my hand, and we traveled
To a great city, and entered it. In the city
We had entered, the people spoke
Of a monstrous omen. It was like placing
A scorpion on me. 'A misfortune will fall
Upon Kōvalaṉ.' Hearing it, I pleaded

Lines 33–50

Before the king who protects. 'A misfortune will fall
Upon the city together with the king,' I vowed.
I won't speak further as it seemed a foul deed.
O woman with close-fitting bangles! If you
Heard about the foul deed inflicted on me,
And its joyous outcome to me and my husband
You will laugh."
Glowing with ornaments,
Tēvanti replied:
"O woman with golden bracelets!
You aren't disliked by your husband. In a previous birth
You had failed to keep a vow on his behalf.
To wipe out the evil as a result of it, go
To the place where the Kāviri takes its waters
To the roaring sea. There is a seaside grove
Where the blue lily opens its petals,
And where there are two holy tanks, the tank
Of the moon and the tank of the sun. Women
Who bathe on their steps and worship at the temple
Of Kāma nearby will enjoy this world
Together with their husbands. To heaven, the land
Of pleasures, they will go and be reborn there.
We will one day go there to play in the water."

Resplendent in jewels, Kaṇṇaki replied:
"It doesn't make me proud." Later, a maid
Came to her and said: "Our Kōvalaṉ has arrived
At the gate. It appears he will protect us
For a long time."
Kōvalaṉ too entered the bedroom

Lines 50–66

Of the glorious Kaṇṇaki, saw the wasted form
Of his wife with fine bracelets, saw her grief,
And said:
"By keeping company with a liar,
Full of deceitful conduct, I have lost
The mountainous hoard of wealth left to me
By my family. The poverty has brought shame on me."

Her bright face lit up with a consoling smile,
She said: "My anklets. Here! Take them."

Kōvalaṉ replied:
"O woman with beautiful ornaments!
Listen. With this anklet as the capital, I will recover
All the jewels and wealth I've lost.
Arise, O woman with petals of flower in your hair!
Go with me from here to the towering city
Of Maturai of renowned fame."
Reconciled
To the karma of his previous birth, he accepted
Its inevitable course and left before the sun
In a blaze of light thinned out the darkness.

ENVOI

The dream of the beloved Kaṇṇaki made
The words of Mātavi of the dark, wide eyes
Empty. Reconciled to the karma
Of his previous birth, he accepted
Its inevitable course and left before the sun
In a blaze of light thinned out the darkness.

Lines 66–83

Canto 10
Country Scenes

In the last watch of the night before daybreak
When the eye of heaven had not opened,
The pale moon had vanished from the sky,
Incandescent with stars. In the pitch darkness
Of that final quarter Kōvalaṉ set out
With Kaṇṇaki, his mind moved by his karma.
They passed through the corridor of their home
With its famed, tall, wide, bolted door
On which the ram, yak, and swan with its soft down
Wandered about with a sense of kinship. After going round
The temple of Maṇivaṇṇaṉ reclining in a state
Of yogic trance on the fair, glistening serpent,
They moved on, and went by the seven Buddhist temples
Built by Indra. Superhuman beings moved
In the air, and carefully explained the holy words
Of the Buddha who had sat in the comely, radiant shade
Of the green-leaved bo tree, its five branches
Spread high. They worshiped and went round
The bright moonstone seat built
By all the Jaina householders for the convenience
Of sages, who would come on the festival
Of the first freshes and the festival of the lofty car,
In the thick, glowing shade of the golden-flowered aśoka,
Near the fine, spacious courtyard beside the temple
Of the arhat where the five junctions sacred
To the five classes of yogis came together.
Gathered there were noble men who had given up

Lines 1–20

Eating meat, taken the vow of speaking the truth,
Purified themselves of sins, understood
The nature of things, restrained their senses,
And known the true way.
Jostling with the crowd,
They emerged from the corridor that led
To the world of Pukār and seemed a long river
That rose in a hill, and came to the royal park.
The lake there, covered with fine, shady trees
Thick with many flowers, was offered together
With spring and the Potiyil breeze
As a tribute to the king by the bodiless god, Kāma.
They crossed the high road shaded
On either side by parks with trees bent low
That led to the bathing ghat where women
Sported at the mouth of the Kāviri.
Going westwards, they entered
A flowery grove on the north bank of the Kāviri
Of fertile waters. Ten miles
They walked from there, and reached the home
Of Kavunti in a thick grove of flowering trees.
Kaṇṇaki was tired and footsore, her waist
Thin as a vine. Breathing hard,
She of the thick, fragrant hair
In an ageless voice inquired, showing
Her sharp, bright teeth: "Which is the ancient city
Of Maturai?" With a smile, Kōvalaṉ replied:

"O you who have five, fragrant plaits
Of hair! It is near—three hundred miles

Lines 20–43

From our spacious country."
He saw,
With his sweet-voiced wife, the revered Kavunti
Who lived there and worshiped her feet.
Kavunti said:
"O you who have good features,
A noble family, impeccable conduct,
And observe the proper austerities enjoined
By the holy words of the arhat! What
Is your reason for leaving home and coming,
Like wicked people, this far?"
Kōvalaṉ replied:

"O you who have done penance! I have
No answer to your inquiry. In the ancient city
Of Maturai I wish to seek my fortune."

The ascetic said:
"Her small feet,
Brightened with anklets, cannot bear the hostility
Of pebbles. It is difficult to pass through
The forests that one frequently comes across
In the country. Looking at her nature, do you
Think she is strong enough? But who knows
What your karma has in store for you?
If I ask you to give up the journey
As being unsuitable, I know you won't.
Single-minded I am to visit flawless Maturai
In the good Tamil country of the south,
And to worship the arhat there by listening to the word

Lines 43–59

Of dharma of the holy sages who have cleansed
Themselves of impure utterances. I will,
Therefore, go with you. Shall we leave?"

With raised hands, Kōvalaṉ then worshiped
The ascetic Kavunti and praised her thus:
"O sage! if you would be so gracious, I shall be rid
Of anxiety for this one who has armlets
On her shoulders." Kavunti said:
"Kōvalaṉ,
Look here! Many troubles will assail us
On our way. Listen to them: Should we
Pass through the grove thick with flowers
With this tender girl who can't bear the severe heat,
We may face overwhelming grief
That strikes people who won't be careful
About false pits made by men
Who pulled out roots buried in the cleft soil
And covered over with the pollen of withered champaks
Fallen down. If we avoid these withered flowers
Fallen down and walk on, ripe, sweet jackfruits
Might, like inveterate enemies, knock us down.
If we step into the garden where the turmeric
And ginger, entangled in confusion, grow,
The stones from the reddish pulp of jackfruits
Might hurt the feet as if in enmity. O loving husband
Of the girl with wide, fish eyes!
Should we cut through the plowed fields,
This girl will be frightened by the otters too
That chase away the snarling fish in ponds

Lines 59–78

Redolent of flowers, and grab the scabbard fish
With its long back when it leaps across the field
Where the eels roll. There the large hives,
Pendent from sugarcanes, fall apart and blend
With the pure water of the pond hugged
By bees. Her mind worn out, she might,
To slake her unbearable thirst, scoop out
The water with the palm of her hand and drink it.

"Those who pull the weeds out would have flung
The blue lotuses with her buds about to open
On the bank where the beetles with spots and stripes
Will be lying about in knots. Tired from the strain
Of the journey, your feet may unknowingly tread
Upon them. Unmindful of the beautiful, spotted crabs
And snails, if we walk along the bank
Of a canal, treading the beaten path,
We might step on them and cause them pain.
It won't be possible for us to bear the suffering
That will follow. Except through the fields and groves,
There isn't a way anywhere. O you who have
A long, black tuft of hair! Keep these places in mind,
And without causing pain go carefully
With this fair woman."
Then the ascetic Kavunti
Picked up in her hands the holy begging-bowl,
The sling to be thrown over her shoulder,
And peacock's feathers, praying:
"May the lord
Of the five holy letters guide our steps!"

Lines 78–100

With the immaculate and esteemed Kavunti, Kōvalan̲
And Kaṇṇaki began their journey. Even if Śani
Fumes and comets blaze, and Śukra
With outstretched rays travels south,
On the windswept top of the Kuṭaku hills
Clouds swollen with water pour down,
To the roar of thunder, the blessing of rain.
Born in those hills, the first freshes
Of the Kāviri flow swiftly, bursting with riches,
Split open the estuary and oppose the treasures
Of the sea, leap over the sluice gate and fall.
Except this there is no other sound. It drowns
The noise of the bucket, the water-lift,
The very loud well-sweep, and the basket
Used for bailing water.
In the thicket
Of fresh lotuses rising from ponds
Caressed by splendid paddy fields
And sugarcane are heard, as on a battlefield
Where two kings fight for victory,
Various kinds of clamorous sounds
Made by waterfowls, screaming cranes,
Red-footed swans, green-footed herons,
Wild fowls, cormorants, snipes,
The ūral water-birds, large herons
And other birds. Buffalos enter and immerse
Themselves in the soft, unplowed mire.
With the hair on their bodies unwashed, eyes
Red, they come and rub
Their itching backs against the unspoilt, straw bins,

Lines 101–122

Thus loosening the twisted strands that hold them.
The bins come apart spilling the rich grain
Stored inside with sheaves of excellent paddy
That resemble chowries.
One heard
The noise of the loud talk of laborers
With strong arms and farmers standing
In knots. One heard the sound
Of songs in new styles by lowborn women
Who turned on by strong wine worked in the fields.
Eyes wide like red minnows,
They bandied indecent words and looked
Singularly charming in their clothes splashed
With mud that also glazed their breasts and shoulders
Clasped by armlets. From their hair they picked
The fragrant flowers and thrust seedlings instead.
One heard the plowmen's song of praise
As they stood by their plows and worshiped
With folded hands. They appeared to break open
The earth radiant with wreaths bound
With shining ears of rice, plaited
With blue lotuses and the thick, vinelike hariali grass.

One heard the mukavai song
When they drove the buffalos to thresh
The sheaves of paddy cut and heaped
On one side for fine grain, and the clamor
Of the joyous music of the round kettledrum,
Smeared with mud, played in a frenzy
By dancers beating the kiṇai drum.

Lines 122–139

One after the other, the travelers heard
These sounds along the banks of the great river.
The joy in their hearts banished weariness.

Because of the triumph of the Cōḻa king
With his tiger-bannered chariot, they saw
Everywhere sacrificial smoke made as an offering
By holy brahmans in the hearths of their tall houses
With sloping roofs. They seemed
Like glorious fog-covered hills that make
The clouds sweat with rain. They saw
Farmers too, the sons of Mother Kāviri
Of expansive waters, who by their plowing helped
The needy multitude and the triumphant king.
In the smoke that rose from the sugarcane press
Over heaps of unwinnowed grain,
The old and thriving villages seemed
Like hills topped with black clouds.
They saw the land interwoven with villages,
And didn't travel more than ten miles a day.
Beyond that they rested.
After many days' journey,
One evening they reached Araṅkam
That veiled the river. Close by was the abode of the gods
Heavy with redolent flowers on one side
Of a thick grove crowded with trees
And fenced with exquisite, bent bamboos.
A sage appeared there who talked of dharma,
Full of the perfect truth of the three excellences
Of the arhat. He was returning from the outskirts

Lines 140–163

Of Pukār where the renowned householders
Had built together the bright moonstone seat
From which the arhat hadn't moved. Kavunti
Who had recognized the sage fell at his feet
And touched them—so did Kōvalaṉ and Kaṇṇaki—
Praying: "May the deeds of our former births
Perish." By the light of his wisdom the sage
Knew the reason for their coming and wasn't upset:
He was a saint who had totally overcome desire
And hatred.
"O Kavunti of great and abounding excellence!
You will realize," he said, "that karma is inexorable.
It makes us experience what should be avoided.
Like a seed when planted, it will sprout
And fulfill itself. When its time is ripe,
It will be impossible to stop it. Like a burning lamp
In a wide, open plain, blown out
By strong winds, so does life flee the body.

"The omniscient arhat, he who has exceeded
The limits of understanding, the all-merciful being,
The victorious lord, the accomplisher, the divine being,
The first cause of dharma, the chief,
The all-righteous, the ultimate reality, the pure,
The ancient one, the all-wise, the one
Who has overcome anger, the master, the lord
Of salvation, the supreme being, the possessor
Of virtues, the light that shines in heaven,
The great truth, the all-humble, the sage,
The major cause, the yogi, the sovereign,

Lines 163–183

The superior person, the brilliant light,
The one who dwells in everything, the guru,
The embodiment of nature, our king, the one
Of everlasting fame, the great king
Of virtues, the all-prosperous, the highest god,
The self-born, the four-faced one, the bestower
Of the aṅgāgama, the arhat, the gracious sage,
The one god, the possessor of the eight powers,
The indivisible primordial substance, the celestial,
The first cause of the Āgamas, and the shining light.
No one can escape the prison-house
Of the body's rebirth unless he is blessed.
With the light of the revealed Āgamas."

Thus spoke the sage.
Hearing his holy words,
Kavunti, foremost in penance, folded
Her hands above her head and said:
"My ears
Won't open except to listen to the holy words
Of wisdom revealed by him who has overcome
The three, that is, desire, anger, and delusion.
My tongue won't speak except to recite
The one thousand and eight names of him
Who has won over Kāma. Though they see the feet
Of other gods near my hands, my eyes
Won't see anything except the two feet of him
Who has overcome the five senses.
My useless body won't touch anyone
On the earth except the holy body of him

Lines 183–201

Who has out of his grace taken virtue upon himself.
My two hands won't come together to worship
Anyone except the knower who explains dharma
To arhats. The top of my head won't suffer
Any flower except the flowerlike feet of him
Who walked on flowers. My mind won't overturn
Itself to repeatedly utter anything
Except the holy words of the god of unending love."

Hearing these sweet words spoken
In praise of the arhat, the sage became one
With the supreme being. Getting up from the paved seat,
He rose to a height of one cubit.
Saying: "Kavunti, may the bonds that cause
Rebirth perish," through a path in the sky
He vanished. As he left, they worshiped
And prayed: "May our bonds perish."
Later, Kavunti of infinite penance, the woman
And her husband entered a boat at the long waterfront
Of the great river Kāviri with cloud-capped groves
Of flowers. They reached the southern shore
Of peerless temples where they rested.

In a flowery grove surrounded by fallen flowers,
A rake chattering aimlessly with his newfound whore
Accosted them in the grove of fragrant flowers.
They asked Kavunti:
"Who are
These two here that look like Kāma and Rati?

Lines 201–221

We would like to know. O woman of penance
Whose body is wasted by ceremonial fasting!
Who are these people that go with you?"
Kavunti replied:
"They are my children.
Look here, they are human beings!
Leave them alone. They are tired from the journey."
The strangers asked:
"Is it possible for those
Born of the same parents to live together
As man and wife, O you have learned and known all?"
Hearing these cruel words, Kaṇṇaki
Shut her ears and trembled before her husband.
A curse born of her penance Kavunti
Threw on them:
"Since these two seem
To insult my girl who looks like a wreath
Of flowers, they shall become old jackals
In a thorny forest."
The curse took effect.
Where is he who won't understand what had happened?
Kaṇṇaki, her hair adorned with fragrant flowers,
And her husband heard the long, protracted howl
Of the small jackals, and trembled. They said:

"Those who stray from the path of virtue
Speak unnaturally. We must know
They do so only because of their ignorance.
O you who have done penance! When will you say
Is the hour of expiation for those

Lines 221–240

Who have done wrong in your presence?"
She replied:

"They who have attained lower forms
Of birth due to ignorance will wander, suffering
Pain, for twelve months in the forest
Outside the Uṟaiyūr fortress. In this way
They will get back their original forms."

After their release from the curse had been uttered,
The ascetic Kavunti, unrivaled in penance,
Kaṇṇaki and her husband, with joy, entered
Uṟaiyūr built on the spot where long ago
A feathered rooster routed in a fight
An elephant with ears as broad as a winnowing fan.

CODA

Here ends "The Book of Pukār." It sings
Of the descendants, among the three crowned kings,
Of the Cōḻa line who shone with their powerful arms
Resplendent with bracelets; of the king's virtues,
Triumphs, and heroism; of the preeminence
Of the glorious, old city of Pukar;
Of the splendor of its festivals; of the coming of the gods;
Of the endless joy of its subjects; of the abundance
Of food; of the divine glory of the Kāviri
That wipes out evil; of the unfailing clouds
That bring fresh rain; of the stages,
Dances, tūkku, and vari; of the pārati-virutti
Whose fame has spread all over the world; of the song

Lines 240–260

About the five phases of love and other kinds
Of songs, and all these suited to the many kinds
Of lutes; of the specialty of the fourteen-stringed lute;
Of the intermediate pālai raga; of the elaboration
Of the seventh note; of the four ragas;
Of the beauty of Pukār; and of the colorful songs.
All these things, including others as well, reflect
The nature of Iḷaṅkō's incomparable art.
Only a glimpse of it is offered here.

ENVOI

Like the sun that rises and spreads its light
In the morning, and the moon that appears in the evening,
May Pukār live forever, resplendent with fame,
A wreath across the sea-encircled earth.

Lines 260–272

The Book of Maturai

Canto 11
The Scenes of the Forest

Under three elegant parasols, like three moons
One on top of the other, sat the arhat
Whose existence had no origin, who outshone
The glorious light of the rising sun.
Kavunti of the great penance worshiped him
In the thick shade of the aśoka tree
Bent with flowers. To all the ascetics
In the temple of the Nirgrantha in the vast grove
Near Araṅkam she graciously conveyed
The good and commendable words uttered
By the sage. With Kōvalaṉ and Kaṇṇaki, she spent
That day at the temple. They wished
To go south, and left Uṟaiyūr
In the last watch of the night before daybreak.
When the sun began to light up the eastern sky,
They entered a house in a grove of young trees.
Around it swarmed rich fields and ponds
Brimful with water. A revered brahman came there
Who praised the Pāṇṭiya king of impeccable fame:

"May our great king who protects this world
From one age to the next live forever!
May Teṉṉavaṉ who rules the southern country,
Widens it by taking the Gaṅgā and the Himālaya
In the north live forever! To reveal his might
To other kings he trampled on the shore,
Hurled at the cruel sea his perfect spear

Lines 1–22

That intolerant of an old enmity swallowed
The river Pahṟuḷi and Kumari hill
Together with a range of nearby hills.
May he live forever who wore on his radiant
Chest the potent wreath of Indra
Of the thousand red eyes to the glory
Of the excellent line of the Moon! 'He smashed
The bracelet set on our Lord Indra's crown,'
Said the heavy rains, and with peals
Of thunder withheld themselves. The Pāṇṭiyaṉ
Imprisoned the clouds to ensure the land
Is blessed with prosperity from an unfailing harvest.
May he live forever!"
                    Kōvalaṉ asked the brahman:
"Which is your village? Why have you come here?"
The brahman of undiminished excellence replied:

" 'With my own eyes let me see it.'
Thus troubled by my heart, I came here to see
The splendor of Viṣṇu praised and adored
By many as he lies, with Lakṣmī reposing
On his chest, on the firm couch of the serpent,
Its thousand hoods raised and spread out
In the islet caressed by the rolling waves
Of the mighty river Kāviri, just as the blue clouds
Lie stretched out on the high, golden mountain.
I came to see the splendor of red-eyed Viṣṇu,
Holding in his elegant lotus hands
The wheel that augurs death to his enemies,
And the milkwhite conch, who appears radiant

Lines 22–51

In a cloth of golden flowers, with a wreath
Of tender blossoms flung over his chest.
On the peak of the sublime hill known as Vēṅkaṭam,
Bathed by waterfalls in spate, he lives—
The hill erect as a dark cloud,
Robed in lightning and brightened with a rainbow,
Its lofty heights washed by the outspread rays
Of the sun and moon. I am from Māṅkāṭu
In the Kuṭaku hills. Since my eyes rejoiced
To see the glory and great doings
Of the Pāṇṭiya kingdom, I stopped here blessing
The king. This is the reason for my coming here."

Hearing what the brahman who has excelled
In virtuous deeds said, Kōvalaṉ asked:

"O first among brahmans! Please tell us
The best way to Maturai."
The brahman replied:

"You have come with your wife in the season
When the forests and hills have shed their nature,
Lost their fresh looks by taking the form
Of a wasteland, thus causing great hardship.
With his minister, Spring, King Sun,
His nature muted by the severe heat,
Is like a great kingdom whose ruler has lost
His sovereignty by flouting it on the advice
Of his minister. If on this long, rough journey,
You swim across rocks, hills,

Lines 51–64

Difficult and giddy paths, and mirages,
And enter Koṭumpai on the shore of a great lake,
You will come to a spot that forks
Into three paths like the devouring trident
Held by the god Śiva whose tuft
Is lit up with a crescent. If you resolve
To take the path that lies to the right,
You will see the cadamba with its branches
Spread out, the dried toothbrush tree,
The sirissa with its scorched stem, the bamboo
With its withered leaves, the spot
Where the striped and shriveled bowstring hemp
Lies about burnt, forests where deer
Stand and cry aloud thirsty and panting
For water, and the wilderness where hunters live;
You will then reach the Pāṇṭiyaṉ's Little Mountain.
Visible by its glimmer, it is thickly covered
With wild rice, sugarcane with severed joints,
Millets ready for plucking, ragi that grows
On fertile soil, garlic, turmeric,
Lovely kavalai vines, plantains,
Arecas, bunches of coconuts hanging low,
Mangos, and jackfruits. If you keep walking
To the right of that hill, you will reach
The great city of Maturai.
"If you don't take
That path, but take the one to the left,
You will hear the rustle of water
From the ponds to the low-lying fields,
Of groves with cool flowers, and of forests

Lines 65–90

With many rough paths. You will then reach
Mount Viṣṇu where there is a cavern that wipes out
All illusions, and leads to three ponds that sparkle
Without imperiling their undiminished fame,
Called holy Caravaṇam, Pavakāraṇi, and Iṭṭacitti.
Their miraculous nature is praised by even the gods.
If you bathe in the holy Caravaṇam,
You will acquire knowledge of the book
Composed by the king of the gods. If you bathe
In the Pavakāraṇi, you will know your past deeds
That caused your present birth. If you bathe
In the Iṭṭacitti, you will obtain the power
To have all that you wish for.

"If you choose to enter that cavern,
Worship the exalted one on that lofty hill
Keeping his lotus feet in your thoughts,
Praising him as you go thrice round the hill.
On the spacious bank of the Cilampāṟu that breaks
Through the earth, there will appear at the foot
Of the ironwood tree strewn with flowers,
A nymph, a golden vine like lightning,
With five plaits of hair like black clouds,
And with armlets on her shoulders. She will say:
'Varōttamai is my name, and I live
At the foot of this mountain. Tell me
What makes this life a joy,
The next life a joy? What is everlasting?
I will be at the service of those who answer
These questions. If your answer is right,

Lines 90–116

I will open the door of the cavern
To the deserving.' She will open the door,
And show many fine tunnels with entrances.
Further down is a corridor with two doors.
Beyond that a vinelike woman, like a painting,
Will appear before you and speak: 'If you
Tell me what is everlasting joy,
You will get one of the three desired things.
If you are unable to answer, I shan't harm you.'
If you answer her, she will take you
To the banks of the three ponds and withdraw.
If you bathe with devotion in the pond
Of your choice, meditate on and recite with equal love
The two great Vedic mantras
Of five syllables and eight syllables,
You will receive blessings that even those
Who do penance are unable to obtain.
If you don't need these blessings, meditate
On the golden lotus feet of the one
Who stands on the hill. And if you do meditate,
You will see the top of the lofty, splendid
Flagstaff with his eagle banner.
After seeing it, his two lotus feet
Will accept you and wipe out the sorrows
Of your former births. Praising him
With joy, go to Maturai of immemorial glory.
This sight in the cavern is worth seeing.

"Besides, if you don't follow either of these paths,
There is a direct path in between them.

Lines 116–142

After crossing many forests linked by villages
That are surrounded by groves of sweet flowers,
You will come to an unusual place
Where lives a troublesome deity. She won't frighten
Travelers, but will appear before them
In a seductive form. She won't harm them,
But will prevent them from going farther.
If you prevail over her, the high road
To Maturai will lie open before you. Go.
It is natural for me to worship the feet
Of Viṣṇu, the lord with a glorious crown
Who measured the entire universe."

Hearing the nature of the paths from the lips
Of the wise brahman, the ascetic Kavunti
Made this remark:
"O brahman, versed
In the four Vedas, who is committed to making us
Know the truth! We have no wish
To enter the cavern. The text composed
By Indra who lives for untold ages
Is clearly seen in our scriptures. Don't you look for
All that was done in past births
In the present one? Is there anything precious
That cannot be achieved by those who protect life
On the earth and are unfailing in truth? Go,
Seek to worship the feet of the god
You love. As befits us we too
Have a long way to go."
These sweet words Kavunti

Lines 142–162

Spoke to the brahman, and rested that day
In a fine village with Kōvalaṉ who hadn't given up
His goal. Later, they took that path.
The next day, the ascetic Kavunti
And the woman of the dark, wide eyes
Stopped at a place on the way, tired
From the journey. From that common spot
That lay across their path, Kōvalaṉ took
A bypass and reached a pond. On its spacious bank
He stood thirsty and panting for water.

A wood nymph smitten with love
Said to herself: "He is the gracious lover
I have pined for." Taking the form
Of Vayantamālai, she fell at his feet
Like a trembling liana, shed precious tears
And moaned:
"Mātavi said to me: 'Guiltless
Am I of the reply inscribed on the fragrant garland.
You must have told him lies. Therefore Kōvalaṉ
Was harsh with me.' Overcome by great sorrow,
She fainted before me. On coming to herself,
She remarked: 'Whether they are sages,
Or whether they are learned men,
Or whether they are those who have the wisdom
To know the difference between good and evil—
All of them think the life of a courtesan
Is despicable, a plague they turn their backs on.'
Red streaks had spread to the far corners
Of her cool eyes. Like white pearls,

Lines 163–185

The tears fell. With her own hands
She tore up a string of frosty pearls
Bright as moonlight. She abandoned
Me too in disgust. Informed by those
Who had met you on the way that you had left
For the ancient city of Maturai, I traveled
With a caravan and suffered great hardship.
You who have the wisdom to know the difference
Between good and evil! What is your command?"

Kōvalaṉ thought: "There is an enchanting nymph
In that huge forest I had been warned about
By the eminent brahman. With a mantra I shall expose
Her trick, and know her who has five plaits
Of hair." The mantra uttered by Kōvalaṉ's tongue
Was a mantra of the goddess who rode a stag.

"A wood nymph am I. I tricked you.
Don't tell your wife, lovely as a peacock,
And the holy one, first among women,
Of my indiscretion. Farewell,"
she wailed,
And vanished.
Taking cool water
In a fresh lotus leaf, he slaked
Their unbearable thirst. As the sun climbed
The sky, the heat from its burning rays
Began to increase. "It is difficult now
To go through this bleak forest," thought Kōvalaṉ,
His woman of the curved earrings, and she who has

Lines 185–206

Done great penance. The expanse of wasteland
Confused them in their paths. They came
To a place bright with a flowery grove
Knit with the bottle-flower, cadamba, ironwood,
And kino trees. Seeing there a temple
Of Aiyai of flawless renown who lives
In heaven adored by the gods, and has an eye
On her forehead, they entered it. No travelers
Were there on those rough, troublesome paths.
Unblessed by the wealth of rains, the hunters
Who lived by the feat of their bows, like Yama,
The god of death himself, took up their fierce bows
And descended on other lands. With great victory
She blessed them, and expected
An offering of splendid manhood as homage.

Lines 206–216

Canto 12
The Song and Dance of the Hunters

NARRATIVE INTERLUDE

1

Fierce was the heat of the sun. Her fragrant hair
Plaited into many braids, Kaṇṇaki
Trembled from exhaustion. She breathed hard,
And from the troubles of the journey her small feet
Turned red. To relieve themselves of the burning pain,
They rested unnoticed in one corner
Of the temple of Aiyai. Later, the oracle
Of the thundering voice became possessed by the spirit
To fulfill the past vows of those born
In the Maṟavaṉ family who with their large hands
Practised the use of bows. The hair
On her body stood on end. She raised
Her hands in the air to the wonder of those that live
In the forest. The Eyiṉaṉs enclosed their village
With a thorny fence. In its midst stood
The meeting place where they gathered
To eat. There the oracle stirred her feet,
Danced in a frenzy, and spoke aloud:
"Herds
Of cattle thrive in the big villages
Of your foes. The meeting places of the Eyiṉaṉs
Are in ruins. Born of the family of the Maṟavaṉs,
They no longer strip travelers of their possessions.
They have become timid like righteous men.
Unless you offer the sacrifice due to the goddess

Lines 1–16

Riding a stag, she won't bless your bows
With victory. O men who live by plunder!
If you wish to spend your days
Drinking palm wine, offer your sacrifice."

The Eyiṉaṉs offered their own heads
As sacrifice so others may count them,
Rather than have them fired by a torch
When they died. From their ancient family
They chose a virgin around whose thick, short hair
They tied a bowstring like the white slip
Of a snake, and twisted it into a long tuft
On her head. For a crescent, they stuck in it
A curved tusk pulled out of a wild boar
That had trampled a well-fenced garden.
A row of white teeth pulled from forcing open
The mouth of a sinewy tiger was the necklace
They put round her as a bridal pendant. She wore
A girdle of tigerskin, its surface a motley
Of spots and stripes. Reluctantly, they bent
A strong bow, put it in her hand,
And mounted her on a stag with twisted antlers.
The Eyiṉaṉ women offered her dolls, parrots,
Wild fowl with small, beautiful feathers,
Blue peacocks, balls, roots,
And praised her, following her
As attendants with paints, powders,
Cool, fragrant pastes, pulses,
Sesame candy, boiled rice
Laced with suet, flowers, incense, and perfumes.

Lines 16–38

As she was taken before the shrine of Aṇaṅku
Who accepts sacrificial offerings as the price
Of victory, there sounded in unison the beating
Of the drum heard during a highway robbery,
The blowing of the trumpet heard at the time
Of plunder, the horn, flute and great bell.
With folded hands, she then worshiped
Aṇaṅku with a swift stag for a mount
And praised her. Possessed by a god, the oracle
Spoke, pointing to Kaṇṇaki of the fragrant hair
Standing with her husband, her small, lotus feet
Swollen with pain:
"This is the Koṅku lady,
The woman from the Kuṭaku hills, the beauty
From the south Tamil country, the sprout
Of her former penance. A peerless gem
Is she that will light up the entire world
As its brightest jewel."
Thinking, "The oracle
Spoke in a frenzy," Kaṇṇaki smiled innocently,
Hid behind the broad back of her dear husband.

"The goddess wore the silver petal of the moon
On her head. From her split forehead blazed
An unwinking eye: her lips were coral,
Bright as silver her teeth, and dark
With poison was her throat. Whirling the fiery serpent
As a bowstring, she bent Mount Meru
As a bow. Her breasts smothered
Inside a bodice the venomous fangs of a snake.

Lines 38–59

In her hand, piled with bangles, she bore
A trident. A robe of elephantskin covered her
And over it, as Aṇaṅku, a girdle of tigerskin.
Her radiant, left foot clasped a tinkling
Anklet, a heroic anklet her right.
She is Ko<u>r</u><u>r</u>avai of the triumphant sword
Who stood on the head of the broad-shouldered demon
With two bodies. She is the goddess
Adored by many as Amari, Kumari,
Gaurī, Samarī, the one with the trident,
The blue one, Viṣṇu's younger sister,
Aiyai, the red one, Durgā
On the leaping stag with a sword in her large hand,
Lakṣmī with a fine bracelet, Sarasvatī,
The goddess of learning, the woman shining
With rare gems, the ever-young virgin
Robed in the vesture of Kumari whom her kinsmen,
Viṣṇu and Brahmā, came to adore."

Thus the oracle praised Aiyai. The Ma<u>r</u>ava<u>n</u>s too
Lauded the oracle's dance and gestures as divine.

Lines 60–74

THE GLORY OF THE COURTYARD

2

In the courtyard of the goddess' altar
Where she rules as part of the lord's body,
Who has an eye in his forehead, the gamboge
And fragrant orange branch out, the sāl
And sandalwood grow tall everywhere,
And crowded together are the cē and mango.

3

In the sacred courtyard of the goddess
With a crescent moon in her matted locks,
The kino sheds its golden flowers,
Red petals from the boughs of the silk-cotton
Are heaped together, and the beech scatters
Its white pollen from its branches.

4

In the sacred courtyard of the goddess,
The younger sister of Tirumāl, the cadamba oak,
Bignonia and laurel are fragrant,
The bottle-flower and ironwood blossom.
On their boughs swarms of bees
Hum as if playing the lute.

THE DANCE OF THE KUṞAVA GIRLS

5

This girl with golden bracelets that stands
Adorned with Koṟṟavai's ornaments:
What penance did she do?
The best of all tribes is the tribe
Of hunters who live by their bows:
It begot the family that begot
The girl with golden bracelets!

6

This girl with a mound of love
Like a hooded cobra who stands
Adorned with Aiyai's bright ornaments:
What penance did she do?
The best of all tribes is the tribe

Of hunters with their bows showering arrows:
It begot the family that begot the girl
With a mound of love like a hooded cobra!

7

This chaste girl with excellent bracelets
That stands adorned with the ornaments
Of the goddess with a leaping stag:
What penance did she do?
The best of all tribes is the tribe
Of hunters with bamboo bows:
It begot the family that begot
The chaste girl with excellent bracelets!

IN PRAISE OF THE GODDESS

8

You once stood on the black head
Of the wild buffalo robed
In elephantskin and tigerskin.
Now you stand, unwearied,
The sprout of wisdom, the Veda beyond
Vedas, adored by the gods.

9

You once stood on a stag
With black, twisted horns to kill
The great Buffalo Demon, holding a sword
In your hand piled with striped bangles.
Now you stand, the shining light,
With undying rays spread on the lotus heart
Of Hari, Hara, and Brahmā.

10

You once stood on the back of a lion
With red, angry eyes holding
The conch and wheel in your lotus hand.
Now you stand praised by the Vedas
As a consort on the left side of him
Who has an eye in his forehead
And is adorned with Gaṅgā in his tuft.

THE DANCE OF VICTORY

11

There, with a garland thick with flowers
And plaited with laburnum and basil leaves
Thrown over your shoulders, you were taken up
With the dance, in the guise of Kumari,
To rout the demons and please the gods.

ENGROSSED IN THE DANCE

12

As her anklets filled with bits of fine gold,
Her bracelets and girdle jingled again and again,
Our goddess on stilts did the sword dance
To rout the tricky demons armed with swords.
If our goddess on stilts does the sword dance
To rout the tricky demons armed with swords,
The gods will praise her who has the color
Of the kāya blossom, and rain flowers with their hands.

THE CATTLE RAID

13

When a fierce warrior of a small village
Is eager to wear a garland of veṭci flowers

As he goes forth to steal cattle,
He invokes Ko<u>rr</u>avai with her bright sword.
Eager to wear a garland of veṭci flowers,
If he invokes Ko<u>rr</u>avai with her bright sword,
The king crow in the forest that encloses the enemy village
Will sound an ominous call with its hoarse voice.

A NOTE ON THE CATTLE RAID

14

When the woman refuses to sell palm wine
To the hunter because he won't pay,
Offended, he will draw his bow, follow the omens
Of birds and go forth with the enemy's cows in mind.
Following the omens of birds, when he goes forth
With the enemy's cows in mind,
Even Ko<u>rr</u>avai will raise the banner
In her hand and walk in front of his bow.

THE GIFT

15

O young and pale Eyi<u>n</u>a<u>n</u> girl!
Look at these herds of cows, hunted
And given away by your elders yesterday.
They fill the courtyards of blacksmiths, drummers
And famous bards who on their fine lutes
Combine with skill song and beat.

16

O girl with a fresh smile like the root
Of a peacock feather! Look at these herds of cows
Lifted by your elders as enemy warriors howled.
They fill the courtyards of women who sell
Palm wine, foresters who are expert spies,

And astrologers who read the omens of birds.

17

Girl with kohl-tinted eyes like kāya blossom!
Look at these herds of cows lifted
By your elders as the enemy village howled.
They fill the courtyards of old, gray-bearded Eyiṉaṉs
Of coarse speech and their old women.

A SACRIFICIAL OFFERING

18

We have adored your two feet
That lovingly remove the troubles of ascetics
And gods who travel with the sun.
Accept the blood that flows from our severed necks.
This is the debt we offer at your feet,
The price of victory you showered on the Eyiṉaṉs
Who have the courage to kill.

19

We have adored your lotus feet,
You who have the color of sapphire!
The crowned gods and their king bow to you.
Accept the blood that spurts from our flesh.
This is the debt, the price for helping
The Eyiṉaṉs slay their enemies
And seize in triumph their herds of cows.

20

Like tigers stalking their prey,
The Eyiṉaṉs come at midnight
To the exploding sound of hourglass drums,

Small kettledrums and horns.
Virgin goddess, this blood that flows
From our severed necks is the debt
Towards unfulfilled vows offered at your feet.

THE GIFT OF SACRIFICE

21

O Śaṃkarī, Antarī, Nīli who wear
In your matted locks the redeyed snake
And the crescent moon! Accept the offerings
Of the Eyiṉaṉs with strong bows and arrows.
May the number of travelers who come our way
Increase and make us rich with their wealth.

22

When other gods drink nectar and die,
You drink the poison that no one else
Can drink and live. Be merciful!
Accept the offerings made by the cruel Eyiṉaṉs
Who lay waste sleeping villages
To the roar of the hourglass drum.

23

You walked between the maruta trees
And kicked the tricky rolling wheel
Sent by your uncle. Be merciful!
Accept the offerings made by the merciless Eyiṉaṉs
Who strip travelers of their possessions
And rub salt in their wounds.

POSTLUDE

24

May the Pāṇṭiyaṉ, eager for victory,
Wear the veṭci flower that spells ruin
For his enemy's forest and rescue of cattle.
For he is the lord of the Potiyil with lofty peaks
Where lives the sage Agastya, born
After Śiva who knew the Vedas well.

Canto 13
Waiting on the Outskirts of the City

After the girl had finished playing the goddess Ko<u>rr</u>avai,
Kōvala<u>n</u> touched the perfect feet of Kavunti,
The first among the pure at heart,
And said:
"This girl cannot endure
The sun's fierce heat: unaccustomed are
Her small feet to the pebbles in the sweltering forest.
The Pāṇṭiya<u>n</u> of the upright scepter, whose great renown
Has spread everywhere, rules this land: the bear
That has the strength to crush its foe won't uproot
The harsh anthill; the flaming striped tiger
Won't fight a herd of deer; the snake,
The goblin, the crocodile bent on its prey,
And the thunder won't hurt friends. No harm
Will befall us if we cross this forest at night
Through roundabout paths by the light of the moon
That nourishes many living things,
Instead of in daylight."
The holy one welcomed
His suggestion. Just as the people bide their time
For a king with a cruel scepter to pass,
So the three of them waited for the fierce sun
To vanish and for the moon, the Pāṇṭiya<u>n</u>s' progenitor,
To appear with its train of stars, spreading
Its milky rays.
"No starlike necklace
Of pearls nor sandalwood paste has so far graced

Lines 1–20

Your firm, lovely breasts. You haven't suffered
Your hair to be laced with the pollen
Of the purple water lily braided
With fresh flowers into a garland. You haven't suffered
The fair sprout of your body to be smothered
With wreaths of sandalwood shoots and the small petals
Of other flowers. Born in the Malaya hills,
Nourished in Maturai, and familiar to the tongues
Of poets, the south wind blew over you
As the moon bathed you in its milk-white rays,"

Mother Earth spoke these words
Of Kaṇṇaki. Exhausted, she breathed hard
And fell asleep. Looking at Kaṇṇaki, tired
From the journey, Kōvalaṉ said:
"Fierce tigers
Will roam, owls screech and bears
Grunt. You should walk unafraid."

She rested her fair arms, shining
With bangles, on his shoulder. All ears
To the omniscient and revered Kavunti's holy words,
They passed through a strange forest till wild fowls
Hidden in a thicket of bamboos, scorched
By the heat, sounded the approach of dawn.

Soon they arrived in a village where lived
Brahmans who wore the sacred thread,
But had taken to singing as they had turned away
From the Vedas. With the ascetic Kavunti,

Lines 20–40

Kōvalaṉ left his loving wife
In a safe and comfortable place, slipped through
A hedge of thorns, and walked along an open path
In search of water for his morning wash.
Thinking of the troubles he had gone through
With her in their trek through the forest, he sighed
Like bellows puffing and blowing in a forge.
Even his appearance had changed, racked as he was
With grief and troubled in his mind. The young
Brahman Kaucikaṉ was unable to recognize him,
And wondered if it was Kōvalaṉ. Standing beside
A green-leaved mātavi arbor, he apostrophized:

"O mātavi! Unable to stand the heat,
You have withered away and shed all your flowers,
Like Mātavi with wide, flower-dark eyes
Who is drowned in grief following her parting
From Kōvalaṉ."
These words of Kaucikaṉ fell
On Kōvalaṉ's ears, and he asked:
"What
Is it you were saying?"
When Kōvalaṉ came
Near him, the young brahman Kaucikaṉ
Exclaimed:
"My worries now are over. I have found
Him."
He then told Kōvalaṉ what had led
To his coming there:
"You had gone away. Like a snake

Lines 40–58

That had lost its jewel, your rich father
And good mother grew weak. All
His close relations drowned themselves in a sea
Of sorrow like bodies from which life had fled.
In every direction his servants have gone
To find you and bring you home. The great hero,
Rāma, left for the strange forest,
Saying:
                'As his eldest son, my father's command
I obey. A trinket the kingdom.'
Like Ayodhyā at Rāma's departure,
All of Pukār is indignant at your going away.

"All this Mātavi heard from Vacantamālai,
And her skin turned pale. She fell ill,
And took to the bed in her room in the middle
Of her tall mansion. Hearing of her great suffering,
I too in pain went to see her one day.
Grief-stricken, she implored:
                                        'I fall
At your feet, and beg of you to free me
Of my pain.'
                Then on a palm leaf she wrote
With her flowerlike hands, and said:
                                                'Please give
This to him who is dearer to me
Than the jewel of my eye.' Sealing it
She put it in my hands."
                                With this palm leaf
The brahman of noble and wise mind

Lines 58–78

Wandered in many lands. To Kōvalaṉ
He now gave the palm leaf given to him
By the vinelike Mātavi with flowerbuds in her locks.
The seal brought back the fragrance of the perfumed oil
That Mātavi rubbed into her thick hair
During their time together. Therefore, he was reluctant
To break it open. Finally, he unwrapped the palm leaf,
And began to read the message inscribed there:

"My lord! I fall at your feet, and beg of you
To forgive my indiscreet words. Why did you leave,
Without even the knowledge of your old parents,
Before dawn with your wife of noble birth?
I don't understand how I am to be blamed
For this? Aimlessly my mind wanders. You must
Free me of my great suffering. O noble one
Who lives without blame seeking only the truth!
I worship you!"
Kōvalaṉ then grasped
The exalted words of Mātavi,
And thought:
"Most blameless is she.
It's all my karma."
His depression left him.
Returning the palm leaf to the young brahman
Kaucikaṉ, Kōvalaṉ said:
"The contents
Of this sealed letter will make clear my present state.
They are fit for the ears of my parents.
I bow to the lotus feet of my flawless parents.

Lines 78–98

Young Kaucikaṉ! Please show them this.
It will banish their anxiety. Go straight
To them and remove the suffering that has clouded
Their noble minds."
He returned
To the place where the holy and immaculate Kavunti
Was resting with his chaste and blameless wife.
There he joined a pride of skilled bards
Who were singing and dancing in praise
Of Antarī's dance. He took up
A seven-stringed lute and tuned its scale
By tightly fastening the leather straps
On the curved arm. He placed the bridge
Along the fingerboard, and tuned the strings
Beginning with the fourth and ending with the third.
On his ear he then tested the mode
That had seven notes in its descending scale
And five in the ascending, and was dear to the goddess
Of the leaping stag. He played it
With three variations according to tradition.
After playing the notes with the bards, he asked
Them:
"Tell me, how far is Maturai from here?"
They replied:
"The south wind
From Maturai blows here. Feel it.
It is redolent of the divinely fragrant, thin, soft mix
Of the eaglewood paste, the aroma of the saffron,
The civet, the goodness of sandalwood paste,
And musk blended together. On its way it hovers

Lines 99–118

Near the wreaths of pollen-laden, red water lilies,
And the newly opened petals of the campak,
The mātavi, jasmine, and homegrown mullai.
It caresses the smoke from kitchen fires,
The smoke from the broad streets, lined
With shops, where appam and cakes are fried,
The fumes of incense swirling from terraces
Where men and women have fun together,
The smoke of sacrificial fires, and other
Odorous fumes. It comes laden
With many indistinct odors from the palace
Of the triumphant Pāṇṭiyaṉ, his broad chest
Wreathed with Indra's garland, and fills
Every nook and corner with its oppressive perfume.
It is unlike the south wind that blows
From the renowned Potiyil hills, praised
By the unfailing tongues of poets. Therefore,
That ancient, prosperous city isn't very far from here.
Even if you go alone, no one will stop you."

As was their practice before, Kōvalaṉ and Kaṇṇaki
Set out on their journey at night with the woman
Of great penance. Nearer dawn, they heard,
Like distant thunder, the sound of the morning drums
Being beaten with exquisite fervor in the great temple
Of Śiva and in the famous palace of the renowned king,
Punctuated by the sounds of other instruments,
The chanting of hymns by brahmans who knew
The four Vedas, and the voices of those doing
Great penance reciting the holy names

Lines 118–142

Of gods. They heard the everyday sound
Of the timbal, in praise of the king who never returned
From the battle without victory, sounded
By warrior-swordsmen, the loud trumpeting
Of war elephants seized in battle,
The screams of wild elephants captured
In forests, the neighing of horses standing
In a row, the sound of the hourglass drum
Played at dawn by singers, and other clamorous sounds,
Coming from Maturai, that excelled the roar
Of the dark sea. These sounds fell
On the ears of the travelers as if to welcome them
And end all their woes.
The date palm,
The ape-flower, the silk-cotton, the kino,
The white cadamba oak, the gamboge,
The redwood, the maruta, the jasmine, the pear,
The tall hampak, and the trumpet-flower opened
Their petals. The flowers of the mātavi, the golden jasmine,
The bindweed with its thick vine, the ivorywood,
The flowering wild jasmine, the white convolvulus,
The bamboo, the volubilis with its thick vine,
The piṭavam, and the Arabian jasmine seemed
To be braided with one another. The steep bank
Of the river, with its rows of flowers, seemed
A girdle worn over a woman's mound
Of love. A glorious sight it was.
The flowery islets, broad at the bottom
And pointed at the top, their sides thickly covered
By many flowering trees, that shine

Lines 143–163

Facing one another—her young and radiant breasts.
The red petals shed by the kino
That grow on the banks—her red lips.
The mullai flowers washed ashore
By the current—her lovely teeth. The minnows
That dart here and there—her wide eyes.
The unmoving, ribbed, black sand—
Her dark hair. Full of lofty ideals,
She protects and feeds the world.
A flowering vinelike woman, ever alive
On the tongues of poets.
Called Vaiyai,
Of everflowing fertility, she is the royal banner
Of the Pāṇṭiyaṉ. As if she knew beforehand
The coming troubles of Kaṇṇaki, with the holy robes
Of fragrant flowers she covered
Her body, and held back the flood of tears
That filled her eyes to the brim.
"This is no river
Of waters, but a river of flowers,"
praised
Kaṇṇaki of the swanlike step and her husband.
They didn't go by the way of the great port
Where boats rocked, their prows shaped
Like the heads of horses, elephants and lions,
But crossed the river on a raft with the ascetic Kavunti
And reached a fragrant grove full of sweet flowers
On the southern bank.
Thinking, "If one went round
The city, the seat of the gods, one will acquire

Lines 163–182

Great merit," they went round
The moat enclosed by the protective forest.
As if they knew for certain the coming troubles
Of Kaṇṇaki and Kōvalaṉ who had traveled this far,
The stems of the long, dark water lily,
The white lily, and the lotus trembled
With grief, their eyes filled with tears,
As bees swirled about. The wide banners,
Seized in war from his foes, flew aloft
On the ramparts of the Pāṇṭiyaṉ, and appeared to stop
Them with a show of hands, warning: "Don't enter."

Passing through fields and groves alive
With birds, they entered the outskirts
Of the ancient city—no one lived there
Except those who practiced dharma—dotted
With bright hospices, crisscrossed by streams
Bursting with water, coconut trees
Bent with fruits, plantains, betel palms,
And booths made of thick bamboos.

Lines 182–196

Canto 14
The Sights of the City

In groves on the outskirts of the city, in gardens
Flooded with water, in fields ripe
With crops, was the clamor of birds
That had risen from sleep. At daybreak, the sun
Adored by the entire world, opened
The petals of the red lotuses in the pond,
Woke up the people of immortal Maturai
Of the Pāṇṭiyaṉ who wielded the sword and made
The heads of his foes tremble. The roar
Of the morning drums, the echo
Of the pure, white conches sounded in unison
From the temple of Śiva with an eye in his forehead,
The temple of Viṣṇu with the eagle-banner,
The temple of Balarāma who brandished the plow
As a weapon, the temple of Murukaṉ with the cock-banner,
The temples of the arhats who expound dharma,
And the palace of the victorious king.

In a reflective mood, Kōvalaṉ went
To pay his respects with folded hands
To the ascetic Kavunti, and said:
"Contemptible
Am I, for I have strayed from the right path.
I have disgraced myself by letting this girl,
Whose body is tender as a flower, tremble
And go through untold suffering by wandering
In strange lands. O you who have done penance!

Till I return from telling the merchant princes
Of this ancient city about my state, this girl
Of shining bracelets will be in your care.
Will she be a burden to you, O holy one?"
And Kavunti replied:
"O you who have suffered much
With your loving wife because you hadn't done
Enough penance in your former births!
Though virtuous men shout themselves hoarse
Beating the drum of their mouths with the stick
Of their tongues: 'Avoid evil deeds,
For you will taste their fruits. Strong
Indeed is karma,' still men with no control
Over themselves won't take this to heart.
But when an evil deed wreaks havoc
On them, they will go mad with grief
That comes of ignorance. Wise and learned men
Won't lament when the time for reaping the fruits
Of their unavoidable actions draws near. In meeting
And parting, the torments of love, and the heartache
Kāma, the formless one, inflicts
Are natural to those who enjoy the favors
Of curly-haired women. They don't touch
Those who observe celibacy. In this world
Those who regard women and food
As their sole pleasure bring untold suffering
On themselves. Wise men have renounced
Both. Embroiled in love and trapped by it,
They have floundered hopelessly and ended up
In despair. This is true today; so it was

Lines 21–44

In the past. It's old, this unhappy state.

"When Rāma's father ordered him, he went
With his wife to the forest where he suffered
Unspeakable troubles. He was indeed Viṣṇu,
The father of him who revealed the Vedas.
Don't you know this? But that's a long story.

"Nala lost his kingdom in a gambling court,
And entered the sweltering forest
With his wife. Nor was he out of love with her.
And she too wasn't of a base and evil nature.
Yet he walked out on her in the dead of night.
Isn't this the work of almighty karma?
Even if there was reason to believe it was all
Damayantī's fault, will you too say that of her?
You aren't like them. Inseparable in life
Are you and your wife. Go untroubled
To the Pāṇṭiyaṉ's city of Maturai, and return
After you have found a place to live."

He entered the city through a tunnel
Made for herds of elephants with long
Trunks to pass, that led from the invincible moat
With its expanse of rippling waters enclosed
By a closely guarded protective forest.
Unnoticed by the Yavana soldiers, who armed with swords,
Kept a close watch over the fortress-gate
That inspired fear in enemies, Kōvalaṉ slipped through.
In a blaze, the city snapped open before him

Lines 45–69

Like the yawning treasure chest of thousand-eyed Indra.
In the street where flags sputtered in the west wind,
Courtesans with their handsome lovers strolled
Toward the park with its tall marutam trees
On the banks of the ever-flowing Vaiyai,
And on the white sand dunes sprinkled with flowers.
They played in boats with high cabins,
In canoes, and climbed on to bright rafts,
Eager to sport in water.
In a spacious grove
Of that ancient city, courtesans like golden lianas
Gently put cool, fragrant mullai blossoms,
Blue lotuses that flowered in deep waters,
And water lilies that opened like eyes
In their hair lit up with wreaths of white flowers,
Jasmine, the pollen of the cool, red lily,
And braided with pearls from the great harbor
Of Koṟkai. With rich sandalwood paste
From the southern Malaya hills, they rubbed
Their bodies. And at the hour of sunset,
On moonlit terraces they rolled
On their flower-strewn beds with their lovers
Who praised their lavish clothes.
When the rains
Came, they wrapped around their waists
Fine, scarlet silks, and stuck in their hair,
Twisted into a knot on their heads, new flowers:
The mountain jasmine, the red convolvulus,
And the fragrant kuṟiñci that flowers on the slopes
Of the Little Mountain. With red saffron paste

Lines 69–92

They painted their breasts, and brightened them up
With wreaths of the rich flowers of the leadwort.
They threw a string of pearls
Over their bodies glowing with red powders.
It was the time when the king of the clouds
Arrived with the north wind, splashed red
All over the noisy city of Maturai
Which he showed to Indra, lord of the thunderbolt,
Who had clipped the wings of the mountains.

During the cold season, timid women
Sat by the fire, lit with eaglewood,
With their lovers whose chests were anointed
With sandalwood paste. They shut the lattice windows
In their high mansions, grazed by clouds,
And built by architects expert in the books.
During the season of early dew, the sun
With outspread rays rolled south,
Scattering the white clouds. With their lovers
The women eagerly waited on the moonlit terraces
Of their large mansions for the warmth of sunshine.
Where is the king of late dew who comes
In Pairkuḻ when the festival of the bow
In honor of Kāma of the cruel eyes
And great spear is observed in the Pāṇṭiya city
Of Maturai? It is then with the south wind
A fleet of ships enters that scours the high seas
And brings, as a tribute from Toṇṭi, incense,

Lines 92–112

Silks, sandalwood, perfumes, and camphor.
Where is sweet spring who brings together
Joyous lovers in the royal city of Maturai,
And comes with the south wind
From the Pāṇṭiyaṉ's Malaya hills? He makes
The mātavi plant put on thick creepers,
And with sweet flowers fills woods and groves.
Women, delicate as vines, with their noble husbands
Remembered the passing of seasons in springtime
That cured them of their grief.
                                        The lord of spring,
Who entered Maturai with the west wind
And ruled over it, thought of traveling
To other lands on the last day of spring.
Herds of elephants with their calves trembled
As the sun burnt the hills
In the fertile mountain regions. The fierce heat
Spread everywhere as if the forest itself was on fire.

Women, adorned with gold bracelets,
Made love to the king, their lives inseparable
From his. As gifts from him they received
Carriages, palanquins, beds with jeweled legs,
The joy of lovemaking in pleasure gardens,
White yaktail fans, gold betel-cases,
And sharp swords. In cups of pure gold
They drank sweet wine poured by their maids
And got drunk. With their fragrant garlands
They tried to drive away the spotted bees
Hovering over them, but struck places

Lines 113–135

Where the bees were not.
Faint smiles,
Like pearls, gleamed on their faces with lips
Red as the petals of the silk-cotton. They spoke
Cruel words with their blue-lotus eyes
To their lovers when they quarreled. The words
Stuck in their throats when they began the eight modes
Of singing, and aroused only laughter. The corners
Of their wide, fishlike eyes, red like the open buds
Of the radiant water lily, spoke of their anger.
Their fierce, bowlike eyebrows curved inwards.
On their foreheads, bright with the tilaka, drops
Of perspiration formed. Men of noble families
Eagerly looked forward to the end of the women's quarrels
In love. These streets of Maturai, where the courtesans
Resided, gave pleasure to the ruler of the earth.

Kōvalaṉ walked past the big street
With its two rows of elegant mansions
That crowned kings, renowned for their upright scepters
That remove injustice, visited in secret.
They were the homes of courtesans exempt from having
To carry on their heads red bricks as a punishment
For misconduct. They knew well the two styles
Of dancing, the vēttiyal and potuviyal,
Which they scrupulously performed following tradition.
They knew the dance, songs, time-beats
And tūkku, and the instruments played with them,
The four kinds of gestures and seven scales.
Many of them had been honored with the sacred rod,

Lines 136–154

Among them dancing girls who sang the vāram,
The opening and middle songs, and who acted
In four different ways. Those who touched
The eighth note while singing were offered
Unfailingly one thousand and eight pieces of gold.

Trapped in the nets of their goddesslike eyes,
Wise men took leave of their senses.
Even sages turned into young men
As they pursued these women like bees
Plundering honey from one flower to another.
Embroiled in Kāma's revelries, some made fools
Of themselves, and spent their days in a trance
With them. Expert in the sixty-four arts,
Their sweet voices put to shame
The music of ragas and parrots' talk.

In the marketplace were sold carriages, two-wheeled carts,
Ornamented chariots, coats of mail
For the entire body, fine goads
Inlaid with gems, leather gloves,
Useful medicines, curved bludgeons,
White yaktail fans, boar-faced shields,
Leather shields, bucklers with a picture
Of the forest on them, pikestaff studded
With pearls, workers in copper and bronze,
Ropemakers, makers of garlands, saws
And other tools, workers in ivory, incense,
Sandalwood, and wreaths of flowers. The envy
Of kings, they were spread out in rich profusion.

Lines 155–179

In the wealthy neighborhoods, unmolested by enemies,
Were shops glittering with diamonds without faults,
Such as crow's-foot, spot, hole, or line.
They had no natural flaws that an expert
Could detect, and had the color of the four castes.
Emeralds of brilliant green, free of dark spots,
Lines, and curves; rubies called the red lotus,
Sapphire, pearl, and flawless crystal;
The puṣparāga stones covered in gold
And resembling a cat's eye; the pure sardonyx,
The color of honey and sunlight; the onyx
Like clear darkness; two-colored opals;
The fine, lucky gems that came from the same mines
And had the colors of sunset. White and pink pearls,
Pearls of the finest quality that sparkled
Without any fault, caused by wind, sand,
Stone, or water, lay in heaps,
As also branches of red coral without holes,
Not bent with stones in them or twisted.

Kōvalaṉ passed through the renowned goldsmiths' street
Flying tiny pennants to help dealers
Identify the four kinds of gold:
Natural gold, gold the color
Of parrots' wings, āṭakam, and cāmpūnatam.

In the cloth merchants' street, he picked
His way though bales piled high,
Each containing a hundred lengths,
Woven of cotton, hair, or silk.

Lines 180–207

In the grain merchants' street, traders
Wandered about everywhere with balances,
Measures and bushels. There were bags of grain
And black pepper in all seasons.

Kōvalaṉ walked through the streets of the four castes,
The crossings of three or four streets,
The marketplace, meeting places, little streets
And lanes. From the shade of an arbor
Overhanging with green creepers that even the fierce rays
Of the sun blazing in the heavens cannot pierce,
He saw the Pāṇṭiyaṉ's great city
Of Maturai and rejoiced in his heart.
Later, he emerged from among the vines.

Lines 208–218

Canto 15
The Refuge

Resolute was the Kauriyaṉ in performing his duty
And his rule, favored by the riches of the land,
Was a blessing. He was renowned for his upright scepter,
His cool, royal parasol and his heroic spear.
Never once did his people think of deserting
His capital, the ancient city of Maturai,
Known for the profusion of its wealth. Kōvalaṉ,
After seeing the city, entered a grove
On the outskirts where lived sages who expounded
Dharma. As he spoke to the ascetic Kavunti
Of flawless Maturai and the Pāṇṭiyaṉ's valor, Māṭalaṉ
Of Talaiccеṅkāṉam, enclosed by a shallow moat, the first
Among brahmans, versed in the four Vedas, and filled
With goodness, arrived there. After going round the Potiyil,
Sacred to the great sage Agastya,
And bathing on the ghats of the Kumari, he was returning
To his own family. To seek relief from the strain
Of the journey, he entered the grove
Where Kavunti was. Kōvalaṉ went up to him
And fell at his holy feet. With a gift for eloquence,
The brahman introduced himself, and began to speak:

"Mātavi, her body tender as a mango sprout,
And renowned for the honor bestowed on her by the king,
Gave birth to a child. The time of pollution over,
The old courtesans said:
'A splendid name

We shall give Mātavi's daughter.'

"Those sweet and fitting words you too heard
And answered:
'Once, in the dead of night, the boat
Of one of my ancestors was wrecked by the roaring waves
Of the wide sea. Many good deeds
He had done in his former birth,
And so was able to keep himself alive by swimming
For a few days unable to reach shore.
A goddess appeared before him and said:
"I live here
On Indra's orders. Here I am. Fear not.
I am Maṇimēkalai. The fruits of your good deeds
Are not lost. Rid yourself at once of pain
And cross this ocean of suffering."
'Through the sky
She carried him ashore, and relieved him of his pain.
She is my family deity. Give my daughter
Her name.'
"Then a thousand courtesans
In jeweled girdles blessed the child
With the name Maṇimēkalai. On that day you too
With the happy woman Mātavi rained a shower
Of gold with your fair hands. One who had reached
The limits of knowledge came hobbling along
With the help of a stick to receive gifts.
A mad elephant that even its trainer was unable to restrain
Rushed here and there to the roar of the drum, picked up
With its trunk that old brahman with the humped back.

Lines 26–47

Shouting, 'Oy,' at once you stopped the elephant
In its path and freed that brahman from its grip.
O merciful hero! You slipped between its legs,
Climbed the white tusks it swings
When provoked, stood on its nape like a Vidyādhara
On a black hill, and curbed its great fury.

"Again, a brahman journeyed north out of grief
For a mongoose his wife had killed. He left her,
And when she followed him, replied:
'If I ate
The food you offered, my life wouldn't be right.
Give this palm leaf inscribed with a Sanskrit verse
To good people.'
"She wandered through the marketplace
And the homes of merchant princes, flourishing
The palm leaf at every door, screaming:
'Rid me
Of my sins and acquire grace.'
You called out
To her and inquired:
'What's your trouble?
And what's this?'
"She told you of her great suffering,
And said:
'Take this palm leaf and read it.
Give me money and rid me of my suffering.'

"And you answered:
'Fear not! I will rid you

Lines 48–69

Of the pain that gnaws at your heart.'
"Gifts
You offered as the scriptures prescribed to absolve
The woman of the sin of killing, and banished
Her pain. You sought out her husband who had left
For the forest and brought him back, showered
Gifts on them from your infinite riches,
And made them live together as a family,
O you who have unlimited wealth!

"Once, a man defamed a chaste woman,
Went to her husband and gave false evidence.
A goblin that seizes slanderers and devours them
Caught him in its net. His mother, seeing him
Trapped in the net, broke down. Her agony
You saw, felt pity, and at once entered
The net and pleaded with the good and kind goblin:

'Take my life and spare his.'
"The goblin
Refused, saying:
'It is unnatural to exchange
The life of a good man for that of a bad one.
I would thereby forfeit the joys of the other world.
Perish the thought.'
"When it had devoured him
In your presence, you went with his mother,
Devastated by grief, and like a dear relation
Saved his family and all its branches from hunger
For many years, O best among householders!

Lines 69–90

"O Gopāla of keen mind! I know
Of all the good things you have done
In this life, but the fruits of your past actions
Make you suffer here with your jewel of a wife
Who is Lakṣmī herself."
Kōvalaṉ answered:

"Because of a contemptible person, the girl
With five, redolent plaits of hair
Trembled and suffered pain in the great city
Of the Pāṇṭiyaṉ who protects. Stripped of my clothes
By strangers, I got on a horned buffalo.
Later, with the girl of choice ornaments
And fine, curly locks I attained
Salvation having cut the bonds of rebirth.
I saw Mātavi entrust Maṇimēkalai
To the care of a Buddhist saint of great glory
Thereby making Kāma, the god love,
Hurl his flower-arrows in the air and weep
Inconsolably. All this I saw in a dream
In the middle of the night. Therefore I have come
Here in haste."
In one voice the ascetic Kavunti
And the brahman Māṭalaṉ spoke to Kōvalaṉ:

"The outskirts of this city are unsuitable for anyone
Except ascetics. Leave this place and enter,
In the heart of the city, the homes of the rich merchants
Who will know you from your past reputation
And welcome you. Before sunset, leave

Lines 91–114

For the great city of Maturai with its tall mansions."

Seeing the ascetic Kavunti, an old herdswoman,
Mātari, fell at her feet. She was on her way
From the shrine of the flower-eyed Yakṣiṇī
To whom she had offered rice boiled with milk
On the outskirts of the old city full of arhats
Whose minds were set on dharma. Then thought
Kavunti:
"The life of cowherds that tend cattle
And offer what they get isn't harsh.
This woman is old, faultless, virtuous,
And kind. I see no harm
In leaving Kaṇṇaki in her care."
She told Mātari:

"Listen! If anyone knows who the father
Of this girl's husband is they would,
As if they have come into a big fortune,
Embrace him like an honored guest,
And take this woman with large, dark eyes
And her husband into their stately homes.
Until she goes to the homes of the rich merchants,
To your care, herdswoman, I'll entrust her.
Give this good woman a bath,
Put kohl in her wide eyes, red
As a minnow; adorn her soft, fragrant hair
With flowers; dress her in clean clothes;
And look after this woman with fine ornaments
As her maid, guardian, and mother as befits

Lines 114–136

The highborn. Before this Mother Earth hadn't known
The lovely, small feet of this vinelike girl
Who has come here with me. A flowering vine,
She was unmindful of her own suffering
When her tongue parched by the sun's fierce heat
Began to wither. Instead, she felt keenly
Her husband's suffering. A goddess, she has taken
The vow of faithfulness essential to women
Devoted to their husbands. We have seen
No shining goddess but her. Don't you know
The old saying that in a land where women
Are virtuous, the rains never fail, prosperity
Never declines, and the triumphs of the king
Of this vast world never diminish?

"Listen, again.
Even if what is entrusted to your care by ascetics
Is small, it affords great pleasure.
Once a mighty god came and stood before the sage
Expounding dharma from the radiant, paved stone
Built by Jaina householders in the timeless shade
Of the flowering aśoka in Pukār, the town
On the Kāviri. Bright like the rainbow his appearance,
Adorned with wreaths of flowers and gems,
Gold ornaments, with a godlike form
Adored by many and not seen in this world,
But with a monkey's hand with black fingers.
All the Jaina householders worshiped the sage
And inquired:

'Why has he come here?'

Lines 136–162

"The sage replied:
'There was once a merchant
Named Eṭṭi Cāyalaṉ. In his home he fed
Regularly men who had taken the vow of fasting.
One day, an ascetic, foremost in penance,
Ate there. The mistress of the house received him
With the words:
"May your sins perish."
'At that time,
A small monkey from that village entered
The house and fell at the ascetic's feet.
In a rage of hunger, it had what remained
Of the food the ascetic had eaten and of the water
He had drunk. Its hunger assuaged,
With joy it looked at his face.
The ascetic of firm mind rejoiced
In his heart and said:
"O mistress of the house!
Consider this monkey too as one of your sons."

'The words of the ascetic she followed.
The monkey died. Thereafter, every time she gave alms,
She also gave on behalf of the monkey saying:

"Let its sins perish."
'As a result, that monkey
Was born as the only son of Uttaragautta of Vārāṇasī
In the middle country. Renowned for his beauty,
Riches and wisdom, and noted for his charities,
He died at the age of thirty-two,

Lines 163–182

Changed into a god, came before me
With a monkey's hand on one arm and said:

"All the blessings of the wealth I've inherited
Arise from my guardian's charities. It was she
Who helped me. Remember, I owe this form
To the charities of Cāyalaṉ's wife." '

"Wise words the sage then uttered.
The mistress of that house and her husband gave
Generously as the sage had instructed. The pious men
Of that city, the Jaina householders who restrained
Their desires, and Cāyalaṉ and his wife, as a result
Of the fruits of their charities, ascended to the world
Of everlasting bliss. Since you too have listened
To my words, go with this woman
Adorned with flowers without losing any time,"

Advised Kavunti. Mātari rejoiced in her heart,
Praised the ascetic Kavunti, and was eager
To take care of Kaṇṇaki. Full of youth and beauty,
Firm breasts, shoulders like arched bamboo,
A row of white teeth like a bulrush sprout,
Wise Kaṇṇaki went with Mātari
To her home as the evening sun was fading.
Cows in search of their calves mooed aloud.
Herdsmen with lambs on one shoulder, axes
And poles with hoops on the other, and herdswomen
With shining bracelets around them walked.

Lines 183–206

Mātari entered her home with Kōvalaṉ's wife
After passing through the rampart-gate, where the flag
Waved throughout the day, enclosed by a protective forest
And a moat, by arbalests for shooting arrows,
A clutch with black pincers in the shape of a monkey,
Catapults for hurling stones, cauldrons
For pouring boiling oil on enemies,
Big pots for melting copper, a forge
For smelting iron, baskets heaped with stones,
Traps shaped like the fabulous āṇṭalai bird,
Sharp poles, hooks, chains, iron rods,
Quivers of arrows, archers' bastion,
Fearful beams, needles for torturing the fingers,
The kingfisher engine for plucking out the eyes,
Boarshaped engines, bolts, wooden braces
For keeping doors in place, clubs,
Missiles, darts, spears, inner mounds
Of a fort that protect bowmen, and other engines
Of war that abounded in the Maturai fortress.

Lines 207–219

Canto 16
The Scene of the Murder

The herdswoman Mātari, overjoyed to take
Dear Kaṇṇaki under her care, did not put her up
In the lowly huts enclosed by fences
Of the cowherds who sold buttermilk, but took her
To a secure and imposing cottage, plastered
With red mud and shaded by an arbor in the front.
Together with some women with radiant bangles,
She bathed Kaṇṇaki, soft flowers in her hair,
And praised her thus:
"You have come here
With unadorned beauty as if to shame the women
Of Maturai decked in rare and costly ornaments
Of gold. This is my daughter Aiyai.
She will wait upon you. O woman
With beautiful flowers in your hair! I will care
For you as if you were gold. Please live here
With me. The woman of great penance, Kavunti,
Has rid you of the troubles of the journey,
And brought you to a faultless place. Are you
Still anxious about your husband? Since he is
A pious Jaina householder, let us have
New vessels that Kaṇṇaki needs
To make his lunch with the help of her husband's sister."

The herdswomen brought vessels for the noble people,
Some ripe jackfruits that never flower,
Striped cucumbers, green pomegranates,

Lines 1–25

Mangos, sweet plantains, fine rice,
And milk from their cows, saying:
"O lady
Of round bracelets! Please take this."

When Kaṇṇaki cut the many green vegetables
With a curved knife, her slender fingers
Turned red, sweat dripped from her face,
Blood rushed to her fair eyes,
And she turned away from the smoking oven.
Then with the help of Aiyai who had lit the fire
With straw, she cooked a good meal
For her husband. Kōvalaṉ seated himself on a mat
Cleverly woven from white palm leaves
By a skilled woman. With her flowerlike palms,
She sprinkled water from a clay pot
And washed the feet of her husband. As if to remove
The heat of Mother Earth, she sprinkled water
On the floor, caressed it with her hands, spread
A tender plantain leaf, and said:
"Here, my lord,
Is your food! Please eat."
After the special rites
Prescribed for a merchant while eating had been performed
With care, Aiyai and her mother looked at them
With pleasure, and said:
"This lord who eats
Good food is Kṛṣṇa himself, his skin
The color of the purple ironwood flower,
Nursed by Yaśodā in the village of cowherds!

Lines 26–48

This lady with many armlets who rescued
The lord, whose color is that of sapphire, on the banks
Of the Yamunā is the shining light of our people.
Our eyes cannot bear to see this bright vision."

To the noble Kōvalaṉ, pleased with his dinner,
Kaṇṇaki of the cool, black hair offered
Tender betel leaves and nuts. He said:

"Come here. Do the slender feet of this lady
Have the strength to walk through forests, over pebbles
And stones?"
Recalling her agony at crossing
The harsh desert, he sighed and went on:

"What hell our old parents have gone through!
Is this a dream, or the work of invincible karma?
Confused, I have been thoughtless in everything.
With slanderers and whoremongers I have passed my days.
Encouraging idle talk and unseemly laughter,
Wise men's words I threw to the winds.
I have forfeited my reputation. I flouted
The advice of my old parents to set me right.
I brought misery on you, young but ripe
In wisdom. I never thought it was wrong
To ask you to go with me. I asked you to leave
Our great city for Maturai. You rose at once
And followed me. What have you done?"
Kaṇṇaki answered:

Lines 48–70

"I was unable to offer alms
To those who observe dharma, to honor brahmans,
To wait upon ascetics, to entertain guests
Befitting our forefathers. Your good mother
And your renowned and excellent father,
Honored by the king, had come to see me.
Your father at that time hid from me the rage
You had thrown him in. With love in their hearts
And kind words on their lips, they consoled me.
I hid from them the pain of our separation
And the agony that followed. Seeing the false smile
That brushed my lips, they suffered.
You have done things that good men
Would have stayed clear of. As for me, I have lived
A blameless life. Therefore, I got up and followed you."

Kōvalaṉ said:
"Your parents, relations,
Servants, foster mother and companions,
You have given them all up, and accepted
As your constant guides modesty, faith,
Good conduct and virtue. You came with me
And rid me of my troubles. O purest gold,
Vine, girl with fragrant locks of hair!
O modest girl, light of the wide world!
O sprout of virtue, elegant lady!
With one of the anklets that shines on your tender feet,
I will go and return after trading it
For money. Till then don't lose faith."

Lines 71–94

He embraced his wife of the dark, fishlike, wide eyes
And was heartbroken at seeing her alone
And without her maids. Tears rose in his eyes.
He passed by the huts of cowherds, rich in cattle,
And with tired steps went down the street.
Before him appeared a humped bull: his people
Did not know it was a bad omen. He passed
Beyond the meeting place, the pollen of flowers
All over it. Walking through the street of courtesans,
He arrived at the marketplace. There he saw
A goldsmith in court dress, marching at a distance,
Pincers in hand, followed by a hundred goldsmiths
Renowned for their skill in melting gold
And making fine jewels. Thinking,
"This is the celebrated state goldsmith
Appointed by the Pāṇṭiyaṉ," Kōvalaṉ asked him:

"I have an ornament that can grace a queen's ankle.
Can you estimate its price?"
He was
Like Yama's messenger. With folded hands,
He replied:
"Your servant is ignorant of this,
But he can make crowns and other ornaments for kings."

Kōvalaṉ then opened the bundle with the precious anklet.
The goldsmith, an incorrigible cheat, examined
Closely the workmanship of the exquisite anklet
Made of fine gold and filled with precious
Rubies and diamonds in sockets, and said:

Lines 95–120

"Except for the great queen no one else ought to wear
This anklet. I shall inform the victorious king
About this and return. Till then please wait
Near my little hut."
Then Kōvalan̲ went
To the shrine beside that common man's home
And entered a small room. The hardened thief
Thought to himself:
"Before anyone
Finds out that it was I who stole the queen's anklet,
I will accuse this stranger from a foreign land
Of the theft and expose him before the king,"

And moved on. Thinking, "The king's heart
Has been charmed by the sight of the dancing girls
Of Maturai, by their many songs, and the wealth
Of their ragas," the great queen covered up
Her jealousy with a feigned quarrel, and pretending
A headache left him. When the council of his ministers
Ended, the king made his way to the great queen's chamber
Accompanied by maids with wide, glowing eyes.
The goldsmith saw him at the end
Of the guarded entrance, fell at his feet,
Praised him in a hundred ways and said:

"Without either a crowbar or pikestaff, the thief
With only sleep-inducing spells made drowsy the guards
At the door and stole the royal anklet.
He has taken shelter, even how hiding from the watchmen
Of our great and clamorous city, in my small hut."

Lines 121–147

It was the hour the Pāṇṭiyaṉ's karma became ripe:
For he who wore a wreath of margosa flowers
Without an inquiry called out his guards that watch
Over the city and ordered them:
"If you find
The anklet of my queen, who looks like a garland
Of flowers, in the hands of the expert thief,
Kill him, and bring that anklet back."

Pleased with the king's orders, the goldsmith
Who had stooped to murder said to himself:
"I will finish what I had in mind."
He approached
Kōvalaṉ, now trapped in the net of his cruel karma,
And said:
"These men have come here to see the anklet
On orders from the king of the victorious army."

The scheming goldsmith showed them
The finer points of the anklet's workmanship.
They observed:
"This man appears
Decent to us, not one who ought to be killed."

The evil goldsmith smiled with contempt
At those strong men, and went on:
"Spells,
Witchcraft, drugs, omens, deceit,
Place, time and tools are the eight methods
Used by men that follow the unholy business

Lines 148–169

Of thieving. If you expose yourselves to their drugs,
You will invite the wrath of the renowned king.
If you chant their spells, you will become invisible
Like the children of gods. If they could make
Gods appear, they could surely walk past you
Unseen, flaunting their stolen things.
They can render you insensible with their drugs,
Making it impossible for you to get up and leave.
Unless there is a good omen, they will not touch
A thing, however costly, even if it falls into their hands.
If they dip into their bag of tricks,
They can even make the garland on Indra's chest
Vanish. If they have chosen a target
For stealing, who is there to track them down?
If they have chosen a time to lay their hands
On something, even the gods cannot stop them.
If they use their tools and pick up rare objects,
Who in this wide world will get them?
To them there is neither day nor night.
If you listen to them talk about thieving,
There is no way you can get the better of them.

"Once a thief hovered about the palace gates
Like a spy. In the dead of night, disguised
As a woman, he entered it unnoticed.
Slipping into the shadow cast by a lamp,
He snatched the necklace of bright diamonds
From the crown prince. When the prince woke up
And found the necklace gone from his shoulders,
He drew his sword which the thief caught

Lines 169–196

Hold of and turned away all the blows.
At this he thought of wrestling with him,
But the thief, skilled in his trade, vanished
After making the prince take on a pillar
Covered with jewels. If there is anyone until now
Who has laid eyes on him, let us see him.
In this world the thief has no one to match him."

A youth with a perfect spear in his broad hands
Who had heard the evil goldsmith out said:

"Once on a dark, rainy night when the entire village
Was fast asleep, like a fierce tiger on the prowl,
A thief appeared with a chisel for splitting the earth,
Dressed in blue robes, and eager
To steal ornaments. When I drew my sword,
He tore it from my hands, and vanished
Right under my nose. Amazing are the exploits
Of thieves. The king too will trouble us if we flout
His orders. Brave soldiers, tell us what is to be done."

Just then an ill-bred lout in a frenzy hurled
The bright sword in his hand at Kōvalaṉ.
It cut him across. The blood that spurted
From his wound rushed in a tide over Mother Earth
Who rolled in great agony. The king's scepter
Turned crooked. Struck
By his inevitable karma, Kōvalaṉ fell.

Lines 196–217

ENVOI

O the wrong done to Kaṇṇaki's husband
By inexorable karma warped the Pāṇṭiyaṉ's scepter
That was never once bent in this world!
Good and bad actions by turns bear fruit.
May virtue bless your life forever.

Lines 218–22

Canto 17
The Round Dance of the Herdswomen

PRELUDE

1

"On the forehead of the Himālaya the Pāṇṭiyaṅ had carved
The fish, and near it the Cōḻa and Cēral, their tiger and bow.
All the kings of the land of the Rose-Apple Tree
With its cool groves, including the Cōḻa and Cēral,
Accept him ruler of the whole earth.
The morning drum roars with a loud voice
In the palace of the Pāṇṭiyaṉ, renowned for his white parasol
Wreathed in flowers. Today it is our turn to make butter."

Thus spoke old Mātari, calling her daughter
Aiyai who appeared with the rope and churning-stick.

NARRATIVE INTERLUDE

2

The milk in the pot hasn't curdled. Tearful
Are the eyes of the big humped bulls.
Some evil is about to happen.

3

The sweet butter in the hanging pot doesn't melt.
The lambs lie down and don't romp about.
Some evil is about to happen.

4

Herds of cows with four-nippled udders tremble
And moo. The bells slip from their necks.
Some evil is about to happen.

THE PREDICTION

5

"The milk in the pot won't curdle; the handsome eyes of the big humped bulls are tearful; the butter in the hanging pot won't melt; the lambs lie down and don't romp about; and the bells fall on the ground. Some evil is about to happen," Mātari turned to her daughter and said. "Don't be upset. To rid the cows and calves of their pain, we shall perform the round dance in the presence of Kaṇṇaki, that jewel among the daughters of the earth. It is one of the boyhood dances of Māyavaṉ and Balarāma with Piṉṉai of the wide, spearlike eyes performed in the open courtyard of the village of the cowherds."

THE THEME

6

This girl with a wreath of honey flowers
Loves him who leaps without fear on the black bull.

7

The shoulders of this girl with gold armlets belongs
To him who tames the bull with red spots on its forehead.

8

This girl with jasmine in her curly hair belongs
To him who mounts the strong, young bull.

9

The shoulders of this vinelike girl belong
To him who tames the bull with small, white spots.

10

The soft breasts of this vinelike girl belong
To him who tames the bull with gold spots.

11

This girl with laburnum in her hair belongs
To him who mounts the victorious young bull.

12

This girl like a newly opened flower belongs
To him who tames the pure, white bull.

EXAMPLES

13

Mātari turned to her daughter and said:

“These seven young girls have each chosen
A bull from the stable and raised it.”

She made them stand in the traditional order,
And gave the name of a musical note to each:
Sa, Ri, Ga, Ma, Pa, Dha, and Ni. Mātari of the fragrant hair
Gave these names which also represented
Clockwise their positions in the round dance.

14

Sa played Māyavaṉ; Pa, the victorious Balarāma;
And Ri, the herdswoman Piṉṉai. Other girls
Were named in the order mentioned before.

15

Piṉṉai and Ni stood next to Māyavaṉ;
Ma and Dha, next to Balarāma; Ga,
To the left of Piṉṉai; and Dha, to the right of Ni.

16

Among them, Piṉṉai puts the garland of rich basil
On Māyavaṉ and begins the flawless round dance.

"It is our own Piṉṉai, her arms ringed with bangles,
That turned the gaze of the lord, renowned for striding
All the three worlds, away from his consort,
Lakṣmī, ensconced on his chest. Ha! Ha!"

Thus spoke Mātari.

PARTICIPATION IN THE DANCE

17

In the circle they took their exact positions,
Held one another's arms with the crab's grip,
And studied the rhythm for the dance. The girl
Who was Sa turned to her neighbor Ri, and said:

"Let us sing the sweet jasmine raga in praise of Māyavaṉ
Who pulled out the citrus tree in the broad uplands."

18

Sa began to sing on a low note;
Pa, on a median note; and Ri, on a high note.
Dha, on a low note, sings for her friend Piṉṉai.

THE SONG OF MĀYAVAṈ

19

O friend! Māyavaṉ struck down the fruit
With a calf as his stick. Today if he came
Among our herd of cows, won't we hear
The sweet laburnum flute at his mouth?

20

O friend, Māyavan̠ churned the ocean
With a serpent as his rope. If he came here
Among our herd of cows, won't we hear
The sweet bamboo flute at his mouth?

21

O friend! Māyavan̠ pulled out the citrus tree
In our broad uplands. At daytime if he came
Among our herd of cows, won't we hear
The sweet jasmine flute at his mouth?

THE SONG OF PIN̠N̠AI

22

We will sing of the beauty and virtue of Pin̠n̠ai
As she danced with the lord on the banks of the Yamunā.

23

How can we describe his presence who hid
The clothes of the girl with a waist so thin
It might have snapped had she bent?
How can we describe the sweet, tender face
Of the girl who fainted when he hid her clothes?

24

How can we describe the beauty of the girl
Who stole the heart of the lord
Who tricked her in the waters of the Yamunā?
How can we describe his presence who cheated
The girl, who stole his heart, of her virtue and bangles?

25

How can we describe the face of the girl who covered
Herself with her hands when she lost her clothes and bangles?
How can we describe his presence who burns with love,
And is troubled on seeing the face of the girl
Who covered herself with her hands?

SONGS WITH ONE BEAT

26

To the left of our Pi<u>nn</u>ai with flowering buds
In her hair stood Māyava<u>n</u>, the sea-colored god
Who hid the sun with his wheel. To her right
Stood his elder brother, Balarāma,
With a body fair as the moon. The Vedic sage,
Nārada, marked the time by strumming the first string.

27

To the right of our Pi<u>nn</u>ai, with her neck bent,
Stood Māyava<u>n</u>, bright as a peacock's neck.
To her left stood his elder brother, Balarāma,
With a body fair as the stem of a flower.
Nārada, who plays the lute,
Marked the time by strumming the first string.

IN PRAISE OF THE DANCERS

28

Splendid was the round dance, praised by Yaśodā,
And performed in the open courtyard, scattered
With pollen, by Māyava<u>n</u>, his elder brother Balarāma,
And Piṇṇai of the striped bangles. It threw
The wreaths of flowers in the herdswomen's hair
Over the back of their necks, as they with measured steps

Beat time with their hands ringed with bangles.
Mātari said:
"Friends, let us all sing together
The masquerade song and praise the god
Who rides on the bird Garuda. Let us praise him."

IN PRAISE OF THE MASQUERADE DANCE

29

The Pāṇṭiya king's chest shines with a garland
Painted with sandalwood paste from the Potiyil,
A string of pearls from the sea, and the jeweled garland
Of the king of the gods. It is said
That the king who wore the garland of the king of the gods
Is the one who herded cows in Gokula
And tore apart the citrus tree.

30

The Cōḻa king Vaḷavaṉ who carved the tiger
On the forehead of the golden Himālaya, and ruled
The world, is the king who rules in walled Pukār.
It is said that the king who rules in walled Pukār
Is the one who wields the golden wheel in war.

31

The Cēral king of kings who entered the sea
And felled the cadamba oak is the king who rules
In prosperous Vañci. It is said that the king
Who rules in prosperous Vañci is the one
Who heaved his Himālayan shoulders and churned the sea.

PRAISING THE LORD TO HIS FACE

32

Lord the color of the sea! Once, long ago, you churned
The belly of the sea with the northern mountain
As a churning-stick, and the serpent Vāsuki as a rope.
Your hands that churned are the hands Yaśodā bound
With her churning rope. Lord with a flowering lotus in your navel!
Is this your māyā? Your ways are strange!

33

"He is the supreme being." Thus the immortals adored
And praised you. You devoured the entire universe
Though hunger does not trouble you. Your mouth
That devoured is the mouth that licked the butter
Stolen from the hanging pot. Lord with a wreath of rich basil!
Is this your māyā? Your ways are strange!

34

Tirumāl whom the host of gods adore
And praise! You strode the three worlds
With your two red-lotus feet to rid them of darkness!
Your feet that strode are the feet that paced
As the Pāṇḍava's envoy. O Narasiṃha! Destroyer of foes!
Is this your māyā? Your ways are strange!

PRAISING THE LORD TO HIS BACK

35

Ears are not ears that haven't heard of the glory
Of the old warrior who kept his promise
Through a clever ruse, and paced the three worlds
In two strides; who went to the forest
With his younger brother though his lotus feet

Turned red; who wiped out in battle
The fortress of Cō, and left ancient Laṅkā
Unguarded. Ears are not ears
That haven't heard of the glory of Tirumāl.

36

Eyes are not eyes that haven't seen the dark lord
With red feet, eyes and lips;
The great lord, Māyavaṉ, who appeared as a god
And clasped the entire world in his navel
Of the flowering lotus. Eyes are not eyes
That blink on seeing the lord.

37

Tongues are not tongues that haven't praised the lord
Who frustrated the wiles of foolish Kaṃsa;
Who went as an envoy of the Pāṇḍavas to the sound
Of Vedic chants, and was praised in all four directions
By a hundred people. Tongues are not tongues
That haven't uttered the name "Nārāyaṇa."

POSTLUDE

38

May the god praised in the round dance
That we performed remove the troubles
Of our cows! May the drumstick of our Pāṇṭiyaṉ,
His shoulders radiant with armlets, who split
The crown of Indra whose weapon
Is the triumphant thunder, strike terror
In his enemies and every day shout his victory!

Canto 18
The Wreath of Sorrow

The dance ended, the elderly herdswoman
Of ineffable charm went to bathe, and adore
With flowers, incense, sandalwood paste and wreaths
The feet of Neṭumāl on the bank of the swollen Vaiyai.
In the city someone heard a clamor
And rushed back. She spoke to none, but stood there
Without speaking to Kaṇṇaki who begged of her:

"Speak to me! Listen everyone! I don't see
My husband. My mind is confused. The sighs
From my heart exceed those from a bellows
Puffing and blowing in a forge. If the sighs
From my heart exceed those from a bellows
Puffing and blowing in a forge,
Won't you tell me what it is everyone
Is talking about? May you live long, friend!
Even during the day I tremble with fear.
Not seeing my love, my heart bleeds.
If my heart bleeds at not seeing my love,
Won't you tell me what it is people
Are talking about? May you live long, friend!
Help me, friend! I don't see my lord returning.
I fear deceit and my heart swoons.
If I fear deceit and my heart swoons,
Won't you tell me what it is strangers
Are talking about? May you live long, friend!"

Lines 1–23

The woman repeated what was said:
"Saying,
'He is the thief who quietly stole the precious anklet
From the king's palace. He is the thief who quietly stole,'
The men who wore loud anklets slew him."

Hearing this, Kaṇṇaki sprang up in a rage
And fainted, as if the moon bursting with light
Had dropped on the wide earth with the clouds.
She wept till her eyes turned red,
And cried her heart out for her husband,
"O where
Are you?" and fainted. She recovered and went on:

"Like the unhappy women who keep painful vows
After their dear husbands vanished in the pyre,
Must I suffer and be ruined
Because I lost my husband through the fault
Of a king despised by his own people?
Like the unhappy women who lost their husbands
With chests resplendent with fragrant wreaths,
And went and bathed in holy rivers,
Must I suffer and be ruined,
O foolish goddess of dharma, through the fault
Of the king whose scepter is bent by evil?
Like the unhappy women drowned in the vows
Of widowhood after their dear husbands vanished
In the pyre, must I give up fame in this life,
Cry my heart out and be ruined
Through the fault of the Pāṇṭiyaṉ

Lines 24–45

Whose scepter turned away from dharma?
Look at me! All you good herdswomen
Who have come and gathered here, and performed
The round dance with foreboding, listen to me!
All you good herdswomen who have come
And gathered here, won't you listen to me?
O lord of the flaming rays! You that see all
That happens in this world clasped by the swirling waves
Tell me, is my husband a thief?"

"He is not a thief, O woman of dark, fishlike eyes!"
Spoke a voice, "A raging fire will burn this city."

Lines 45–53

Canto 19
Kaṇṇaki Goes Round the City

The Sun spoke thus. Not for a moment did Kaṇṇaki,
Her shoulders radiant with armlets, wait there.
Taking the other anklet in her hand, she cried out:

"Virtuous women who live in this city
Ruled by an unjust king! Listen to this!
I have suffered a blow past cure,
When my troubles were about to end, unlike anything else
I had suffered before. Will I recover from it?
Listen to this. My husband isn't a thief.
Reluctant to pay the price of my anklet,
They killed him. Listen to this! Will I ever see
My dear husband in your presence, O virtuous women?
Listen to this. If ever I see my dear husband,
I shall hear from only his lips the real truth.
If I don't hear the real truth, condemn me,
Saying, 'She alone brought misery on him.' Listen to this!"

The sight of Kaṇṇaki in tears and distraught
Beyond endurance moved the people
Of the rich city of Maturai. Confused, they said:

"Untold harm has been done to this woman.
The king's upright scepter is bent!
How did it happen? Eclipsed is the glory
Of the Pāṇṭiyaṉ, the king of kings of the moonlike parasol
And spear! How did it happen?

Lines 1–20

The victorious king's parasol that kept the land
Cool under its shade now throws off heat!
How did it happen? Before us has come
A new and mighty goddess bearing in her hand
A golden anklet! How did it happen?
Her beautiful, red eyes stained with kohl
And spurting tears, she laments inconsolably,
As though filled with godhead. How did it happen?"

Raising indignant voices, the people of Maturai
Lamented thus with Kaṇṇaki, and comforted her.
In the tumult someone showed Kaṇṇaki
Her husband's body. She, the golden vine,
Saw him, but he saw her not.
It was the hour the red-eyed sun
Withdrew his fierce rays and vanished
Behind the big mountain plunging this wide world
In darkness. On that amazing evening,
The flowering, vinelike Kaṇṇaki wailed aloud,
And the entire city echoed with her cry.
Only that morning she had with joy received
From her husband a wreath he had himself worn,
And she had adorned her hair with it. The same evening
She saw him in a pool of blood that spurted
From his open wound. Numbed by the agony
Of his not being able to see her, she mourned:

"Seeing me grief-stricken, won't you think,
'She will suffer?' Is it right that your body,
Fair as gold, should lie sprawled in the dust?

Lines 21–40

Won't they say, 'This is the doing of your own karma,'
That forced the king in his ignorance to cause
This grief? Is it right that on this amazing evening,
With no one to comfort me in my grief,
Your fair chest heaped with wreaths
Should lie clinging to the earth? Won't they say,
'This is the doing of your own karma,'
That forced the Pāṇṭiyaṉ's error the whole world
Condemns? Is it right that you should lie here
In the dust with blood spurting from your open wound
Before this weak, unfortunate one, her eyes
Brimful of tears? Won't they say, 'This is the doing
Of your own karma,' that forced the king
To murder for which his people condemn him?

"Are there women here, are there women?
Are there women who would allow such vileness
Done to their own husbands? Are there
Such women here? Are there good people here,
Are there good people who cherish and rear
Their own children? Are there such good people here?
Is there a god? Is there a god?
Is there a god in this Maturai whose king
Erred with his fierce sword? Is there a god?"

As she raved, and caressed the chest
Of her husband where Lakṣmī had ensconced herself,
It seemed that he rose to his feet, and said:
"O! the bright, full-moon face has paled,"
And wiped her tears with his hands. The fair woman

Lines 41–64

Collapsed on the ground and clasped
The precious feet of her husband with both hands,
Radiant with bangles. Again he rose,
Cast aside his human form,
And ascended to heaven with a host of gods, saying:
"Girl with bright, flowerlike eyes
Shaded with kohl! Live here in peace."

Kaṇṇaki cried:
"Is this a vision?
What else is it? Is it a spirit that has tricked me?
Where shall I go and look? Full of truth
Were his words. Till the wrath that burns in me
Is appeased, I will not hold my husband
In my arms. I will confront the evil king
And demand an answer."
She rose, stood up,
Remembered her terrible dream, and wiped the tears
From her wide, fishlike eyes. She stood up, remembered,
Wiped the tears from her wide, fishlike eyes,
And strode toward the palace gates.

Lines 64–75

Canto 20
The Demand for Justice

"Friend! In a dream I saw the scepter
Tumble down with the parasol. I saw the bell
At the palace gate ring by itself and toll.
Friend! I saw the eight points of the compass
Quiver. I saw the night devour the sun.
Friend! I saw a rainbow span the night.
I saw a meteor blazing with heat fall by day.

THE OMENS

"The upright scepter, the white parasol
Fall upside down on the solid earth. The bell
At our king's victory gate trembles
And makes my heart quake. The rainbow spans
The night, and the meteor falls by day.
Some evil is about to happen. I must tell the king,"

Thus spoke the great queen. Maids adorned
With resplendent jewels followed her:
Some held mirrors, some held ornaments,
Some held new clothes, some held silks,
Some held caskets stuffed with rolls of betel,
Some held paints, some held pastes
Some held the paste of the musk deer,
Some held chaplets, some held wreaths,
Some held yaktail fans, some held incense.
Hunchbacks, dwarfs, mutes, and maidservants
Clustered thickly about the queen. Women

Lines 1–20

With sweet flowers in their hair sang
The king's praises:
"May the great queen of the Pāṇṭiyaṉ
Who protects this earth clasped by the sea
Live forever!"
Her companions and guards who sang
Her praises at her every step followed. Thus with her train
The great queen approached the Pāṇṭiya king
On whose chest Lakṣmī is ensconced forever, and told him
As he sat on the lion-throne of her bad dream.
At that hour a terrible cry rent the air.

"Ho gatekeeper! Ho gatekeeper! O gatekeeper of the king
Who has forsaken his wisdom, whose vile heart
Has turned away from justice! Go tell the king
A woman, bearing an anklet from a pair
Of tinkling anklets, who has lost her husband
Waits at his gate. Go tell him."

The gatekeeper came before the king and spoke:

"May our lord of Koṟkai live forever! May the lord
Of the southern mountain live forever! May Ceḻiyaṉ
Live forever! May Teṉṉavaṉ live forever! May Pañcavaṉ
Whom scandal has not touched live forever!
She is not Koṟṟavai, the goddess of victory
With the fierce spear in her large hand,
Standing on the buffalo's neck that spurts
Continuous blood from its open wound.
She is not Aṇaṅku, the youngest sister

Lines 20–38

Of the seven virgins, who made Śiva dance.
She is not Kālī who lives in the dreadful forest.
She is not Durgā who tore apart the broad chest
Of Dāruka. Pent up with hatred and anger
At the loss of her husband, she stands
At the gate, a golden anklet in her hand."

The king answered:
"Let her come in. And bring her over here."

The gatekeeper led Kaṇṇaki to the king.
She rushed to him. He asked:
"With tears
In your eyes you have come before us,
Young vinelike girl! Who are you?"

Kaṇṇaki replied:
"Impetuous king!
Listen to what I have to say. Pukār
Of great renown is my town. One of its kings
Of spotless glory once rid a dove
Of its suffering to the wonder of the gods.
Another had his only son killed under the wheels
Of his chariot. He was burned to the quick
By the tears falling from the eyes of a cow
That swung the bell at the palace gates.
O king with tinkling anklets! Born in Pukār
As the son of Mācāttuvāṉ, a merchant prince
Of untarnished fame, Kōvalaṉ came to Maturai
For a living, driven by his karma. When he was here

Lines 38–60

To sell my anklet, he was murdered.
I am his wife: Kaṇṇaki is my name."

The king said:
"O divine woman! It is not unjust
To kill a thief. You should know it is the king's duty."

Kaṇṇaki of the shining ornaments replied:

"O lord of Koṟkai who does not dispense justice
Impartially! You should know that my golden anklet
Screams with gems."
Said the king:
"Woman
With a sweet voice! What you have said is true.
Our anklet is filled with pearls. Give me yours."

She gave it, and it was placed before the king.
Her precious anklet she broke open,
And a gem leaped into the king's face.
He saw the gem. His parasol rolled,
His scepter bent, and he spoke up:

"Am I a king? I listened to the words of a goldsmith!
I alone am the thief? Through my error
I have failed to protect the people
Of the southern kingdom. Let my life crumble in the dust."

He fell down in a swoon. His great queen
Shuddered in confusion, and said:

Lines 60–80

"There is no refuge
For a woman who has lost her husband."
That woman
Of soft words touched her husband's feet and died.

ENVOI

1

"Dharma itself will become the god of death
To those who do evil." It is no idle thing
That the wise say. O queen of the victorious king
Who acted cruelly and unjustly! A slave am I
Of my karma. See what I shall do.

2

"I am a sinner," cried an onlooker.
Tears pour from her blue-lotus eyes. Her hand
Clasps a single anklet. Lifeless her body.
Like a forest, her dark hair spread about her.
The Pāṇṭiyaṉ saw her, and died of terror.

3

"When the lord of the Vaiyai saw the dust on her body,
Her dark hair undone, the single anklet
Blazing in her hand, he lost heart. Her words
Pounded his ears, and he gave up his life."

Lines 80–93

Canto 21
The Crown of Wrath

"Consort of the great king! A slave am I
Of cruel karma. By nature I am innocent.
You will see that whoever harms another
In the morning will find himself harmed
By the afternoon,"
Kaṇṇaki told the great queen.

THE SEVEN CHASTE WOMEN

1

At midday a woman with flowing hair
Offered her kitchen and the mesquite as witnesses
To her virtue before some wise men.

2

A woman with a wide, striped mound of love
Was told by her friends while playing on the banks
Of the Poṉṉi: "This image of sand is your husband."
Because of what they said, she stood there
And did not go home. Around her swirled the waves:
They left the image untouched.

3

The renowned Cōḻa king Karikālaṉ's daughter,
Ātimanti, followed the Kāviri in flood
When it carried away her husband, Vañcikkōṉ.
She called out, "Lord with shoulders like hills!"
The sea itself came and offered him to her.

Lines 1–14

Embracing him, the golden vine of a girl returned home.

4

In the seaside grove covered with sand
A woman turned herself into a stone, and peered
At the returning boats. When her husband stepped
Ashore, she turned into her usual self.

5

A woman with spearlike eyes dropped her own child
Into a well when the child of her husband's second wife
Fell into it. She then saved both children.

6

She caught a stranger making eyes at her, and said
To herself: "Into a monkey face will I turn
My bright full-moon face." When her absent husband
Returned, that flowerlike woman,
A girdle set with rubies blazing over her mound of love,
Then ripped off her monkey face.

7

Bright as a golden icon, a girl overheard
Her mother talking to her father:
" 'A woman's understanding, however fine, is often
Childish.' I paid no attention to this remark
Of learned men. Once, while playing with toy houses,
I innocently told my maid: 'Woman
Of bright ornaments! If I should give birth
To a daughter and you, to a son, he alone

Lines 15–28

Will be my daughter's husband.' Now she holds
Me to my word. It pains me to hear it:
I choke with grief. I am truly unfortunate."

Hearing this, the girl robed herself in silks,
Knotted the locks of her hair, and with bowed head
Went forth to the maid's son, took him
As her husband, and returned with him on her head.

"I was born in the city where such virtuous women
With fragrant locks of hair were born.
If I too am truly a virtuous woman, forbearing
I will not be, but bring ruin on Maturai and the king.
The force of my vengeance you will see,"

Thundered Kaṇṇaki as she walked out of the palace.
In a rage she cried out:
"Men and women
Of Maturai of the four temples! O gods in heaven
And ascetics, listen! I curse this city. Its king erred
In killing the man I loved. Blameless am I!"

She wrenched off her left breast with her hand,
And grief-stricken went round the city of Maturai
Three times. And with a curse she hurled
Her fair breast on its pleasant street.

Before Kaṇṇaki, who had cursed, appeared Agni,
The god of fire, in the guise of a brahman,
Blue in color, with a red tuft and milkwhite teeth.

Lines 28–49

He said:
"Virtuous woman! Long ago I was told
To burn this city the day you are wronged.
Who shall now live in it?"
Kaṇṇaki, the golden vine,
Was in a rage, and ordered the god of fire:

"Brahmans, good men, cows, chaste women,
The old and children—spare these. Go
After the wicked."
Fire and smoke smothered the city
Of Maturai of the king with the lofty chariot.

ENVOI

As the fire of virtue burned the renowned Pāṇṭiyaṉ,
His wives, palaces, legion of shining bows,
Horses and elephants, the gods and deities
Of Maturai became invisible through their powers.

Lines 50–61

Canto 22
The Great Fire

The flaming mouth of Agni, the messenger
Of the gods, opened. Their doors
The guardian deities closed. To wipe out
The disgrace of his crooked spear, Ce̱liyaṉ,
The warlike king of kings, forfeited his life.
He gave up his life on the throne itself
To reassure Mother Earth that his rule
Was just. The great queen of unblemished virtue
Also died with him. Not aware of this,
The royal priest, the brahman judges,
The astrologer, the treasurer, accountants who write
The king's commands, servants, maids
With small bracelets remained speechless
As in a picture. The elephant riders, cavalrymen,
Charioteers, and foot soldiers with terrible swords were
confused
By the fire spewing from the victory gate
Of the king's palace, and they ran to put it out.

The lord of the brahmans' demigods shone
With a bright, pearl necklace. He lighted
The three sacrificial fires, following the rites
Established by Brahmā. The lord of the warriors' demigods
Shone with the coral's luster. He ruled
This earth clasped by the sea, and in his hands
Held the sweet victory drum, the white parasol,
The yaktail fan, the tall pennant,
The famed elephant-hook, the fierce spear

Lines 1–23

And iron chains. In battle he put to flight
Numberless kings of great renown, and seized
The entire world which he ruled with an upright scepter.
He wiped out evil deeds, established justice,
And protected the world like Neṭiyōṉ himself.
As his fame grew, he was praised by everyone.
The lord of the illustrious merchants' demigods
Shone with the color of pure gold.
He wore every ornament except the crown
Of the renowned king of the fierce spear.
He served the wide world as becomes a merchant:
A plow and a pair of scales he bore
In his hands. As lord of the farmland, he led
The simple life of a peasant tilling the soil.
He resembled Śiva with the crescent moon
In his radiant knot of hair. The lord
Of the farmers' demigods, appeased with sacrifices
In noisy Maturai, shone like a polished sapphire.
He wore a robe of bright cloth,
And was skilled in the ways of dance and music.

The four demigods spoke:
"We have known
That the day the king's justice fails
This city will be devoured by fire. Since this is right,
Is it not proper that we should leave?
The four guardian deities quit their regions
Long before the heroic woman wrenched off her breast.
There was excitement in the grain merchants' street,
The chariot street festooned with banners,

Lines 23–51

And the four streets of the four castes
As on the day a fire raged in the Kāṇḍava forest.
The flames spared the homes of the virtuous
But destroyed those of the wicked. Unharmed
By the fire, cows and calves returned
To the broad streets of the good cowherds.
Fierce elephants, herds of cow elephants
And swift horses escaped beyond the ramparts.

On soft, wide beds women lay unconscious
Beside their men drowned in love and wine.
Their young breasts were redolent of unguents,
Their eyes darkened with kohl, and their hair
Braided with wreaths of flowering buds
That spilled perfume in the air. Pollen floated
On their breasts red with kumkum and sparkling
With pearl necklaces. Women with fair mounds
Of love and perfumed hair rose from their sleep
On soft beds. Lisping with red lips
Their children toddled along with gray-haired women.
Women who dutifully kept house and honored
Guests rejoiced. They adored and praised
The god of fire whose flames leaped high, and said:

"This woman has lost her husband whose chest
Glowed with fair wreaths, but was victorious
With her anklet. This tumult her breast has caused,
Is it wrong? No, no, no."
In the infamous street
Of courtesans skilled in the sixty-four arts,

Lines 52–81

One heard the thunder of drums, the sweet notes
Of flutes, and the echoes of singing lutes
From variations in tone. Dancing girls
Who lost their theater in the fire asked:

"Where is this woman from? Whose daughter
Is she? It is amazing that a woman who has lost
Her husband has, with her anklet, brought a rash king
To his knees and burned this city."
Stripped
Of its evening festivals was the great city,
Of Vedic chants, the lighting of sacrificial fires,
The adoration of gods, the burning of lamps in homes,
The balm of night, and the drum's loud roar.
Unable to bear the heat of the raging fire,
The goddess of Maturai appeared before
The heroic woman ravaged by grief.
Devastated by the loss of her dear husband,
She sighed like a bellows puffing and blowing
In a forge, and blindly roamed the streets and lanes,
Faltered in her steps, dazed and stupefied.

ENVOI

The goddess of Maturai appeared before her
Who had wrenched off her fierce, youthful breast,
Whose triumph equaled that of Lakṣmī, Sarasvatī,
And Kālī who slew the Buffalo Demon.

Lines 82–103

Canto 23
The Explanation

The goddess of Maturai was the family deity
Of the king who ruled over the cool port
Of Koṟkai, the port of Kumari, and Mount Potiyil.
His kingdom extended to the Himālaya in the north.
On her head blazed a crescent. With matted hair,
Blue-lotus eyes, luminous face,
Coral mouth with sparkling teeth,
Her body was dark blue on the left side
And golden on the right. In her left hand
Was a golden lotus, in her right a fierce sword.
A heroic anklet shone on her right leg,
And a tinkling anklet on her left. She was reluctant
To face the elegant and grief-stricken woman,
The heroic wife who in her despair had wrenched off
Her breast. She came behind her and said:

"Blessed woman! Won't you listen to my words?"

And Kaṇṇaki, her face shriveled with pain,
Turned to her right and asked:
"Who are you
Following me? Can you fathom the depth
Of my sorrow?"
The goddess of Maturai replied:

"O woman adorned with bright jewels!
I know your great sorrow.

Lines 1–21

I am the guardian deity of this vast city
Of Maturai. I wish to speak with you.
I too care about what happened to your husband.
O woman with golden bracelets! Listen.
O noble woman! Listen to this. O friend!
Won't you hear of the pain that is gnawing
At my heart? Listen, O woman, to the consequences
That followed our kings' actions in their former births.
Listen to the fate that overtook your husband
And heaped ruin on him.

"My ears have heard
Only the chant of the Vedas, and not the tolling
Of the bell of justice. But for the slander of kings
Who come to pay tribute and fall
At our Pāṇṭiyaṉ's feet, his scepter has never troubled
His people. Fair women make discreet eyes at him
Stirring up passions in his heart that put his reason
To sleep, like a young elephant
That its skilled trainer is unable to control.
No blemish this on the king, heir
To a noble and virtuous line.

"Haven't you heard
Of the Pāṇṭiya king who with his own hands
Split the golden crown and sparkling bracelets
Of the king of the gods clasping a thunderbolt?
One day he knocked on the doorless house
Of Kīrantai whose life had no use for anyone,
And overheard his wife complain: 'You went
To a distant land, leaving me in this open courtyard.
You said that no fence was stronger

Lines 22–45

Than the king's protection. Has that fence stopped
Protecting us today?' The king shut his ears
As if pierced by a red-hot nail. Hurt to the quick,
He trembled with fear, and cut off
His hand to keep an upright scepter.
Untarnished is the name of this royal line.

"Listen again. Another king, who held a polished spear,
Lavishly fed his soldiers, brought peace to the land
And held a public reception. A learned brahman
Parāśara arrived from the fertile kingdom
Of far-famed Pukār whose king held
An upright scepter and a victorious sword.
One of its kings weighed his flesh
To save a dove, and another dispensed justice
To a cow. The brahman had heard of the Cēral's
Generosity: he had offered the heavens themselves
To a Tamil brahman poet. He said to himself:
'I must see this heroic Cēral of the great spear.'

"Beyond the high Potiyil, he passed through forests,
Towns and villages. He had learned dialectics
In the traditional way from the twice-born
Who strove to become one with the infinite
By lighting the three ritual fires
As ordained in the four Vedas and performing
The five sacrifices and six duties. In debates
He overcame his opponents, and was honored
With the title of Victorious Brahman. On his way
Home, rich with gifts, he stopped

Lines 45–73

At the village of Taṅkāl of the upright Pāṇṭiyaṉ
And virtuous brahmans. In the village, he rested
On a seat under a bo tree, thick with green leaves,
With his staff, bowl, white umbrella,
Fire-sticks, a small bundle, and slippers.
He said: 'May the victorious king live forever
Whose royal parasol comforts and ensures
His success! May the protector live forever
Who tore apart the cadamba oak from the sea!
May the king live forever who inscribed his bow
On the Himālaya! May the Poṟaiyaṉ live forever,
Guardian of the cool and lovely Porunai river!
May King Māntaraṉ-Cēral live forever!'

"A group of children crowded round him,
Some with curls, others with tufts of hair.
Some lisped with their coral mouths
And had wandered from their homes. Parāśara
Said to them: 'Young brahmans! If you can recite
The Vedas after me, this bundle of jewels
Is yours to keep.' Then Ālamarcelvaṉ,
The son of the famous brahman Vārttikaṉ,
His red lips still fragrant with his mother's milk,
Lisping before his playmates, recited the Veda
With pleasure, flawlessly keeping the rhythm.
The old brahman rejoiced at this child
Of the south, and gave him a sacred thread
Of pearls and bright jewels, bangles and earrings.
He then resumed his journey home.

Lines 74–99

"Envious of Vārttikaṉ because his son had been honored
With fine ornaments, some guards accused him:
'This brahman has embezzled treasures that by law
Is the king's.' They imprisoned him. Kārttikai,
Vārttikaṉ's wife, became desperate. She cried
And rolled on the ground. At this the goddess Durgā
Of impeccable glory bolted the doors
Of her temple. It could not be used for worship.
The king of the fierce spear heard
That the doors of the temple would not open.
He was confused and asked: 'Has there been
Any injustice? Let me know if you hear
Of our having failed in our duties to Durgā.'
His messengers bowed to the king who protects
And told him about Vārttikaṉ. 'This is unjust,'
Raged the king, and said to Vārttikaṉ:
'You must forgive me. My just rule
Still lives, though it was thwarted by ignorant men
From the right path.' The king gave him Taṅkāl
With its rice fields watered by ponds,
And Vayalūr with its huge yield. He fell
At the feet of Vārttikaṉ, Kārttikai's husband,
To appease her wrath. The temple door of the goddess
Who rode on the stag opened loud. Down
The long and broad streets of that ancient city,
Thick with towered mansions, it echoed.

"The victorious king then sent a drummer
On elephantback round the city to proclaim
His orders: 'Free all prisoners. Remit

Lines 100–131

All unpaid taxes. Let those who find a treasure
And other unclaimed objects enjoy them.'

"Now listen how even such a king could swerve
From justice. It was foretold that a great fire
Would devour renowned Maturai and bring ruin
On its king in the month of Āṭi,
The eighth day after the full moon rose
On a Friday when Kṛttikā and the Ram are in the ascendant.

"Listen, O woman of shining bangles!
The kings Vasu and Kumāra of valiant spears
Who ruled wisely with their armies over Kaliṅga,
Enclosed in thick woods, became enemies.
One ruled in Ciṅkapuram amid lush fields,
And the other in Kapilapuram in the bamboo forest.
They were kinsmen, heirs to an old family
Of untold wealth. As the fighting raged, no one
Could come within thirty miles of the battlefield.

"A merchant named Caṅkamaṉ, eager to swell
His fortune, came unnoticed with his wife,
As if they had fled the country. On his head
Was a large bundle, and he began to sell
His precious goods in the marketplace at Ciṅkapuram
Of immortal fame.

"O woman with gold bracelets!
Your husband, Kōvalaṉ, in a former birth
Was known as Bharata. He gave up his vow
Of nonviolence while in the service of the brave king

Lines 131–155

Vasu. He mistook Caṅkamaṉ for a spy,
Caught him, and in the presence of the king
Of the victorious spear, he beheaded him.
With no prospect of refuge, Caṅkamaṉ's wife
Nīli roamed the streets and courtyards
Howling in rage: 'O king, is this your justice?
O merchants, is this justice? O common people,
Is this justice? O townsmen, is this justice?'
For fourteen days, she raved aloud,
And excited by the thought that it was a holy day
She walked up a cliff to rejoin her husband
And leaped down with a curse: 'He who has brought
This suffering upon us will himself suffer one day.'
Her irrevocable curse is now upon you.
Listen to the explanation. When actions performed
In a former life by the wicked bear fruit
No penance can reverse it. O woman
With thick locks of hair! In fourteen days
You will see your loving husband
In his heavenly, but never again in his earthly, form."

After carefully explaining what happened
To the virtuous Kaṇṇaki, the goddess of Maturai
Put out the great fire in the city.
Kaṇṇaki vowed:
"Till I have seen the husband
My heart has known, I will neither sit nor stand."

Her gold bracelets she then broke in the temple
Of Koṟṟavai, and wept:

Lines 156–181

"With my husband
I entered this city through the East Gate:
I now leave by the West Gate, alone."

Along the bank of the Vaiyai in flood, she wandered
Unconscious of night or day. Sad
And inconsolable, unaware when she fell
Into a ditch or climbed a slope, she walked
Step by painful step up the sacred hill
Of Neṭuvēl who swirls the long, fierce spear
That ripped open the sea's bowels, scooped out
The mountain's heart, and routed the demons.
In the shade of a grove of flowering kino trees,
She cried:
"O! I am a great sinner."

Thus passed fourteen days. Indra,
Lord of the immortals, with other gods
Thought that day to be right for worship,
Praised the glorious name of this revered woman,
Rained unfading flowers upon her, and adored her.
In a heavenly chariot, by the side of Kōvalaṉ
Slain in the royal city, Kaṇṇaki, her hair
Thick as a forest, ascended to heaven.

ENVOI

It is true that even the gods adore her
Who adores no god but her husband. A jewel
Among the women of the earth, Kaṇṇaki became
A goddess and a guest of the women of heaven.

Lines 181–204

CODA

Here ends “The Book of Maturai.” It sings,
Among the three crowned kings, of the virtues,
Triumphs and heroism of the Pāṇṭiya line
That wielded the renowned spear;
Of the preeminence of the glorious, old city
Of Maturai; of the splendor of its festivals; of the coming
Of the gods; of the endless joy of its subjects;
Of the abundance of food; of the fertility lavished
By the great Vaiyai river; of the unfailing clouds
That bring fresh rain; of the two types of drama
Known as ārapaṭi and cāttuvaṭi, with the songs
And round dances in which they are shown.
All these things, including others as well, reflect
The exemplary rule of law of the Pāṇṭiyaṉ Neṭuñceḻiyaṉ
Who routed the army of the northern Āryas
And brought peace to the southern Tamil country,
And who died in harness on his throne,
As if asleep, with his queen of unblemished virtue.
Only a glimpse of it is offered here.

Lines 205–224

The Book of Vañci

Canto 24
The Round Dance of the Hill Dwellers

NARRATIVE INTERLUDE

1

“We came to the mountains to scare away
Little birds, to frighten off parrots,
To play in the waterfalls, to plunge in the springs.
Wandering at will we ran into a woman, and asked her:
‘O lovely woman who looks like Vaḷḷi!
Who are you that stands in the shade
Of the sweet kino tree having lost a breast?
We shudder in our hearts.’ She replied:
‘My unhappy fate it was to lose my husband
On that terrible day when joyous Maturai
And its king were destined to fall into ruin.’ ”
Hearing this, the hill dwellers were overawed
And adored her with raised hands
Sparkling with bangles, as the gods rained flowers:

“In our presence and before other mountain folk
The gods took her to heaven with her husband.
Until now our people have never had a goddess like her.
O people of small huts! O people of small huts!
Let us honor this woman as our goddess, O people
Of small huts! Let us honor this goddess
In the cool shade of the kino whose buds
Scatter perfume on the mountain slopes
Ribbed with bright waterfalls, O people

Lines 1–15

Of small huts! Sound the great drum,
Sound the little drum, blow the horn,
Ring the loud bell, sing the kuṟiñci raga,
Offer strong incense, and rain flowers
In honor of this woman who has lost a breast
So that our mountains are forever blessed with plenty."

Lines 15–22

THE THEME
her friend speaks to her

2

You will see nothing there, girl with fine jewels!
Look here. We will bathe in the mountain waterfall
That sparkles and flows, bright as Indra's bow,
A blend of powders: the kohl, musk and sindura.

3

Let us bathe, friend! Let us bathe! Though the lord
Of the mountain had us and departed, saying:
"Fear not," we will bathe in the mountain waterfall
That rises from the grove shrouded in mist.

4

We see no reason to envy the fresh waters
That swirl, clasping the rocks of his mountain.
With whom else shall we play, friend, if not the fresh waters
That swirl, clasping the rocks of his mountain?

5

We see no reason to envy the fresh waters
That swirl, reveling with the gold of his mountain.

With whom else shall we play, friend, if not the fresh waters
That swirl, reveling with the gold of his mountain?

6

We see no reason to envy the fresh waters
That swirl, bearing the flowers of his mountain.
With whom else shall we play, friend, if not the fresh waters
That swirl, bearing the flowers of his mountain?

INTERLUDE

again the friend speaks to her

7

Girl of sweet speech! Plunging deep into the pure water,
We bathed till our eyes, black with kohl,
Turned red. Let us join in the round dance, friend,
And sing, praising the lord of the fierce spear
That slew the demon in the form of a mango tree in the sea.

8

The spear held by the lord of the eternal hills—
Centil, Ceṅkōṭu, Veṇkuṉṟu and Ērakam—
Is the bright, leaflike spear that killed
A long time ago the mango-tree demon,
Pushing him into the sea that clasps the earth.

9

The spear held aloft by the peerless god
With six faces and twelve hands
Is the bright spear, praised by the king
Of the gods, of the lord riding a peacock
Who routed the demons and eclipsed their greatness.

10

The spear that graces the hand of the lord
Nursed by six mothers in the lily pond
Of Caravaṇam is the long spear that brought down
The Kuruku mountain, splitting open the heart
Of the demon whose home it was.

INTERLUDE

she speaks to her friend

11

Good woman with striped bangles!
This makes me laugh: Mother who hasn't heard
The village gossip thinks I am possessed by Katampaṉ.
She has called the shaman to perform the dance
To rid me of this illness caused by the man
From the cool mountain on which peppercorns grow.

12

Good woman with fair bangles!
This makes me laugh: if the lord who brought down
The Kuruku mountain comes here, he is a bigger fool
Than the shaman who comes to rid me of the illness
Caused by the man from the high mountain.

13

Good woman with arms ringed with bangles!
This makes me laugh: if the son of our lord
Who drank poison and sat under the banyan tree
Comes here, he is a bigger fool than the shaman
Who comes to rid me of the illness caused
By the man from the mountain of strong fragrance.

14

Good woman with fine ornaments!
This makes me laugh: if our lord with a wreath
Of cadamba flowers that blossom in the rains
Comes here, he is a bigger fool than the shaman
Who comes to rid me of the illness
Caused by the chest of the man from the mountain.

INTERLUDE

her friend speaks to her

15

The son of the lord seated under the banyan tree
And his wife will come on his peacock
To the courtyard where the shaman performs the dance.
When he comes, we will ask his blessing for our marriage
With the man from the high mountain.

16

Son of the lord of Mount Kailāsa! We adore
Your feet red as aśoka flowers and your wife,
Vaḷḷi, daughter of the mountainfolk, with a crescent
On her forehead, the color of peacock.
We ask you to bless our love marriage with this man.

17

Son of the mountain's daughter! We adore
Your feet and Vaḷḷi, with a crescent on her forehead,
Daughter of the folk that inhabit these old mountains.
We ask that our man talk of our marriage to everyone.

18

Lord of six faces! We adore your feet

And the mountain girl of our tribe.
We ask that our man who touched your holy feet
And promised to wed have a true marriage
And end our lovemaking in secret.

INTERLUDE

her friend speaks—he within earshot

19

Our man from the mountain with a fragrant garland
Hid himself and was all ears as we sang.
Before he departed, I went to him,
Touched his feet with my hands, and stood.
Friend, may you live forever! Listen to what I said:

20

"You came to our village wearing a cadamba garland
And holding a spear for the sake of our girl
But you do not have a fine peacock, the mountain girl
Vaḷḷi, and broad shoulders. The people
Of the small huts, being foolish, will not accept you
As the god wreathed in a cadamba garland."

INTERLUDE

again the friend speaks to her

21

When he heard what I told him of the gossip
In our village, he left with a broken heart.
It seems the man from the mountain will marry you.
We will sing a song in honor of the chaste woman
Who burned down the glorious city of Maturai
With her breast, who was shown her husband
By a host of gods, and is worshiped by many.

22

Come, let us sing. May you live forever, friend!
Let us sing. We will sing in praise of the woman
Who burned down the city of Maturai with its tall mansions
When the king's justice vanished. We will sing
In praise of the woman who burned down the city
And ask for our marriage with the man from the mountain.

23

Chaste women of the fertile land!
Praise and worship the lovely woman
With a mound of love like a cobra's hood.
When the gods restored her husband to her,
They did not stop from praising the lovely woman
With a mound of love like a cobra's hood.

24

The immortal gods of heaven praised
And worshiped the woman who stood in the shade
Of the fragrant kino of the forest. The woman
Who stood in the shade of the fragrant kino
Of the forest will live in heaven
With her husband and not be sent back.

25

If we sing in honor of the woman
Who will not be sent back from heaven, a favor
Will be bestowed on this village. A favor is bestowed
On our village, a favor is bestowed on it. A favor
Is bestowed on our village, of seeing the marriage
Of the woman with gold bangles and her husband.

26

In the same way, our lover will come to this place
While we sing our songs and perform
The round dance. May the king of the west country
Who ruled over the Kolli hills
And inscribed his bow-emblem on the Himālaya
Live in endless joy in the days to come.

Canto 25
The Choice of a Stone

King Ceṅkuṭṭuvaṉ of the fearless sword,
Born in the illustrious line of the Cērals,
Tore apart the cadamba oak, fenced in
By the immense sea, to the amazement of the gods,
And engraved his bow-emblem on the Himālaya.
Once while resting with his queen, Iḷaṅkō Vēṇmāḷ,
Near a fountain in his silver palace, he was keen
On seeing the mountain where the groves were thick
With clouds and the waterfalls leaped with the roar
Of drums. Followed by a train of women
Pressing along the route, he left the environs of Vañci,
Appeared like Indra of the fierce spear
Who wished to amuse himself with the heavenly women
That lived in the grove bursting with flowers.
He mounted his great elephant,
And his train wound to a distance
Of twelve hundred and sixty miles
Through avenues of trees with flowers of gold,
Expansive river banks, islets sparkling
In their waters, groves crowded with young trees,
Playhouses and public halls.
                                        Ceṅkuṭṭuvaṉ
Reached the finc sand dunes
Of the Periyār river that tumbled from the high mountain
And resembled a wreath on Viṣṇu's chest.
Its swift waters carried with them
Fully opened flowers from the cottonwood, kino,

Lines 1–23

The laburnum in clusters, gamboge, redwood,
And fragrant sandalwood. Swarms of bees
And insects hovered over them. Here he stopped.

Songs of the hill dwellers accompanying their dances
Floated in the air, laced with hymns
Chanted by priests in honor of the victorious god
Of the red spear, the vaḷḷai song
Of those who pounded grain, the clamor of guards
In the fields, the cries of men as they split open
Honeycombs, the roar of waterfalls like the striking
Of drums, the trumpet of elephants as they ran
Into tigers, the shouts of watchmen from their lookouts,
The noises of mahouts as they lured elephants
To their traps, and the tumult of his retinue.
Like defeated kings come to pay tribute
And wait for an audience at the court in Vañci,
Overflowing with a profusion of riches,
The hill dwellers came before him. They carried
Gifts on their heads: white tusks
Of elephants, piles of eaglewood, whisks
Of deer hair, pots of honey, sticks
Of sandalwood, lumps of sindura, kohl
And orpiment, stalks of cardamom and pepper,
The flour of arrowroot, rich millet,
Coconuts, ripe mangos, wreaths of green leaves,
Jackfruits, garlic, sugarcane, flowering creepers,
Clusters of areca nuts from rich palms,
Bunches of sweet plantains, cubs of lion
And tiger, baby elephants, young monkeys,

Lines 24–50

Small bears, mountain hinds, fawns,
The young of deer, musk deer, harmless mongooses,
Peacocks with brilliant feathers, civet cats,
Wild hens, and sweet-talking parrots.

They addressed the king:
"For seven generations
We have been your vassals. May your glory live
Forever! Under a kino tree in the forest stood a woman
With one breast torn off and distressed
Beyond words. Praised by the gods, she ascended
To heaven. We do not know where her home is,
And whose daughter she is. We know she came
To your kingdom. May your line live
For hundreds of years!"
The famed Tamil poet,
Cāttaṉ, who had observed all this with wonder,
Then spoke to the king of the long spear,
The joy of the world:
"Noble and mighty king,
Hear me! I shall relate what happened
To the woman of radiant bangles and her dear husband
Because of an unfortunate anklet. I shall also relate
How that lovely woman pleaded before the king
Of strong armies, flourishing her anklet,
And how the glorious, old city of Maturai
Was burned to ashes from the fire born
Of the young breast of this chaste woman
Who flung her precious anklet before the queen,
And left in a rage, crying: 'Lady with five plaits

Lines 50–75

Of hair! Know this: "The Pāṇṭiya king who sat
On the lion-throne, with Lakṣmī glowing on his breast,
Fainted and died, not knowing what to do
With the ordeal of the woman with fair wreaths."
Without fully hearing Kaṇṇaki's words, the great queen,
Reeling under the shock, touched the king's lotus feet,
And said: 'Let me follow my lord,' and died,
As if she tried to reach out to her dear husband.
Perhaps she wanted to tell you, O great king,
Of the terrible injustice done to her
By the mighty Pāṇṭiyaṉ, and so came to your kingdom,
Rather than go back to her own home. O king!
May your glorious rule last from one age to the next."

Indignant was the Cēral king of kings
At the foul deed of the Pāṇṭiyañ. He said:

"By crowned kings the Pāṇṭiyaṉ lies condemned.
And before the news reached our ears, it is well
He gave up his life. Now the king's death has made
The scepter upright, bent by the inexorable hand
Of fate. When the rains fail, disaster strikes.
If men suffer injustice, fear grips the land.
To forswear tyranny and ensure the welfare
Of his subjects is the king's duty. Born
Of a noble line, suffering is his lot. His throne
Is not to be envied."
The gracious king spoke thus
To the poet who had related the unhappy tale,
And turned to his wife:

Lines 75–106

"One chaste woman
Gave up her life the moment her husband died.
Another in a rage came to our kingdom.
Good woman, tell us who is the better of the two?"

When the king asked her, the great queen replied:

"May the joys of heaven wait upon the queen
Who gave up her life before she felt the pain
Of surviving her husband. And may the goddess
Of chastity who has come to our good land be honored."

The king of the white parasol wreathed in flowers
Welcomed her answer, and turned to his councillors
Who then spoke:
"An image of her should be made
With stone brought from the Potiyil hills
Or from the great Himālaya where the bow-emblem
Is engraved. Both are holy: one is washed
By the floods of the Kāviri, and the other by the Gaṅgā."

The king replied:
"It does not redound to the good name
Of kings born in our family of fierce swords
And great valor to get a stone
From the Potiyil hills and lave it in the waters
Of the Kāviri. In the Himālaya live brahmans
With matted hair, wet robes,
Three-stringed cords across their chests,
And the power of their three sacrificial fires.

Lines 106–127

If the king of mountains refuses us the stone
To carve the image of the goddess of chastity,
With garlands of willow around our necks,
We will show the evil men that survived
Our earlier onslaughts the uncertainty of lives
That do not follow the right path, perform
The marriage rites of the young Umā,
Born in an old family, to Śiva
Glowing with the crescent on his head, and attack
The northern king. We will rob the Himālaya
Of his crown, radiant like the moon, and glowing
With a wreath of mantāram flowers strung together
With kino blossoms. We will attend to this."

With these rousing words, the king adorned
His elephant-soldiers with garlands of willow,
Celebrated the day the royal parasol was taken out,
The success of the Cēral, the excellence of winning
The title "Great King," the glorious victory
After setting fire to the enemy's camp,
The imperishable fame achieved by feeding
His soldiers, and the prowess of a king on the eve of battle.
He ordered his troops to put on their battledress
And wreaths of unbroken palm leaves, and said:

"Outside the golden city of unfading Vañci
We shall wear chaplets of willow
That will befriend our fierce swords."
Villavan̠ Kōtai,
His minister, then said:

Lines 128–151

"May your upright rule
Last for many years! On the bloodstained field
Of Koṅkaṇ you routed your equals
Who forfeited their banners with the emblems of the tiger
And the fish. This news has spread to the four corners
Of the earth. My eyes will not forget the scene
Of your elephant among the Tamil hosts that overcame
The armies of the Koṅkaṇas, Kaliṅgas, cruel Karunāṭaṉs,
Paṅkalaṉs, Gaṅgas, Kaṭṭiyaṉs renowned for their spears,
And the Āryas from the north. We cannot forget
Your courage when you escorted your mother
To bathe in the swollen Gaṅgā, and fought alone
Against a thousand Āryas that the cruel god
Of death was stunned. No one can stop you, if you wish,
From imposing Tamil rule over the entire world
Clasped by the roaring sea. Let a message be sent forth:
'It is our king's wish to go to the Himālaya
To bring a stone for engraving the image
Of a goddess.' Close it with your clay seal
That bears the imprint of the bow, fish
And tiger, emblems of the Tamil country,
And dispatch it to the kings of the north."

Aḻumpilvēḷ then spoke:
"The spies of every country
In the Land of the Rose-Apple Tree never leave
The outskirts of our capital, Vañci. Won't these spies
Inform their kings renowned for elephants
That are richly caparisoned? We shall therefore announce
Your expedition by drumbeat within our own city."

Lines 151–177

The king of the Cēral legion invincible in war
Agreed. On his return to the unfading city
Of Vañci, bursting at the seams with tribute
Collected on expeditions, the news was announced
By drumbeat from the back of a state elephant:

"May our gracious king live forever! May he protect
The world from one age to the next. Our king
Marches north to get a stone from the Himālaya
Engraved with his bow-emblem. O kings
Of the northern countries! Go forth and pay
Him tribute. Remember the heroic acts
Of our king who tore apart the cadamba oak
From the sea, and engraved his bow-emblem
On the forehead of the Himālaya. If you refuse
To listen, leave your wives and become
Hermits. May the army live forever,
Dear as his own face to the king of victorious anklets."

Lines 178–194

Canto 26
Removing the Stone

When the drum was beaten the king mounted
The lion-throne of his ancestors. The royal priest,
The chief astrologer, the renowned ministers,
And the commanders of the army came together
And blessed him:
"May our king of kings live forever."

They asked him to tell them about his intention
To march northwards. The Cēral whose white parasol
Was taller than those of other kings
With great armies spoke aloud in public:

"It would be unbecoming of us to ignore the talk
Of northern kings of insecure lives reported
To us by sages from the Himālaya when they traveled
Here. That way lies humiliation to kings
Such as ourselves. If my invincible sword fails
To help me in persuading the northern kings
To bring on their heads the stone on which the image
Of the goddess is to be carved, and if I also fail
To put down rebellious kings who wear anklets
And are ferocious in battle, may my own scepter
Turn into an instrument of torture and harrass
The people of our rich and fertile land."

The royal priest said:
"O unfailing victor

Lines 1–24

In battle! Your words are true of only the Cōla
And the Pāṇṭiya who put on wreaths of fig leaves
And margosa, and wear resplendent crowns.
O you who have the Himālaya for a boundary!
Is there a king who can survive your wrath?
None dares to offend you. So put away your anger."

Next the astrologer, versed in the lore of the stars
And the influence of the planets in the twelve signs
Of the zodiac, stood up and said:
"Mighty king!
May you be strong forever! It is the auspicious hour
When the kings of this world will fall over backwards
To touch your lotus feet. Be ready
To leave in the direction you intended to go."

When the ever-victorious king heard this,
He ordered that his sword and royal parasol
Should be carried in the northern direction.
Bards cheered and war drums thundered:
The serpent Ādiśeṣa who supports the earth
Bent down his head. Jeweled lamps trimmed
The darkness of the night. Its banners flying
Closely, the army, the five great groups
Of the king's councillors, the eight great sets
Of courtiers, the royal priest of the king,
Rich in swift horses and elephants,
Tax collectors, guards and officials spoke aloud:

"May the ruler of the entire world live forever!"

Lines 24–42

His sword renowned for its exploits and his white parasol
Wreathed in flowers were placed on the nape
Of the state elephant, used to eating immense balls
Of rice. It was then led to its place near the ramparts.
The king, glowing with a wreath of palm leaves
Braided with the flowers of the willow, entered
His hall of audience and feasted the army commanders
Excited by the prospect of war. The king
Of the fierce sword adorned his crown
With willow flowers from unfading Vañci
When the morning drum roared at the gate
To inform other kings of the world to offer
Their tributes. On his wreathed head he placed
The sandals of Śiva, who manifests in himself
The whole universe and wears a crescent
In his matted hair. His head he bowed,
That bowed to no one, before the holy shrine
And he went round it. His wreath lost
Its splendor from the fine smoke that rose
From the sacrificial fires lighted by the brahmans.
He then mounted the nape of his brave elephant.

Brahmans appeared with offerings from Viṣṇu
Who sleeps in a trance at Āṭakamāṭam and blessed him:

"May Kuṭṭuvaṉ, the lord of the west, be victorious
Forever!"
Since the king had placed the sandals
Of the lord, whose matted hair carries the Gaṅgā,
On his crown, he received the offerings

Lines 43–66

And placed them on his fair, ornamented shoulders.
As he set out, dancing girls came in knots from theaters
All over the town. With arms crossed, they spoke:

"O triumphant king! Ensconced in the shadow
Of your white parasol on the elephant, its forehead
Wreathed in sirissa, white dead nettle and palm,
May your presence ravish our eyes and make
Our sparkling bangles fall from our hands."

Poets, bards and panegyrists praised
His victories on the battlefield. Elcphant riders,
Horsemen and footsoldiers with bright swords
Praised the strength of the king's sword.

Like Indra setting forth from heaven to fight
The demons, the king left Vañci.
The army, with its commanders and vanguard,
Appeared to spread as far as the seashore,
Forced the backs of mountains to bend
And the plains to tremble. Thus the king rode
With his horses chafing at the bit and chariots
Till he reached the foothills of the Blue Mountain.
There the elephants, chariots, horses, and footsoldiers
Encamped for the night, protected by guards.
Radiant as the sun, the king graced Mother Earth
With his holy feet, and as he withdrew
Into his tent, he was praised by his brave men.

Curious to see this ruler of the spacious world

Lines 66–94

Who was like Indra, sages flying through the air
Stopped at the king's tent, their bodies incandescent
Like lightning. The king rose and bowed to them.
They said:
"Listen, O Cēral, born in Vañci
Through the grace of Śiva of the matted hair!
We are on our way to the Malaya hills,
And it is your duty to protect the learned brahmans
Who live there."
They blessed him and left.
Dancers from the Koṅkaṇa country came next,
And said:
"Long live the king of the sea-encircled world!"
The fierce Karunāṭaṉs in colorful robes
And ornaments came with their girls, wreaths
Glowing in their dark, curly hair:
Their young breasts shone with necklaces,
And their wide eyes flashed like minnows. They sang:

"Black cuckoos hurl their notes,
Bees imitate the music of the lute.
Summer has come when buds flower,
But he hasn't come, our lover."

Then came the folk from the Kuṭaku country
With their dancing girls with fine bangles
And wide, fishlike eyes. They chanted the song
Of the round dance appropriate to the winter:

Lines 94–121

"O woman with elegant bangles! Put on
Your jewels. Watch the hour. Clouds gather
To the rumble of thunder. His task done,
My lover has returned in his chariot."

The panegyrists too came to bless the king:

"May our king with the fierce sword triumph
In his expedition, and live forever with his large host
Of friends and retainers."
The king, whose spear
Struck terror in the hearts of his enemies,
Rewarded those who sang his praises, as ordained
By the master of dances, with rare jewels
Of whose value they were unaware. As he was resting,
A guard arrived and reported:
"O king
Of the upright scepter on whose lofty banner
A bow appears! One hundred and two dancing girls,
Two hundred and eight singers, one hundred jesters
From the ninety-six heretical sects, one hundred tall chariots,
Five hundred robust elephants, ten thousand horses
With cropped manes, twenty thousand carts
Piled with bales of merchandise from the northern country
But unknown elsewhere, their contents shown by pictures,
And a thousand messengers, their hair all done up,
Have arrived at the gate with Saṃjaya as their leader."

The king replied:
"Let Saṃjaya come in

With the officials, dancing girls, singers, and musicians."

Saṃjaya then entered the king's tent,
Bowed to him, praised him lavishly, and presented
In order the chief officials and the one hundred
And two dancing girls. Then he said:

"O king of the upright scepter!
King Śātakarṇi, who is friendly
And bears no enmity towards you, has said:

'If the Cēral king's expedition to the north
Is to choose a stone to engrave the image
Of a goddess, we will get it from the lofty Himālaya,
Lave it in the swirling waters of the Gaṅgā
And bring it to him. We can do it ourselves.'

May you live forever to rule over the sea-encircled earth."

The king whose army, endless as the sea,
Could swallow the lives of his rival kings
And their fierce spears, answered:
"Kanaka and Vijaya,
Sons of Bālakumāra, and other northern kings
With unbridled tongues poured scorn
On the Tamil kings during a banquet, ignorant
Of their courage. Like the god of death, this army
Marches forth with untamed fury. Inform
King Śātakarṇi and ask him to get ready
For us a large fleet of boats to cross the holy Gaṅgā."

Lines 145–165

When Saṃjaya had gone, the thousand, fine-spoken messengers
Brought sticks of sandalwood and pearls
From the deep sea, with tributes sent by the Pāṇṭiyaṉ.
The guardian king ordered his scribes
To send, through them, to all the kings, letters
Sealed with clay. When the messengers had left,
The ruler of the sea-encircled world received
The homage of the local chiefs, broke camp
And marched to the holy Gaṅgā which he crossed
By boats provided by the kings, and reached
The north bank where they received him with joy.
He went farther into the enemy country,
North of the Gaṅgā, enclosed by a vast sheet
Of water. There he and his army set up camp
Near the battlefield.

Opposed by such a warrior,
Uttara, Vicitra, Rudra, Bhairava,
Citra, Siṃha, Dhanurdhara, Śiveta,
And other northern kings, followed by Kanaka and Vijaya
Marched at the head of an army boundless as the sea.
They said:

"Let us see the courage
Of the southern Tamil kings."

As a famished lion
Stalking for prey rejoices at the sight
Of a herd of elephants, so did Ceṅkuṭṭuvaṉ rejoice
Seeing his foes march towards him. Wreathed
In a garland of portia, he hurled his troops
Against the enemy. The canopy of banners eclipsed
The sun's rays. The earth trembled

Lines 166–194

With the clamor of war drums, stretched taut
With hides, white conches, resounding drums,
Long trumpets, and sweet cymbals.
The thunder of the royal war drum, covered in skin,
Echoed above this tumult, and seemed ready
To devour the lives offered in sacrifice.
The cloud of dust stirred up by archers
With bows on their shoulders, by lancers with fierce spears
In their hands, by foot soldiers with leather shields,
By lofty chariot riders, by riders on elephants
With gleaming tusks, and by swift horsemen,
Smothered the battlefield, blinded people,
Made hoarse the throats of bells suspended
From the necks of war elephants, and choked
The far-sounding conches of the standard bearers,
And stopped them from adding to the terror.

Confusion reigned as the vanguard of the two armies
Met. Heads and shoulders flew
In all directions, as archers piled corpses.
Cut by swords, the headless trunks
Danced to the music of ghosts with eyes
Like drumheads. Goblins clustered together, danced
And drank the blood spurting from corpses
Together with pieces of human flesh.
The brave warriors of the Ārya kings,
Whose chariot forces were renowned for slaughter,
Fell, and their bodies piled up on the battlefield.
Their lofty chariots, hosts of war elephants
And troops of swift horses were destroyed

Lines 194–203

And piled high by the Cēral with the resounding anklet.
On his head he now wore a wreath of white
Dead nettle, braided with palm leaves,
And appeared on the battlefield to the Ārya kings
Like the god of death himself, riding a buffalo
And devouring all the lives in the span of a day.
The brave spearmen, Kanaka and Vijaya,
Their fierce spears clutched in their hands,
And their fifty-two chariot soldiers who had hurled
Insults at the Tamil kings, now bit the dust
Before Ceṅkuṭṭuvaṉ's wrath. Trying to escape,
Some braided their hair into plaits, some wore
The robes of a monk, some smeared themselves
With ash, some sat like hermits with peacock feathers,
Some looked like minstrels, some like dancers,
And some had lutes on their shoulders. Casting aside
Swords and lances, they fled in every direction.

Those who guarded the elephants trembled with fear.
Ceṅkuṭṭuvaṉ yoked the animals like oxen,
And with swords as sticks he threshed the enemy.
Goblins applauded him who plowed the battlefield
With his spear. With their long hands, shaking
With bangles, they raised the crowned heads
Of the dead. Flaunting them they danced
Before the war-chariot, and compared this battle
With the ones fought at the time of churning
The ocean, and in seablown Laṅkā, and the one
In which the seablue god drove the chariot.
The goblins then danced behind the war-chariot

Lines 204–241

In that cremation ground, the battlefield, to mark
The victory. With crowned heads for an oven,
Broken heads for pans, shoulder blades for ladles,
The goblin chef fed all the goblins. Smacking
Their lips, they gave thanks:
"May the king
Of the upright scepter who fought and won
This just battle live forever."
Ceṅkuṭṭuvaṉ
Of the fearless spear, with victory in his palms,
Then spoke to his messengers:
"Go and promise
Our support to all those in the northern country
Who honor the Vedas, and lead flawless lives
By lighting the sacrificial fires."
Later, the guardian king,
Who had won the war and achieved his end
With Villavaṉ Kōtai, led several regiments of his army
To the gold-browed Himālaya to get a stone
To engrave the image of the goddess Pattiṉi.

Lines 241–254

Canto 27
The Lustration

The image of the goddess Pattiṉi, giver of rain,
Was engraved on the stone brought from the renowned
  Himālaya
In the north, and placed on the shining crowns
Of Kanaka and Vijaya who had challenged Ceṅkuṭṭuvaṉ
Of the fierce spear, the lord of the radiant anklet.
For seven hours he had taken over the task
Of the god of death, and devoured many Ārya kings
Who had treated the power of the southern kings
With scant respect. The world, enclosed by the sea,
Added this to the battles fought in turn
For eighteen years, eighteen months,
And eighteen days. With his army of fearless spears,
Ceṅkuṭṭuvaṉ had killed in one day on the battlefield
The entire hosts of his enemies. He returned
To the banks of the immortal Gaṅgā, and had the stone
With the image of the goddess Pattiṉi bathed
In the way ordained by the scriptures with the help
Of brahmans expert in ritual. On the south bank
Of the clear Gaṅgā, the king settled in a camp
Built for him by the Ārya kings in an open plain.
It included a spacious palace, fine arches,
Golden islets, canopies rich with flowers,
Apartments, expansive groves, lily ponds,
And theaters to suit the needs of that illustrious king.
He sent for the sons of those warriors—
Who had killed ambitious kings and made the nymphs
Of heaven wed them; who had fought bravely

Lines 1–24

And lay with their heads and shoulders cut off,
Defeated but valiant still; who had trounced
Their enemies, though mercenaries, with their spears
Before their own bodies were hacked to pieces
On the battlefield; who had fallen with swords,
Their noble line praised in a round dance
By goblins with sunken eyes; who had died
With their comrades and thus forced their wives,
Necks sparkling with jewels, to take their own lives;
Who had, as the vanguard of the army, worn
On their crowns chaplets of sirissa flowers
As a token of having killed with their spears
The enemy's frontline; who had fallen near
The lofty chariots with their painted banners
And stood up dripping blood. He sent for
The soldiers who had held the battlefield after cutting off
The dark, crowned heads renowned for their valor,
And those whose breastplates had been ripped open,
Thus wounding their chests. The god of death himself
Was moved to pity. By his great victory, the king
Had covered himself with glory which the poets
Praised. To each soldier, he said:
"Come here."
A golden sirissa flower he offered him. More
He couldn't have given even on his birthday.
With a wreath of palm leaves and white dead nettle,
He adorned himself to commemorate the great victory.
As he sat on the throne, the brahman Māṭalaṉ approached him
And said:
"May our king live forever! The song

Lines 24–50

Of Mātavi in the seaside grove burdened the crowns
Of Kanaka and Vijaya. Ruler of the world,
Clasped by the sea, may you live forever!"

The king replied:
"You have spoken in riddles.
Some of these enemy kings will not understand you.
O brahman, learned in the four Vedas,
What did you say? Explain yourself."

The brahman Māṭalaṉ replied:
"The girl Mātavi
Had a lover's quarrel with Kōvalaṉ as they amused
Themselves on the cool seashore. Inspired by fate,
She sang the songs of the seaside grove
To accompany her dance. Instead of reuniting them,
The songs made them drift apart. He returned
To his virtuous wife, and they came
To the old, towered city of Maturai.
Its king, wreathed in leaves, went to heaven
Because of Kōvalaṉ's murder. It is his wife,
O lord of the west, who has entered your country.
On their crowned heads the northern kings
Now carry her.
"Be gracious enough to listen
To the reason why I came here, O king of kings
Of the resplendent spear! I had gone round
The Potiyil hills, sacred to Agastya,
And bathed in the renowned waters of the Kumari.
I was returning home when pressed by fate

Lines 50–70

I entered Maturai of the illustrious Pāṇṭiyaṉ
Of the fierce sword. When Mātari heard
That the fair girl had defeated the Pāṇṭiyaṉ
Of the invincible army with her anklet, she spoke aloud
In the open space smeared with cowdung
And covered over with pollen: 'Cowherds! No wrong
Has Kōvalaṉ done. Only the king has erred.
And I have lost her who was in my care.
Have the king's parasol and scepter fallen
From the true path?' With those words,
She leaped into the fire in the dead of night.
Enraged was Kavunti of the great penance.
She calmed down when she heard of the death
Of the king, renowned for his upright scepter.
And she moaned: 'Was this the fate of those
Who were my companions?' She vowed to starve
Herself to death. So ended her life.

"All this I heard in detail, and of the destruction
Of the glorious city of Maturai, ruled by the Pāṇṭiyaṉ
Of the golden chariot. Grief-stricken, I returned
Home to Pukār, capital of the Cōḻas,
And informed all the notable men there.
When Kōvalaṉ's father heard of what had become
Of his son and daughter-in-law and also of the just king
Of Maturai, he was distraught. He gave away
All his wealth and entered the sevenfold monastery
Of Indra. There he observed severe vows
Like the three hundred monks who roam the heavens,
Having renounced the world to escape from rebirth.

Lines 70–95

His wife, too, reeling from the shock
Of her son's terrible death, gave up her life.
Kaṇṇaki's father, too, gave away his wealth,
Took the holy vows before the Ājīvikas,
Like sages observing rigorous penance.
Within a few days, his noble wife gave up her life.

"Mātavi heard this and said to her good mother:
'I must now lead a virtuous life.
Maṇimēkalai should be spared the life of a courtesan
Which is full of troubles.'
Her hair, wreathed in flowers,
She removed, and entered a Buddhist nunnery
And was taught the holy word. Hearing the news
From me, they had all died. And therefore I have come
To bathe in the holy waters of the Gaṅgā
To absolve myself. May you live forever, O king of kings!"

The great king of the Cērals, wreathed
In unfading willow, palm leaves and white dead nettle,
Asked:
"May we hear what became
Of the fertile Pāṇṭiya kingdom after the king's death?"

The brahman Māṭalaṉ then spoke:
"O king
Of the vast world, may you live forever!
In one day you broke the nine parasols
Of nine kings who had formed a league
Against your cousin, Kiḷḷivaḷavaṉ.

Lines 96–120

They would not accept him as the crown prince,
Flouted his orders, and brought the Pāṇṭiya country
To the brink of ruin. You restored the golden wheel.

"O Poṟaiyaṉ! A wreath of palm leaves
You wore to celebrate the success of your sword,
Brandished in your right hand, in tearing apart
The margosa tree guarded by the Paḻaiyaṉ.
Be gracious enough to listen to me.
The victorious Vēṟ-Ceḻiyaṉ, ruler of Koṟkai,
Offered a sacrifice of one thousand goldsmiths
In a single day to the goddess Pattiṉi
Who had wrenched off one of her breasts. It was then
Ancient Maturai lost her glory,
And troubles dogged her steps because of injustice.
A Pāṇṭiya king of the moon's lineage,
Which was known for the way it protected the people
Of the southern kingdoms, ascended the throne
Of Maturai. He was like the crimson Sun
Who mounted at dawn his one-wheeled chariot
Drawn by seven horses with bells
Around their necks. May our king live forever,
Crowned with glory, who guards the world
From one age to the next!"
Night spread
Its wings over the land as the king sat
Listening to the brahman's tale. The sun gave way
To twilight: the western sky turned red.
A wisp of a crescent showed. He was lost
In its beauty as the court astrologer rose

Lines 120–148

To speak:
"Thirty-two months have passed
Since we left Vañci. May the ruler of the world live
Forever!"
Later, the king passed through
The street of the chariots in his camp, lined
With posts and surrounded by high canopies.
He looked at the mounds of tents everywhere,
Small and large, and walked beyond his tent
Down a side lane and mounted his golden throne
Finely decorated by royal craftsmen.
He sent for Māṭalaṉ and asked him:

"Since the princes of the fertile Cōḻa kingdom
Are now dead, does the new king rule justly?"

Māṭalaṉ, the peaceful brahman, blessed him:

"May you live forever, O my king! The fierce spear
Of the Cōḻa that, to the amazement of the gods who shine
With radiant ornaments, destroyed the three fortresses
Will never stray from the right path. This cannot be true
Of the upright scepter of the king who cut off
His own flesh and offered it to a famished hawk,
And thus saved a dove in pain limping on its feet.
No harm can come to a king, even in times
Of danger, whose land is watered by the Kāviri."

Hearing these words of Māṭalaṉ, foremost among
Learned brahmans, the great king

Lines 148–172

Who holds a spear and is wreathed in palm leaves
Rejoiced and said:
"O brahman Māṭalaṉ,
Please accept this."
He gave him fifty measures
Of gold equal to his own weight.
He then told the hundred northern kings:
"Return to your fertile lands." He ordered
His thousand messengers, known for their ready wit,
To show to the two great Tamil kings
The princes of the large armies who fled
The battlefield disguised as ascetics; the Ārya eunuchs
Noted for their high cheeks, dark locks
Of hair, wide fishlike eyes, red at the corners,
Bright earrings, red lips,
White teeth, thin bamboo-like arms
Ringed with gold bracelets, small breasts,
A waist slender as lightning, and anklets
On their small feet; and the captive kings,
Kanaka and Vijaya, who fought because they questioned
The valor of the Tamil kings whose emblem
Was the flawless palm.
As dawn broke,
Bees woke up from flowering lotuses
In the endless plains watered by the Gaṅgā,
And made lutelike music in the air.
On the far peaks of the eastern hills,
The sun rose and poured its soft rays.
Ceṅkuṭṭuvaṉ, the conqueror of the west, adorned
His wreath of sirissa flowers with the white dead nettle

Lines 172–197

Of the north, walked round his camp, and began
His journey south with his triumphant army.

The goddess of prosperity resides forever
In the palace of many stories that touch the skies.
A flowery canopy topped the golden harem.
Made by expert hands, it was decorated
With strings of pearls and flowers, and blazed
With the glitter of diamonds and gems fastened
By gold thread. The queen's gold bed
Was covered with the soft down of mating swans.
Sleep wouldn't come though she lay there.
Maidservants had heard of the victory
Of Ceṅkuṭṭuvaṉ's chariot and sword on the battlefield.

Skilled in conveying good news,
They wished her long life and, singing,
Praised her:
"Renounce your sorrow at the parting
Of your dear lord."
The dwarfs and hunchbacks
Came up to her and said:
"Let beauty reappear.
The noble lord is come. Brighten up
Your fragrant hair with everyday ornaments."

The songs of the hill dwellers floated down:

"Short be his way who returns on top

Lines 198–222

Of the speeding elephant, wreathed in willow
And the white dead nettle of the north."

From their lookouts, they observed the forest guard.
Reeling from the honey taken from honeycombs
On bamboos, he forgets to hurl rocks
From his slingshot at elephants that trample
On the vast millet fields and sleep in them.
The plowman's loud song was also heard:

"The lord of the west is come who pulled down
The big fortresses of the northern kings
And plowed the enemy's land with asses
And sowed white millet. O bullocks!
Tomorrow you can lay down the plow.
It is the king's birthday. Prisoners will be freed."

Colorful as Indra's bow in the sky
Were the renowned steps leading down to the river
Āṉporunai, splashed with the paints,
Scented powders and flowers of the bathers.

"With herds of cows the bowman comes
From the famed Himālaya. O cows! You will play
And leap with them."
So cowherds piped on their flutes
As they knotted their tufts with chaplets of the blue lotus
Nursed by the swirling bee, and with fragrant lilies
With open petals. They stood on the stems
Of the flowering screw pine after bringing

Lines 222–241

The king's cows to their watering hole.
Fisherwomen sang the well-turned love song:

"Our king Vāṉavaṉ is come to fondle
The shoulders and firm breasts of his queen.
Girls! Let us sing the willow song
In praise of his white dead nettle braided with palm leaves."

Under the laurel tree the fisherwomen gathered
On the sands washed by the sea to play with balls.
They collected in their hands, ringed with bangles,
Bright pearls scooped out of open shells.

The great queen listened to these songs
And removed her tight bangles. The conches
Sounded. Throned atop a speedy elephant,
Under a wreathed parasol, Ceṅkuṭṭuvaṉ
With a chaplet of white dead nettle on his crown,
And cheered by his subjects, in a procession of carts
Drawn by elephants, entered Vañci.

Lines 242–256

Canto 28
The Dedication of the Memorial Stone

Evening, when flowers open and men pray,
Took hold of the ancient city of Vañci,
Famous for the wealth of its great king's triumph
Over the world, for his victorious sword
And tall, golden parasol that like the full moon
Cools the earth. Before a lamp glowing
With a white flame, girls with radiant bangles
Offered fresh flowers, and prayed:
"May the king of the wide world live forever!"
Women, their eyes lined with kohl,
And their breasts firm and round, embraced
The sword-warriors covered with chaplets
Of palm leaves and gold chains wrought with flowers.
The chests of some were gored by elephant tusks;
The chests of others bore the mark of spears;
Arrows had pierced the shining chests of a few;
And fierce swords had cut the chests of others
Glowing with jewels.
"Like the arrows of flowers
Of the fish-bannered god, my love shot
Her quick glances from curved lashes
Set in a moonlike face among clouds of thick hair,
Scented with eaglewood fumes. I welcome
The evening as a balm," so thought a warrior.
A crescent of a smile hovered over her lips
Red as ripe mangos. It was pleasant to behold
Her eyes flash like minnows, and her bright teeth

Lines 1–24

Split with laughter. His chest adorned,
The warrior was thus told of his heart's desires.
The evening also provided a banquet of pleasures
In the form of women with beautiful faces
Luminous with the scented tilaka. Their curly hair
And wreaths crowded with bees slipped
During their embraces, and they tidied themselves
Before mirrors. With ease, they removed
Small lutes from their cases, thrummed
The strings and played in the pālai mode
By taking the first note itself as the tonic.
Then they played in the kuṟiñci mode
By taking the second note as the tonic.
Evening gave way to the splendor of the moon
That came to receive the homage of the earth.
To the people of ancient Vañci, the moon
Recalled the face of Ceṅkuṭṭuvaṉ in his audience hall
As subject kings touched his anklets
With their crowns.
The lovers and their women obeyed
The commands of the god of love, the archer
Who shot flower-tipped arrows. He ruled
Over moonlit terraces, groves covered with flowers,
Theaters with floors of soft earth,
Pavilions strung with flowers, beds,
And balconies with awnings. Over all of them fell
The cool rays of the moon. The audience hall
Of the golden palace was in the center of the ancient city
With its flagged ramparts. It rose like Mount Meru
From this good earth encircled by the sea.

Lines 25–50

Vēṇmāḷ, the good and chaste queen, came
To look at the moon. She was followed by maids
With shining bangles carrying lamps
And wishing the queen a long life;
By players on drums smeared with mud,
And lutes, and by those who sang sweet songs;
By dwarfs and hunchbacks carrying pastes
Of musk and sandalwood; by eunuchs in women's clothes
Carrying incense; by maids with mattresses
Spread with flowers, incense, and other perfumes;
And by others carrying mirrors, clothes, and vessels.
The ruler of the sea-encircled earth,
Together with his queen, walked up to the terrace.

Then a Cākkaiyaṉ, an expert in dance from Paṟaiyūr
Renowned for brahmans proficient in the four Vedas,
Performed for the king's pleasure the koṭṭiccētam
Danced by Śiva, with Umā as part of himself,
To the rhythm of the tinkling anklet on his feet.
The hourglass drum echoed in his graceful
Hand; his red eyes expressed many moods;
And his red, matted hair flew in all directions.
Her anklet did not stir; her bracelet was still;
Her girdle was silent; her breast did not shake;
The jewels on her head were undisturbed;
And her knotted hair did not become loose.
When the dancer had sung the praise of the ruler
Of the wide world, the gatekeeper informed
The king of the arrival of the brahman Māṭalaṉ,
Nīlaṉ and the messengers. The king went

Lines 51–83

To his audience hall. Nīlaṉ offered his respects to him
Through the courtiers, and said:
"O king who wears
A wreath of white dead nettle and an anklet,
Emblems of success in battle! We went
To the ancient city of Cempiyaṉ with the Ārya kings
And offered our respects to him through his courtiers.
Seated in the fine audience hall
Built for him by the kings of Vajra, Avanti,
And Magadha, he spoke to the commander
Of his chariot corps, foremost in the army:
'To capture in the open battlefield those who fled,
Disguised as common people, throwing away
Parasol and sword after showing great courage,
Is not something to boast about.' We took leave
Of the noble Cōḻa, his chest wreathed in a garland,
O king of the upright scepter, and went to see
The king of far-famed Maturai. The Pāṇṭiyaṉ
Of the fierce spear said: 'Strange
Is this victory in which kings that fled the battlefield
And put on the robes of monks were abused.
It is even stranger that Ceṅkūṭṭuvaṉ should use
The staff of the white parasol that the Ārya kings
Placed on the neck of their elephants as the sacred rod
Of Jayanta, and worship Śiva and his consort Umā
At Kuyilāluvam on the slopes of the Himālaya.' "

As Nīlaṉ reported the indiscreet comments
Of the two kings, Ceṅkuṭṭuvaṉ roared with laughter
And his red-lotus eyes blazed. The learned Māṭalaṉ

Lines 83–112

Stood up and said:
"O king of kings,
May your valor live forever! May you live
Forever! You destroyed Viyalūr, famed
For its clusters of dark lilies and elephants
Who sleep in the mountains thick with pepper.
At Nērivāyil you routed nine kings
Who wore garlands of fig leaves. Camping
On the outskirts of Iṭumpil with your force
Of lofty chariots, you fought a battle
On the sea, following your enemy to a great distance.
You defeated the Ārya kings
Who marched on the banks of the Gaṅgā in flood.
O king, crowned with a victor's wreath
And lord of an immense army! O lion
Among kings, full of the wisdom of great men,
Give up your anger! Ruler of the earth,
May the days of your life be as innumerable
As the grains of sand in the cool river Āṉporunai!
Ruler of the earth clasped by the sea,
May you live forever! Be gracious enough to listen
To my words. Fifty years have passed
Since you ascended the throne: you perform
The sacrifice of war but not religious sacrifices.
O king who kept your promise with a sword
In your right hand and a wreath of palm leaves!
One of your forebears in this city covered himself
With glory by uprooting the cadamba oak
From the sea; another showed great courage
By engraving his bow-emblem on the Himālaya;

Lines 112–136

Another helped a Vedic brahman to ascend
To heaven as a reward for composing poems;
Another forced death's messengers
To take lives only in the order he indicated;
Another Cēral entered the fertile kingdom
In the high mountain of the ill-bred Yavanas.
Still another Cēral drove his enemy away
From the fierce battlefield and attacked his fortress
In the hills; another in that illustrious line
Of kings bathed in the Ayirai river
And in the waters of the two seas; another
Invited the spirit of the crossroads to Vañci
And offered him a sacrifice of wine. None
Of them escaped death. This body is fragile.
Didn't you see in your war with the Ārya kings,
Who had scorned the courageous Tamils, that wealth
Will not remain forever with men who live in this world?

"O just king! It is unnecessary to remind men
Of wisdom that youth will not last forever. O guardian king!
Lakṣmī resides in your chest though you see
Your body covered with grey hair. Souls
In divine bodies are often reborn in human bodies,
And souls in human bodies may be reborn
In animals. Souls that leave the bodies
Of animals may be reborn in the bodies of demons.
Men are actors on a stage: they don't play
One role forever. The actions of former births
Determine life after death. No empty words, these.
O king, whose chest is adorned with a wreath

Lines 137–169

Of seven crowns, may your wheel add luster
To your illustrious line! Of king of the fierce sword!
Not for soliciting gifts have I thus spoken.
I cannot bear to see a good soul
Inside a good body tread the common path.
You have gone beyond the limits of knowledge.
Therefore you should perform that great sacrifice
With the help of priests versed in the four Vedas
So that you may attain the path the gods approve.
A good deed may not be put off till tomorrow,
For your soul, blessed by the Vedas, may even today
Leave your body. No one on this good earth,
Clasped by the sea, knows how long he will live.
May you live forever with your queen, adored
By princes who fall at your feet in submission!
May our illustrious king live from one age
To the next protecting this world!"
The tongue
Of the brahman, expert in the Vedas, plowed
And sowed the seeds of wisdom in the king's ears.
In good time, those seeds sprouted.
Eager to enjoy the rich harvest of virtue,
The king of the loud anklets, invited
Sacrificial priests, instructed by teachers
Expert in the four Vedas. They were asked
To begin the festival of rites as advised
By Māṭalaṉ.
He ordered the Ārya kings
Removed from prison and taken outside the city
Of Vañci of great renown to Vēḷāvikkō Palace,

Enclosed by ponds and cool groves.
They were informed they could return
To their cities at the end of the sacrifice. He rejoiced
In saying:
"Villavaṉ Kōtai! Look to their comfort
As befits princes."
Orders were sent
To Aḻumpilvēḷ and to revenue officers to proclaim
In distant towns with fields brimming
With water:
"Throw open all prisons. Remit
All taxes due from the citizens of our state."

The Cōḻa king, who wears a wreath
Of fig leaves, shone as an example.
Pattiṉi whom the whole world now worships
Had proved the truth of the Tamil saying:
"The virtue of women is useless if the king
Rules unjustly." She made the Cōḻa realize it.
She made the Pāṇṭiyaṉ, lord of the south,
Realize, "The king cannot survive if his scepter
Is crooked." She made the Cēral,
Lord of the west, realize, "The wrath
Of kings will not be appeased till their vows
Are fulfilled, and made known to the kings
Of the north."
In her rage, Pattiṉi lit
A fire from one of her breasts and burned down
The ancient city of Maturai, entered
Our country, and stood in the golden shade

Lines 198–221

Of the cool branches of the kino. With the help
Of brahmans, royal priests, astrologers,
And expert sculptors, a shrine was dedicated
To that revered woman and built
According to established rules so that wise men
May approve it. The image of Pattiṉi was installed
In it, engraved by skilled hands on the stone
Brought from the slopes of the Himālaya, the home
Of the gods, after prayers to Śiva who resides there.
She was adorned with precious ornaments
Exquisitely crafted and worshiped with flowers.
Images of the guardian deities stood
At the entrance to the temple. The lion among kings,
Who had extended his rule over the northern countries,
Performed the dedication and ordered:
"Worship
The goddess every day with offerings and festivities."

Lines 221–234

Canto 29
The Benediction

PREFACE

1

Once Ceṅkuṭṭuvaṉ defeated the Koṅku in a fierce battle, and then marched to the banks of the great Gaṅgā. He returned to Vañci where he remained in a foul mood. He was the son of Cēralātaṉ who ruled all the land from the Kumari to the Himālaya. His mother was the daughter of the Cōḻa, illustrious descendants of the sun. Many holy men from the north came to Vañci and told him that the northern kings, gathered together on the occasion of a princess' marriage, ridiculed the valor of the Tamil kings of the south who had once fought against them and carved on the slopes of the Himālaya their emblems of the bow, fish, and tiger. They boasted: "There were no crowned kings then as powerful as ourselves." The decision to bring a stone from the Himālaya for the image was like a stick that turns a hoop. It inspired Ceṅkūṭṭuvaṉ to fight and defeat the kings of the land of the Āryas. Having done this, he remained for some time on the banks of the Gaṅgā as a guest of the Ārya kings. He made some of them carry a stone for the image of the goddess on their crowned heads after bathing it, as custom required, in the holy Gaṅgā. Thus he appeased his wrath. He returned to Vañci, and dedicated the image of Kaṇṇaki, whose breast had caused an upheaval, in a temple. She was worshiped there by many crowned kings with tributes.

Shortly after, Mācāttuvāṉ became a monk. He had heard from the noble brahman of the agony of Kaṇṇaki, whose moon-like face overflowed with tears from her fish eyes, and whose dusty hair tumbled over her back. It was thus she upbraided the god of righteousness for the injustice done to Kōvalaṉ which resulted in his death at the hands of a contemptible person. She stood before the king with tears flowing from her eyes until he fell dead. His wife too gave up her life.

Hearing this, the foster mother, her close friend, and Tēvanti, who had taken refuge with Cāttaṉ, were distraught and went to see Kaṇṇaki in the great city of Maturai. There they were told of the upheaval caused by her wrenched-off breast. They visited the herdswoman Aiyai, the daughter of Mātari, who died after she lost Kaṇṇaki who was in her care. All of them traveled along the Vaiyai, and crossed the lofty hill. They entered the palace of Ceṅkuṭṭuvaṉ, who had built a temple to the goddess of chastity, and spoke to him of their relationship with Kaṇṇaki.

WHAT TĒVANTI SAID

2

Know me as the friend of that goddess,
The three crowned kings protect and worship,
Born in the northern Himālaya, and bathed
In the swirling waters of the Gaṅgā,
Whose shoulders are ringed with armlets.
Know me as the friend of the woman of the Cōḻa country.

WHAT THE FOSTER MOTHER SAID

3

Know me as the foster mother of the woman
With wide eyes, who did not give vent to her anger
Toward the fair and pleasant Mātavi,
But hand in hand walked with her dear husband
Through the terrible forest where even a handful of water
Could not be found in the wells.
Know me as the foster mother of the woman of cool Pukār.

WHAT HER CLOSE FRIEND SAID

4

Know me as the friend of the woman
With gold bangles, who said not a word

To the mother who gave her birth,
To the foster mother who raised her, or even to me,
But followed her husband as a dutiful wife.
Know me as the friend of the woman of Pūmpukār.

TĒVANTI'S LAMENT
before the image of Kaṇṇaki

5

I haven't done penance. I didn't know
The nature of your dream when I heard it.
What have I done? The day your mother
Heard of the troubles your torn-off breast had caused,
O woman with beautiful locks of hair,
She died of grief. And did you hear, friend,
Your mother-in-law too died? Did you hear that, friend?

THE FOSTER MOTHER'S LAMENT

6

Mācāttuvāṉ heard of the evil done to Kōvalaṉ
By the wretched man, and of the death
Of the guardian king. He lost heart
And wished he were dead. He gave away
His wealth and renounced the world.
Did you hear that, mother? And did you also hear,
Mother, of the renunciation of Mānāykaṉ?

THE CLOSE FRIEND'S LAMENT

7

Mātavi heard of your lover's death,
Of your agony, and of the people's outrage towards her.
She lost heart. She went to the sages
That live under the bo tree, gave away her wealth,

And entered a nunnery. Did you hear that, friend?
And did you also hear, friend,
Of the renunciation of Maṇimēkalai?

TĒVANTI'S LAMENT

what she said to Aiyai

8

This unmarried girl is the daughter
Of the old woman who gave up her life, saying:
"I embrace the fire. I failed
To protect the woman left in my care
By the ascetic of untroubled vision." Do you see, friend,
Aiyai of the pretty teeth? Do you see, friend,
This fair daughter of your aunt?

WHAT CEṄKUṬṬUVAṈ SAID

9

What! O, what is this? O, what is this?
O, what is this? I see a vision in the sky,
Of a lightning figure with gold anklets,
A girdle, bangles round her arms, earrings
Of gold set with rare diamonds,
And other ornaments of pure gold.

WHAT KAṆṆAKI SAID

10

Blameless is the Pāṇṭiyaṉ, now an honored guest
In the palace of the king of the gods.
I am his daughter. I am going to play
On Veṉvēlāṉ's hill. Friends, come there, all of you!

WHAT THE GIRLS OF VAÑCI SAID

11

O girls of Vañci, girls with waists
Like the willow. Girls whose feet are painted
With lac, who are a part of the king's following.
Come, all of you. Come, sing of her
Who burned down Maturai with her breast,
And humbled a king with her anklet.
Let us all sing of Teṉṉavaṉ's daughter.
She came to our country, and the king praised her:
"Pāṇṭiya kings will die if their tall scepter bends."
Let us all sing of the lovely woman.
Come, let us all sing of the Pāṇṭiyaṉ's daughter.

THE GIRLS' CHORUS

12

We said she was our king's daugher.
She said she was the vinelike daughter
Of the king of the Vaiyai. We shall praise Vāṉavaṉ.
Let the gods praise the king of the Vaiyai.

THE BLESSING

13

Let us praise the king who gave up his life
Burned by the tears of the woman
Who suffered the outcome of past fate.
May the old dynasty of kings that rules
Over the people of Maturai, enclosed by the rising waters
Of the Vaiyai, live forever! May it live forever!

14

Let us praise the king who placed the stone

From the Himālaya on the crowned heads
Of the northern kings. May the old dynasty
Of the kings of Vañci live forever,
Enclosed by the rising waters
Of the Āṉporunai! May it live forever!

15

Let us all sing of the lord of the Kāviri land.
Girls with flowers in your hair,
Let us sing of Pukār!

SONG OF THE WOODEN BALL

16

Ammāṉai, who is the strong king
That ruled over the world enclosed by the sea
And guarded the tall fortress of the king of the gods?
Ammāṉai, the strong king that guarded
The tall fortress is the Cōḻa king who pulled down
The three fortresses hanging from the heavens.
Ammāṉai, let us sing of the Cōḻa city, Pukār.

17

Ammāṉai, who is the victorious king
Praised by heaven that sat on the scales
And offered a piece of his own flesh
For the sake of a dove?
Ammāṉai, the king that offered a piece
Of his own flesh is the guardian who sought justice
For the sake of a cow.
Ammāṉai, let us sing of that king's city, Pukār.

18

Ammāṉai, who is the king that engraved
The tiger-emblem on the northern mountain,
While elephants of the eight directions
Stared and never batted an eyelid?
Ammāṉai, the king that engraved the tiger-emblem
On the northern mountain is the victorious king who swept
All the eight directions under his one parasol.
Ammāṉai, let us sing of that king's city, Pukār.

19

Ammāṉai, why do women with fine jewels
Hold wooden balls in their hands
And sing inside their homes?
Ammāṉai, women sing inside their homes
So that the king should embrace their full breasts,
Ammāṉai, if the king should embrace their full breasts,
We will sing of the beautiful city of Pukār.

THE SONG OF THE BALL

20

Girl, like a shining creeper of gold,
With a gold necklace, to the echo
Of our jeweled girdles that flash like streaks of lightning
We will run and strike the ball, saying:
"May the king of the southern countries live forever!
May Teṉṉavaṉ live forever!"
Let us strike the ball, saying: "May the king whose chest
Is adorned with Indra's garland live forever."

21

Let us run forward, sit, dart back and forth,

Moving in all directions, as if the climber of the sky,
Lightning, has struck the earth.
Let us run and strike the ball, saying,
"May the king of the southern countries live forever!
May Teṉṉavaṉ live forever!"
Let us strike the ball, saying, "May the king whose chest
Is adorned with Indra's garland live forever!"

22

We throw the ball. It does not stay
In our hands. It does not rise to the heavens
Leaving the earth behind.
Let us run and strike the ball, saying:
"May the king of the southern countries live forever!
May Teṉṉavaṉ live forever!"
Let us strike the ball, saying: "May the king whose chest
Is adorned with Indra's garland live forever!"

THE SONG OF THE SWING

23

Let one of us standing near Aiyai
Be seated on the ornamental swing hanging by ropes.
Let us stretch out our hands and begin
A one-beat rhythm. Shall we not swing,
Rolling our eyes shaped like curved palms,
Singing of the king who pulled apart the cadamba oak?
Shall we not swing, singing of the king's curved bow?

24

Shall we not swing tossing our long, black hair,
Singing of the valor of the lord of the mountain,
The Cēral king, Poṟaiyaṉ, who offered

An enormous amount of food in the war
Between the five Pāṇḍavas and the hundred Kauravas?
Shall we not swing, singing of how
The cadamba oak was pulled apart?

25

Shall we not swing bending our lightning-thin waists,
Singing of the glory of our king of kings,
The guardian of the earth with his bow, fish
And tiger banners, and the ruler of the fertile lands
Of the Yavanas of weird speech
And of Kumari spiked with rocks?

THE SONG OF THE PESTLE

26

Using sweet sugarcane as pestles,
The women of Pukār pound choice pearls
In the shade of the flowering portia tree.
This song is the song of Cempiyaṉ
With broad shoulders wreathed in fig leaves,
A strong chariot, and the emblem of the wheel.
This song is the song the women sing.

27

Using red coral pestles
The women of Maturai of tall towers
Pound pearls, sung by poets.
This song is the song of Pañcavaṉ
With shoulders bright with the garland of the king
Of the gods, and a banner with the emblem of the fish.
This song is the song of his margosa garland.

28

Using white ivory pestles,
The women of Vañci pound rare pearls
In sandalwood mortars. This song is the song
Of the Cēral king with a garland of palm leaves,
Whose fame for crossing the sea and pulling apart
The cadamba oak has spread across the world.
This song is the song
Of his palmyra garland that excites the heart.

29

Those who do not worship the holy feet
Of Poṟaiyaṉ of the great bow will find it
Difficult to bless our lord of the good earth.
The renowned daughter of our king, Kaṇṇaki,
Spoke the benediction: "May our Ceṅkuṭṭuvaṉ live forever."

Canto 30
The Granting of a Favor

The great king who had subdued the north
Saw Kaṇṇaki in her divine form.
He turned to Tēvantikai and asked her:

"Who is this Maṇimēkalai for whom you cried
Your eyes out? Why did she renounce the world?
Tell me."
Tēvantikai blessed the king:

"May the king's fame grow forever! May his kingdom
Flourish!"
She then told him of Maṇimēkalai's great
Renunciation. Known among dancers
With exquisite girdles, her dark hair
Had grown thick and could be braided into five plaits.
Her cool eyes, red in the corners,
Had a simple charm she was unaware of.
Behind her coral lips, the pearlwhite teeth
Were not quite grown. Her breasts had risen;
Her chest, broadened; her slender waist,
Become thinner; her fair mound of love,
Widened; her thighs were rounded; her tender feet,
Unable to bear the weight of her ornaments, shone.
Men of noble families did not consider her
A dancer as she had not yet been taught the art.

"Mātavi's good mother, Citrāpati,

Lines 1–23

Asked her: 'What do you have in mind?
What should I do?' Mātavi turned
To Maṇimēkalai and said: 'Come here, dear innocent girl,'
And removed her locks of hair braided with flowers.
Enraged, the god of love threw down
His sugarcane bow and his flower arrows.
She entered a Buddhist nunnery and obeyed its rules.
When the king and the people heard about this,
They were as unhappy as if a priceless jewel
Had been dropped into the sea. The monk
Who received her said: 'The lovely girl
Spoke to me of her wish to renounce.'
I was sad to see her change her fair appearance
In the prime of life."
After speaking to the king,
Tēvantikai entered into a trance. The flowers
Shook from her locks of hair; her brows
Throbbed; her lips shut; a faint smile
Passed over her teeth; her speech was unusual;
Sweat ran down her face; her eyes reddened;
And her hands rose as if to threaten. Then she moved
Her legs and stood up. Her wisdom went unnoticed.
Still in a trance, her dry tongue spoke
Inspired words before the king of the mountain slopes
Where the kuṟiñci flowers.
"Among the good, modest,
And beautiful women who came here for the dedication
Of the goddess are the twin girls born to the wife
Of Araṭṭaṉ Ceṭṭi, and the little daughter of Cēṭakkuṭumpi,
Employed in the service of the lord resting

Lines 23–52

On the divine serpent in the golden temple.
Near the temple of Maṅkalatēvi, there is a hill
That touches the sky. On its red summit
Is a bowlike rock with many pools.
Springs leap from them with white stones
Like small, mustard seeds, and red stones
Like coral-tree flowers. Those who bathe
In these pools recall their past births.
I brought that water and gave it to you,
O brahman Māṭalaṉ, when you were resting
At the gate of that temple and said: 'Take this.
Look after it. Aren't you keeping it in the pot
Inside the string bag in your hand? The water
Will not lose its power till the sun and moon
Vanish. If you would, therefore, sprinkle it
Upon these three little girls, they will recall
Their past births. I am the god Pācaṇṭaṉ,
Speaking through the body of this brahman woman.' "

Ceṅkuṭṭuvaṉ was struck with wonder, and turned
To Māṭalaṉ who said:
"O king, hear this!
May all your troubles end. Once, the woman Mālati
Offered milk to the child of her husband's second wife
When fate decreed that it should die. In her despair
For the child she was inconsolable. She fell,
Pleading for grace, at the feet of Pācaṇṭaṉ
Who appeared to her in the form of her child
And said: 'Mother, grieve no more,' and rid her
Of her suffering. After this miracle, he grew up

Lines 53–81

In the care of his foster mother and the rival wife
In the old family of the Kāppiyas. He married
Tēvantikai by going round the fire. For eight years
He lived with her, and then showed her his divine form
And vanished, saying: 'Come to my temple.'
When I was in the temple of Maṅkalatēvi, this god
Came before me in the form of a brahman, gave
This string bag with a pot in it, asked me
To keep it safe, and went away. He never came back,
And I took it with me. He reappears now
In the form of the brahman woman and says:
'Sprinkle that water.' Let us, therefore, O king,
Sprinkle it on these girls and learn the truth."

When he sprinkled the water, the girls recalled
Their past births. One of them, Kaṇṇaki's mother,
Cried:
"O my daughter, my partner! When your husband
Abandoned you, I sympathized with you.
Unconcerned, you went to a strange city alone
With your husband and suffered. My dearest!
Won't you come back and rid me of my great sorrow?"

Another, the mother of Kōvalaṉ, said:
"Alone,
In the dead of night, you vanished and left
My good daughter-in-law to live with me. Heartbroken
Over your departure, I raved. I can't endure
This anymore. Won't you come back, my son?"

Lines 81–107

The third, Mātari, said:
"I left for the steps
Leading to the river Vaiyai in flood.
When I returned, I heard the news
From some young people of the renowned city.
I didn't see you in my home.
O my dear, my dear, where did you hide yourself?"

And so the three little girls, their arms
Glowing with bangles, with childlike lips
Spoke their elders' words, grieving again and again
Before the king with gems sparkling on his chest.
Wearing a garland of palm leaves and the victor's anklet,
He turned to Māṭalaṉ, the brahman
With the holy thread across his chest, who blessed him
And told him what he remembered:
"O king of kings,
May you live forever! These three women
Were, in their past births, attached to the wife
Of Kōvalaṉ who wrestled with an elephant's tusk
To save a brahman in pain, and thus secured
A place in heaven. They could not follow Kaṇṇaki
To the other world as they had not done
Any other virtuous action. Because of their great love
For the golden vine of a girl, who unafraid
Entered this glorious city of Vañci,
The two were born as twins, to the delight
Of the good wife of Araṭṭaṉ Ceṭṭi. The old herdswoman
Mātari, who too was devoted to Kaṇṇaki and performed
A round dance, is now reborn as the daughter

Lines 108–135

Of Cēṭakkuṭumpi, employed in the service of Viṣṇu.
It is not uncommon that people who do good
Enter heaven, and that people who are attached
To things of this earth are reborn. Good and bad
Actions have their own reward. Those who are born
Die, and those who die are reborn. Old truths, these.
You were born through the grace of Śiva
Who rides the holy bull, and have won praise
As a king all over the world. Clear as an object
Held in the palm of your hand, you saw the results
Of good actions and the forms of sages.
May you live forever from one age to the next
Guarding the earth! May you live forever,
Noble king!"
Rejoicing over what the brahman Māṭalaṉ
Had said, the king offered grants
To the temple of the immortal Pattiṉi who had wrenched off
Her breast and set fire to the noisy city
Of the great Pāṇṭiya kingdom that poets have sung about.
He ordered that festivals be observed every day
And that Tēvantikai be responsible for offering flowers,
Perfume, and incense at the temple. Thrice
The king of the world went round the temple
And stood before the deity to pay his homage.
In front of him were the Ārya kings released from prison,
Kings set free from captivity, the Koṅku ruler
Of the west, the king of Mālva, Gajabāhu,
The king of sea-encircled Laṅkā—all prayed
With feeling to the deity:
"Please grace our countries

Lines 135–163

By your presence, as you have done this holy day
At the Cēral's sacrifice."
A voice rose
From the heavens:
"Your wish is granted."

Then Ceṅkuṭṭuvaṉ, the other kings and their strong armies
Praised the goddess in impeccable words,
As though they themselves had achieved salvation.
With the seeker of truth, the brahman Māṭalaṉ,
And kings with faint anklets, Ceṅkuṭṭuvaṉ
Entered the sacrificial hall. I also went in.
Before me stood Tēvantikai, possessed by a god.
She said:
"In the elegant audience hall
Of the ancient city of Vañci, you were seated
Beside your father. When the astrologer predicted
You would inherit the throne, you disapproved of him
To relieve the pain of Ceṅkuṭṭuvaṉ, renowned
For his chariot corps and his garland of cottonwood flowers.
You went away to the cloister at the East Gate
And before the sages there renounced the burdens of this world
To gain the kingship of the land of everlasting bliss
Beyond the reach of the human mind.
"Good people!
You have now heard the kind and holy words
Of the daughter of the gods who told my story.
Disregard both pleasure and pain and follow
The right path.
"Know God, and serve those

Lines 163–187

That have known him. Fear to tell lies.
Avoid spreading rumors. Give up
Eating meat. Do not hurt any living thing.
Be charitable and do penance. Do not forget
The good others have done. Despise
Bad company. Do not give false evidence.
Do not distort the truth. Keep the company
Of the virtuous. Stay away from the wicked.
Avoid other men's wives. Care for the dying.
Uphold domestic virtues. Reject the bad.
Keep off drinking, theft, falsehood,
And bad company. Youth, wealth, and the body
Are unstable. Few are the days of your life.
You cannot escape from your fate. Seek
The best help to reach heaven. Follow these
Precepts, O people who live on this good earth."

CODA

Here ends "The Book of Vañci." It sings
Among the three crowned kings, of the virtues,
Triumphs, and heroism of the ruler
Of the western kingdom, a wreath of flowers
Glowing on his chest, born in the Cēral line;
Of the preeminence of the glorious, old city
Of Vañci; of the splendor of its festivals; of the coming
Of the gods; of the endless joy of its subjects;
Of the abundance of food; of the songs and dances
With their fine interrelationships; of his army
Of sword-warriors who won decisive victories
In battle by fair methods; of his success

Lines 187–214

In following the enemy for a long distance
In the wide, foaming sea; and of his expedition
To the banks of the holy Gaṅgā. All these things,
Including others as well, reflect the career
Of Ceṅkuṭṭuvaṉ. Only a glimpse of it is offered here.

Lines 214–217

Epilogue

Here ends the *Cilappatikāram*. It ends, in truth,
With the story of *Maṇimēkalai*. Like a mirror
Reflecting the far hills, it reflects the essence
Of the cool Tamil country, enclosed by the Kumari
And Vēṅkaṭam, and by the eastern and western seas.
It comprises the five landscapes of pure and impure Tamil
Where live gods and humans following their duty
And practicing virtue, wealth, and love.
Its noble language expresses in perfect rhythm
Good sense, the themes of love and war,
Exquisite songs, the lute, musical mode, chants,
Drama, acts and scenes, dances
That conform to the established rules of the vari
Round dance and cētam, put in simple and perfect Tamil.

Lines 1–18

A Note on the Text

In making this translation I have used U. Vē. Cāminātaiyar's text (8th printing, 1968), together with Po. Vē. Cōmacuntaraṉār's (1969). I have also consulted the text of Na. Mu. Vēṅkaṭacāmi Nāṭṭār (1942). I have omitted from canto 22 lines 17–33, 37–50, 67–84, 89–96, and 111, considered to be spurious by both Cāminātaiyar and Cōmacuntaraṉār. These lines, notes Cāminātaiyar, "are not found in some manuscripts" (p. 490, fn. 1), and Cōmacuntaraṉār informs us that even the author of the *Arumpatavurai,* an old commentary on the poem, has "not glossed any of the words" from these lines (II:293, note.). I have, on the other hand, included two *veṇpā*s from cantos 4 and 6 from Cōmacuntaraṉār's text, not found in Cāminātaiyar's.

Reproduced below is an ancient editor's note that accompanies the prologue. Cōmacuntaraṉār writes that Aṭiyārkkunallār, the medieval commentator, believed it to be Iḷaṅkō's work (p. 31). Scholars now, however, believe it to be the work of an editor. Since it is not integral to the narrative, I have moved it here.

1. Since that day, it stopped raining. Famine stalked the Pāṇṭiya country, followed by smallpox and leprosy. The victorious Vēṟ-Ceḻiyaṉ, who ruled at Koṟkai, killed a thousand goldsmiths, and offered them as a sacrifice to Pattiṉi at a festival. He thus propitiated her. Then, it rained: the land overflowed with abundance. Hardship and disease passed away.

2. The Kōcar rulers in the Koṅku country heard that. They propitiated Pattiṉi in their country. Then, it rained: the land was tilled continuously.

3. Gajabāhu of Laṅkā, enclosed by the sea, heard that. He built a temple with a sacrificial altar for Pattiṉi to whom daily offerings were made. Thinking, "She will end hardship, and bestow favors," he established an annual festival in the month of Āṭi. Then, it rained without interruption: the crops never failed, and the land overflowed with abundance.

4. Peruṅkiḷḷi, the Cōḻa king, heard that. He built a temple at Uṟaiyūr for Pattiṉi, thinking, "She is the goddess Pattiṉi who will bestow all manner of favors." He established a festival, and the ritual of adorning the goddess everyday.

Postscript

"After the last line of a poem," observes a poet, "nothing follows except literary criticism."[1] This postscript invites the reader to share with the translator the excitement of reading together a poem written some fifteen hundred years ago. It attempts to situate the poem in the context of the Tamil literary tradition, both oral and written, to examine the poem's origin in myth, and to speak of the religious and political circumstances surrounding it.

What Kind of Poem is the *Cilappatikāram*?

Even for the native speaker, the *Cilappatikāram* is an unfamiliar and difficult poem. We shall look at two classical Tamil poems, and explore their poetics as the first step in learning how to read a poem such as the *Cilappatikāram*. The purpose of this enterprise is to help readers unacquainted with Tamil to experience the poem in a modern English verse translation, and to enhance their appreciation of it by examining some of the elements of its composition. Attempts to identify the genre of the poem, specifically its "epic" features, have resulted in numerous definitions. We shall consider some of them, and also pursue new directions for formulating a poetics of the Tamil "epic." We shall also study the compositional features of the first book of the *Cilappatikāram*, "The Book of Pukār," in an attempt to reconstruct the theoretical and aesthetic issues involved and to open a window through which to view the work.

The Making of a Tamil Poem

Except for the thief, there was no one.
And if he lies, what shall I do?
A heron too was there,
its thin legs yellow as millet stalks,
looking out for sand eels in the running water
the day he took me.

Kapilar, *Kuṟuntokai* 25[2]

A woman confides in her friend, and we overhear their conversation. The memory of past intimacies overwhelms the present, now threatened by the fear of betrayal. Of all the elements that compose this scene, it is the heron with its rapacious appetite that stands out in the woman's mind. The heron is oblivious of the world around it in its pursuit of food. The woman's lover is the heron, and she is the helpless eel in its beak.

The heron is the only witness to their lovemaking—an indifferent witness at that. The world is also indifferent to the private woes of individuals. The heron presides over the woman's life as a bird of ill omen foreboding a lonely future for her, though it does not utter a sound. The stillness of the heron is in contrast to the flowing water. This contributes to its ominousness. The heron is totally absorbed in itself. So is the lover. Hence the danger and threat. The epithet "thief," referring to her lover, further reinforces the idea: he stole her innocence, and what is worse, from her point of view, he may even deny the whole thing, and then abandon her. And if he does so, she will not be able to call him to account. She is obviously in desperate straits.

The woman does not, however, openly accuse her lover of possible betrayal. To do so would be discourteous and in bad taste. She only hints at the possibility, obliquely, through her references to the heron and the thief who are both predatory by nature. We are offered evidence of this in the heron's behavior towards its prey. A thief, it is implied, behaves in the same fashion. He takes what belongs to another, without any right to do so. Also implied is the notion of acting secretly or unseen.

The figure of the heron, "looking out for sand eels in the running water," dominates the scene. The figure is not simply decorative; it is functional. It discreetly alludes to her lover's behavior and its implication for the future of their relationship.

The *Tolkāppiyam* (The Old Composition, 5th c. C.E.), the earliest work on Tamil grammar and poetics, refers to this device as *uḷḷuṟai uvamam,* "indirect suggestion."[3] Only the object of comparison (the heron) is explicitly described. Readers are offered the barest of hints to establish relationships (the heron and her lover) and discover the subject (the fear of her lover's betrayal) on their own. A love poem such as this, which explores the inner world, is classified as *akam,* "the inner," one of the two great categories of Tamil discourse. The other category is *puṟam,* "the outer."[4] In an akam poem the burden of the discourse is borne by the figure whose resonances are knit together into a mosaic and inlaid into the poem. Uḷḷuṟai uvamam is thus a mode of understanding through indirect suggestion. A puṟam poem depends less on the image than on a statement to make its meaning explicit. One is reductive in its approach; the other is expansive. The two categories are not exclusive; they often overlap.

It is this unobtrusive drama in miniature, at once contemporary and perennial, that Kapilar invites the reader to witness. The reader can be expected to be more sympathetic than the heron. Though Kapilar works by the ground rules of convention, he is able to rise above them and, in the process, shape a poem that continues to resonate in the mind long after the readers have heard it. The entire poem of five lines in the original Tamil is compressed into one sentence of twenty-five words. This is a common syntactic feature of the akam poems. The opening lines construct the frame in which the drama is enacted. The punch line ("the day he took me," "*maṇanta ñāṉṟē*") appears at the end of the poem and completes the sentence. Here and elsewhere, when a poet wishes to depict one of the phases of love, all he does is to conjure with a few deft strokes the appropriate landscape, including the several elements integral to it. Eventually, the poem that emerges is at once concrete and universal: all traces of personal accents have been refined away to a vanishing point.

A famous verse in the Songs of Songs offers a parallel:

Awake, O north wind; and come, thou south;
Blow upon my garden, that the spices thereof may flow out.
Let my beloved come into his garden,
And eat his precious fruits. The Song of Songs 4.16[5]

The Shulamite invokes the wind to arouse her physically to enable her lover to smell her out and possess her completely. Social conventions inhibit her from being more explicit. So she withdraws behind the veil of language and cries her heart out in metaphors. The garden is herself; its fruits and spices are her physical charms, which are her lover's alone.

Love and war are the two primary motifs in the Song of Songs, one representing the inner world (akam) and the other, the outer (puṟam). The two worlds, however, come together in Solomon's inspired phrase describing the Shulamite's beauty: "Terrible as an army with banners."[6] The beauty of a woman can very well strike a man as having this overwhelming force. It is an unusual simile for praising a woman's beauty, but appropriate. The ancient Israelites were constantly under the threat of invading armies from abroad, such as the Assyrians, Persians, and Romans. A Tamil poet likewise compares the beauty of a woman's eyes to spears: "Her red eyes, lined with kohl, are spears/ with sharp blades thrust high in the din of battle."[7] In ancient Tamil society, the king and his exploits in war were the common subject of bardic poetry. Both king and woman were the loci of sacred power; hence, the association of the two is not unusual.

Literary traditions often overlap, and in the Song of Songs we have tentative evidence of a remarkable cross-fertilization of two traditions—the Hebrew and the Tamil. 1 Kings 10:22 mentions imports of apes, peacocks, and ivory in Solomon's time, the trip taking three years to reach its destination. The Hebrew word for peacock, *tukki,* is borrowed from the Tamil word for peacock, *tōkai.* Further evidence of contact with Tamils early in the first millenium B.C.E. is found in the names of Indian products in Hebrew, like *ahalot,* for the spicewood aloes, from the Tamil *akil.*

Both the Tamil and Hebrew poems share a common theme of women in love expressing their thoughts—not explicitly for that would violate social norms: women were expected to be chaste and not display their emotions—but implicitly through a set of poetical conventions. Both poems illustrate the paradox of the language of omission in which women for centuries were conditioned by society to express themselves. Chaim Rabin, to whose scholarship I owe this insight, goes so far as to suggest that the genre of the Song of Songs may owe something to the Tamil love poems that probably made their way to Tarshish along with the apes, peacocks, and ivory.[8]

A puṟam poem, on the other hand, explores the outer world. It is firmly tethered to a specific place and time.

> "On the weak, shriveled arms of the old woman
> the veins stand out. Her stomach is flat
> as a blade of lotus. Unnerved by the fighting,
> her son had turned his back on it." So folks talked.
> "If he had fled in the heat of battle,"
> she thundered in a rage, "these breasts that nursed him
> I'll tear to pieces." Sword in hand, she groped
> in the bloodstained field, turning over
> one lifeless body after another. When
> she saw her son lying prostrate, hacked to bits,
> she rejoiced more than on the day he was born.
>
> Kākkaipāṭiṉiyār Nacceḷḷaiyār, *Puṟanāṉūṟu* 278[9]

A woman, incensed by the rumor that her son had lost heart in battle and fled, rejoices on discovering that he had died heroically on the battlefield, his body hacked to bits. It is dishonorable to perish with wounds in one's back. In *Puṟanāṉūṟu* 65, we learn of King Cēramāṉ Peruñcēralātaṉ facing north and ritually starving himself to death to atone for the spear wounds in his back. The battlefield, soaked in blood and burdened with the dead, is the object of the poet's praise. It is contrasted with the shriveled old woman whose breasts and womb can no longer support life. She vows to renounce that emblem of femininity, her breasts, should her son prove to be a coward. If he had fallen wounded in the back, she would have cut up his body and dispatched him to heaven.

The poem oscillates between the akam and puṟam worlds, between a mother's love for her son and his heroic death on the battlefield. In case of a conflict between the two, as is evident here, puṟam takes precedence over akam, war over love, death on the battlefield over death at home. The poem represents, in microcosm, the values of a heroic age when the sword was

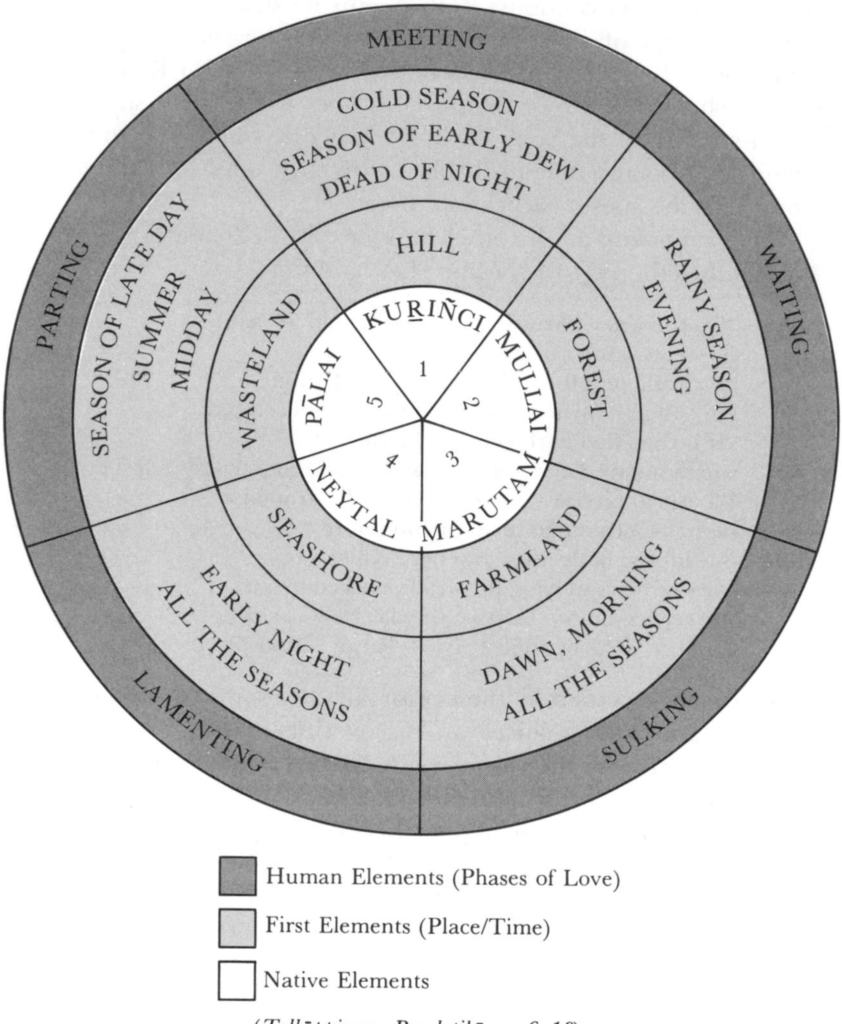

(*Tolkāppiyam. Poruḷatikāram 6–18*)

For a list of the native elements, see Ramanujan (1967:107; 1985:242) and Zvelebil (1973:100).

Figure 1: A Map of Akam Poetics

mightier than the plow, and a good name was cherished above life itself.

Tamil Poetics: Akam and Puṟam

Classical Tamil poetics is original, and not indebted to Sanskrit. It comes as an exciting revelation to those who stumble onto it. The most comprehensive statement of Tamil poetics is the third book of the *Tolkāppiyam*. It is basically a handbook for the making of poems. Poetry is classified into akam and puṟam, categories that extend, however, beyond poetry to permeate a whole way of life.

The akam poems have as their focus the individual within the matrix of familial relationships, foremost among them being love between man and woman, which is explored vertically, that is, archetypically. The bias is impersonal: the experience itself is rarefied and frozen in the shape of a poem. The puṟam poems, on the other hand, are centered outside the matrix of familial relationships, and are occasional in character. They explore the relationship between man and the world around him horizontally, that is, historically, with reference to a specific place and time.

Women preside over the akam poems, which are redolent of their ambiance and sacred power *(aṇaṅku)*. Premarital love *(kaḷavu)*, and marital and extramarital love *(kaṟpu)* in all their phases are the subject of akam proper, which includes the whole gamut of the experience: meeting, waiting, sulking, lamenting, and parting. The characters of the akam poems include the heroine, her friend, mother, and foster mother, the hero, his friend or bard, the concubine, her friend, and passersby. A typical situation would include the heroine speaking to herself or to her friend, as in *Kuṟuntokai* 25 above. The audience overhears what is said. The utterance is in the form of a monologue, the genre preferred by the poet who never directly addresses his audience. In fact, the poet himself is nowhere in the picture, a feature quite uncommon in much romantic verse. The monologue emphasizes the primacy of speech, the relation of poetry to the spoken voice. Men preside over the puṟam poems, which reverberate with the exploits and prowess in battle of heroes.

Three distinct elements blend together to shape a poem. They provide the specific context for its realization.

> When we study the contents of a poem
> only these three things excel in the act of composition:
> the first elements, native elements and human elements.[10]

The first elements (*mutal*) are place and time. Place refers to the seven landscapes (*tiṇai*s), of which five are basic, into which the world of akam is divided, the tiṇai being a complex of "land, class and behavior pattern."[11] The tiṇais are named after their characteristic flowers or trees and are presided over by deities. They are *kuṟiñci* (hill/conehead), *mullai* (forest/jasmine), *marutam* (farmland/arjuna tree), *neytal* (seashore/dark lily), and *pālai* (wasteland/ivorywood tree). Time includes both the seasons of the year and the hours of the day and night. The seasons are the rains (August–September), the cold season (October–November), the season of early dew (December–January), the season of late dew (February–March), early summer (April–May), and late summer (June–July). A day has six parts: dawn, morning, midday, evening, early night, and the dead of night.

The native elements (*karu*) comprise an entire taxonomy of interrelationships between humans and nature. They include human beings, their occupations and pastimes, musical instruments, ragas, animals, birds, trees, and flowers. One or more of these elements usually occurs in a poem as a concrete symbol of one of the phases of love.

The human elements (*uri*) are the phases of love (meeting, waiting, sulking, lamenting, and parting) that correspond to the five tiṇais. In practice, the elements of one tiṇai often blend harmoniously with those of another in a "fusion of tiṇais" (*tiṇaimayakkam*) to deepen the poem's resonance. *Kuṟuntokai* 25, discussed above, is a poem that hovers between kuṟiñci and marutam, refusing to be tethered to one or the other tiṇai. The elements that compose the text are drawn from both kuṟiñci (lovers' meeting, millet stalks) and marutam (fear of betrayal, heron, sand eels, running water). This indeterminacy of genres is characteristic of akam poems.

Two phases of love the *Tolkāppiyam* considers not suitable for love poetry are unrequited love (*kaikkiḷai*) and mismatched love (*peruntiṇai*).[12] Their corresponding tiṇais, with identical names, are not included in the study of the five akam tiṇais. Peruntiṇai also includes the socially accepted practice of *maṭalūrtal,* where a man rides on a horse made of the stems of the palmyra leaves to declare his love for a woman.[13] The horse is dragged through the streets. As it moves, the stems inflict cuts, and he bleeds. He then publicly claims her hand. Convention prohibits a woman from riding a maṭal. The *Tirukkuṟaḷ* states:

> A woman, even when troubled by love as intense
> as the waves of the ocean, does not resort to maṭalūrtal.
>
> *Tirukkuṟaḷ* 1137[14]

The maṭalūrtal has a distant relation in skimmington, a noisy rural English procession assembled in order to ridicule an unfaithful wife and often including effigies and a mock serenade. Lucetta, in Thomas Hardy's *The Mayor of Casterbridge,* is thus mocked by an effigy of herself on a donkey.[15] Skimmerton and shivaree are the American variants of this custom.

In the poetics of akam, kuṟiñci for example stands for lovers' meeting in the hills because of the secrecy they afford; the time frame is the cold season, or the season of early dew, and the dead of night. "Millet stalks," in our example (*Kuṟuntokai* 25), are one of the elements of the kuṟinci landscape where millet is raised as a staple food. The phrase evokes at the same time the theme of lovers' meeting.

The world of puṟam also comprises seven tiṇais. They correspond to those of akam. Six of them are named after flowers or trees. Flowers, appropriate to each phase of combat, are worn as garlands by warriors. They are *veṭci* (scarlet ixora), for cattle raiding; *vañci* (Indian willow), for invasion; *uḻiñai* (balloon vine), for siege; *tumpai* (white dead nettle), for pitched battle; and *vākai* (sirissa tree), for victory. *Kāñci* (portia tree), for the impermanence of life, and *pāṭāṉ,* for the praise of kings, were not considered suitable for poetry.

The akam/ puṟam classification may be regarded as a unique contribution of Tamil poetics.[16] The genres are not exclusive: they complement each other. Often, they overlap, even fuse together to speak passionately and with sophistication of an ancient way of life. Elaborate as this "grammar of poetry" is, it is not mechanistic. It is a part of the received tradition of poets who put it to effective use in making poems and in achieving their poetic effects. A knowledge of this grammar is, therefore, essential for understanding classical Tamil poetry.

Iḷaṅkō's Poetics

Tamil poetics speaks of two kinds of love: premarital love (kaḷavu) and marital and extramarital love (kaṟpu). An old text, the *Akapporuḷ* (The Meaning of Love) of Iṟaiyaṉār (5th–6th c. C.E.), treats premarital love in the context of the five landscapes (tiṇais). It treats marital love separately, and gives the following causes of a husband's separation (*pirital*) from his wife: (1) the search for knowledge; (2) the pursuit of wealth; (3) the service of the king; (4) the protection of the land; (5) the appeasement of enemies; and (6) consorting with harlots.[17]

Harlots *(parattai)* are classified into three types: (1) concubines (*iṟparattaiyar*); (2) courtesans (*kātaṟparattaiyar*); and (3) whores (*cēriparattaiyar*). Concubines were generally the daughters of courtesans. They married into prominent families and were faithful to their spouses. The courtesans were accomplished dancers (*ātaṟkūttiyar*) and had a select clientele among the ruling class. The whores were public women (*potumakaḷir*) and along with the courtesans kept alive the fine arts among the Tamils.[18]

In "The Book of Pukār," Iḷaṅkō explores aspects of both marital and extramarital love in Kōvalaṉ's relationships with his wife Kaṇṇaki and the courtesan Mātavi. When Kōvalaṉ abandons Kaṇṇaki for Mātavi, Iḷaṅkō contrasts Kaṇṇaki's situation (love-in-separation, Ta. *pirital,* Skt. *vipralambha-śṛṅgāra*) with that of Mātavi's (love-in-enjoyment, Ta. *puṇartal,* Skt. *saṃbhoga-śṛṅgāra*). Before long, Kōvalaṉ is disillusioned with Mātavi, and by the end of the book, he is back with Kaṇṇaki, a repentant spouse. A well-known poem by Pālaipāṭiya Peruṅkaṭuṅkō (2d c. C.E.) poignantly evokes the situation of the abandoned woman, separated from her lover—in this instance, both Kaṇṇaki and Mātavi.

> He avoids our street though he lives
> in the same town. Should he visit us,
> he won't take me, lovingly, in his arms.
> Unseeing, he walks past me as if I were
> the burning ground of strangers. Once,
> I was unashamed when passion had robbed me
> of my senses. But now, like an arrow

sent flying from a bow, it has landed far off.
Pālaipāṭiya Peruṅkaṭuṅkō, *Kuruntokai* 231[19]

Kaṇṇaki, too, is abandoned by Kōvalaṉ for the courtesan Mātavi with whom he lives for some years and fathers a child, Maṇimēkalai. Suspecting Mātavi of infidelity, he returns to Kaṇṇaki, who accepts him without complaint, and the two are reunited. But their reunion is brief; shortly afterwards, Kōvalaṉ is killed by the Pāṇṭiya king on a false charge. Kaṇṇaki avenges his death and ascends to heaven; Mātavi enters a nunnery.

Iḷaṅkō consciously uses four of the seven akam tiṇais to organize and enrich the narrative in "The Book of Pukār:" (1) mullai, the patient endurance of a woman during the time of separation from her lover; (2) marutam, the infidelity of lovers; (3) neytal, the anxiety caused by separation; and (4) pālai, elopement and separation from the family. Akam themes overlap these tiṇais and further indicate Iḷaṅkō's dependence on the conventions of erotic poetry. Each of the four tiṇais used in "The Book of Pukār" has a strong undercurrent of erotic themes (*turais*) that throw light on the events of the narrative, and give it a structural unity. We shall now identify some of the themes under the four tiṇais as they occur in cantos 7 through 10.

Patient endurance during the time of separation (mullai):

parattaiyirpirivu, forsaking one's wife, and seeking the company of a harlot.[20] Kōvalaṉ leaves his wife Kaṇṇaki for the courtesan Mātavi. He squanders his fortune on her (3.171–76; 4.33–43; 6.125–27). Though devastated, Kaṇṇaki does not complain and patiently awaits his return (4.61–74). We are told nothing about how she feels at Kōvalaṉ's betrayal. She drops out of the narrative at this juncture, to reappear only in canto 9 as Iḷaṅkō focuses on the relationship between Kōvalaṉ and Mātavi.

The infidelity of lovers (marutam):

ūṭal, lovers' quarrel, arising from jealousy.[21] Both Kōvalaṉ and Mātavi suspect each other of infidelity. They convey their suspicions, indirectly, through songs (7:11–24; 7:28–46; 7:48–52).

The anxiety caused by separation (neytal):

orutalaiyuḷḷutal, a woman's constant thought of her lover.[22] Consumed by her love of Kōvalaṉ and separated from him, Mātavi pours her heart out in a letter to him (8.67–77).

Elopement and separation from the family (pālai):

pālai, temporary separation from one's family—to recoup one's fortune, for example.[23] Unbeknownst to their parents, Kōvalaṉ and Kaṇṇaki leave Pukār for Maturai (9.110–18; 10.59–67).

Through the use of indirect suggestion (uḷḷuṟai uvamum), Iḷaṅkō in canto 4, "In Praise of the Evening," brings home both the agony of Kaṇṇaki and the joy of Mātavi. Kaṇṇaki's situation is represented by the earth personified as a woman lamenting the approach of twilight when neither of her two spouses, the sun and the moon, will be with her. He further emphasizes Kaṇṇaki's waiting for Kōvalaṉ's return by introducing motifs from the mullai (forest) tiṇai: cowherds returning from their pastures on the edge of the forest, the evening filled with the sound of their flutes, and the smell of jasmine in the air (4.20–22). But Kaṇṇaki is not fated to be a part of this idyll. She remains outside it. Kōvalaṉ fails to protect her. Mātavi's situation is represented by a lake personified as a woman opening at dawn "Her eyes of radiant blue lotuses" (4.101) after a night of love. Iḷaṅkō offers precise details that indicate a further polarization in their situations. He describes Kaṇṇaki's situation with one negative particle, such as "no," "not," or "without," after another:

> No anklets sounded
> On her small graceful feet. No girdle
> Blazed over her mound of love wound
> In a soft white garment. No vermilion
> Rouge was painted on her breasts. Except
> Her bridal pendant, she wished for no ornament.
> (4.61–66)

Contrast this with his opulent description of Mātavi's situation:

> In the bedroom,
> Mātavi's couch was sown with homegrown
> Mullai petals, musk jasmine
> And other flowers. Undone was her red,
> Coral girdle that blazed over her mound
> Of love, and the fine garment unwound
> From her waist. (4.33–39)

Iḷaṅkō resorts to the subterfuge of indirect suggestion and negation because he is perhaps reluctant or unable to expatiate on

Kaṇṇaki's agony. There is tension in the discourse: it forewarns the reader that Kaṇṇaki's situation is unnatural and will not be tolerated for long, just as it is unnatural for the earth to be separated, even for a moment, from the sun and the moon. The latter form part of an invariable and established cosmic order.

Again, both earth and water are primarily feminine symbols. The earth is not only the womb out of which all life originates, but also the grave into which it returns. Hence, it corresponds to the Mother Goddess (*Tēvi*) and foreshadows Kaṇṇaki's apotheosis into Pattiṉi, one of the forms of the Mother Goddess. Unlike the earth, a solid element, water is a transitional element. Buddha, in his Assapuram Sermon, regarded the lake, whose transparent waters reveal at the bottom shells and fishes, as a symbol of redemption. This points to Mātavi's renunciation: she enters a Buddhist nunnery and takes the holy vows. Canto 4 is a touchstone of Iḷaṅkō's virtuosity as a poet. At the same time, it reveals the extent of his indebtedness to the Tamil poetic tradition.

Instead of openly reproaching Kōvalaṉ for his infidelity, Iḷaṅkō hints at it through the motifs of the marutam (farmland) tiṇai in canto 5, "The Celebration in the City of Indra's Festival": dawn (5–8), festival (177), river (2), lotus (238), and Indra (73). In the classical poems, the hero returns home at dawn after spending the night with a courtesan. Kōvalaṉ, on the other hand, does not return home to his wife. Canto 6, "Bathing in the Sea," is replete with motifs from the neytal (seashore) tiṇai: seashore (6.130), summer (6.133), bathing (6.129), screw pine (6.172), and fish (6.159). Together with the following canto, it prepares the reader for the imminent breakup of Kōvalaṉ's liaison with Mātavi.

Kōvalaṉ and Kaṇṇaki leave behind the familiar environs of Pukār and travel through the wilderness to reach Maturai. The narrative is interspersed with motifs from the pālai (wasteland) tiṇai. They will never again set eyes on Pukār. Thus, in "The Book of Pukār," Iḷaṅkō employs the conventions of akam poetry to make explicit the emotional and psychological overtones that are not directly addressed by the narrative. Motifs from the kuṟiñci (hill) tiṇai occur, however, only in "The Book of Vañci" in canto 27, "The Lustration," which describes Ceṅkuṭṭuvaṉ's reunion with his queen, Iḷaṅkō Vēṇmāḷ, on his triumphant return from the Himālaya: millet fields (240), elephant (239), bamboo (238), and songs in the kuṟiñci mode (232).

Iḷaṅkō follows the conventions of heroic poetry in "The Book of Vañci." The narrative is interspersed with six of the seven puṟam tiṇais: (1) vañci, the preparation for war with a view to taking over the land of one's enemies; (2) uḻiñai, the siege of a fortress or a city; (3) tumpai, the pitched battle; (4) vākai, the celebration of victory; (5) kāñci, the belief in the impermanence of life as a prelude to achieve liberation; and (6) pāṭāṉ, praising a warrior's fame and munificence. Puṟam themes (tuṟais), especially those connected with the ritual of installing a memorial stone (*naṭukal*), link these tiṇais and further indicate Iḷaṅkō's dependence on the conventions. The *Tolkāppiyam* mentions the different stages of the ritual: (1) *kāṭci,* the choice of a stone; (2) *kālkōḷ,* removing the stone; (3) *nīrppaṭai,* the lustration of the stone; (4) *naṭukal,* the installation and dedication of the stone; (5) *vāḻttu,* praise and benediction.[24] The *Cilappatikāram* leaves out one stage, *perumpaṭai,* the inscription of the exploits on the stone. These themes are, in fact, the titles of five of the seven cantos of "The Book of Vañci," and they emphasize the ritual underpinnings of the poem and the intimate relationship in Tamil society between the king and the goddess. By installing the stone for the heroic Kaṇṇaki, Ceṅkuṭṭuvaṉ confirms the place as sacred. By entering this sacred place, he is able to share in the goddess' power. He thus institutionalizes the cult of the goddess. Simultaneously, he installs himself as a universal emperor (*cakravartin*) who enjoys the protection of the goddess.

The Greeks also had a cult of stones. At Delphi, which they believed to be the exact center or navel (*omphalos*) of the earth, there was a beehive-shaped stone that was sacred to Apollo. The city was famous for its oracle, which figured prominently in myths. Mircea Eliade reports that "the *omphalos,* in every tradition, is a stone consecrated by a superhuman presence. . . . [It] bears witness of something, and it is from that witness that it gets its value, or its position in the cult."[25]

Each of the six tiṇais that comprise "The Book of Vañci" has an intricate network of heroic themes that not only carry the burden of the narrative but also provide a coherent structure to the poem. It would not be an exaggeration to say that the *Cilappatikāram* derives its structure from the conventions of Tamil erotic and heroic poetry. We shall now identify some of the themes under the six tiṇais as they occur in cantos 25 through 29.

The preparation for war (vañci):

1. *koṟṟavañci,* praising a king who destroys his enemies with his sword.[26] Villavaṉ Kōtai, Ceṅkuṭṭuvaṉ's minister, praises the Cēral king's prowess in battle with the Cōḻa and Pāṇṭiya kings and the Ārya kings of northern India (25.157–73).

2. *vañciṉakkāñci,* a king declaring that he may be accursed if he does not succeed in subduing his enemies.[27] Ceṅkuṭṭuvaṉ vows to destroy his own kingdom if he fails in his expedition (26.1–21).

3. *kuṭainilai* and *vāṉilai,* sending, in advance at an auspicious time, the royal umbrella and sword of a king who intends to set out on an expedition.[28] Ceṅkuṭṭuvaṉ orders that his royal parasol and sword be carried north ahead of him to inform the rulers of those lands of his expedition to the Himālaya (26.36–52).

4. *peruñcōṟṟunilai,* a king throwing a feast for his soldiers on the eve of battle.[29] Ceṅkuṭṭuvaṉ entertains his army to a feast prior to its departure from Vañci (26.53–56).

The siege of a fortress or a city (uḻiñai):

koṟṟavuḻiñai, the march of a king with his army to capture the enemy's city.[30] Ceṅkuṭṭuvaṉ marches north to subdue the Ārya kings, especially Kanaka and Vijaya, who had spoken ill of the Tamil kings (26.88–100; 26.163–72).

The pitched battle (tumpai):

1. *tāṉaimaṟam,* the heroism of a king who regardless of the consequences rushes forward at the call of battle.[31] Ceṅkuṭṭuvaṉ rejoices seeing his enemies spoiling for a fight (26.193–215).

2. *vēḷvi,* praising a warrior for destroying his enemies so that demons might feast on their corpses.[32] Demons rejoice at the carnage inflicted by Ceṅkuṭṭuvaṉ's sword (26. 216–64).

3. *pērāṇmullai,* a wrathful king becomes the master of the situation on the battlefield.[33] The Ārya kings of northern India bite the dust before Ceṅkuṭṭuvaṉ's wrath (26.224–45).

4. *maṟakkaḷavaḻi,* a victorious king described as plowing the battlefield.[34] The demons praise Ceṅkuṭṭuvaṉ for plowing the battlefield with his spear. Ceṅkuṭṭuvaṉ also threshes the enemy, yoking elephants like oxen (26.246–50).

5. *muṉṟērkkuravai,* a king's dance on the rostrum of his char-

iot, joining hands with his warriors in celebration of his victory.[35] Demons dance in front of Ceṅkuṭṭuvaṉ's chariot to commemorate his victory (26.250–56).

6. *piṉṟērkkuravai,* Koṟṟavai, the goddess of war and victory, and her retinue dancing in joy behind the chariot of a victorious king.[36] Demons dance behind Ceṅkuṭṭuvaṉ's chariot elated at his victory (26.257–59).

The celebration of victory (vākai):

vākaiyaravam, a grateful king honoring his warriors with chaplets of sirissa flowers as a token of victory.[37] Ceṅkuṭṭuvaṉ rewards his warriors with golden sirissa flowers to celebrate his victory (27.25–53).

Endurance, and belief in the impermanence of life (kāñci):

1. *kāñci,* a warrior defending his position wearing a garland of portia flowers.[38] Ceṅkuṭṭuvaṉ, wreathed in a garland of portia, overpowers the kings of northern India (26.187–215).

2. *peruṅkāñci,* the teaching of wise men about the impermanence of life.[39] The brahman Māṭalaṉ reminds Ceṅkuṭṭuvaṉ that life is uncertain and he should therefore perform the rājasūya sacrifice to "attain the path the gods approve" (28.131–96).

3. *mutumoḻikkāñci,* wise men (and women) giving instruction on dharma, *artha,* and *kāma* to the people.[40] Tēvantikai, the wife of the god Cāttaṉ, instructs the people on dharma (30.178–98).

The praise of the hero's fame and munificence (pāṭāṉ):

1. *maṟakkaḷavēḷvi,* praising a warrior for killing his enemies.[41] The brahman Māṭalaṉ praises Ceṅkuṭṭuvaṉ for destroying his enemies and urges him to perform the rājasūya sacrifice (28.131–96).

2. *vāḻttiyal,* the praise bestowed on a king by a bard.[42] As emperor of the Tamil imperium, Ceṅkuṭṭuvaṉ is praised for his territorial conquests, which include the Yavanas of northwestern India (29:23–25). Kaṇṇaki herself, as the tutelary deity of the Cērals, blesses Ceṅkuṭṭuvaṉ (29:29).

It is in "The Book of Vañci" that the three aspects of the poem, the erotic, the mythic, and the heroic, come together. Twice separated from Kōvalaṉ—temporarily in Pukār, and permanently in Maturai, following his death—Kaṇṇaki is eventually reunited with him in heaven. Separated from Kōvalaṉ, Mātavi finds solace in renunciation: she becomes a Buddhist nun. Her response is extreme, and it at once absolves her from continuing to suffer the "pangs of despised love." The erotic aspect thus comes full circle. As a renouncer himself, Iḷaṅkō is only too aware of the sense of *sic transit gloria mundi*. He makes no exception of love. In fact, the theme of the impermanence of life, included in the poetic situation of kāñci, is repeatedly stressed in "The Book of Vañci," as in the brahman Māṭalaṉ's good counsel to Ceṅkuṭṭuvaṉ:

> O just king! It is unnecessary to remind men
> Of wisdom that youth will not last forever. . . .
> Men are but actors on a stage: they don't play
> One role forever. . . .
> A good deed may not be put off till tomorrow,
> For your soul, blessed by the Vedas, may even today
> Leave your body. No one on this good earth,
> Clasped by the sea, knows how long he will live.
> (28.158–82)

This is a faithful reflection of the Tamil view of life that is as old as the epic itself. We come across it in *Gilgamesh* in Siduri's advice to the hero in his quest:

> Gilgamesh, whither runnest thou?
> The life thou seekest thou wilt not find;
> (For) when the gods created mankind,
> They allotted death to mankind,
> But life they retained in their keeping.
> *Gilgamesh*, tab. X, col. iii.1–5[43]

Anthropologists talk about the crossroads city and the walled city.[44] The order in the first is a social order; that in the second, a moral order. Maturai is a walled city; the king must be destroyed because he violates the moral order. In a crossroads city Kōvalaṉ would not have been spotted as a stranger. In the walled city of Maturai he is immediately recognized as a stranger by the goldsmith. This recognition sets Kōvalaṉ's death in motion.[45]

The *Cilappatikāram*, like the *Mahābhārata* and the *Rāmāyaṇa*, contains a journey through a forest that signifies dangerous ground—a journey through liminality, through land without settlements, through communities that are not fully social. Heinrich Zimmer notes that, in contrast to the city, the forest harbors all kinds of dangers.[46] That is why forests were among the first places to be dedicated to the cult of the gods, and why propitiatory offerings were hung from trees. The journey to Maturai represents an irrevocable break with the past. It is, in fact, a rite of transition from a preliminal to a postliminal world, to use Arnold van Gennep's terms.[47] By traveling to Maturai, Kōvalaṉ expects to recoup his fortune and be incorporated into the social order. But that was not to be. His karma intervenes, and he is executed by the Pāṇṭiya king on a false charge. A sort of incorporation does, however, occur when fourteen days later both Kōvalaṉ and Kaṇṇaki are reunited in heaven. Further, we witness the transfiguration of Kaṇṇaki into a goddess.

The forest represents a descent (Ta. *iṟakkam,* Skt. *avatāraḥ*) into the unknown, and the Jaina nun (*āryikā*) Kavunti helps Kōvalaṉ and Kaṇṇaki negotiate their rough passage through it. As their spiritual guide, she speaks to them in parables that emphasize that karma is inexorable and that each one of them must follow his or her own path to its destined end. This is repeated by the Jaina sage (*cāraṇar*) whom they meet in Śrīraṅkam:

> Like a seed when planted, it will sprout
> And fulfill itself. When its time is ripe,
> It will be impossible to stop it.
> (10.232–34)

In a memorable image he brings home to them the impermanence of life:

> Like a burning lamp
> In a wide, open plain, blown out
> By strong winds, so does life flee the body.
> (10.234–36)

Kōvalaṉ's karma comes full circle in "The Book of Maturai" and opens the way for Kaṇṇaki's apotheosis. Events beyond her control succeed in thrusting Kaṇṇaki from her role as a patient and submissive wife into the public role of a goddess with a cult status.

Landscape is thus one of the most resonant of Iḷaṅkō's symbols, for it reflects both the outer and inner worlds. He uses landscape to define emotional and spiritual conditions. The particular landscapes that he chooses for symbols come from the traditional division of the Tamil country into five regions that are evoked in hundreds of early Tamil poems. It is the geography of the mind and imagination, *le paysage intérieur,* that

Iḷaṅkō explores. "[Interior] landscape," writes Marshall McLuhan, "is the means of presenting, without the copula of logical enunciation, experiences which are united in existence but not in conceptual thought."[48] The state of mind is distilled in the landscape, the scene, from which comment and reflection are withheld. The landscape embodies, rather than expresses, meaning. Iḷaṅkō chooses only a few details, but they are enough to evoke the total landscape, one that becomes the inner landscapes of mind, heart, and spirit that are ineffable. The landscape grounds the poem in the actual by invoking a specific place. Iḷaṅkō's evocations of the Tamil country move me deeply. We may tend to overlook this sense of the actual in our preoccupation with his religious or philosophical thought.

Kaṇṇaki's life begins at Pukār on the sea and ends on a mountain-top near Vañci where she arrives from Maturai after traveling through farmland, wasteland, and forest. This is both a physical and symbolic journey. Mountains symbolize the union of heaven and earth, and therefore of spiritual ascent. Spiritually important events take place on them: Moses, for instance, receives the Ten Commandments on Mount Sinai. Indra's heaven is on Meru, the golden mountain in the center of the earth. We are told in the Ṛgveda (X.14.1) that Yama, the first mortal to die, reaches heaven after crossing the high mountain paths.[49] It is, therefore, appropriate that Kaṇṇaki ascends to heaven from a mountain. Iḷaṅkō's use of landscape as a symbol of Kaṇṇaki's transformation from an ordinary mortal to a divinity therefore follows established convention.

The Genre of the *Cilappatikāram*

Genres are culture-specific, and the significance of generic categories resides in their being exponents of a culture. Each culture chooses its own generic labels for the linguistic artifacts it creates. The *Cilappatikāram* is a poem with songs, blended with prose, as the prologue informs us.[50] Aṭiyārkkunallār (12th–13th c. C.E.) in his commentary defines the form of the poem as a composition with its stanzas interlinked by the theme, and having elements of poetry, music, and dance,[51] that is, a kind of poetic sequence. Naccinārkkiniyar (14th c. C.E.), in his commentary on the *Tolkāppiyam,* cites the *Cilappatikāram* as an example of a *toṉmai,* which the *Tolkāppiyam* defines as follows:

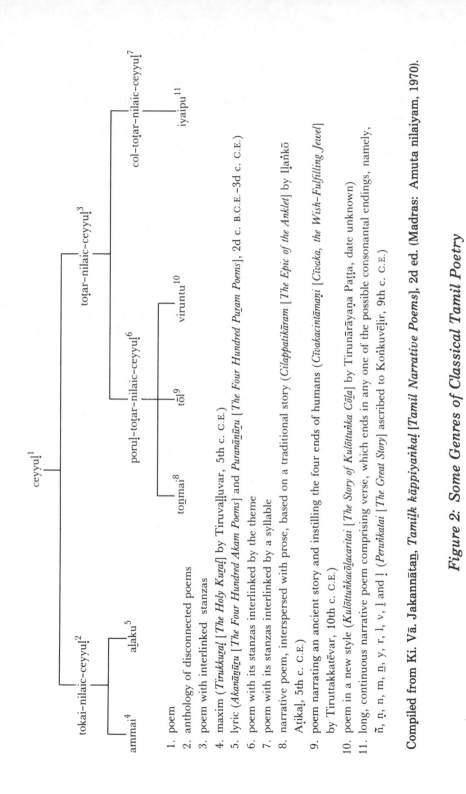

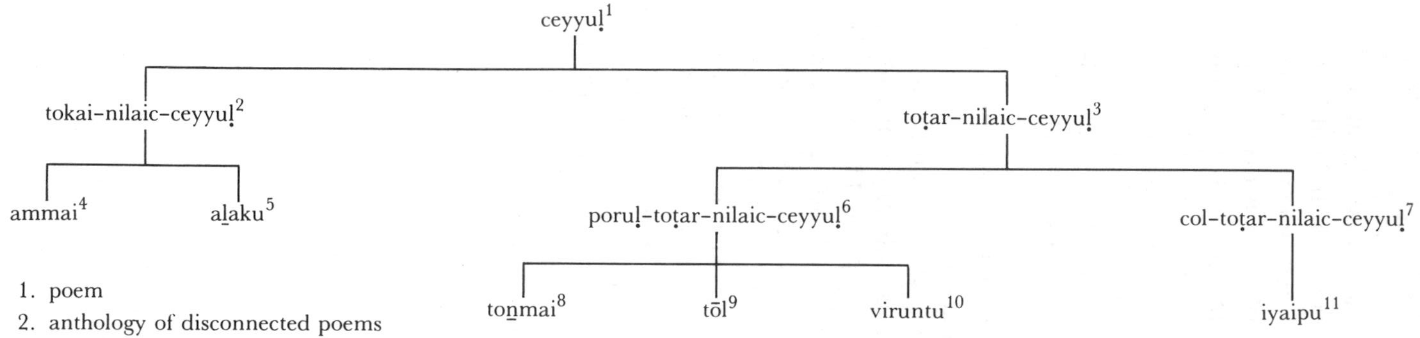

1. poem
2. anthology of disconnected poems
3. poem with interlinked stanzas
4. maxim (*Tirukkuṟaḷ* [*The Holy Kuṟaḷ*] by Tiruvaḷḷuvar, 5th c. C.E.)
5. lyric (*Akanāṉūṟu* [*The Four Hundred Akam Poems*] and *Puranāṉūṟu* [*The Four Hundred Puṟam Poems*], 2d c. B.C.E.–3d c. C.E.)
6. poem with its stanzas interlinked by the theme
7. poem with its stanzas interlinked by a syllable
8. narrative poem, interspersed with prose, based on a traditional story (*Cilappatikāram* [*The Epic of the Anklet*] by Iḷaṅkō Aṭikaḷ, 5th c. C.E.)
9. poem narrating an ancient story and instilling the four ends of humans (*Cīvakacintāmaṇi* [*Cīvaka, the Wish-Fulfilling Jewel*] by Tiruttakkatēvar, 10th c. C.E.)
10. poem in a new style (*Kulōttuṅkacōḻacaritai* [*The Story of Kulōttuṅka Cōḻa*] by Tirunārāyaṇa Paṭṭa, date unknown)
11. long, continuous narrative poem comprising verse, which ends in any one of the possible consonantal endings, namely, ñ, ṇ, n, m, ṉ, y, r, l, v, ḻ and ḷ (*Peruṅkatai* [*The Great Story*] ascribed to Koṅkuvēḷir, 9th c. C.E.)

Compiled from Ki. Vā. Jakannātaṉ, *Tamiḻk kāppiyaṅkaḷ* [*Tamil Narrative Poems*], 2d ed. (Madras: Amuta nilaiyam, 1970).

Figure 2: Some Genres of Classical Tamil Poetry

A toṉmai is a composition in verse,
interspersed with prose, that speaks of old times.[52]

The commentator interprets it as an extended narrative poem based on traditional stories.

The toṉmai, in fact, bears a family resemblance to the *ākhyānas* that form the core of the *Mahābhārata.* Commenting on the ākhyāna as the origin of epic poetry in Sanskrit, Hermann Oldenberg remarks:

The oldest form of epic poetry in India was the *ākhyāna,* a tale in a mixture of prose and verse, the speeches of the persons only being in verse, while the events connected with the speeches were narrated in prose. . . . This theory is supported by the fact that not only in Indian but also in other literatures the mixture of prose and verse is an early form of epic poetry. We find this form, for instance, in Old Irish and Scandinavian poetry.[53]

The *Mahābhārata* grew to its present form probably from the kernal of an old epic song of the tenth century B.C.E.

Vaiyāpurip Piḷḷai identifies the *toṭar-nilaic-ceyyuḷ* (see note 56), poetic sequence, with the toṉmai, narrative poem, on the basis of Pērāciriyar's (13th c. C.E.) commentary on the *Tolkāppiyam: Poruḷatikāram* 313.[54] The poetic sequence, as understood here, first appears in the *Taṇṭiyalaṅkāram* (Taṇṭi's Book on Ornament [in Poetry], ?10th c. C.E.), an adaptation in Tamil of the *Kāvyādarśa* (The Mirror of Composition, 8th c. C.E.) of Daṇḍin. We may assume that Pērāciriyar and other commentators owe their use of the term to the *Taṇṭiyalaṅkāram.*

The *Arumpatavurai* (The Meaning of Difficult Words, 9th c. C.E.), an old glossary, calls the *Cilappatikāram* "a *kāvya* that combines verse and prose."[55] The term *kāviyam,* narrative poem, is not found in the *Tolkāppiyam.* It entered Tamil probably around the eighth century C.E. after the *Cilappatikāram* and similar works were written down, and it was replaced around the twelfth century C.E. by the term toṭar-nilai, poetic sequence. Later, this term itself fell into disuse largely because of a lack of clarity in its definition, and was in turn replaced by the term kāviyam or *kāppiyam,* narrative poem. Vaiyāpurip Piḷḷai reports that "poetic sequence" has once again reappeared in Tamil because of the resistance, at the present time, to words of Sanskrit origin.[56] He cites the instance of a Tamil textbook for the Secondary School Leaving Certificate examination for 1950 published by the University of Madras where Kampaṉ's *Irāmāvatāram* (The Descent of Rāma, 12th C. C.E.) is referred to as a toṭar-nilai, poetic sequence.

The genre in classical Tamil literature approximating the kāvya, narrative poem, is the toṭar-nilaic-ceyyuḷ, poetic sequence. Both had as their objective the promotion of the four great ends of humans (*puruṣārtha*): duty, wealth, desire, and liberation, an objective stressed by the texts on grammar and poetics. It is the special prerogative of the narrative poem, especially of the great narrative poem (*mahākāvya*), the most prestigious of all forms of Indian literature, to promote these four ends.

The Poetic Sequence: Its Origin and Development

The poetic sequence as a genre evolved in three distinct phases.[57] The first phase includes works such as the *Pattuppāṭṭu* (The Ten Long Poems, 150 B.C.E.–250 C.E.), an anthology of poems in each of which a central theme is developed with elaborate descriptions. For example, the *Paṭṭiṉappālai* (A Pālai [Separation] Poem on the City), a long poem of 301 lines, deals with the grief of a bard's wife as he leaves for Pukār, the Cōḻa capital. But this theme is incidental as the poem is a fulsome panegyric on the Cōḻa king Karikālaṉ and his capital. The bard praises the king in expectation of gifts from him. The descriptions of the hero and his land in the narrative poems are modeled on the descriptions of the king and his capital. In the second phase, the theme is usually a traditional story, especially one that occurred in the Tamil country. The *Cilappatikāram* and *Maṇimēkalai* are cited as examples. The third phase is characterized by the imitation of Sanskrit models, for instance, *Cīvakacintāmaṇi*.

Let us now consider Mīṉāṭcicuntaraṉ's observation that the narrative poem itself evolved from the genres of classical Tamil poetry, later collected in the *Eṭṭuttokai* (The Eight Anthologies, 150 B.C.E.–250 C.E.) and the *Pattuppāṭṭu*.[58] The two works include 2,381 poems. The extent of the poems varies from three lines in the discontinuous stanza (*taṉippāṭal*) to 782 lines in the long poem (*pāṭṭu*). In some of the long poems, the akam and puṟam genres blend together through a fusion of the erotic and heroic elements. The *Cilappatikāram* exhibits precisely such a fusion of the akam and puṟam. Moreover, descriptive and narrative modes also overlap to produce an indeterminate form that bears a family resemblance to both.

The *Cilappatikāram* comprises three books (*kāṇṭams*). Each book consists of story-songs or cantos, *kātais* (Skt. *kathā*, "story;" *gāthā*, "song, poem"). Mīṉāṭcicuntaraṉ regards the kātai as an extended lyric and the poem itself as an aggregate of such lyrics.

The earliest Tamil poems are short isolated lyrics invariably spoken by one persona. Gradually, they were strung together and organized thematically into clusters. In this way they expanded in length and like the *Maturaikkāñci* (The Counsel [Given] at Maturai) assumed the shape of long poems. This was possibly how a poetic sequence originated. And we see this form emerging in the *Cilappatikāram,* the first great unmistakable exemplar of the genre. It would not, therefore, be inappropriate to regard the *Cilappatikāram* as a collection of thirty distinct long poems, twenty-five of which are story-songs or cantos, and five of which are song cycles that appear at critical junctures and function as choruses unobtrusively commenting on the action. The cantos only comment, explain, and amplify the story line. In fact, each canto is more or less static. It does not always evolve from the previous canto because there is no compulsion from the plot to do so. Of course, each contains hints and allusions to the story. When these are read sequentially, they form a composite whole.

The stringing together of isolated lyrics and their expansion into long poems is not an eccentric mode of composition among poets. The practice is confirmed by Edgar Allan Poe (1809–49) in his essay, "The Philosophy of Composition" (1846), and explored in detail in a recent study.[59] Poe observes:

> What we term a long poem is, in fact, merely a succession of brief ones—that is to say, of brief poetical effects. It is needless to demonstrate that a poem is such, only inasmuch as it intensely excites, by elevating, the soul; and all intense excitements are, through a psychal necessity, brief.[60]

Elaborating on Poe's definition, Rosenthal and Gall note that the long poem consists of a group of lyric poems, each radiating from a "center of intensity."[61] Its structure is essentially lyrical though it includes narrative, dramatic, and ratiocinative elements, and the poet aspires to epic scope. What ultimately helps to make the structure of the *Cilappatikāram* an organic whole is not its narrative or dramatic threads of discourse but its "succession," to use Poe's phrase, of "brief poetical effects." We will shortly examine the ways the *Cilappatikāram* achieves these poetical effects.

These observations on the structure of the *Cilappatikāram* are, again, supported by John Brough's remarks on the structure of the great narrative poem in Sanskrit:

> The stanzaic structure was doubtless in part responsible for the fact that in such epics the actual narrative is, typically, not dominant. Although two or more stanzas are not infrequently linked syntactically to form a single sentence, the tendency is to have a series of descriptive verses on one point of the story, and then a few linking verses to carry the narration on to the next important point, where another topic is similarly elaborated.[62]

Thus it would appear that the great narrative poem in both Sanskrit and Tamil evolved from the lyric.

The long poem is an ongoing form embodying the knowledge of a culture. The epic process is encyclopedic and inclusive, though the epic itself may not be so. In the beginning, the epic was a multiform; now, it is not.

The *Taṇṭiyalaṅkāram* and the Great Narrative Poem

We have so far considered some of the latent forms of the epic as a genre that already existed in Tamil before Sanskrit models replaced them. We have also observed a certain lack of clarity in the definition of terms for the epic. The *Tolkāppiyam* does not consider the poetics of the great narrative poem. A later work, the *Taṇṭiyalaṅkāram,* does. With the appearance of this text on rhetoric and poetics, it was possible for the first time to offer a definition of the narrative poem.

The *Taṇṭiyalaṅkāram* classifies narrative poems into the great narrative poem (*peruṅkāppiyam*) and the narrative poem (*kāppiyam*), and defines the former as follows:

> A great narrative poem should begin with one or more of the three elements: a song in praise of God, invocation, and an introduction to the subject. The four ends of humans should form its content. It should have a hero of incomparable greatness. It should contain descriptions of mountains, the sea, land, city, the six seasons and six parts

> of the day, sunrise and moonrise. It should further describe the consummation of a marriage, a coronation, the enjoyment of gardens and water sports, pleasures of intoxication, the bearing of children, lovers' quarrels, and sexual love. The state council (with the king and his ministers), diplomatic missions, invasions, battles, and victories should be a part of it. It should be divided into chapters called *carukkam, ilampakam,* or *pariccētam* (cantos). Ripe with moods and emotions, it should please, and be the work of a learned man.[63]

The subject of the great narrative poem is the four ends of humans, while the narrative poem has as its subject any three of the four ends. This convention was not present in classical Tamil poetry.

However, many of the elements of the great narrative poem that the *Taṇṭiyalaṅkāram* mentions were already present in Tamil poetry.

1. The beginning: a song in praise of God, invocation, and an introduction to the subject. These are the three ways of beginning a great narrative poem. In the Tamil tradition, however, it was the usual practice to begin a work with verses in praise of God. Besides God, six others may be praised in the beginning: ascetics, brahmans, kings, cows, rain, and the land. These comprise the six kinds of praise.[64]

The *Cilappatikāram* begins with verses in praise of the sun, moon, rain, and the city of Pukār. An element not found in the poem is the apologia.[65] In *Cīvakacintāmaṇi,* the poet Tiruttakkatēvar speaks of the loftiness of his theme and of his own inability to deal adequately with it. He asks his readers to overlook the flaws in his work.

Again, the prologue or epilogue (*patikam*), usually written by someone other than the poet himself, provides an introduction to the subject of a poem. This element can be traced to the *Rāmāyaṇa* where Nārada tells Vālmīki the story of Rāma at the beginning of the poem (*Bālakāṇḍa* 1.1–79).[66]

2. In the Tamil tradition, ethical works like the *Tirukkuṟaḷ* expound the first three ends of humans. The four ends are, however, exemplified in the great narrative poems by the characters themselves as they evolve in the course of the story.

The *Cilappatikāram* deals with only three of the four ends, that is, duty, wealth, and desire.[67] *Maṇimēkalai,* which continues the story of the *Cilappatikāram,* deals with only duty and liberation. On the grounds that neither of them by itself deals with all the four ends of humans, Aṭiyārkkunallār suggests that they be considered together as one great narrative poem.

3. Characterization of the hero and heroine. Kōvalaṉ and Kaṇṇaki are depicted as idealized types rather than as individuals. This is in keeping with the conventions of the great narrative poem which stipulates heroes and heroines of incomparable greatness. They are expected to live according to their dharma and are, therefore, not free to act on their own. Their actions are predestined, and reflect little or no freedom of choice. Indeed, we sense a foreboding of tragedy in Kōvalaṉ's description:

> The fame of his son Kōvalaṉ,
> Only sixteen years old, had already shrunk
> The earth. Over and over again, in voices
> Seasoned by music, with faces luminous
> As the moon, women confided among themselves:
> "He is the god of love himself,
> The incomparable Murukaṉ." For it was love
> That made them speak thus of the handsome Kōvalaṉ.
> (1.35–42)

Kōvalaṉ's liaison with Mātavi impoverishes him and he dies in the process of retrieving his fortune. His execution is attributed to his karma: he had killed a merchant named Caṅkamaṉ in a former life.

As a chaste and devoted wife (*pativratā*), Kaṇṇaki is cast in a traditional role—a role she shares with Sāvitrī and Gāndhārī. She is glorified in the poem and repeatedly paired with the ideal heroines of tradition like Arundhatī, an exemplar of conjugal chastity. This elevation to a universal type turns her into a paragon. In spite of her exaltation, Kaṇṇaki fortunately does not become an abstraction. Up until Kōvalaṉ's death (cantos 1–16), she hovers in the background, suffering without complaint the indignity of her husband's desertion. With Kōvalaṉ's death, she comes into her own. She takes charge of the situation and heaves the story forward to its destined end. The poem breathes and pulsates with her presence as she rises to her full stature in her encounter with the king. This is the poem's climactic scene. She exposes the hollowness of the king's justice and extracts the ultimate price from him. Her motivation is not vengeance but the removal of an unjust king. The ritual cleansing by fire is necessary for the restoration of dharma.

Kaṇṇaki's actions are consistent with her role as a chaste wife. We are told in the *Mahābhārata* that Gāndhārī had the power to burn the world, and to stop the planets in their orbits:

> Because of the power of your austerities,
> You are able, most blessed one, to burn
> With your eyes inflamed with rage the whole earth
> With whatever moves or is immovable in it.
> *Mahābhārata: Śalyaparvan* 9.62.60[68]

Kaṇṇaki lives up to her role with a fury unexpected in someone who initially appears meek and self-effacing. Her task accomplished, she departs this world and ascends to heaven, a goddess. In classical Tamil poetry, the erotic and heroic genres often overlap. In the *Cilappatikāram,* too, the genres come together. Kaṇṇaki's personal deprivation engulfs the Pāṇṭiya kingdom. Through the power of her chastity, she metamorphoses herself into a goddess.

We are stunned by Kaṇṇaki's courage and by the enormity of her tragedy. Despite the traditional role assigned to her by Iḷaṅkō, she does manage to break out of it to assume instead the role of an unfortunate individual whom we immediately recognize and empathize with. It is, therefore, not Kōvalaṉ but Kaṇṇaki who is the real protagonist of the *Cilappatikāram.* In all of Tamil literature, she has no peer. The *Cilappatikāram,* it may be noted, contains the earliest record in the Indian tradition of the apotheosis of a woman not of the brahman or kṣatriya, but of the vaiśya, class—a woman of the people, exalted to the pantheon not for any heroic deed but simply for being a chaste wife.

4. Descriptions of mountains, the sea, land, city, etc. It is part of the Tamil narrative tradition to begin with utopian descriptions of the land, river, or city. This practice goes back to the concept of the five tiṇais in classical poetry. One of the elements of the tinai is the landscape or region. Through an overlap or fusion, the five landscapes are collapsed into one ideal region overflowing with abundance. Thus the descriptions of Pukār, Maturai, and Vañci in the *Cilappatikāram* are utopian.

5. Consummation of a marriage. Canto 2 (The Setting up of a Home) is an intensely erotic lyric that captures the idyllic life of Kōvalaṉ and Kaṇṇaki. The envoi collapses their several moments of love together, and freezes them into one unforgettable image:

> Like snakes coupled in the heat of passion,
> Or Kāma and Rati smothered in each
> Other's arms, so Kōvalaṉ and Kaṇṇaki
> Lived in happiness past speaking,
> Indulged in every pleasure, thinking:
> "We live on earth but a few days."
> (2.112–17)

The reference to coupling snakes is indeed ironic. In Tamil folklore, the sight of copulating snakes is believed to presage some great evil.[69] Epics seem to begin with some evil or malfeasance. Kōvalaṉ soon abandons Kaṇṇaki to live with the courtesan Mātavi. That is when his woes begin.

6. Invasions, battles and victories. King Ceṅkuṭṭuvaṉ's expedition to the Himālaya and his defeat of northern kings such as Kanaka and Vijaya form the subject of canto 26 (Removing the Stone). There are vivid battle scenes that follow the conventions of the heroic genre.

7. Moods and emotions. Unlike the great narrative poems of Sanskrit, the *Cilappatikāram* shows no evidence of being written with the theory of *rasa/ dhvani* (the suggestion of mood) in mind. No one dominant mood pervades the entire poem. Love in union and separation is the mood of "The Book of Pukār," while heroism is the mood of "The Book of Vañci." In fact, they correspond to the akam and puṟam genres. The *Cilappatikāram* is, however, reticent in describing the love-in-union of Kōvalaṉ and Mātavi.

> He entered Mātavi's residence: came
> Under her spell the instant he took her in his arms.
> He forgot himself, and wished never to part from her.
> (3.173–75)

How do we account for this? It could be that Iḷaṅkō is reluctant to praise extramarital relations. Mātavi is after all a courtesan, whereas Kaṇṇaki is a chaste wife.

The Book of Pukār

The genre of the *Cilappatikāram* is, as we have seen, indigenous to Tamil. The poetic sequence evolved from the long poems of classical Tamil poetry. Viewed against this background, the *Cilappatikāram* appears as a sequence of thirty individual long poems. We shall now examine "The Book of Pukār" in this light.

Canto 1 (The Song of Praise) begins by praising the sun, moon, rain, and Pukār, identifying each with the Cōḻa king. In fact, it is the king who is really praised, and the blessing of the elements is sought on his behalf. The description of the Cōḻa capital is idealistic:

In fame Pukār rivals
Heaven itself, blinds the Serpentworld in pleasures.
(1.19–20).

It is Kaṇṇaki and not Kōvalaṉ who is introduced first. This suggests that Kaṇṇaki will be playing a greater role in the poem than Kōvalaṉ. Her elevation ironically foreshadows her later humiliation:

She is Lakṣmī herself, goddess
Of peerless beauty that rose from the lotus,
And chaste as the immaculate Arundhatī.
(1.27–29)

This idealistic note is again sounded in the blessing invoked on the couple when they are married—a foretaste of the events that will devastate them both:

Your arms forever knotted
In embrace, inseparable in love may you
Remain. (1.73–75)

Iḷaṅkō appropriately rounds off the canto with a prayer for the Cōḻa king always to remain invincible in battle. Note here the conflation of the domestic (akam) and public (puṟam) realms, of chastity and kingship, and of love and war that are the chief concerns of the poem as a whole. They will reappear in other cantos of the book. Two-thirds of the 82 lines of canto 1 comprise descriptions. Only a third takes upon itself the burden of the story. The rest of the cantos in "The Book of Pukār" follow this pattern.

Canto 2 (The Setting up of a Home) is an extended lyric of 117 lines, half of which is taken up by Kōvalaṉ's extravagant praise of Kaṇṇaki's beauty (2.46–99), a classic Tamil example of the Welsh poetic figure known as dyfalu, in which a person or object is compared to different things in a series of metaphors. It is preceded by a description of the opulence of Pukār, the bedroom on the upper floor of Mācāttuvāṉ's spacious mansion in which Kōvalaṉ and Kaṇṇaki "abandoned themselves to love," and the open terrace to which they later repaired. The canto concludes with seven lines of narration which inform us that Kōvalaṉ's mother set up Kaṇṇaki in a home of her own, and that Kōvalaṉ and Kaṇṇaki lived there happily for some years. The envoi sums up this happy period of their life together to which they will never again return. It foreshadows the events that later undo them both. Perhaps such happiness as they experienced was the prerogative of the gods. The canto is thus overwhelmingly descriptive. The narrative seems to intrude almost as an afterthought.

Canto 3 (The First Performance) presents one of the climactic situations in the poem. It leads to Kōvalaṉ's separation from his wife and to all that follows. Briefly, it gives an account of Mātavi's first performance before the king and of his recognition of her talent. He presents her with a garland and 1,008 pieces of gold.

Custom requires that Mātavi now take a lover. She dispatches her maid, the hunchback Vacantamālai, to the city square with the garland. The maid offers it for sale, adding that whoever purchases it becomes Mātavi's lover. Kōvalaṉ buys it and moves in with Mātavi. He abandons Kaṇṇaki. This incident is narrated in the last 13 lines (164–76) of the canto before the envoi. The preceding 163 lines constitute an elaborate discourse on music and dance. Mātavi's own teachers, and others who perform in her dance such as the drummer, flutist, and lute player, the dimensions of the stage, and her first performance are meticulously described.

What is the relevance of this digression to the poem? Clearly Iḷaṅkō is not parading his knowledge of the fine arts to impress the reader. This canto is a turning point in the poem. Kōvalaṉ is swept off his feet by Mātavi's beauty and accomplishments. He deserts Kaṇṇaki for her. His infatuation with Mātavi is the beginning of all his troubles. Iḷaṅkō's excursus is intentional.

His objective is to distract the reader's attention from Kōvalaṉ's illicit liaison with the courtesan Mātavi, coming so soon after his idyllic life with Kaṇṇaki described in canto 2. We have seen him there adoring Kaṇṇaki with a litany of ecstatic phrases. Yet in the very next canto Iḷaṅkō confronts the reader with Kōvalaṉ's unexpected turnabout. It is, to say the least, confusing. Skillful artist that he is, he too says as little as possible about Kōvalaṉ's indiscretion, preferring to instruct his reader in the niceties of music and dance. The digression, however, underscores Mātavi's consummate artistry that Kōvalaṉ found so irresistible. It is, therefore, essential that Iḷaṅkō lavish some attention on Mātavi's talents. In canto 1, we are told that women raved about Kōvalaṉ as "the god of love himself,/ The incomparable Murukaṉ" (40–41). An explanation for Kōvalaṉ's behavior is perhaps to be sought in this description of him. Thus, within the structure of this canto, description far outweighs narration. Yet the narrative element, minimal though it is, is crucial to the development of the story.

Canto 4 (In Praise of the Evening) is an isolated lyric of 119 lines describing an ordinary evening in Pukār. Interwoven with the description is the plight of women, including Kaṇṇaki, parted from their husbands. Shorn of all adornments, Kaṇṇaki presents a desolate picture. There is a brief reference to Kōvalaṉ and Mātavi taking their pleasure. The canto underscores the theme of parting and the behavior of faithful wives as opposed to that of courtesans. For Kaṇṇaki, Pukār in spite of its prosperity is only a wasteland (pālai), the landscape associated with parting. The canto is entirely descriptive, adding little to the progress of the story. The digressions are introduced into the poem to break the linearity of the narrative.

Canto 5 (The Celebration in the City of the Festival of Indra) presents a utopian description of the city of Pukār on one of the festival days, including the occupations of the people, their customs, and their beliefs. Again, Kōvalaṉ and Mātavi put in a brief appearance. The festival of Indra itself is the centerpiece. Description predominates, and the canto does not substantially contribute to the story.

On the last day of the festival, crowds throng the seashore for fun and games. Mātavi, eager to participate in the revels and dressed in all her finery, arrives there with Kōvalaṉ. Canto 6 (Bathing in the Sea) offers an elaborate account of the occasion, and is thus a continuation of canto 5. It also offers a description of the eleven kinds of dance in which Mātavi excels, together with an inventory of the ornaments with which she decks herself. But the focus of attention is the revels themselves. Kōvalaṉ and Mātavi only feature as part of the scene. The canto is an exquisite cameo. Again, the narration flounders without making any significant advance.

It is possible that Iḷaṅkō made use of a variety of folksongs in composing the song cycles in the *Cilappatikāram*. Folksongs are classified as *paṇṇatti* which the *Tolkāppiyam* defines as follows:

> A paṇṇatti makes the theme of poetry
> its own, and has the quality of songs.[70]

Cāminātaiyar lists 56 varieties of folksongs, 13 of which figure in the *Cilappatikāram,* including the *kāṉalvari,* love songs of the seaside grove and the *kuravai,* song of the hill dwellers.[71]

"The Love Songs of the Seaside Grove," the song cycle between cantos 6 and 8, comprises 19 songs in the form of monologues of an imaginary hero, his friend, the heroine, and her friend. Kōvalaṉ and Mātavi sing nine songs each, and Mātavi's friend sings one song. It is the end of the festival of Indra, and all of Pukār has converged on the seashore for the occasion. Kōvalaṉ and Mātavi join in the revelry and amuse each other with songs. But the event becomes a turning point in their relationship. It signals the end of Kōvalaṉ's liaison with Mātavi, and his return to his wife.

The songs are modeled on the classical akam poems. In fact, the song cycle as a whole is replete with the motifs of the neytal tiṇai (the seashore). Let us consider it in this light, beginning with the human elements. The phase of love that corresponds to this tiṇai is lamenting. The heroine fears that her lover may abandon her and she worries herself to death thinking about it. She bemoans her bitter fate. The native elements include the sea, salt-marsh, seaside grove, sand, conches, pearls, the occupations of selling fish and salt, shark, crocodile, tigerclaw tree, laurel, hedge of screw pine, blue and white lilies, the *nāvāy* drum, the *cevvaḻi* raga, and Varuṇa. The first elements are the seashore and early night. The festival itself occurs in Cittirai (April-May).

Both Kōvalaṉ and Mātavi begin their duet with river songs (*āṟṟuvari*s 1 and 10) in praise of the Cōḻa king and his country watered by the Kāviri. The songs eloquently reiterate the themes of chastity and kingship that are the overriding concerns of the poem. The river is spoken of as the king's wife and extolled for her patience. The king's upright scepter ensures the prosperity of his realm through his triumphs in war and the fidelity of his wife. The songs evoke the vision of a Tamil imperium based on dharma. Observe the conflation of the domestic and public realms and their interdependence. The songs thus prepare the way for Kōvalaṉ's reunion with Kaṇṇaki.

Songs 2 and 11 refer to the growing estrangement between Kōvalaṉ and Mātavi. Some of their compositional features, especially the themes and motifs, appear in *Akanāṉūṟu* 110 by Pōntaip Pacalaiyār:

> If mother finds out, let her.
> And if this lovely little street with its loose mouths hears, let it.
> Before the god at Pukār with swift whirlpools,
> I swear this is all that happened.
> In the grove, I and my garlanded friends played in the sea,
> made little houses and heaped up play rice.
> Then we were resting a bit,
> waiting for our tiredness to go,
> when a man came up and said,
> "Innocent girls with round, soft arms as supple as bamboo!
> The light of the sun has faded and I am very tired.
> Would there by anything wrong if I ate a guest's meal
> on a soft, open leaf,
> and then stayed in your noisy little village?"
> Seeing him, we lowered our faces,
> and, hiding ourselves, we politely replied,
> "This food is not for you.
> It is moist fish, eaten only by low people."
> Then suddenly someone said,
> "There, can't we see the boats coming in
> with their tall, waving banners?"
> At that we kicked over our sand houses with our feet.
> Of all those who were leaving,
> he looked straight at me and said,
> "O you who have the lovely face, may I go?"
> so I felt I had been ruined.
> I answered, "You may,"
> and he, staring at me all the while,
> stood tall, holding the staff of his chariot.
> Still it seems to be before my eyes.
>
> Pōntaip Pacalaiyār, *Akanāṉūṟu* 110[72]

A girl is accosted by a stranger in a seaside grove. They exchange a few words, perhaps even make love. Then the man leaves in his chariot. The girl is in despair. The motif of the sand house overrun by waves suggests the fragility of her life under pressure from the outside world. Thus, a single image often recapitulates a whole tradition, firmly rooting a present work in the literature of the past. We hear the echo of the classical poem, however faintly, in these exquisite songs.

Again, the motif of "furrows" is part of the classical repertoire. As Sally Noble points out, furrows in the sand recall the motif of plowing used in the poems of the mullai tiṇai (the farmland) to suggest the hero's union with the heroine.[73]; She cites a poem, *Kuṟuntokai* 131, by Ōrēruḻavaṉār as an example.[74] In the neytal tiṇai, the furrows in the sand are made not by the plow but by conches or the wheels of the hero's chariot. Again, she quotes a poem, *Kuṟuntokai* 227, by Ōta Ñāni which implies this through indirect suggestion.

What Her Girlfriend Said

In the seaside grove
where he drove back in his chariot
the *neytal* flowers are on the ground,
some of their thick petals plowed in
and their stalks broken

by the knife-edge of his wheels' golden rims
furrowing the earth.

Ōta Ñāni, *Kuṟuntokai* 227[75]

The motif of furrows appears in song 3. The hero is in pain as he remembers the moments of union with the heroine, now parted from him. She alone can remove his pain. Likewise, in song 13, the furrows remind the heroine of the lover who has deserted her.

Songs 4, 5, and 7 explore the hero's rather mixed feelings about the heroine whom he begins to perceive as a femme fatale who has enmeshed him in her charms. Song 8 goes a step further and identifies her as Kūṟṟam, the god of death. And in song 9, the hero warns other men to stay away from her. Thus, in songs 1 through 9, Kōvalaṉ examines the entire gamut of his feelings for Mātavi, realizes the folly of his infatuation, and resolves to go back to the wife he had abandoned.

A narrative interlude (*kaṭṭurai*) comments on Mātavi's response to Kōvalaṉ's songs. She feels that he has left her for another woman and that it is all over between them. In fact, song 11 poignantly evokes, in the figure of the sand house discussed earlier, her feelings of betrayal and helplessness. It speaks for women who are taken advantage of and are therefore unable to face the world. Their loss of innocence is irreparable.

> In Pukār, our town,
> Waves pull down our sand houses. And women,
> Tears welling up from spearlike eyes,
> Long wounds fresh on moon-faces,
> Scoop sand by the handful to fill the sea.
>
> (7.30)

Songs 12 and 16 focus on the heroine's suffering. Alone and helpless, she feels that the whole world has turned against her. In her pain, she remembers the happy times spent with her lover and resolves never to forget him. And in song 18, the heroine is finally reconciled to her lover's desertion. Her world has truly come to an end.

The "Kāṉalvari" (The Love Songs of the Seaside Grove) song cycle shows Iḷaṅkō at his finest as a poet and composer. Though firmly rooted in tradition in terms of themes and motifs, the songs have a delicate touch and are totally free from artifice.

The song cycles (*icai*) in fact exploit the use of indirect suggestion. They elucidate what is only implied in the narrative and function as a subtext, periodically illuminating the literary narrative (*iyal*). The singers function as a chorus. They not only intensify and distance the emotions associated with a specific phase of love but also mediate between the protagonists and the reader. The chorus responds to the events as an audience in miniature by publicly expressing its hopes, fears, joys, and sorrows out of its repertoire of traditional wisdom in its attempt to make explicit the meaning of an event it finds difficult and unfamiliar. Its function is thus almost ritual. For this reason, the *Cilappatikāram* is sometimes referred to as a narrative poem of threefold Tamil, that is, poetry (iyal), music (icai), and dance (*nāṭakam*).

After the musical interlude of the "Kāṉalvari," the narrative picks up in canto 8 (The Coming of Spring). Mātavi sends

Kōvalan̲, through her maid Vacantamālai, a conciliatory letter that he refuses to accept. Despite Kōvalan̲'s rejection, she entertains hopes of seeing him again. The reader, however, knows that Kōvalan̲'s decision is irrevocable.

Kōvalan̲ describes to Vacantamālai the eight varieties of the masquerade dance (*varikkūttu*) in which Mātavi is an expert, perhaps implying that her love for him was only a pretense. He concludes that she is, after all, only a dancing girl and he should have known better than to expect her to love him. Observe that he does not explicitly spell out his disappointment. It would violate the norms of social behavior. He has recourse to indirect suggestion, which Iḷaṅkō employs especially when the situation demands the utmost delicacy. As before, this digression is structurally relevant. Again, almost two-thirds of the canto are descriptive.

Canto 9 (The Nature of the Dream) is the only canto in "The Book of Pukār" that is entirely narrative in its thrust. It tells of Kōvalan̲'s return to his wife and of his decision to leave for Maturai to retrieve his fortune. It also narrates the episode of Cāttan̲ and Tēvanti, a Jaina couple. It is obviously one of those cautionary tales the Jainas are so fond of. However, it is to Tēvanti that Kaṇṇaki confides her bad dream that foreshadows the coming events of "The Book of Maturai": Kōvalan̲'s murder, the destruction of Maturai, and Kaṇṇaki's ascent to heaven.

The canto furnishes a touching example of Kaṇṇaki's patience. When Kōvalan̲ returns, he complains of having squandered his entire fortune on Mātavi. Kaṇṇaki, under the impression that he has returned for more ornaments to lavish on Mātavi, at once offers him her anklets:

> Her bright face lit up with a consoling smile:
> She said, "My anklets. Here! Take them."
> (9.108–109)

Coming as it does toward the end of "The Book of Pukār," the burden of the story appears to have fallen to this canto.

Canto 10 (Country Scenes) is a breathtaking pastoral on the Cōḻa country that spreads across the Kāviri, through which Kōvalan̲ and Kaṇṇaki pass on their way to Maturai. They are joined by Kavunti, the Jaina ascetic. At Śrīraṅkam, all three encounter a Jaina sage. Iḷaṅkō uses the occasion for a spiritual discourse by the sage to underscore the great narrative poem's concern with the four ends of humans, especially its bias toward enlightenment. This canto continues the narrative trend of the earlier one, but it remains substantially descriptive in its form.

This analysis of the composition of "The Book of Pukār" shows that the disproportion between the modes of description and narration is the most notable feature of every canto, and that description predominates in all the cantos but one. This bias, of course, goes back to the origins of the narrative poem itself in the long poems of classical Tamil, which are primarily descriptive. Each canto is an individual poem in its own right and it employs the conventions of akam and puṟam poetry for "poetical effects." It is rooted in tradition, which it has both deepened and enriched by its example.

Our investigation of the genre of the *Cilappatikāram* encourages us to conclude that it is indigenous to Tamil. The genre, the toṭar-nilaic-ceyyuḷ, poetic sequence, originated in the long poems of classical Tamil poetry and later came to be known as the kāppiyam, narrative poem. It tells the reader clearly how the poem may be read, which was in effect the thrust of our inquiry. The kāppiyam bears a family resemblance to the epic as we understand it. If the association is not pushed too far, epic is a useful term to keep in mind when discussing the genre of the *Cilappatikāram*.

The *Cilappatikāram* and Oral Tradition

The Vedas, the earliest literary texts of the Indo-Europeans, are the classic example of oral poetry. Composed about 1500–1000 B.C.E., they were orally transmitted by the *śrotriyas*, brahmans learned in the Vedas, more or less unchanged for centuries. If we keep in mind the function the Vedas performed as ritual texts in Hindu society, their lengthy oral transmission becomes clear. No doubt memorization played a significant role in the preservation of a text such as the Ṛgveda, which alone comprises 40,000 lines. It is possible that at some stage writing contributed to fixing the text as we have it today. However, Indian society to this day remains essentially glottocentric rather than chirocentric. Moritz Winternitz reminds us that

> In India, from the oldest times, up till the present day, the spoken word, and not writing, has been the basis of the whole of the literary and scientific activity. . . . Not out of manuscripts or books does one

> learn the texts, but from the mouth of the teacher, today as thousands of years ago. The written text can at most be used as an aid to learning, as a support to the memory, but no authority is attributed to it. Authority is possessed only by the spoken word of the teacher. If today all the manuscripts and prints were to be lost, that would by no means cause the disappearance of Indian literature from the face of the earth, for a great portion of it could be recalled out of the memory of the scholars and reciters. The works of the poets, too, were in India never intended for readers, but always for hearers. Even modern poets do not desire to be read, but their wish is that their poetry may become "an adornment for the throats of the experts."[76]

In fact, the brahman priesthood, the keeper of the Vedas, regarded writing with suspicion, even as an impure activity.

Now, what precisely was the role of the poet in the Indian tradition? In the Ṛgveda we are told:

> Varuṇa confided in me, the wise one:
> "Thrice seven names has the cow. Who knows the trail
> Should whisper them like secrets, if he is to speak
> To future generations as an inspired poet."
>
> Ṛgveda VII.87.4[77]

According to Sāyaṇa, a commentator, speech (*vāc*) in the form of a cow (*aghnyā*) has 21 meters corresponding to her breast, throat, and head. Only after the intervention of Varuṇa does the poet who is the wise one (*medhira*) become the inspired one (*vipra*). His exceptional knowledge imposes a responsibility on him. He is both the keeper and transmitter of the tradition.

The tradition has regarded poetry as a way of knowledge, as a way of putting one's "house of Being" in order, to borrow Martin Heidegger's phrase.[78] Poetry, for that matter every word we speak, is composed of breath. On this most intangible foundation rests the way of poetry. It offers both the poet and his listeners the unique opportunity of finding order, integrity, a way. This we take to be the function of language itself, rather than an exclusive property of poetry. However, poetry exhibits this property to an unusual degree. It was believed that the spoken word, properly formulated, could produce a physical effect on the world. The word was invested with sacred power.

There is in the West generally a reluctance to endow language with such power. Heidegger (1889–1976) is an exception. In a series of lectures, first delivered at the University of Freiburg in 1957–58, titled "The Nature of Language," he says:

> "What is it that the poet reaches? Not mere knowledge. He obtains entrance into the relation of word to thing. This relation is not, however, a connection between the thing that is on one side and the word that is on the other. The word itself is the relation which in each instance retains the thing within itself in such a manner that it 'is' a thing."[79]

Patañjali (2nd c. B.C.E.), in fact, had gone further than Heidegger in his attempt to empower the word. This is what he says in his classic formulation of the view in his great commentary on the *Grammar* (*Vyākaraṇa-mahābhāṣya*) of Pāṇini: "A single word, well used and perfectly understood, and conforming to the sacred texts is, in heaven and in the world, the sacred cow to fulfill every wish."[80] In the Indian tradition, literature (*sāhitya*) was a way of realizing the Absolute (*Brahman*) through the mediation of language. "Therefore, the attainment of faultless speech," states Bhartṛhari (5th c. C.E.) in the *Vākyapadīya* (Of the Sentence and the Word) "is the attainment of Brahman. He who knows the secret of its functioning enjoys the immortal Brahman."[81] The literary artefact in itself had no significance. It was this metaphysical bias that distinguished Indian literature from every other literature.

A poem can be oral in one or more of its aspects: composition, transmission, and performance. Writing often plays a role in each of these. An orally composed poem may be transmitted through writing. Or, a poem may be orally performed with the help of a written text. In oral culture, where the performer is unlettered, he composes in performance, and the poem is orally transmitted by one bard to another. Writing, as Walter J. Ong points out, "introduces into his mind the concept of a text as controlling the narrative and thereby interferes with the oral composing processes. . . ."[82] The idea of a fixed text is borrowed from writing: it is alien to oral poetics. So are the ideas of "authorship" and "originality" associated with writing. In oral culture, tradition is the legitimate author. It is the *Kunstsprache* that "does the thinking for the poet." Mikhail Bakhtin puts it well: "Epic discourse is a discourse handed down by tradition. By its very nature the epic world of the absolute past is inaccessible to personal experience and does not permit an individual, personal point of view or evaluation."[83] The discourse of oral poetry is, moreover, highly intertextual: oral poems freely borrow from one another and develop through a process of elaboration. No text is free of other texts. In fact, it is a commonplace of literary theory that texts are continually in dialogue with other texts, literary and nonliterary, over time and space. In oral culture, a text presupposes in its composition a shared knowledge between the bard and his audience. It is dependent on its context to help explicate its meaning. Text and context are therefore inseparable.

It is generally accepted that the *Cilappatikāram* existed long before it was put down in writing. Scholars are of the opinion that the epic, with the rest of early Tamil literature, must have had a long oral existence before it acquired its present form.[84] For generations, bards (*pāṇaṉs*) have recited or sung the story of Kōvalaṉ throughout the Tamil country, embellishing it with myths. It was this story from the oral tradition that was at some point transcribed by a learned poet (*pulavaṉ*). Thereafter, both the oral and written versions freely circulated, each drawing upon the other. One such written version that has come down to us from the distant past is attributed by tradition to Iḷaṅkō Aṭikaḷ, a prince of the Cēral royal family and Jaina monk. The poet tells the story in the *āciriyam* meter, a recitative (*akaval*) meter that is the staple of early Tamil poetry. By the time of the poem, northern Sanskritic ideas had become a part of the Tamil worldview. The *Cilappatikāram* is thus a syncretic work that unites and harmonizes elements drawn from various sources. These include Sanskrit kāvya literature that offered Iḷaṅkō examples of rhetorical conventions; Hindu myths; Jainism and its heterodox traditions, notably karma, nonviolence, and renunciation; and memories of Aryan invasions of southern India. The poem also exploits, as we have observed, the conventions of classical Tamil poetry to achieve new heights of expressiveness.

We notice that both the oral and written traditions coexist in the Indian situation, often interacting with one another. It is not unlikely that numerous versions of the Kōvalaṉ story arose in the centuries following Iḷaṅkō's poem. The most notable among the versions that have survived is a folk ballad (*nāṭṭuppāṭal*), *Kōvalaṉ katai* (The Story of Kōvalaṉ), attributed to Pukaḻēntip Pulavar (12th-13th c. C.E.), and first published in 1873. The ballad, together with the publication of the *Cilappatikāram* in 1892, revived interest in the tale of Kōvalaṉ and Kaṇṇaki in the twentieth century. My knowledge of the several versions of the Kōvalaṉ story, excluding the one collected by Mary Frere, is based on Sally Noble's unpublished study, "The Tamil Story of the Anklet."[85] The *Kōvalaṉ katai,* as Noble reports, is associated with the Tiyākarācacuvāmi temple in Tiruvoṟṟiyūr near Madras where Kaṇṇaki is worshiped as Vaṭṭappāṟaiammaṉ, "the Goddess of the Round Stone."[86] We learn that prior to the 1930s temple dancers (*devadāsīs*) used to perform the story of Kōvalaṉ during the goddess' festival in Cittirai (April-May). *Kōvalaṉ katai* represents a significant departure from the *Cilappatikāram.* The Jaina bias, prominent in the epic, is replaced by that of popular Hinduism. Kaṇṇaki, for instance, is depicted as an incarnation of the goddess Kālī. References to Iḷaṅkō Aṭikaḷ, Kavunti, Maṇimēkalai, and to the beliefs and practices of Jainism are expunged. The folk ballad reflects the ascendency of Hinduism, and the decline of the heterodox religions. By "re-visioning"[87] Iḷaṅkō's work, Pukaḻēnti has composed it from a new perspective that could be regarded as subversive. Other differences are examined below in connection with the folktale, "Chandra's Vengeance."

Kōvalaṉ kaṇṇaki nāṭakam (Kōvalaṉ and Kaṇṇaki: A Play) by Vīrapattiraṉ, based on the folk ballad, but incorporating the conventions of the *terukkūttu,* a genre of folk play performed in the open as ritual, was published in 1889. A musical play (*icai-nāṭakam*), *Kōvalaṉ carittiram* (The Story of Kōvalaṉ's Life), by Ṭi. Ṭi. Caṅkaratās Cuvāmikaḷ, also based on the folk ballad, was regularly performed between 1910 and 1922, and published in 1925. Two other musical versions, *Caṅkīta kōvalaṉ* (Kōvalaṉ: A Musical Play) by M. R. Muttuccāmi, performed between the 1950s and the 1980s, and *Kaṇṇaki katai: villuppāttu* (The Story of Kaṇṇaki: A Bow Song), published in 1953, attest to the popularity of the story. The bow-song versions are invariably based on the *Cilappatikāram.* They are not ritually oriented, and seek to encourage in their audience an interest in Tamil culture. In one of the versions, that of C. Taṅkaiyā collected by Noble, the fire that burns Maturai originates in a tear Kaṇṇaki sheds when she learns of Kōvalaṉ's death. In the classical epic, the source of the fire is Kaṇṇaki's breast, which she wrenches from her body and hurls at the city. Performers of bow songs are thus innovative, though they often adapt their repertoire to suit the expectations of their sponsors. Thus the texts are context-sensitive.

The poet Pāratitācaṉ (Kaṉaka Cuppurattiṉam, 1891–1964) rewrote Iḷaṅkō's poem in modern Tamil in his *Kaṇṇaki puraṭcik kāppiyam* (The Epic of Kaṇṇaki's Revolt, 1962), but the work is flawed: he replaces Iḷaṅkō's universal outlook with a narrow, insular one. Mu. Karuṇāniti (b. 1924) likewise politicizes Iḷaṅkō's epic in his *Cilappatikāram: nāṭakak kāppiyam* (The *Cilappatikāram:* An Epic Play, 1967) to reflect the aims of the Dravidian Progressive Party of which he is a leader. In the early 1970s, he produced a film version, *Pūmpukār,* of his play which helped to popularize the story among the Tamils.[88] The transmission of the Kōvalaṉ story in different genres since the late nineteenth century offers the best proof of the fact that the Tamil-speaking peoples have opened their hearts to it, and become its ultimate custodians.

I would like to introduce at this stage the term "oral residue," proposed by Ong as a useful tool for investigating a text's orality. Ong defines it as "habits of thought and expression tracing back to preliterate situations or practice, or deriving from the dominance of the oral as a medium in a given culture, or indicating a reluctance or inability to dissociate the written medium from the spoken."[89] In view of the long history of the cult of the Mother Goddess in the Indian tradition, Kaṇṇaki's apotheosis into the goddess Pattiṉi makes sense, especially if we consider the etymologies of the names of Kōvalaṉ and Kaṇṇaki. Etymology provides an opportunity to explore the idea of oral residue. "Kōvalaṉ" derives from the Sanskrit *gopālaka* (Ta. *kōpālakaṉ*), "a guardian of the cow," a cowherd. And the cow being one of the forms of the Mother Goddess, it is only appropriate that her spouse is a gopālaka. The irony of Kōvalaṉ's name is not entirely lost. In the *Cilappatikāram,* he fails Kaṇṇaki as her guardian by abandoning her soon after their marriage for the courtesan Mātavi. He does return to Kaṇṇaki, but their reunion is brief. He is murdered within hours of their arrival in Maturai. Having failed to protect Kaṇṇaki, Kōvalaṉ even fails to protect himself. But then his death is essential for Kaṇṇaki's apotheosis. Folk etymology derives "Kaṇṇaki" from the Tamil *kaṉṉi* or *kaṉṉikai,* "a virgin." In the oral tradition, Kaṇṇaki remains a virgin even after her marriage to Kōvalaṉ, but this is not the case in the *Cilappatikāram,* where Kōvalaṉ and Kaṇṇaki are compared to Kāma and Rati "smothered in each/ Other's arms . . ." (2.113–14). Could Kaṇṇaki be perhaps derived, as the *Tamil Lexicon* suggests, from the Tamil *kaṇ,* "eyes" + *akam,* "beautiful" + *i,* the feminine singular suffix to mean "she who has beautiful eyes?"[90] This would appropriately relate her to the Mother Goddess who is known by similar epithetical names, for example, Viśālākṣi, "she who has large eyes."

The oral residual dimension of the *Cilappatikāram* is, again, evident from the presence of folktales embedded in the text. In canto 15, the brahman Māṭalaṉ narrates a tale from the *Pañcatantra* (The Five Books, c. 200 B.C.E.) in the course of praising Kōvalaṉ's nobility (57–61). A brahman woman kills a mongoose (*Herpestes nyula*) suspecting it of having killed her child. To atone for the sin, her husband leaves her and travels north to bathe in the Gaṅgā. When she follows him, he gives her a note in Sanskrit asking her to show it to people who can understand it. Note in hand, she wanders about and eventually runs into Kōvalaṉ. He reads the note and comforts her. He lavishes gifts on her and hopes her merits will remove her sins. He also restores her husband to her and offers them enough money to help them support themselves. The phrase *vaṭamoḻi vācakam,* "Sanskrit verse," is an explicit reference to the following lines in the *Pañcatantra:*

> aparīkṣya na kartavyaṃ kartavyaṃ suparīkṣitaṃ|
> pascād bhavati saṃtāpo brāhmaṇī nakule yathā||
> *Pañcatantra* 5.18[91]

> Let the well-advised be done;
> Ill-advised leave unbegun:
> Else, remorse will be let loose,
> As with the lady and mongoose.[92]

The presence of similar folktales in the epic suggests an oral provenance.

We examined some folk versions of the Kōvalaṉ story above. One version of the story, called "Chandra's Vengeance," was told to Mary Frere, the daughter of Sir Bartle Frere (1815–84), Governor of Bombay Presidency (1862–67), by her nanny, Anna Liberata de Souza, in "broken English" in the winter of 1865–66.[93] Anna had heard the story, probably in Kannada, from her grandmother, who was a Lingayat from Calicut, Malabar province, then a part of Madras Presidency. The de Souza-Frere version was published in London by John Murray in 1868, five years before the Pukaḻēnti ballad (1873), and 24 years before Iḷaṅkō's epic (1892). It therefore has the distinction of being the first version of the Kōvalan̲ story to ever appear in print. Here is the story.

Once upon a time there was a sahukar's (banker's) wife who was childless. She told her husband, the sahukar, that she would not rest till she had seen Mahadeo (Śiva) and asked him to grant her a child. Much against his wish she left her home and traveled through the jungle for months. She finally arrived in the Madura Tinivelly country where she met two women at the riverside. One of them was Rani Coplinghee, and the other, a nautchgirl. Soon they fell to talking among themselves, and the sahukar's wife learned that they too were childless like herself and had vowed to seek Mahadeo to ask him for a child. At her request, all three traveled together in search of Mahadeo. They traveled for years till they were utterly worn out. One day, in the middle of the jungle, they saw a great river of fire swirling away. Rani Coplinghee and the nautchgirl lost heart at the sight of the river. Undeterred, the sahukar's wife waded through the fire and crossed over. She was not burned. The two women promised to wait for her till she returned.

Now the sahukar's wife had been wandering for twelve years in search of Mahadeo. From his throne in Mount Kailās, Mahadeo saw her and took pity on her. He made a shady mango tree grow beside a round well in her path and, disguised as a fakir, stood by the tree. But the sahukar's wife did not stop to refresh herself with a drink of water, nor did she notice the fakir. When he called out to her, she would not stop. At last, removing his disguise, he revealed his true self to the sahukar's wife who then fell at his feet. He gave her a mango from the tree and asked her to eat it so that she could have a child on returning home. She told Mahadeo about her two companions waiting for her on the other side of the river. He asked her to share the mango with them so that they too could have children. On rejoining her companions, she squeezed the mango and offered its juice to the rani, its skin to the nautchgirl, and herself ate its pulp and stone.

On their return, the sahukar's wife gave birth to a son, Koila ("He of the Mango Stone"); the rani, to a daughter, Chandra

Bai ("The Moon Lady"); and the nautchgirl, to a daughter, Moulee ("She from the Sweet Mango Pulp"). Chandra was born with two golden anklets filled with precious stones. A brahman warned Chandra's father, the raja, to get rid of her. He said that the princess would one day burn and destroy the country. Chandra was then put inside a golden casket, which floated down the river and was carried to the land where the sahukar's wife lived. It so happened that the sahukar was down by the river to wash his face. He saw the casket and retrieved it with the help of a fisherman. He took the child home, and his wife brought her up as her own daughter. When Chandra was a year old she was married to Koila.

The years passed, and both the sahukar and his wife died of old age. Koila and Chandra grew up to be the handsomest couple in their country. Moulee also grew to be a pretty woman. One day, Moulee traveled with her people to the land where Koila and Chandra lived. She had a beautiful voice that could be heard from far off. Once Koila heard her sing and was charmed by her voice. Determined to find her, he arrived near Moulee's tent where, garland in hand, she was dancing. The people urged her to marry one of them, and Moulee agreed to wed the man on whose neck her garland would fall. She swung the garland and threw it, and it fell around Koila's neck. He was told that Moulee had chosen him as her husband. When he hesitated, declaring he already had a wife, he was offered a powerful drink that made him forget Chandra. He was then forced into marrying Moulee. After some months, Moulee's mother insisted that he pay for his support. To raise money, Koila returned to his homeland and begged Chandra for one of her anklets. A furious Chandra at first refused to part with her anklet. She later agreed if he let her go with him. Together, they set off for the Madura Tinivelly country. On the way the god Krishna, who was playing a game of cards with his three wives, saw Koila and Chandra. He told his wives that Koila was going to be killed and that Chandra in anger would burn the whole country. The goddesses, disguised as fortune-tellers, tried to stop Koila from entering the Madura Tinivelly country, but he brushed them aside.

Koila and Chandra came to the outskirts of the raja's capital and stopped for the night at the house of an old herdswoman. The next morning, Koila entered the city to sell Chandra's anklet. Shortly before their arrival, Rani Coplinghee had sent her two anklets to a jeweler for cleaning. In the backyard of the jeweler's house, two eagles had built a nest where their young ones constantly screamed aloud, disturbing the jeweler's family. Unable to stand the noise any longer, the jeweler's son tore down the nest and killed the young ones. When the eagles saw what had happened, they were bitter. They swooped down to the jeweler's porch where one of the rani's anklets was kept and flew away with it. The jeweler was at his wit's end. After some delay, he returned the other anklet to the rani, telling her that its companion would soon follow. So when he came across the anklet that Koila was trying to dispose of, he first pretended to be Koila's friend, then betrayed him to the Raja's police. He accused Koila before the raja of stealing the Rani's anklet and told the raja to put him to death. Meanwhile, the anklet was sent to the rani for confirmation, and she recognized it as Chandra's. She pleaded with the raja to examine the case further, but he refused. The rani then locked up Chandra's anklet in a cupboard. Koila was taken away by the guards to the jungle where he asked them permission to die by his own hand. He then fell down on his sword, cutting his body in two.

The next morning, when the old herdswoman took Chandra a bowl of milk to drink, it turned to blood in her mouth. Chandra was certain that Koila was dead. The herdswoman confirmed this after visiting the city. Chandra then rushed to the raja's palace and charged him with the murder of her husband. At the sound of her voice her anklet, that the rani had locked up in a cupboard, came rolling to her feet. The raja was speechless. Chandra fell on her knees and tore her hair. As the hair started falling, fire rose from it and burned the city. The old herdswoman pleaded with her to spare the Purwari lines beyond the ramparts where the houses of the outcastes were located. Chandra spared them. The fire burned the palace, as the brahman had predicted, and the raja and rani perished in it. So did the jeweler, whose heart Chandra tore out and offered to the eagles. Moulee and her mother also perished in the fire.

Then Chandra ran to the place where Koila's body lay. As she wept over it, a needle and thread fell at her feet from heaven. She quickly sewed Koila's body together and prayed to Mahadeo to restore her husband to life. This he did. Koila and Chandra returned to their homeland to live happily ever after.

The sequence of events narrated in "Chandra's Vengeance" corresponds to that in the first two books of the *Cilappatikāram*. However, the differences between the two are striking enough to invite comment. Though the supernatural element is a common motif, it is treated differently. Koila, Chandra, and Moulee are all born as a result of their mothers eating a mango, a gift from Mahadeo. Their births are therefore supernatural. Remember that the mango blossom is the most potent of Kāma's five flower arrows. On the other hand, Kōvalaṉ and Kaṇṇaki are born naturally to their mothers without any divine intervention. Chandra is born a princess: her mother is rani Coplinghee (a corruption of Kōviliṅki, the Pāṇṭiya queen in the *Kōvalaṉ katai*), and her father, the raja of the Madura Tinivelly country. In several folk versions, Kaṇṇaki is the Pāṇṭiya king's daughter, who eventually destroys him. In the *Cilappatikāram*, Kaṇṇaki is the daughter of a noble merchant of Pukār.

Following Chandra's birth, a brahman warns the raja that she will destroy his country, and burn it down. He advises the raja to get rid of her. The raja puts her in a golden casket and floats it down the river. Koila's father discovers the casket and takes Chandra home to be raised as his own daughter. We are reminded of the Egyptian queen Hatshepsut who discovers Moses in a papyrus basket among the reeds of the Nile as she steps into the river to bathe. This motif is not present in the epic.

The folktale comes up with a plausible explanation for Koila's misdemeanor. He forgets Chandra under the influence of a powerful drink fed to him by Moulee's people. He is then forced into marrying Moulee. Infatuated by Mātavi, Kōvalaṉ buys her garland for 1,008 pieces of gold; it does not fall around his neck. He abandons Kaṇṇaki of his own free will and lives with Mātavi. Since she is a courtesan, a marriage with her would be socially unacceptable. The folktale does not recognize such considerations.

In the classical story, the royal goldsmith steals the queen's anklet, thus betraying her trust. His cupidity brings ruin on the kingdom. The jeweler in the folktale does not steal Rani Coplinghee's anklet. Two eagles carry it away from his porch to avenge the death of their young ones at the hands of the jeweler's son. The induction of birds into the narrative is quite common in folktales. When Chandra's anklet is produced before Rani Coplinghee, she recognizes it as her daughter's and locks it away in a cupboard. This motif is not present in the epic. Though both Koila and Kōvalaṉ are condemned to death, there is a difference in the way they die. Unable to put up with the indignity of being accused as a thief, Koila takes his own life by falling on his sword. Kōvalaṉ is offered no such option. He is executed as a common thief by one of the king's guards. The two women establish their husbands' innocence differently. An enraged Chandra accuses the raja of Koila's death. Hearing her voice, her anklet rolls out of the cupboard and stops at her feet leaving the king speechless. In the climactic scene of the epic, Kaṇṇaki breaks open her anklet filled with gems in the king's presence. When one of the gems leaps into his face, the king realizes his blunder and dies from the shock. For the queen's anklet contained not gems but pearls. It is the anklet in both stories that challenges the king's scepter and exposes his justice as a sham. The king himself is not spared the consequences of his unlawful action. It is significant that in the folktale the anklet remains whole and unbroken, an allusion perhaps to Chandra's virginity.

Chandra then kneels down and tears her hair. Fire at once bursts from her hair and destroys the city. Everyone who had injured her dies, including Moulee and the jeweler, whose heart Chandra tears out and offers to the eagles. She, however, spares the outcastes. This scene is even more dramatic in the *Cilappatikāram.* In her rage, Kaṇṇaki wrenches her left breast from her body and hurls it at the city. It turns into a ball of fire that devours Maturai. Kaṇṇaki spares brahmans and cows, besides chaste women. The polarity of the social classes that are spared the great fire betrays the ideological biases of the folktale and the classical poem. We are told in the epic that Mātavi enters a nunnery, but it is silent about the fate of the goldsmith.

While Chandra sews together the two halves of Koila's body with a needle and thread that fall from heaven and prays to Mahadeo to restore her husband's life, Kaṇṇaki ascends to heaven, a goddess, in Indra's chariot. Kaṇṇaki is reunited with Kōvalaṉ in heaven; Koila and Chandra live happily ever after on earth. The differences, with a few exceptions, that "Chandra's Vengeance" reveals are precisely those that it shares in common with the *Kōvalaṉ katai,* suggesting the possibility that it ultimately derives from the folk ballad.

The Ritual Origin of the Poem

Myth, rather than history, is more often the route a nation takes to understand itself. It finds solace in idealizing myths to dissipate quotidian tensions. India is no exception. Its national imagination is mythopoeic, and this aspect has survived into the present day. In India, mythology as presented in the narratives of the *Mahābhārata* and the *Rāmāyaṇa* has served the function of history. The myths of Kṛṣṇa, for example, are not fictitious stories but real events the people believe in. Even the discourse of contemporary Indian politics bristles with the idiom of myth. The term *Rāmarājya,* "the reign of Rāma," is often used to evoke a golden age. Myths enable the past to be forever present and to inform the future. Mark Schorer's observations on myth are appropriate here. "Myths," he writes, "are the instruments by which we continually struggle to make our experience intelligible to ourselves. A myth is a large controlling image that gives philosophical meaning to the facts of ordinary life; . . . [it unifies] experience in a way that is satisfactory to the whole culture."[94] Some myths have their origins in rituals. We can, therefore, talk of a myth as a "rite spoken." Epics in India are closely associated with ritual performances unlike their counterparts in Europe. In temples and at festivals across the country, Hindus relive the stories from the epics. Epic heroes and heroines are considered divine, as they invariably ascend to heaven on their death. They become objects of religious cults and *māhātmyas* are composed in praise of their greatness. The *Cilappatikāram* may have originated from the desire to account for the existence of rituals associated with the cult of the goddess Pattiṉi. The rise and spread of the cult in the Tamil country are central to the poem whose spiritual bias is embedded in the myth of Kaṇṇaki. What Iḷaṅkō does in the *Cilappatikāram* is to expose the mythic underpinnings: the apotheosis of Kaṇṇaki into the goddess Pattiṉi. "Goddesses," remarks A. K. Ramanujan, "come out of ordinary women who are desecrated; they do not come out of the churning of the ocean."[95] The aphorism offers one explanation of Kaṇṇaki's transfiguration. Her deprivation is more than compensated for by her ultimate spiritual triumph—her apotheosis into a goddess. The implications of the myth become clear: we must risk losing ourselves to gain everlasting life. The myth's religious significance is complete. Kaṇṇaki's ascent to heaven, to use Eliade's phrase, is "a passing to what is beyond, an escape from profane space and human status."[96] The Virgin Mary's Assumption, that Pope Pius XII proclaimed as a dogma on November 1, 1950 by the bull *Munificentissimus Deus,*[97] offers an interesting Western parallel to Kaṇṇaki's ascent.

The story of Kōvalaṉ and Kaṇṇaki is told in the first two books, "The Book of Pukār" and "The Book of Maturai," cantos 1 through 23, and it ends with Kōvalaṉ's death and the burning of Maturai by Kaṇṇaki. "The Book of Vañci," cantos 24 through 30, deals entirely with the apotheosis of Kaṇṇaki into the goddess Pattiṉi. With the death of the Pāṇṭiya king Neṭuñceḻiyaṉ, who was responsible for the execution of Kōvalaṉ, and with the fall of Maturai, Kaṇṇaki's wrath is appeased and dharma is restored. The book is an attempt to provide legitimacy to the cult of the goddess Pattiṉi. The ritual traditions of the cult are, therefore, an important part of the poem's intention. This appears, however, to be overshadowed by the poet's attempt to sing the praise of the Tamil imperium spread over the three kingdoms of the Cōḻa, Pāṇṭiya, and Cēral, in strong contrast to the northern, Aryan India.

The myth also has an ethical and political bias: the chastity (kaṟpu) of a woman is inviolable, and it is the duty of a king to protect and uphold it; he can do so only if he rules justly. If he swerves from justice (*nīti*), he puts his kingdom in danger. We observe here the conflation of the domestic and the public, of akam and puṟam. Nowhere is this more eloquently stated than in the following lines:

> Pattiṉi whom the whole world now worships
> Had proved the truth of the Tamil saying:
> "The virtue of women is useless if the king
> Rules unjustly." She made the Cōḻa realize it.
> She made the Pāṇṭiyan, lord of the south,
> Realize, "The king cannot survive if his scepter
> Is crooked." She made the Cēral,
> Lord of the west, realize, "The wrath
> Of kings will not be appeased till their vows
> Are fulfilled, and made known to the kings
> Of the north." (28.210–20)

Kaṇṇaki's apotheosis occurs in three stages: (1) she is a chaste and uncomplaining wife who is deserted by her husband; (2) she turns into a destructive force; and (3) she becomes a tutelary deity whose cult is institutionalized.

The king's dependence on the support of a virgin is a familiar theme in Indo-European mythology, as Georges Dumézil clearly shows.[98] He discusses the myth of Yayāti and his daughter Mādhavī as the *locus classicus* of this theme. The myth is told in the fifth book of the *Mahābhārata*.[99] King Yayāti is expelled from heaven because of his pride. His restoration can be effected only by his grandsons through a sharing of their merits with him. Mādhavī, who is unmarried and a virgin, readily obliges and bears sons. Accordingly, four sons are born to her from four different kings. She thus saves her father. In the end, however, she regains her viginity. She commits no sin, for she acts throughout out of regard for dharma.

In the oral versions of the *Cilappatikāram,* Kaṇṇaki is invariably a *virgo intacta.*[100] Ceṅkuṭṭuvaṉ establishes a temple in her honor to acknowledge her support and protection as the tutelary deity of his kingdom. Tamil society to this day regards Kaṇṇaki as an ideal of chastity. For the Tamils, chastity goes beyond mere sexual abstinence; it represents sacred power (*aṇaṅku*). A phrase in *Akanāṉūṟu* 73, for instance, makes this explicit: "chastity filled with sacred power" (*"aṇaṅku uṟu kaṟpu"*)[101] with reference to a woman who is disconsolate in her husband's absence. Tamil literature is replete with examples of chaste women who are held up as ideals. Kaṇṇaki represents this ideal best. She is a resonant cultural symbol that has remained unchanged for two thousand years. Hanumān, in Kampaṉ's *Irāmāvatāram,* for instance, refers to Sītā as "the jewel of chastity" (*"kaṟpiṉukku aṇiyai"*).[102] The tale of Sāvitrī in the *Mahābhārata* demonstrates the power of the chaste wife. Sāvitrī wins over Yama, the god of death, by strictly observing her dharma: she is an exemplary wife; cares for her parents-in-law; observes fasts and penances to discipline herself; and does not give up on her husband. It is these qualities that overwhelm Yama, and he restores Satyavat to life. She recalls Alcestis, traditionally the ideal wife, who willingly dies in place of her husband Admetus, but is restored to life by Persephone, the goddess of the underworld. It must be said, however, that no such power is attributed to chaste men; nor are men expected to be chaste or faithful to their wives. The symbol of Kaṇṇaki has pulled together the different strands, religious, social, and political, in the Tamil cultural experience.[103] At its extreme, it demarcates Tamil India from the rest of the subcontinent.

Further, the Tamils identify chastity with female spirituality. Kaṇṇaki embodies this best in the Tamil tradition. Her chastity empowers her to dispense justice (nīti): she humbles the Pāṇṭiya king and burns down Maturai. Her spiritual authority thus supersedes the purely temporal one of the king, notwithstanding the gender and class differences between subject and ruler. For, as Iḷaṅkō tells us:

> It is true that even the gods adore her
> Who adores no god but her husband. (23.209–10)

Or, as Milton puts it:

> Or if Vertue feeble were,
> Heav'n it self would stoop to her.
> *A Mask Presented at Ludlow-Castle, 1634,* 1022–23[104]

Again, the mythical aspect comes full circle in Ceṅkuṭṭuvaṉ's dedication of Pattiṉi's memorial stone (naṭukal), thus institutionalizing her worship in his kingdom. To appease the goddess' wrath, the Cōḻa king Vēṟ-Ceḻiyaṉ sacrifices a thousand goldsmiths. All those who had wronged Kaṇṇaki have now been punished, and her rehabilitation is complete. Though Kaṇṇaki has passed into the heavens (Ta. *viṇṇēṟutal,* Skt. *ārohaḥ*), her spiritual presence remains on the earth. Her apotheosis invests her with power and dominion in heaven and earth. As the goddess Pattiṉi, she can now perpetually intercede on behalf of her followers. While the Sanskrit epics, the *Mahābhārata* and the *Rāmāyaṇa,* deal with the descent of gods (Kṛṣṇa, Rāma) in human form, the Tamil poem deals with the ascent of a human (Kaṇṇaki) to divinity. The heterodox religions, Buddhism and Jainism, emphasized a human being's innate ability to obtain salvation on his or her own.

In *The Cult of the Goddess Pattini,* Obeyesekere examines the status of the cult in contemporary Sri Lanka after its diffusion there from southern India around the tenth century C.E. My source for much of the information on the cult is Obeyesekere's study. Though the cult has disappeared from southern India, or has been absorbed into the cults of the Hindu Mother Goddess, it flourishes in parts of Sri Lanka among the Buddhists and Hindus. The central shrine of the goddess is in Navagamuva in Sabaragamuva province. *Gammaḍuva,* "hall in the village" and *aṅkeḷiya,* "horn game" are the two ritual expressions of the cult. The former is a postharvest thanksgiving ritual performed by the priests of the Pattiṉi cult known as *kapurālas*. The aṅkeḷiya is, on the other hand, a ritual game in honor of the goddess in which the entire village participates. The *pantis kōlmura,* "thirty-five songbooks," comprise the ritual texts of the cult, and they primarily deal with the myths relating to Pattiṉi. These texts are available in Hevawasam (1974)[105] They incorporate Pattiṉi into a Buddhist ethos.

Among the Tamil-speaking Hindus of the Eastern province, especially Batticaloa district, Pattiṉi is worshiped as Kaṇṇaki Ammaṉ. An annual festival, the Vaikāci caṭaṅku, is celebrated in Vaikāci (May–June) in her honor when the song, *Kaṇṇaki vaḻakkurai* (Kaṇṇaki's Demand for Justice), is recited. Another ritual song, *Kaṇṇaki Ammaṉ kuḷirtti pāṭal* (The Song of the Cooling of the Goddess Kaṇṇaki), ends on this uplifting note:

> Let everyone praise the *Cilappatikāram*
> Whose words are sweet as honey.
> Let them, daily, sing those songs forever.
>
> Let those who, today and forever,
> Honor this great story live forever.[106]

It is believed that the Kālī-Bhagavatī temple in Koṭuṅkoḷūr, Cranganore district, Kerala was originally a Pattiṉi shrine. Pilgrims visiting the temple refer to the goddess as *oṟṟaimulaicci,* "the woman with one breast," even though this description does not fit the deity. Chummar Choondal reports that the female pilgrims "remove their bodice and expose their naked breasts" while singing and dancing.[107] Pattiṉi, as Obeyesekere reminds us, is the only goddess in Indian mythology with one breast.[108] Likewise, Taṭātakai may well be the only Hindu goddess with three breasts, one of which disappears when she meets Śiva, her future husband. In her discussion of the Hindi oral epic *Ālhā,* Karine Schomer mentions the temple of the goddess Śāradā Devi in Maihar, Madhya Pradesh built on the spot where one of Pārvatī's breasts fell. The temple commemorates the myth of the goddess' dismemberment.[109] The German ethnographer Hermann Ploss narrates an interesting legend about St. Agatha (3d c. C.E.) that states she had her breasts dismembered for refusing the Consul Quintianus. Ploss also mentions that during the festival of Hathor, the Egyptian Mother Goddess, held at Dendera on New Year's Day when her image was taken out in procession the two ritual events were the unveiling of her breasts and their display to her followers.[110]

A genre of Malayalam folk songs, the *tōṟṟam pāṭṭu,* "the song of origin," tells the story of Kōvalaṉ and Kaṇṇaki. These songs have been collected from southern Kerala by G. Sankara Pillai.[111] It therefore appears from Obeyesekere's study that the cult of the goddess Pattiṉi is alive in Kerala in southwestern India and in Sri Lanka, even though it no longer survives in Tamiḻnāṭu.

In view of the paramount important of the myth, it is not improbable that the three stages in Kaṇṇaki's apotheosis furnished Iḷaṅkō with a basis for composing the poem in three parts: the erotic, the mythic, and the heroic, set in the three Tamil kingdoms of the time. Given the Jaina interest in numbers, it is not surprising to find everything occurring in groups of three or multiples of three. Thus there are three principal characters, three kings (*mūvēntar*), three religions, and three books of the poem, comprising thirty cantos.

The Jaina Background

Kaṇṇaki's apotheosis is foretold by the goddess Maturāpati in canto 23 where she explains to her the circumstances surrounding Kōvalaṉ's unexpected death. In a former birth, Kōvalaṉ, as one Bharata, had given up his "vow/ Of nonviolence" (23.160–61) and murdered an innocent merchant, Caṅkamaṉ, whom he had mistaken for a spy. Caṅkamaṉ's wife, Nīli, raved for fourteen days. She cursed Kōvalaṉ and took her own life by jumping off a cliff. The reference to Bharata's "vow/ Of nonviolence" (Ta. *kollāviratam;* Skt. *ahiṃsāvrata*), a cardinal doctrine of Jainism, and one which it carried further than either Hinduism or Buddhism, is one of the many indications that suggest the Jaina provenance of the poem. A layman (*śrāvaka*) takes this vow in the presence of his teacher with the words, among others: "As long as I live, I will neither kill nor cause others to kill."[112] The goddess attributes Kōvalaṉ's death to his karma (23.176–78), again a law that the Jainas developed further than either the Hindus or Buddhists.

A Tamil scholar, Cinnaiah Govindarajan, spent eighteen years (1945–63) trying to identify the places mentioned in the *Cilappatikāram.*[113] He claims that the Maṅkalatēvi temple (30.84) in the Maṅkalatēvi Hills in the High Waving Mountain (Curuḷimalai) of the Western Ghats, about ninety miles to the west of Maturai, is the original temple of Pattiṉi *(Pattiṉikkōṭṭam)* built by Ceṅkuṭṭuvaṉ on the site of Kaṇṇaki's ascension (28.222–37).

After burning down Maturai, Kaṇṇaki vows:

Till I see the husband
My heart has known, I will neither sit nor stand.
(23.185–86)

She visits the temple of Koṟṟavai, and ceremoniously breaks her gold bracelets. Indian women, even today, on the death of their husbands, break or remove the bangles on their wrists. Kaṇṇaki then leaves Maturai for ever.

Along the bank of the Vaiyai in flood she wandered,
Unconscious of night or day. Sad
And inconsolable, unaware when she fell
Into a ditch or climbed a slope, she walked
Step by painful step up the sacred hill
Of Neṭuvēl who swirls the long, fierce spear. . . .
In the shade of a grove of flowering kino trees,
She cried:
"Oh! I am a great sinner."

Thus passed fourteen days. Indra,
Lord of the immortals, with other gods
Thought that day to be right for worship,
Praised the glorious name of this revered woman,
Rained unfading flowers upon her, and adored her.
In a heavenly chariot, by the side of Kōvalaṉ
Slain in the royal city, Kaṇṇaki, her hair
Thick as a forest, ascended to heaven.
(23.191–208)

Govindarajan writes that Kaṇṇaki climbed the "steep hill (Neṭuvēl) and fasted unto death under a vēṅkai tree."[114] There is no reference to Kaṇṇaki's death by fasting either in the text or commentaries. But the idea is not improbable given the Jaina context of the poem. The Jaina nun Kavunti starves herself to death (27.95–96 [*uṇṇānōṉpu,* 27.83]) on hearing of Kōvalaṉ and

Kaṇṇaki's fate. She was, in fact, their spiritual counselor and felt herself responsible for the unfortunate turn of events. Kavunti, as a devout Jaina, undertakes a ritual death by fasting (*sallekhana,* "properly thinning out [the passions and the body]"),[115] enjoined on Jainas in special circumstances. Fasting is a way of spiritual purification. There are references to the practice of death by starvation (*vaṭakkiruttal,* "sitting [facing the] north") in *Puṟanāṉūṟu* 65, 66, 214, 218–20, 223 and 236, and in *Akanāṉūṟu* 55.[116] A king starves himself to death facing the north to atone for his loss of face. Cēramāṉ Peruñcēralātaṉ resorted to vaṭakkiruttal when he was wounded on the battlefield. The *Mahābhārata* and the *Rāmāyaṇa* furnish examples of the practice of death by starvation (*prāya*). In the *Mahābhārata,* a king says:

> Sinner that I am, I will sit here and dry up my body. Know that I have now entered death (*prāya upaviśṭaḥ*) in order that I may not be born in other births, a destroyer of family. I will not eat, I will not take water, I will stay here and dry up my dear life.[117]

The king punishes himself for his sin, and welcomes death as an expiation. Warriors in the *Rāmāyaṇa* who have failed in their duty to the king do likewise.[118] E. Washburn Hopkins remarks that "those intending to die touch water and lie on holy *darbha* grass (the ends of the grass pointed south), with their faces to the east."[119]

In the grove of kino trees on Neṭuvēl Hill, Kaṇṇaki confesses: "Oh! I am a great sinner" (23.200). As a wife, she is only too conscious of the fact that she had failed to protect her husband. A vow to end her life by fasting or to undertake severe penances is not an improbable response under the circumstance. Even Mātavi, who was no more than Kōvalaṉ's paramour, on hearing of his death enters a Buddhist nunnery and takes the holy vows (27.18–20).

Again, the god who is present at Kaṇṇaki's apotheosis is Indra. He comes down from heaven, rains unfading flowers upon her by way of adoration, and takes her to heaven in the company of Kōvalaṉ. By the time of the poem, Indra had ceased to be an important god in the Hindu pantheon. He had become, on the other hand, the foremost god of the Jainas and Buddhists. The presence of Indra (Śakra) is, therefore, no fortuitous coincidence but, rather, one more instance of the poem's

Jaina orientation. Indra's importance in the poem is further attested by the description, in cantos 5 and 6, of the god's festival (*Śakradhvajotthana,* "the raising of Indra's standard") as observed in Pukār for twenty-eight days in Cittirai (April-May). As Jan Gonda points out, the May Day festival, with its flower-wreathed maypole forming a center for sports and dances, is the European counterpart of this traditional Indian festival, which was celebrated as a sacrificial rite to ensure the king's welfare and his success in war.[120]

The *Cilappatikāram* offers further evidence of its Jaina ethos. The eponymous author of the poem is Iḷaṅkō Aṭikaḷ. An *aṭikaḷ* is a Jaina ascetic or mendicant (*camaṇācāriyar*) who combines monastic life and outside religious activity. Kōvalaṉ uses the honorific when he addresses the nun Kavunti (10.85). We can infer that both Kōvalaṉ and Kaṇṇaki are Jainas from Kavunti's words: "O you who have good features,/ A noble family, impeccable conduct,/ And observe the proper austerities enjoined/ By the holy words of the arhat" (10.59–62)! The term *arhat,* from the verbal root *arh,* "to be worthy," means "worthy of worship" and is used for a Jaina or Buddhist sage who has reached the stage of enlightenment (*kevalajñāna*). Kavunti herself is on her way to Maturai "to worship the arhat there" (10.79). On reaching the outskirts of that city, Kavunti entrusts Kaṇṇaki, who accompanies her along with Kōvalaṉ, to the care of the herdswoman Mātari. The latter tells her daughter Aiyai: "Since he is/ A pious Jaina householder, let us have/ New vessels that Kaṇṇaki needs/ To make his lunch with the help of her husband's sister" (16.19–22). There are references to an elevated stone platform, built by the Jaina householders (*śrāvaka*s) of Pukār, for arhats to teach dharma from (10.19–21, 10.220–22, 15.163–66); to sages (10.217, 10.261, 15.172) or cāraṇars, whom Cāminātaiyar identifies as Jaina or Buddhist mendicants;[121] to the five holy letters (10.134) or *pañca-namaskāra-mantra,* a prayer to the five holy ones: arhat, *siddha* (perfected being), *ācārya* (spiritual leader), *upādhyāya* (preceptor) and *sādhu* (mendicant), represented by the symbols *a, si, ā, u* and *sā;* and to peacock feathers (10.133) or *piñcchi,* a whisk broom that Jaina monks and nuns carry for dusting the places they sit on to ensure that no insects are harmed.

Iḷaṅkō introduces the Jaina doctrine of karma as a structural element in the narrative. Kōvalaṉ's death is attributed to the karma of his former birth (23.153–81), and Kaṇṇaki's tragedy to her failure to keep a vow on Kōvalaṉ's behalf in a former birth (9.83–88). An explanation such as this diffuses the focus of the poem by subjecting characters to a force outside themselves and over which they have no control. The *Vipāka-śrutam* (The Oral Tradition of Karmic Fruition), one of the sixty Āgamas or canonical scriptures of the Jainas, deals exclusively with karma. Jainism divides all existing things into two classes: *jīva,* "sentient," and *ajīva,* "insentient." The jīva is unable to realize its true nature because of its association with ajīva. This is the work of karma, a subtle matter that collects on the jīva, embroiling it in an endless cycle of birth, death, and rebirth. The jīva can rid itself of its karmic associations by the practice of austerities (*tapas*) and attain nirvana, release from bondage. Jainas believe that karmas can, through tapas, be consciously matured before their time, and shed.

The law of karma functions as a dominant motif in the poem. This is borne out by the many references to it:

1. "His karma now appeared, and found an excuse in the music of the lute. He took his caressing hands off her. . ." (7:52).

2. "In the pitch darkness/ Of that final quarter Kōvalaṉ set out/ With Kaṇṇaki, his mind moved by his karma" (10.4–6).

3. ". . . karma is inexorable./ It makes us experience what should be avoided./ Like a seed when planted it will sprout/ And fulfill itself. When its time is ripe,/ It will be impossible to stop it" (10.230–34).

4. "Avoid evil deeds,/ For you will taste their fruits. Strong/ Indeed is karma" (14.35–37).

5. "O the wrong done to Kaṇṇaki's husband/ By inexorable karma warped the Pāṇṭiyaṉ's scepter/ That was never once bent in this world" (16.230–32)!

6. "When actions performed/ In a former life by the wicked bear fruit/ No penance can reverse it" (23.176–78).

The sage's sermon to Kavunti at Śrīraṅkam (10.229–60) and Kavunti's exhortation to Kōvalaṉ (14.30–55) are characteristically Jaina in their ethical thrust. The sage stresses that karma is inexorable and life uncertain. Therefore it behoves every Jaina to rid himself of his or her karma through the intercession of an arhat: "No one can escape the prison-house/ Of the body's rebirth unless he is blessed/ With the light of the revealed Āgamas" (10.258–60).

The poem's bias in favor of Jainism shows itself in Kavunti's response (11.182–94) to the brahman Māṭalaṉ's counsel to Kōvalaṉ (11.71–179) on their way to Maturai. Māṭalaṉ urges ablutions in three holy lakes in order to know Indra's grammar and one's karmas from former births, and to acquire the power to fulfill all one's wishes. In reply, Kavunti tells Māṭalaṉ that the Jaina Āgamas contain everything he has spoken about. On this friendly note, they part company.

Jaina tradition ascribes the origin of Jainism in southern India to Bhadrabāhu, the great ācārya, and Emperor Candragupta Maurya (4th c. B.C.E.) who on his abdication became a monk (*muni*). To escape a famine then ravaging Magadha, they traveled south to the Kannada country with their followers. Their exodus split the Jaina community into the Digambara, "sky-clad," and Śvetāmbara, "white [cotton]-clad" sects. It was Digambara Jainism that was practiced in Tamiḻnāṭu. Inscriptions at Śravaṇa Beḷgoḷā, Hāssana district, Karnataka refer to Bhadrabāhu's journey to the south with twelve thousand disciples.[122] Candragupta, we are told, ritually starved himself to death in accordance with the Jaina practice. We learn from the *Digambara-darśana* (The Philosophy of the Digambaras) that Vajranandi, a disciple of the ācārya Pūjyapāda, founded a Drāviḍa Saṃgha in Maturai in 470 C.E. for the propagation of Jainism. We can infer from this that Jainas enjoyed the patronage of the Pāṇṭiya kings.[123]

During its heyday in southern India, from the second to the sixth century C.E., Jainism was not only the dominant religion, but the Jaina contribution to Tamil literature was exceptional. The Chinese Buddhist pilgrim, Hsuan-tsang, reports in his *Buddhist Records of the Western World* (*Si-yu-ki*) on the popularity of Jainism in southern India in the early seventh century.[124] The *Cilappatikāram* is thus a mine of information on the condition of Jainas in the Tamil country.

Though the religious underpinnings of the poem are to be found in Jainism, Iḷaṅkō is not intolerant of the orthodox religions. There is, in fact, a great deal of religious eclecticism in the poem that perhaps reflects the situation in Tamiḻnāṭu at the time of its composition.

Hindu Myths: Kṛṣṇa and Cāttaṉ

We examined above the Jaina myth of the goddess Pattiṉi. Here we shall look at two Hindu myths and their implications for the story of Kōvalaṉ and Kaṇṇaki: the myth of Gopāla-Kṛṣṇa in canto 17, and that of Cāttaṉ (Aiyaṉār) in cantos 9 and 30.

In canto 17 Kōvalaṉ, leaving Kaṇṇaki in the care of the herdswoman Mātari on the outskirts of Maturai, departs for the city to sell the anklet. Strange occurrences take place in his absence in the village of the cowherds (*āyarpāṭi*). Taking them for bad omens, Mātari's daughter, Aiyai, fears "Some evil is about to happen" (17.2). It is then that Mātari suggests that they perform one of the boyhood dances (*vāla carita nāṭakaṅkaḷ*) of Kṛṣṇa, Balarāma, and Piṉṉai ("she with the plaited hair") to remove any danger to the village. At this point, except perhaps for Kaṇṇaki, none of them is aware of the danger to Kōvalaṉ's life. Seven herdswomen perform the round dance (*kuravai*) to recreate a famous episode in the life of Kṛṣṇa where he tames seven bulls and marries the women, including Piṉṉai, who raised them. The myth itself survives in the custom of herdswomen, each choosing a bull from the stable and raising it until the time she is married. The herdsman who is able to tame the bull in an open contest earns the right to the woman's hand. V. R. Ramachandra Dikshitar, to whom I owe this information, reports that this custom survives in the festival of Māṭṭuppoṅkal ("the ceremonial boiling of rice to ensure the prosperity of cattle") observed on the second day of Tai (January–February), but without any relation to marriage.[125] Mātari gives each of the seven herdswomen the name of a musical note: Sa, Ri, Ga, Ma, Pa, Dha, Ni. In addition, Sa plays Kṛṣṇa; Ri, Balarāma; and Ga, Piṉṉai. They recreate in song and dance other famous episodes in the life of Kṛṣṇa: Kṛṣṇa becomes a dwarf and takes three steps to trick the demon Bali; he churns the ocean with the Mandara as the churning-stick and the serpent Vāsuki as the rope; he opens his mouth, and his foster mother Yaśodā sees the entire universe inside; he steals the clothes of the herdswomen of Gokula, including Piṉṉai, and is troubled when he sees the look of distress in Piṉṉai's eyes. They also eulogize the Pāṇṭiya, Cōḻa, and Cēral kings for their upright rule and identify each of them with Kṛṣṇa. The canto ends with the herdswomen praising Kṛṣṇa to his face and behind his back.

The incorporation of the myths relating to Kṛṣṇa clearly indicates the extent to which the Tamil worldview had, by the fifth century C.E., been Sanskritized. It offers evidence of the cult of Kṛṣṇa worship in the Tamil country that was to find its noblest expression in the hymns of the *āḻvār*s (6th–9th c. C.E.), the Vaiṣṇava bhakti poets. This aspect of the Kṛṣṇa story, Kṛṣṇa as Gopāla, is first told in the *Harivaṃśa* (300 C.E.), and later expanded in the *Viṣṇu-purāṇa* (4th–5th c. C.E.) where the god's acts are regarded as play (*līlā*). The Gopāla literature culminates in the *Bhāgavata-purāṇa* (9th–10th c. C.E.), the spiritual fountainhead of the cult.[126]

It is ironic that while Kṛṣṇa in the oral tradition wins Piṉṉai after taming the bulls, Kaṇṇaki, for whom the herdswomen expressly perform the round dance of Kṛṣṇa, loses her husband Kōvalaṉ, the god's namesake who is unable to tame his karmic bulls. Kōvalaṉ is killed as a result of a plot by the king's goldsmith.[127] Cāttaṉ (Skt. Śāstā) is the tutelary deity of the village in Tamiḻnāṭu, and has his shrine on its outskirts. In iconography he is represented as a sea-blue god, riding on a white elephant or a black horse, with a whip in his hand, his banner sporting the figure of a cock. His consorts are Pūraṇai and Puṭkalai.[128] Canto 9 speaks of his temple (20–21) in Pukār along with those of Murukaṉ, Indra, and the Nirgrantha, indicating the religious eclecticism of the Cōḻa capital. He is referred to as *Puṟampaṇaiyāṉ* (9.12), one who lives outside the limits of the town. In the Tamil tradition, Cāttaṉ is the offspring of Śiva and Viṣṇu which accounts for his name Hariharaputra. In the *Cilappatikāram,* however, we learn that he is raised in a brahman family of the Kāvya-gotra (30.78–80), that he is learned in the ninety-six heretical doctrines (*pāṣaṇḍaḥ*) (9.24; 30.67), and that he marries one Tēvanti with whom he lives for eight years (30.80–82). On the death of his foster parents, he performs their funeral rites and settles all family disputes among their relations (9.47–50). Then he reveals his divine form to his wife and vanishes into his temple, urging her to visit him there (9.53–55; 30.82–83). Tēvanti spends the rest of her life in the worship of Cāttaṉ. Later, when Māṭalaṉ is in the temple of Maṅkalatēvi, Cāttaṉ appears before him as a brahman. He brings him water from the pools near the temple and leaves (30.59–63).

During the dedication of the memorial stone for Kaṇṇaki,

Cāttaṉ once again appears before Māṭalaṉ. He speaks to him, in the presence of Ceṅkuṭṭuvaṉ, through Tēvanti. He tells him about the miraculous powers of the water he had earlier brought him. If sprinkled on people, it would help them remember their previous births (30.65–68). He asks Māṭalaṉ to sprinkle the water on the twin daughters of Araṭṭaṉ Ceṭṭi, and on Cēṭakkuṭumpi's daughter; the two fathers are employed in the service of the god Viṣṇu at Āṭakamāṭam in the suburbs of Vañci. When the holy water falls on them, the three girls remember their previous births and begin to sob. One remembers herself as the mother of Kaṇṇaki; another, as the mother of Kōvalaṉ; and the third, as Mātari, the herdswoman (30.90–109). These miracles indicate Cāttaṉ's compassion for the unfortunate. The myth also illustrates the ideal of *vairāgyam,* "freedom from desire," that releases one from the endless cycle of birth, death, and rebirth. Because of their attachment to Kaṇṇaki, all three women were reborn. The poem is explicit on this point (30.118–31). Iḷaṅkō once again seizes the opportunity to underscore the doctrine of karma. In this instance, he uses a Hindu myth to do so. "It is not uncommon that people who do good/ Enter heaven, and that people who are attached/ To things of this earth are reborn" (30.132–34).

While the apotheosis of Kaṇṇaki is the primary myth in the poem, Iḷaṅkō is not averse to exploring the myths of the orthodox religions. The myth of Gopāla-Kṛṣṇa is Sanskritic and originates in the great tradition; the myth of Cāttaṉ is Tamil and has its roots in the little tradition of village India. Despite the Jaina bias of the poem, Iḷaṅkō is not an apologist for Jainism. He is fair in his presentation of the Hindu worldview.

The Tamil Idea of Kingship

In spite of its epic and therefore conventional status, the poem is politically subversive. In the Tamil worldview, even a king is not spared if he swerves from dharma. The humblest of his subjects is allowed to interrogate him. The ideal Tamil king is basically a protector (*kāppālar*). This is the sole reason for his existence. Mōcikīraṉār (2d c. C.E.) expresses the idea memorably:

> No, rice isn't life. Not even water.
> The nation's life-blood is the king.

With his army of many spears, it is his task
to know, "I am the life of this wide, open world."
Mōcikīraṉār, *Puṟanāṉūṟu* 186[129]

The Tamil idea of kingship can be gathered from Iḷaṅkō's references to it in all three books. The Cōḻa king is an exemplary ruler. A statue in the public square in Pukār weeps "Whenever swerved/ The king's scepter, and preference was shown/ In court by favoring one side/ Against the rule of law" (5.163–67). Iḷaṅkō eulogizes Pukār as rivaling heaven itself. Maturai, on the other hand, is steeped in pleasures. As Iḷaṅkō tells us, "Even sages turned into young men/ As they pursued these women . . ." (14.198–99). The Pāṇṭiya king bypasses the law; he has Kōvalaṉ executed without a trial in his anxiety to be reconciled to the queen who at that moment feigns a quarrel with him. The king's rashness costs him his life, and Maturai itself goes up in flames.

Of the three kings, it is the Cēral king Ceṅkuṭṭuvaṉ alone who has the ear of our poet. Ceṅkuṭṭuvaṉ describes what kingship entails:

To forswear tyranny and ensure the welfare
Of his subjects is the king's duty. Born
Of a noble line, suffering is his lot. His throne
Is not to be envied (25.103–106)

This idea is elaborated in a discourse on kingship by the goddess Maṇimēkalai for the benefit of Prince Utayakumāraṉ in *Maṇimēkalai:*

If the king swerved from the rule of law,
The planets would step out of line.
If the planets stepped out of line,
The rains would fail. If the rains failed,
Life on the earth would cease. It would be true
To say: "One who rules the world as a king
Should look upon every life as his own."
Maṇimēkalai 7.8–12[130]

She emphasizes the close bond between the king and his subjects on the one hand, and between the king and the cosmos on the other, and underlines the importance of the rule of law for an orderly universe.

Ceṅkuṭṭuvaṉ marches to northern India to realize his vision

of a Tamil imperium that would extend over the subcontinent. In fact, his minister Villavaṉ Kōtai even goes a step further by proclaiming: "No one can stop you, if you wish,/ From imposing Tamil rule over the entire world . . ." (25.171–72). As a universal emperor, Ceṅkuṭṭuvaṉ establishes his hegemony first, by performing the rājasūya, royal sacrifice, and second, by dedicating the memorial stone for the goddess Pattiṉi. The royal consecration implies that he is now a king of kings (*rājādhirāja*) and divinely ordained. The dedication implies that Pattiṉi is now the tutelary deity of his kingdom and that he is under her protection. Ceṅkuṭṭuvaṉ thus sees himself as uniting the three Tamil kingdoms culturally into a single nation (*Tamiḻakam*). Thus, both the king and the goddess become defenders of the realm.

It is no coincidence that Iḷaṅkō is the younger brother of King Ceṅkuṭṭuvaṉ, however apocryphal the kinship might be. Ceṅkuṭṭuvaṉ legitimized the cult of the goddess by building a temple for her worship, thus acknowledging her as the tutelary deity of the Cērals. This is one of the two themes of "The Book of Vañci." Ceṅkuṭṭuvaṉ's victory over the kings of northern India is the other. In keeping with this tradition, would it not be appropriate that a member of his own family compose a māhātmya, a poem in praise of the goddess' power? Such an effort would certainly redound to the glory of the Cēral royal family, besides offering evidence of religious eclecticism in the kingdom.

Commending Ceṅkuṭṭuvaṉ for performing the "sacrifice of war," the brahman Mātalaṉ urges him to perform the "great sacrifice/ With the help of priests versed in the four Vedas" (28.176–77) before it is too late. By performing the royal sacrifice (rājasūya), as Gonda notes, the king is able to identify himself with the gods, especially Indra, the god of rain and fertility.[131] During the celebration of Indra's festival in Pukār, elderly women perform a circular dance round Indra's standard, and chant a prayer:

> May the king of this great land
> Sustaining his kingdom be rid of hunger,
> Disease and enmity. May he be blessed
> Abundantly with rain and prosperity.
>
> (5.85–88)

Early Tamil kings performed Vedic sacrifices to confirm their sovereignty.

Fired by imperial ambition, Ceṅkuṭṭuvaṉ hopes to be a universal emperor. It is, therefore, necessary that he undertake a *digvijaya,* "the conquest of the four quarters." The universal emperor had a special place in the cosmic scheme and was considered to be semidivine. Both Yudhiṣṭhira and Rāma were universal emperors and their example was an inspiration to others. This is one of the many instances in the *Cilappatikāram* that attests to the incorporation of northern, Sanskritic ideas into the Tamil worldview.

In order to fulfill his ambition, Ceṅkuṭṭuvaṉ marches north with the ostensible aim of getting a stone from the Himālaya for Kaṇṇaki's image. Like his father, Imayavarampaṉ Neṭuñcēralātaṉ, he too would carve his emblem, the bow, on its slopes. There are references throughout the poem to Tamil kings marching to northern India and engraving their insignia on the slopes of the Himālaya. This accounts for the epithets *imayavarampaṉ,* "he who has the Himālaya for his boundary," and *vānavarampaṉ,* "he who has the sky for his boundary" that adorn the names of many of these kings, for instance, Imayavarampaṉ Neṭuñcēralātaṉ. Again, Ceṅkuṭṭuvaṉ himself brings the stone for the goddess Pattiṉi's image from the Himālaya, and he makes the Ārya kings, Kanaka and Vijaya, carry it on their heads to the banks of the Gaṅgā. Karikālaṉ, and Ceṅkuṭṭuvaṉ are not just local rulers, but monarchs fired with imperial ambitions. A symbolic march to the Himālaya is, therefore, an appropriate gesture every Tamil king indulged in.

The poem is avowedly ethnocentric. The Tamil kings regarded the kings of northern India with scorn. Ceṅkuṭṭuvaṉ's supposed conquest of northern India, described in cantos 26 and 27, is however an invention of the poet, as P. T. Srinivasa Aiyangar reminds us.[132] There are, however, references in early Tamil poems to the Mauryan invasion of southern India—in *Akanāṉūṟu* 251 and 281 by Māmūlaṉār (3d c. C.E.); in *Akanāṉūṟu* 69 by Paraṅkoṟṟaṉār; and in *Puṟanāṉūṟu* 175 by Kaḷḷil Āttiraiyaṉār.[133] Māmūlaṉār reports:

> The wheels of their bright chariots rolled
> through the Aṟaivāymoḻi Pass, flattened
> by their vast army. Thus descended the Mauryas
> on the battlefield—those strangers to our land.
> Māmūlaṉār, *Akanāṉūṟu* 251.11–14[134]

It was a psychological response to the memory of the Aryan penetration of the south, including Aśoka's, that had culminated in the Kaliṅga War of 260 B.C.E. Historically, the three Tamil kingdoms remained independent of the Mauryan hegemony.[135]

We can see here the beginnings of Tamil separatism that has manifested itself in the mid-twentieth century. Pāratitācaṉ expresses the euphoric mood of the Tamils at the time:

> I rejoice in being able to say:
> "I am not an Aryan."
> Pāratitācaṉ, "Iṉappeyar"[136]

The story of Kōvalaṉ and Kaṇṇaki, from the repertoire of the Tamil oral tradition, provided Iḷaṅkō with a splendid opportunity for fleshing out his intention. It is a fact that the Tamils regard the *Cilappatikāram* as their national epic, a work as uniquely indigenous to the Tamil worldview as the *Tirukkuṟaḷ*.

Following the tradition of Tamil heroic poetry, Iḷaṅkō vividly evokes the war in bold overstatements:

> As a famished lion
> Stalking for prey rejoices at the sight
> Of a herd of elephants, so did Ceṅkuṭṭuvaṉ rejoice
> Seeing his foes march toward him. Wreathed
> In a garland of portia, he hurled his troops
> Against the enemy. The canopy of banners eclipsed
> The sun's rays. The earth trembled. (26.193–99)

The reference to the "garland of portia" (kāñci) indicates the poetic situation (tiṇai) as kāñci, struggle for excellence. We must remember that Ceṅkuṭṭuvaṉ is out to establish himself as a universal emperor, and the poet does not hesitate to pull out all the figurative stops.

The *Rāmāyaṇa* shares the Tamil idea of kingship; the *Iliad* does not. In the *Rāmāyaṇa,* Sītā, the wife of Rāma, king of Ayodhyā, is forcibly abducted by Rāvaṇa, king of Laṅkā. Rāma and his brother Lakṣmaṇa then invade Laṅkā, kill Rāvaṇa, and burn down the city. On his return to Ayodhyā, Rāma bows down to the pressure of his subjects who suspect that Sītā, during her long absence, may have been violated by Rāvaṇa. This, of course, is not true. Rāma does not, however, accept Sītā back. An enraged Sītā (whose name means the "furrow") then demonstrates her innocence by asking Mother Earth to open and receive her. The Earth opens and accepts Sītā. Rāma by his unusual conduct as a king establishes the rule of dharma even at the expense of giving up his wife on suspicion.

The Trojan War begins as a result of Paris carrying away, with her full consent, Helen, the wife of Menelaus, king of Sparta, when he was a guest at the king's court. Paris thus violates the host-guest relationship that is founded on mutual respect and trust. When Paris returns to Troy, Priam, his father, does not reprimand him, nor does he ask him to restore Helen to her husband, Menelaus. Thus the seeds of both domestic and social disorder are sown by this act. By not acting honorably, Priam has forfeited, at least in the Indian tradition, his rights as a king. All hell breaks loose as the Greeks storm the city of Troy. Hector, Priam's favorite son and heir, is killed by Achilles and his body is dragged around the walls of Troy. Priam himself visits Achilles in his tent at night, unseen as an interloper, to beg for the return of his son's body. This is one of the most heart-rending scenes in the *Iliad.* He clasps Achilles' knees, kisses his hands, and speaks:

> Honor then the gods, Achilles, and take pity upon me
> remembering your father, yet I am still more pitiful;
> I have gone through what no other mortal on earth has gone through;
> I put my lips to the hands of the man who has killed my children.
> *Iliad* XXIV.503–506[137]

Priam's family and kingdom are in shambles. If only he had exercised his judgment and restrained Paris, the war with the Greeks could have been averted.

Both the *Rāmāyaṇa* and the *Iliad* are Indo-European epics, but they differ in their idea of kingship. The *Iliad* was composed 600 years earlier than the *Rāmāyaṇa,* when it is possible that notions of kingship among the Indo-European peoples were not sufficiently developed. One thing, however, is clear. The king as the embodiment and upholder of dharma has to have an upright character. If he swerves, he brings ruin on himself, his family, and his kingdom.

The *Cilappatikāram,* a Dravidian epic, shares the *Rāmāyaṇa*'s concern for the uprightness of kings. Neṭuñceḻiyaṉ, the Pāṇṭiya king, puts Kōvalaṉ to death without a trial at the instigation of his goldsmith. Kōvalaṉ is innocent of the theft of the queen's anklet. We learn in canto 16 that the queen has had a quarrel with the king who is, as a result, in a foul mood. The goldsmith informs the king just at that moment that he has apprehended the thief, whereas in fact it is the goldsmith who is the culprit. The king is taken in by the goldsmith's deception and immediately, without a trial, orders Kōvalaṉ's execution. Acting on hearsay and impulse, the otherwise exemplary king is responsible for a serious miscarriage of justice. Having failed to uphold and protect dharma, the king forfeits his life. Even the queen is not spared. Maturai itself, like Laṅkā and Troy, goes up in flames. The poet then explains the king's conduct in terms of the ripening of his karma. The fire cleanses the kingdom and dharma is once again restored. Now a widow, Kaṇṇaki has no reason to live. Fourteen days after the death of her husband she ascends to heaven, exalted as a goddess.

The Discovery of Tamil India

We owe our knowledge of the *Cilappatikāram* and other early Tamil poems to an unusual man who redrew, very much on his own, the literary map of India in the late nineteenth century. Uttamatāṉapuram Vēṅkaṭacuppiramaṇiya Cāminātaiyar was born on February 19, 1855 in the obscure village of Cūriyamūlai in Tañcāvūr district, Tamilnāṭu, the son of Vēṅkaṭacuppiramaṇiya Aiyar and Sarasvatī Ammāḷ. He had no formal education to speak of, as his father was a musician who traveled from one village to another and supported himself by the patronage of local landowners. Early in life Cāminātaiyar had decided to study Tamil instead of English, the key to advancement under the raj. The opportunity to study Tamil with the foremost scholar of his time, Tiricirapuram Mīṉāṭcicuntaram Piḷḷai (1815–76), presented itself in 1871 when Cāminātaiyar was seventeen. Three years earlier, on June 16, 1868, he had married Maturāmpikā, a distant relation. During the next five years Mīṉāṭcicuntaram prepared the groundwork for Cāminātaiyar's knowledge of Tamil. Cāminātaiyar himself tells the story of their warm relationship in his autobiography, *Eṉ carittiram* (1950; *The Story of My Life,* 1980).[138] After the death of his guru, he taught at the Tiruvāvaṭuturai monastery at the invitation of its head, Cuppiramaṇiya Tēcikar, who had now become his patron. On February 16, 1880, Cāminātaiyar was appointed, on the recommendation of Tiyākarāca Ceṭṭiyār, to succeed him as Tamil pandit at the Government College, Kumpakōṇam, a town renowned for its old temples.

Neither Cāminātaiyar nor his guru was aware of the existence of the classics that are the glory of Tamil. Then on October 21, 1880, he met Cēlam Irāmacuvāmi Mutaliyār (1852–92) who had come to Kumpakōṇam as a munsif or district judge on a transfer from Ariyilūr. "My auspicious stars," Cāminātaiyar writes, "conducted me to him. His friendship proved a turning point in my life. As a result of this, I had my first view of the vast expanse that is ancient Tamil poetry" (243). Mutaliyār specifically asked him if he had read *Cīvakacintāmaṇi, Maṇimēkalai,* and the *Cilappatikāram.* He had to confess that he had not. Mutaliyār told him that these and other poems had provided the inspiration for the religious texts that Cāminātaiyar had read with his guru. That fateful day, a new planet had swum into Cāminātaiyar's ken, and he was to become its first intrepid explorer. Four days later, Mutaliyār put in his hands a manuscript copy of *Cīvakacintāmaṇi* (Cīvakaṉ, the Wish-Fulfilling Jewel, 10th c. C.E.), a Jaina poem, and asked him to study it in hopes of Cāminātaiyar's teaching it to him. Cāminātaiyar published *Cīvakacintāmaṇi* in 1887 in a royal octavo edition of 500 copies. He had the book printed at Tirāviṭa Ratṉākara Press in Madras. With the publication of *Cīvakacintāmaṇi,* Cāminātaiyar had begun his life's work of restoring to print the heritage of the Tamils that had for centuries slumbered in palm leaves unbeknownst to them.

Two of Cāminātaiyar's illustrious contemporaries had, however, preceded him in his field: Āṟumuka Nāvalar (1822–79) had, in 1861, published the *Tirukkuṟaḷ* (The Holy Kuṟaḷ, 4th c. C.E.), and Ci. Vai. Tāmōtaram Piḷḷai (1832–1901) had, in 1887, published the *Kalittokai* (The Anthology in the *Kali* Meter, 4th–5th c. C.E.), one of the *Eṭṭuttokai.* These early texts were of immense value to historians who used them to reconstruct the history of Tamil India. Tiru. Vi. Kaliyāṇacuntaram eloquently sums up the contributions of these three great Tamil scholars: "Āṟumuka Nāvalar laid the foundations for the recovery of the classical Tamil texts; Tāmōtaram Piḷḷai raised its walls; and Cāminātaiyar put on its roof and made it into a temple."[139]

From the earliest times, manuscripts were written on palm

leaves of which two varieties were in use: the leaves of the palmyra palm (*Borassus flabellifer*), and those of the talipot or South Indian fan-palm (*Corypha umbraculifera*). The usual width of the first is between 1 and 1¾ inches; that of the second, between 1¾ and 3 inches.[140] Tamil manuscripts were generally written on palmyra palm leaves. Though paper had been introduced into northern India from Samarkand by the Muslims in the fifteenth century, scribes continued to use palm leaves, as the latter had the sanction of age and religion.[141] When Mutaliyār moved to Madras he presented Cāminātaiyar with his manuscript copy of the *Cilappatikāram.* Cāminātaiyar's subsequent odyssey in search of the manuscripts of the poem took him to the remotest villages in Tamiḻnāṭu. One such village he visited was Karivalamvantanallūr in Tirunelvēli district. He had been told that the manuscripts of King Varakuṇa Pāṇṭiyaṉ were deposited in the local temple of Pālvaṇṇa Nātar. He inquired about the location of the manuscripts from an official and was enraged to be told: "You know, sir, it is said that it is improper to let old-time scripts lie about; and that the proper way to dispose them of is to dip them in ghee and offer them dutifully to the god of fire. That is exactly what was done here" (323). In Tirunelvēli itself he was told of other novel ways by which owners got rid of the burden of manuscripts in their possession. One of them piled up all his manuscripts to look like a temple-car and floated them down the river. In another village, a Śaiva religious leader insisted that the title of the poem was really *Ciṟappatikāram!*

Manuscripts elsewhere have not fared better. The poems of Catullus (c. 84–54 B.C.E.), the Roman poet were all but lost for twelve hundred years. According to tradition, the original manuscript, the *Codex Veronensis,* from which all our texts of the poet derive, was discovered in Verona at the end of the thirteenth century, being used to plug a wine barrel.[142] Literary history records other instances of manuscripts that disappeared only to resurface hundreds of years later.[143] In the course of his search, Cāminātaiyar was eventually able to find eight manuscript copies of the text, including two from Jaffna, Sri Lanka, and fourteen copies of an old commentary on the poem by Aṭiyārkkunallār, a medieval scholar. He collated these extant copies in order to establish as far as possible what the author wrote, and prepared the critical edition, which he handed over to the printers, V. N. Jubilee Press, Madras, in June 1891. He provided, in the preface, a census of the manuscripts.

MS	*Location*	*Provenance*
A	Tiricirapuram	Ci. Mīṉāṭcicuntaram Piḷḷai
B	Mitilaippaṭṭi	Aḻakiya Ciṟṟampalak Kavirāyar
C	Tirunelvēli	Cālivāṭīcuvara Ōtuvār
D	Āṟumukamaṅkalam	Kumāracāmip Piḷḷai
E	Tiricirapuram	Aṇṇācāmip Piḷḷai
F	Tirumayilai	Aṇṇacāmi Upāttiyāyar
G	Yāḻppāṇam (Jaffna)	Ti. Kumāracāmi Ceṭṭiyār
H	Yāḻppāṇam (Jaffna)	Vi. Kaṉakacapaip Piḷḷai

MS "B" from Mitilaippaṭṭi helped Cāminātaiyar to correct several incorrect readings and provided titles for many of the songs (334). No other details, especially about the manuscript traditions of the poem, are given.

For Cāminātaiyar, it was an uphill task deciphering the palm-leaf manuscripts (*ēṭṭuccuvaṭi*). The commentary was usually written around the text, often running into the text, and it was difficult to tell one from the other. There were also scribal errors in calligraphy and spelling to contend with. The two "r's," the flapped /r/ and the trilled /ṟ/, were seldom distinguished. Sometimes a palm leaf (*ōlai*) would simply crumble into dust as he picked it up, its succulence drained away by generations of termites. Such were the travails Cāminātaiyar put up with as he collated several manuscripts, and pored over them night after night into the small hours, a hurricane lamp by his side, in the pial of his rented house in Bhaktapuri Agrahāram, Kumpakōṇam. Through the critical edition, he attempted to provide for the first time a single text of the work as close as possible to what he thought the author had written. To Cāminātaiyar we owe the beginnings of textual criticism in Tamil, rudimentary though it was. In a famous passage in his autobiography, Cāminātaiyar speaks of his devotion to the books he edited for press:

> I looked upon the book I had taken up for printing as an image to be worshiped. All I desired to do was to remove the accretions of dirt, and see the image properly attired. It was not for me to take upon myself the work of setting a crooked arm right, or altering the shape of a fingernail. I felt that the image was instinct with divinity most vividly

from head to foot; and that it was one thing to scrub the dirt away, and quite another to alter the formation of its limbs (287–88).

This passage sums up his editorial method of letting the texts "retain the shape in which they were originally cast . . . without [his] meddling" (288) with them.

Both *Cīvakacintāmaṇi* and the *Cilappatikāram* were issued on subscription. He asked subscribers who responded to his proposal to pay the price of the book in advance to enable him to decide on the print run and defray the cost. Often, when subscribers did not pay on time, he had to borrow to settle the printer's bill.

Though Cāminātaiyar's was the first complete edition of the *Cilappatikāram* to be published, an edition of the *"Pukārkkāṇṭam"* ("The Book of Pukār") only, the first of the three books that comprise the poem, by Cōṭacāvatāṉam Cupparāyar Ceṭṭiyār, with Aṭiyārkkunallār's commentary, appeared in 1872. It was followed in 1876 by another edition of the *"Pukārkkāṇṭam"* only, without the commentary, by T. E. Cīnivācarākavāccāriyār. Cāminātaiyar published the *Cilappatikāram* in 1892. This was its first appearance in print after being in circulation in manuscript for fourteen hundred years. It can, therefore, be considered the editio princeps. In fact, all the classical Tamil works that Cāminātaiyar published were editiones principes. Besides the usual editorial matter, the book included Aṭiyārkkunallār's commentary (for cantos 1 through 6, and cantos 8 through 20). In the second edition, published in 1920, he included the old glossary, the *Arumpatavurai.* He tells us, characteristically: "Now that the beloved Tamil Muse had put on her anklets again, and my readers were exhorting me to burnish the other jewels also for me to deck her with, I began to weigh in my mind what publication would be the most suitable to follow the *Cilappatikāram*" (352). *Maṇimēkalai* (Jeweled Girdle, 6th c. C.E.) appeared in 1899. Other works followed, and were published by Cāminātaiyar, after 1903, under the imprint of Tiyākarāca vilācam, named after his house in Madras.

Cāminātaiyar's Himālayan labors in the collection[144] and dissemination of manuscripts are comparable to those of Coluccio Salutati (1331–1406), Chancellor of Florence and a colossus of the Renaissance. A bibliophile, Salutati ransacked the monasteries of northern Italy for Latin manuscripts buried there. He had them edited and translated, and thus gave the ancient Greek and Latin writers a new birth.[145] In 1903, Cāminātaiyar was transferred to Presidency College, Madras where I taught English in 1966–67. A statue of Cāminātaiyar graces the campus on the Marina, overlooking the Bay of Bengal. He continued to teach there until his retirement in 1919. For the next 23 years, he labored untiringly to find and publish the Tamil classics. For a brief period (1924–27), he was the Principal of Śrī Mīṉāṭci Tamil College, Citamparam. He died at the age of 87, on April 28, 1942 at Tirukkaḻukkuṉṟam, near Madras, where he had temporarily moved following the Viceroy Lord Linlithgow's call to evacuate the city in the face of a possible Japanese invasion in October of that year.

Translating the *Cilappatikāram*

During the summer of 1942, as the Second World War threatened to engulf India, I lived with my grandmother in Śrīraṅkam, an island in the Kāviri, to which my imagination constantly returned. Together with the Vaiyai, the Kāviri is the lifeblood of Tamiḻnāṭu, and has always been on the lips of poets. That summer, I began my study of Tamil in a *pāṭacālai,* traditional school, that met for a few hours every morning in the pial of a house on West Chitra Street. Over the years I continued my Tamil studies with pandits.

This translation of the *Cilappatikāram* into modern English verse is one way of acknowledging the debt I owe Tamil, my mother tongue.[146] My assimilation of Iḷaṅkō, the author of the *Cilappatikāram,* is another form of translation—rewriting a poem in English I could not myself write in Tamil. I envied Iḷaṅkō his great epic, and the only way I could possess the poem, make it my own, was to rewrite it in English. By making Iḷaṅkō speak in the accents of English, I hope I have breathed life into the poem and awakened it from its enforced sleep in Tamil.

The Tamil Language

Tamil is the oldest of the four major Dravidian languages, and is spoken mainly in Tamiḻnāṭu in south-eastern India. The language was regularized around 250 B.C.E., and it is this standard language (*centamiḻ*) that is described in the *Tolkāppiyam*. However, the earliest Tamil poetry goes back to a period between 100 B.C.E. and 250 C.E. and is found in numerous anthologies that were later gathered together in two great collections: the *Eṭṭuttokai* (The Eight Anthologies) and the *Pattuppāṭṭu* (The Ten Long Poems).

Throughout its history, Tamiḻnāṭu was relatively isolated and free from the invasions that swamped the rest of the country, except for a brief Muslim interlude (1324–70 C.E.) in Maturai. Though the Aryanization of southern India had been going on since the first millenium B.C.E., Tamiḻnāṭu (and Kerala) were not united with the rest of India till the British period. Again, Tamil, among all the Indian languages, has resisted Sanskritization by preserving archaic features of phonology and morphology. As a result, the spoken and written forms are different from each other. Unlike other Dravidian scripts, Tamil orthography has resisted the inclusion of special characters for writing down Sanskrit sounds.

Tamil is an agglutinative language like Finnish, Japanese, Magyar (Hungarian), and Turkish. Such languages form their derivatives by a process of fusion. Suffixes, themselves meaningful elements, are added to a noun or verb to inflect its meaning. For example, the Tamil word *paṭittatilēyiruntu,* "from what was read," comprises the following elements:

paṭi	*-tt*	*-at*	*-il*	*-ē*
to read	(past tense)	(3rd per. sing. neuter)	(locative case)	(emphatic)

-y	*-iru*	*-ntu*
(phonetic insertion)	to be	(past tense)

Words are thus built up by piling one suffix on top of another.

Again, Tamil and English have distinct phonologies that resist translation from one to the other. Classical Tamil has eighteen phonemic consonants as opposed to twenty-four in modern English. The same letters are used for voiced, unvoiced, and aspirated forms. Tamil has no sibliants (/s/, /ś/, /ṣ/) or aspirates (/h/). However, the dental stop /t/ (as in *tāmarai,* "lotus"), the retroflex stop /ṭ/ (as in *kaṭai,* "shop"), the retroflex lateral /ḷ/ (as in *kaḷvaṉ,* "thief"), the retroflex palatal lateral /ḻ/ (as in *paḻam,* "fruit"), the alveolar trill /ṟ/ (as in *aṟivu,* "knowledge"), the dental nasal /n/ (as in *cantu,* "lane"), the retroflex nasal /ṇ/ (as in *kaṇ,* "eye"), and the palatal nasal /ñ/ (as in *pañcu,* "cotton") are not found in English. Double consonants are frequent in Tamil (as in *kappal,* "ship"; *vaṭṭam,* "circle"). In English they are enunciated only between words (as in fas*t* *t*rain, gol*d* *d*igger). Initial and final consonant clusters (as in *spl*endid, *tr*ibe, ha*tch,* plu*mp*), typical of English, are unknown in Tamil. Again, Tamil has only two diphthongs (/ai/, /au/), whereas English revels in them. Tamil has long and short vowels; English has stress which tends to forward whenever it can. Stress being phonemic, it determines, for example, the noun and verb functions of the same homographs: PERmit (n.), perMIT (v.).

Two examples, one each from English and Tamil, chosen at random, bring home to the translator the impossibility of reproducing their distinctive acoustic features. Lines such as these simply defy translation.

> The moan of doves in immemorial elms,
> And murmuring of innumerable bees.
> Tennyson, *The Princess* 7:206–7[147]

> puḷḷāṅ kuḻalkoṇṭu varuvāṉ—amutu
> poṅkit tatumpunar̲ kītam paṭippāṉ;
> kaḷḷal mayaṅkuvatu pōlē—ataik
> kaṇmūṭi vāytir̲an tēkēṭ ṭiruppōm.
> Pārati, *Kaṇṇaṉ pāṭṭu* 9[148]

Turning to syntax, we find that the normal order of words in an English sentence is SVO (subject + verb + object). In Tamil and other Dravidian languages, the word order is SOV (subject + object + verb): *nāṉ puttakam paṭittēṉ* ("I a book read" instead of "I read a book"). Of course, such a construction is not unusual in English; it occurs in poetry as an inversion: "For thy sweet love remembʼred such wealth brings" (Shakespeare, "Sonnet 29").[149] The inversion of the normal order of words (anastrophe) is a rhetorical device used for dramatic effect. It takes many forms: (1) subject after verb ("Unkempt about those hedges blows/ An English unofficial rose"—Rupert Brooke, "The Old Vicarage, Grantchester"); [150] (2) object before subject ("Nature I loved, and, next to Nature, Art"—Walter Savage Landor, "Dying Speech of an Old Philosopher"); [151] (3) verb after adverbial clause ("When lilacs last in the dooryard bloom'd"—Walt Whit-

506 சிலப்பதிகாரம் [உ. மதுரைக்காண்டம்

விழுவோ ளிட்ட வழுவில் சாபம்
பட்டனி ராதலிற் கட்டுரை கேணீ
உம்மை வினைவந் துருத்த காலைச்
செம்மையி லோர்க்குச் செய்தவ முதவாது
†வாரொலி கூந்தனின் மணமகன் றன்னை
ஈரேழ் நாளகத் தெல்லை நீங்கி
வானோர் தங்கள் வடிவி னல்லதை
ஈனோர் ‡வடிவிற் காண்ட லில்லென
மதுரைமா தெய்வ மாபத் தினிக்கு
விதிமுறை சொல்லி யழல்வீடு கொண்டபின்
கருத்துறு கணவர் கண்டபி னல்ல
திருத்தலு ¶மில்லே னிற்றலு மிலனெனக்
கொற்றவை வாயிற் பொற்றொடி தகர்த்துக்

171 - 2. உம்மைவினை......யுதவாது - உம்மையிற் செவ்விய மனமில்லாதோர்க்கு அக்காலத்துச் செய்தவினை வந்து பலிக்குங்காலத்து முன்பு செய்த நல்வினை யாதும் உதவாது; இத்தீவினைவந்து கொடுப்பதற்கு முன்னே வந்துதவுதல் பின்புதவுதல் செய்யுமித்தனை; அந்நல்வினையும் உதவாமற் போகாது; பாவமானதும் தனியே அனுபவிக்க வேண்டும்.

176. ஈனோர் - ஈங்குள்ளோர். 176 - 8. இல்லென்று மதுரைமா தெய்வம் சொல்ல.

181. பொற்றொடி - பொலிவினையுடைய சங்க வளை; துர்க்கை கோயில் வாயிலிலே தன்கைவளையைத் தகர்த்து.

அடி, 138 - 9 : இச்சாபவரலாற்றை இப்படியே **மணிமேகலையில்** வஞ்சிமாநகர்புக்க காதையிலும்மணிமேகலைக்குக் கண்ணகி கூறியதாகக் கூறினர்; அது வருமாறு :—" வேட்கை துரப்பக் கோட்டம் புகுந்து, வணங்கி நின்று குணம்பல வேத்தி, அற்புக்கட னில்லாது நற்றவம் படராது, கற்புக்கடன் பூண்டு நுங்கடன் முடித்த, தருளல் வேண்டுமென் றழுதுமுன் னிற்ப, ஒருபெரும் பத்தினிக் கடவுளாங் குரைப்போள், எம்மிறைக் குற்ற விடுக்கண் பொறாது, வெம்மையின் மதுரை வெவ்வழற் படுநாள், மதுராபதியெனு மாபெருந் தெய்வம், இதுநீர் முன்செய் வினையின் பயனாற், காசில் பூம்பொழிற் கலிங்கநன் னாட்டுத், தாய மன்னவர் வசுவுங் குமரனும், சிங்கபுரமுஞ் செழுநீர்க் கபிலையும், அங்காள் கின்றோரடற்செரு வுறுநாள், மூவிரு காவத முன்னுந ரின்றி, யாவரும் வழங்கா விடத்திற் பொருள்வேட்டுப், பல்கலங் கொண்டு பலரறி யாமல், எல்வளை யாளோ டரிபுர மெய்திப், பண்டக் கலம்பகர் சங்கமன் றன்னைக், கண்டனர் கூறத் தையனின் கணவன், பார்த்திபன் றொழில்செயும் பரத னென்னும், தீத்தொழி லாளன் றெற்றெனப் பற்றி, ஒற்ற னிவனென வுரைத்து மன்னற்குக், குற்றமி லோனைக் கொலைபுரிந் திட்டனன், ஆங்கவன் மனைவி யழுதன ளரற்றி, ஏங்கிமெய் பெயர்ப்போ ளிறுவரை யேறி, இட்ட சாபங் கட்டிய தாகும், உம்மை வினைவந் துருத்தலொழி யாதெனும், மெய்ம்மைக் கிளவி விளம்பிய பின்னும், சீற்றங் கொண்டு செழுநகர் சிதைத்தேன் " (5 : 34). அடி, 173 : 6. மு : சிலப். பதிகம், 50 - 53.

(பி - ம்.) † 'வாருறு கூந்தன்மணமகன்' ‡ 'வடிவினிற்' ¶ 'மிலனே யிறத்தலும்'

Figure 3. Text of the *Cilappatikāram:* "The Book of Maturai. Canto 23: The Explanation," lines 179–83 (corresponding to lines 185–90 of the translation), with U. Vē. Cāminātaiyar's commentary.

கீழ்த்திசை வாயிற் கணவனொடு புகுந்தேன்
மேற்றிசை வாயில் வறியேன் †பெயர்கென
இரவும் பகலும் மயங்கினள் கையற்
றுரவுநீர் வையை யொருகரைக் கொண்டாங்
‡கவல வென்னா ளவலித் திழிதலின்
¶மிசைய வென்னாண் மிசைவைத் தேறலின்
கடல்வயிறு கிழித்து மலைநெஞ்சு §பிளந்தாங்
கவுணரைக் கடந்த சுடரிலை நெடுவேல்
நெடுவேள் குன்ற மடிவைத் தேறிப்
பூத்த வேங்கைப் பொங்கர்க் கீழோர்
தீத்தொழி லாட்டியேன் யானென் றேங்கி
எழுநா ளிரட்டி யெல்லை சென்றபின்
தொழுநா ளிதுவெனத் ||தோன்ற வாழ்த்திப்
பீடுகெழு நங்கை பெரும்பெய ரேத்தி
வாடா மாமலர் மாரி பெய்தாங்
கமரர்க் கரசன் றமர்வந் $தேத்தக்

---

183. தமியேனாய்ப் பெயராநின்றேனெனச் சொல்லி.

184. இரவும் பகலுமயங்கினள் - இரவும் பகலும் அறியாது மயங்கி.

186. பதறி இழிதலாற் குழியென்று பார்க்கிலள்.

190. நெடுவேள்குன்று - திருச்செங்கோடு. அடிவைத்தேறி யென்றார், அதற்குமுன்பு வருத்தத்தாற் கால் நிலத்துப் பாவாமையால்.

191. வேங்கையின் கீழே நின்றென்க.

192. குறத்தியர்கேட்கத் தீத்தொழிலாட்டியேன் யானென்று சொல்லி; ஏங்கியென்றது - சொல்லியென்றபடி.

193. எழுநாளிரட்டி - வேங்கை நீழலினின்ற நாளளவு. எல்லை யென்றது பகலை. அவணின்ற நாளளவு, அன்று பதினாலாநாளாயிற்று. பதினாலாநாள் பகற்பொழுது சென்றபின் என்க; பதிகத்திலும், "ஈரேழ் நாளகத்தெல்லை" (51) என்றார்.

194-7. அமரர்க்கரசன் தமர்வந்து, கண்ணகி தன்கணவனைத் தோன்றவாழ்த்தித் தொழுநாளிதுவெனக்கருதி இவள்பெயரைச் சொல்லி மலரைத்தூவி ஏத்தினார்; இவள் பெயர் மந்திரோத்தியாதலால்; இன்னும், கண்ணகி கோவலனைத் தோன்றவாழ்த்தி வானவூர்தியேறினாளென்றுமாம்.

194-9. பெரும்பெயரேத்தி மலர்மாரிபெய்து தமர்வந்தேத்த வான வூர்தி ஏறினாளென்க.

அடி, 188-9: குறுந். கடவுள். 4-5. அடி, 190. நெடுவேள்: பெரும்பாண். 75.

அடி, 193-4. மு: 163-4. அடி, 197: சிலப். பதி. 6.

(பி-ம்.) † 'பெயர்வனென்று' ‡ 'கவலென்னாளலைத்திழிதலின்' ¶ 'மிசையாமென்னாண்' § 'பிளந்தே யவுணரை' || 'தொழுது வாழ்த்திப்' $ 'தேத்திக்'

man;[152] (4) preposition after noun ("It was young David, lord of sheep and cattle/ Pursued his fate, the April fields among"—Stella Benson, "Five Smooth Stones").[153]

The verb, in Tamil, is usually in the final position. What are the implications, then, for translation into a non-OV language such as English? The inverted word order has to be normalized in English.

Let us look at an example from the *Cilappatikāram* written in the Tamil script (figure 3), followed by a transcription in roman type. Whatever its origins, Iḷaṅkō's Tamil was not a spoken language. He appears to have embalmed the speech of the pāṇaṉs, who kept alive orally the tradition of the story of Kōvalaṉ and Kaṇṇaki. The diction is elitist and courtly, which is perhaps understandable, as the realm of the epic's passage are the three kingdoms: the Cōḻa, the Pāṇṭiya, and the Cēral.

I. karutturu kaṇavar kaṇṭapi ṉalla
tiruttalu millē ṉiṟṟalu milaṉeṉak
koṟṟavai vāyiṟ poṟṟoṭi takarttuk
kīḻtticai vāyiṟ kaṇavaṉoṭu pukuntēṉ
mēṟṟicai vāyil vaṟiyēṉ peyarkeṉa. (23.179–83)

Let us then separate the constituent elements in each line, and translate them. The virgules indicate phrase/clause boundaries that are marked by Arabic numerals.

II. karuttu-uṟu kaṇavar kaṇṭa-piṉ allatu
iruttalum illēṉ ṉiṟṟalum ilaṉ-eṉa-k
koṟṟavai vāy-iṟ poṉ-toṭi takarttu-k
kīḻ-t-ticai vāy-iṟ kaṇavaṉ-oṭu pukuntēṉ
mēl-ticai vāy-il vaṟiyēṉ peyark(u)-eṉa.

III. /[my] heart-has known [the] husband I have seen-after till/[2]
/sitting there is no standing there is no/[3]-/thus [Kaṇṇaki] vowed/[1]
/[of] Koṟṟavai temple-in [the] [her] golden-bracelets breaking/[4]
/[the] East Gate-through [my] husband-with I entered [this city]/[6]
/[the] West Gate-by/[7b]/[and] grieved/[5] /I leave [now alone]./[7a]

This is how the lines appear in my English version.

IV. Kaṇṇaki vowed:

"Till I have seen the husband
My heart has known, I will neither sit nor stand."

Her golden bracelets she then broke in the temple
Of Koṟṟavai, and wept:
"With my husband
I entered this city through the East Gate:
I now leave by the West Gate, alone." (23:185–90)

English has blurred the focus of the Tamil original as the latter's phonetic template has all but vanished. A brief description of Tamil meter is now in order.

Meter in the *Cilappatikāram*

Classical Tamil prosody developed independently of Sanskrit and is based on totally different principles.[154] The most important of them is the *acai* (*acaital,* "to move, stir"), a metrical unit that comprises one or more syllables (*eḻuttu*). It is unique to Tamil and is not known to Sanskrit prosody. There are two types of acais: the *nēr* and the *nirai.* The *nēracai* is a simple metrical unit of one syllable, long or short (CV̄[C] or CV̆[C]). The *niraiacai* is a compound metrical unit of two short syllables, or of one short syllable followed by a long syllable (CV̆CV̆[C] or CV̆CV̄[C]). It therefore follows that the nēracai may be long or short, and that the first of the two syllables of the niraiacai is always short. However, a short syllable is considered long if it occurs alone, or if it is the final syllable in a foot. Also, if the first syllable in a foot is short, the one following it is considered short, even if it has a long vowel. A nēr is represented here by the symbol (¯), and a nirai, by the symbol (⁼).

A combination of two or more metrical units gives us the *cīr,* "foot." Usually, four feet make up a line (*aṭi*) of poetry. A foot, as a rule, comprises only one word, or words that are closely related. Thus, word boundary and prosodic boundary tend to coincide. It is the line of four feet that predominates in three of the four standard meters: *āciriyam, veṇpā,* and *kali.* Thus a line in the āciriyam meter has four feet or eight acais. A fourth meter, the *vañci,* differs from the other three in that its foot comprises three acais instead of two. The normal vañci line has two feet of six acais.

Besides acai, the other important principle of Tamil prosody is *toṭai,* the stringing together of metrical units into feet and lines. The devices commonly used for the purpose are *etukai,* initial rhyme; *iyaipu,* final rhyme; and *mōṉai,* alliteration. Rhyme in Tamil is in the beginning of the line: the second syllables in each of two or more lines are identical. Final rhyme is the exception in classical Tamil poetry. As regards alliteration, the letter that begins each line should at least begin one other foot in the same line. It is, however, enough if one of its class begins one of the other feet. For vowels, the classes are: (1) a, ā, ai, au; (2) i, ī, e, ē; and (3) u, ū, o, ō. Toṭai is thus the art of knitting together lines to compose a song (*pāṭṭutoṭuttal*). *Toṭuttal* and *yāttal* are other words used in this connection. They are similar to the Greek word *rhapsoidein,* "to rhapsodize," that is, "to stitch songs together."

While the number of acais in a foot is fixed at two, three, or four, the number of syllables in a foot varies. This is because the acai varies from one to two syllables. The rhythm (*ōcai*) of Tamil poetry arises from the succession of acais, unlike that of English poetry, which is determined by the pattern of stressed and unstressed syllables. There is, nevertheless, a strong impression of stress in spite of the uneven number of syllables in a line. The ear recognizes four beats per line that usually fall in the first acai of each foot.

Each of the four Tamil meters has its own distinctive rhythm: *akaval,* "calling," for āciriyam; *ceppal,* "saying," for veṇpā; *tūṅkal,* "swinging," for vañci; and *tuḷḷal,* "tripping," for kali. These terms describe how the verses in the four meters sound to the ear when recited. Akaval, as the āciriyam meter was known earlier, is the oldest Tamil meter. It originated with the *akavunaṉ*s and *akavaṉmakaḷ*s, men and women of a specific clan who told the future. Thus akaval is a "prophetic utterance." Hart mentions that when the akavunaṉ prophesied, he held a bamboo staff in his hand called the *piṟappuṇarttuṅkōl,* "the staff which gives knowledge of the future."[155] As in the case of the Greek hexameter, the connection between meter and ritual existed in Tamil society as well. Āciriyam, with its strong impression of stress, was the meter of bardic poetry. It was recited to the accompaniment of a lute (*yāḻ*); this is clearly suggested by the term akaval to indicate the rhythm that is characteristic of this meter.

Talai, "linking," indicates the mode by which the end of one foot is linked to the beginning of another to form a line. Lines are bound together to form a stanza or verse-form (*pā*) of which there are four types: *āciriyappā, veṇpā, vañcippā,* and *kalippā.* Āciriyappā, the verse-form in the āciriyam meter, is the staple of classical Tamil poetry. Each line comprises four feet of the type known as *iyaṟcīr,* "natural foot," which is of four kinds: nēr nēr (¯ ¯), nirai nēr (= ¯), nirai nirai (= =), and nēr nirai (¯ =). Each of these feet has a mnemonic (*vāypāṭu*) named after a tree: *tēmā,* sweet mango (¯ ¯); *puḷimā,* sour mango (= ¯); *karuviḷam,* wood apple (= =); and *kūviḷam,* bael (¯ =).

A scansion of *Kuṟuntokai* 17 by Pēreyiṉ Muṟuvalār will make our discussion of Tamil meter clear.

	kūviḷam	*puḷimā*	*tēmā*	*kūviḷam*
	– =	= –	– –	– =
	nēr nirai	*nirai nēr*	*nēr nēr*	*nēr nirai*
1.	māveṇa	maṭalu	mūrpa	pūveṉuk
	karuviḷam	*puḷimā*	*kūviḷam*	*kūviḷam*
	= =	= –	– =	– =
	nirai nirai	*nirai nēr*	*nēr nirai*	*nēr nirai*
2.	kuvimukiḻ	erukkaṅ	kaṇṇiyum	cūṭupa
	puḷimā	*kūviḷam*	*puḷimā*	
	= –	– =	= –	
	nirai nēr	*nēr nirai*	*nirai nēr*	
3.	maṟuki	ṉārkkavum	paṭupa	
	puḷimā	*kūviḷam*	*tēmāṅkāy*	*puḷimā*
	= –	– =	– – –	= –
	nirai nēr	*nēr nirai*	*nēr nēr nēr*	*nirai nēr*
4.	piṟitu	mākupa	kāmaṅkāḻ	koḷiṉē.

When love rises to fever pitch,
men will even trot on palmyra stems
for horses; the unopened buds of the *erukkam*
they will wear round their heads like a chaplet
of flowers; endure the bad mouth
of the street; and even give up their lives.

Pēreyiṉ Muṟuvalār, *Kuṟuntokai* 17 [156]

The foot of three acais (¯ ¯ ¯) in line 4, known by the mnemonic *tēmāṅkāy,* "sweet mango fruit," belongs to a different type of feet, the *uriccīr,* "specific foot," and it commonly occurs in veṇpā and vañci meters.

Iḷaṅkō reveals consummate skill in his manipulation of Tamil sounds, as in the following verses in the akaval meter from the end of canto 1, which praise the Cōḻa king to the skies at the conclusion of Kōvalaṉ and Kaṇṇaki's wedding in Pukār. The rhythm has an incantatory quality that arises from the knitting together of the four kinds of natural foot into a complex sound pattern employing assonances and consonances, horizontally and vertically, to create a metrical grid. A scansion of the original verses in terms of their metrical feet and mnemonics is followed by the verses divided into their individual words and translated into English.

	tēmā	*puḷimā*	*karuviḷam*	*tēmāṅkāy*
	– –	= –	= =	– – –
	nēr nēr	*nirai nēr*	*nirai nirai*	*nēr nēr nēr*
1.	ippā	limayat	tiruttiya	vāḷvēṅkai
	tēmāṅkāy	*tēmā*	*karuviḷam*	*tēmāṅkāy*
	– – –	– –	= =	– – –
	nēr nēr nēr	*nēr nēr*	*nirai nirai*	*nēr nēr nēr*
2.	uppālaip	poṟkōṭ	ṭuḻaiyatā	veppālum
	karuviḷam	*puḷimā*	*kūviḷam*	
	= =	= –	– =	
	nirai nirai	*nirai nēr*	*nēr nirai*	
3.	cerumiku	ciṉavēṟ	cempiyaṉ	
	karuviḷam	*tēmā*	*karuviḷam*	*puḷimā*
	= =	– –	= =	= –
	nirai nirai	*nēr nēr*	*nirai nirai*	*nirai nēr*
4.	orutaṉi	yāḻi	yuruṭṭuvō	ṉeṉavē

	ippāl	*i*mayattu	*i*ruttiya	vāḷvēṅkai
1.	on this side	of the Himālaya	inscribed	tiger-emblem
	*uppāl*aip	poṉkōṭṭu	*u*ḻaiyatā	ep*pāl*um
2.	on the other side	golden crest	may abide	forever
	*ceru*miku	ciṉavēṟ	*ce*mpiyaṉ	
3.	great battle	fierce spear	Cempiyaṉ	
	*oru*taṉi	āḻi	*uruṭṭ*uvōṉ	eṉavē
4.	ever-victorious	wheel	whirl	thus chanted

May the t*i*ger-em*b*lem, inscr*ib*ed on the *b*row
Of the Himā*l*aya, dwe*ll* on its go*l*den crest

*F*orever. May Cem*p*iyaṉ, o*f* the s*p*ear *f*ierce
In the great batt*le*, *w*hir*l* his e*v*er-*v*ictorious *w*hee*l*.
(1.79–82)

Second-syllable rhyme (Ta. *etukai;* Skt. *dvitīyākṣaraprāsa*) is a characteristic feature of Tamil prosody. It is the repetition of the second syllable at the beginning of each couplet: *"pāl"* in lines one and two, and *"ru"* in lines three and four. It functions vertically. Then there are assonances (the repetition of similar vowel sounds) and consonances (the repetition of similar consonant sounds) that function horizontally in a line: *"i"* in line one and *"u"* in line two are assonances; *"pāl"* in line two, *"ce"* in line three, and *"ru"* in line four are all consonances. What we have here is a metrical grid in each couplet, as in a tapestry, formed by the linking together of sounds, both vertically and horizontally. Often the translation resembles the wrong side of the tapestry: the design is there but it is confused by extra threads. I have, to a limited extent, tried to imitate Iḷaṅkō's brilliant phonic effects in the translation: the assonances and consonances are all italicized. Though rhyme in English invariably occurs at the end of a line, initial rhymes are not uncommon. Sidney Lanier even offers an example of second-syllable rhyme in English:

We *weave* in the mills and heave in the kilns,
We sieve mine-meshes under the hills,
And *thieve* much gold from the Devil's bank tills,
To relieve, O God, what manner of ills?
Sidney Lanier, "The Symphony"[157]

Poetry begins where prose ends—at the edge of the word. It is the line, as the custodian of the syllable, that controls the shape of a poem. Vowels expand the line; consonants contract it. It is this diastolic and systolic flow of the line that keeps a poem breathing and alive on the tongue. The line, then, is the unit of composition in a poem, not the word. Words, those aggregates of vowels and consonants, fuse together to produce the line—the bloodstream of a poem. Every word in a line enters into an active relationship with every other word. The line is unthinkable without this lexical relationship. It is the divining rod that releases the wellspring of poetry.

Despite all the erosion that has occurred in translation, I have firmly held on to Iḷaṅkō's voice and anchored my English version to it. The voice often peaks as it does in the famous scene above where Kaṇṇaki leaves Maturai after burning it down. Translation is a necessary rite of passage. Exiled from its own language, the poem puts down roots in the host language to begin its life as an immigrant in hopes of eventually becoming a native.

A language and nation remember themselves best in a poem. The *Cilappatikāram* is the well of Tamil undefiled to which the Tamils return to witness their language and identity most vigorously asserted. In translating a poem, one translates nothing less than an entire culture with all its idiosyncrasies. Here is one. Traditionally, an Indian woman's life ends with the death of her husband. She removes the ornaments on her person, stops putting the *tilaka* on her forehead, and shaves her head to indicate her unholy status as a widow. Kaṇṇaki finds herself in this limbo when she vows in the temple of Koṟṟavai that she will not rest till she has seen her husband and ceremoniously breaks her golden bracelets. Iḷaṅkō turns this gesture, dictated by tradition, into a resonant symbol: earlier, in canto 20, Kaṇṇaki confronts the king with his injustice and in his presence breaks her anklet to establish her husband's innocence. The king collapses from the shock. So does his queen. And Maturai itself goes up in flames. Only then is Kaṇṇaki's wrath appeased. A woman's ornaments function metonymically as extensions of her power that even kings may not trifle with. The king rules only at the pleasure of his subjects. Such gestures as Kaṇṇaki's are culture-specific. There is no way a translator, short of erecting a babel of footnotes, can alert his or her English to them. But I want the poem to speak without choking itself on too many footnotes, though I appreciate the fondness some translators have for them.[158]

Translation is a way of reading a poem, of interpreting it in a second language. Given the differences between languages, not every feature of one language can be imitated by another. It is, however, possible to establish a family resemblance. Eventually, the differences are only of secondary importance. For as Max Picard said: "Languages seem like so many expeditions to find the absolute word."[159] Often a single poem may aspire to the status of the absolute word. Such a poem is the *Rāmāyaṇa*.

A translation must first abolish the word in one language before it attempts, with the word, to restore it in another language. Languages orbit by themselves in splendid isolation. Occasionally, they come into close proximity with one another, thanks to the daring of a translator. Translation ensures the survival of a language, even if its speakers have vanished from the face of the planet.

Notes

1. Brodsky, "The Child of Civilization," p. 123.
2. Kapilar, *Kuṟuntokai* 25, p. 60.
3. *Tolkāppiyam: Poruḷatikāram* 298.
4. James J. Y. Liu reports a similar pair of "inside"/"outside" words, *ch'ing* and *ching,* in Chinese poetics. *Ch'ing* refers to "emotion/inner experience," and *ching* to "scene/external world." The critic Hsieh Chen (1495–1575) notes: "The writing of poetry is based on *ch'ing* (emotion/inner experience) and *ching* (scene/external world): neither by itself can complete (poetry); neither is in conflict with the other. . . . When these fuse to become poetry, one can then sum up ten thousand forms with a few words." Quoted in Liu, *Chinese Theories of Literature,* pp. 40–41.
5. The Song of Songs, in Bates, *The Bible as Literature,* p. 778.
6. The Song of Songs, in Bates, *The Bible as Literature,* p. 780.
7. Maturaiyōlaikkaṭaik Kaṇṇampukuntārāyattaṉār, *Puṟanāṉūṟu* 350.
8. Rabin, "The Song of Songs and Tamil Poetry," pp. 205–19. I thank David Shulman for bringing this article to my attention.
9. Kākkaipāṭiṉiyār Nacceḷḷaiyār, *Puṟanāṉūṟu* 278, p. 453.
10. *Tolkāppiyam: Poruḷatikāram* 3.
11. *"tiṇai nilam kulaṉ oḻukkam,"* in the *Cūṭāmaṇinikaṇṭu* (The Crest-Jeweled Glossary) of Maṇṭalapuruṭaṉ (16th c. C.E.). Quoted in Zvelebil, *Tamil Literature* (1974), p. 37, fn. 77.
12. *Tolkāppiyam: Poruḷatikāram* 1.
13. *Tolkāppiyam: Poruḷatikāram* 51.
14. *Tirukkuṟaḷ* 1137.
15. Hardy, *The Mayor of Casterbridge,* pp. 198–216.
16. For an excellent introduction to Tamil poetics, see Hart, *The Poems of Ancient Tamil,* and Ramanujan, tr. *Poems of Love and War,* pp. 229–315.
17. See Zvelebil, *The Smile of Murugan,* pp. 92–93.
18. Manickam, "Harlots in Ancient Tamil Literature," pp. 340–43.
19. Pālaipāṭiya Peruṅkaṭuṅkō, *Kuṟuntokai* 231, p. 439.
20. *Akanāṉūṟu* 204, commentary. Cited in *Tamil Lexicon* (hereafter *TL*), p. 2495.
21. *Akapporuḷviḷakkam* 25. Cited in *TL,* p. 493.
22. *Akapporuḷviḷakkam* 36, commentary. Cited in *TL,* p. 600.
23. *Maturaikkāñci* 314. Cited in *TL,* p. 2631.
24. *Tolkāppiyam: Poruḷatikāram* 60.
25. Eliade, *Patterns in Comparative Religion,* p. 233.

26. *Puṟapporuḷveṇpāmālai* 3, 7. Cited in *TL*, p. 1167.
27. *Puṟapporuḷveṇpāmālai* 4, 9. Cited in *TL*, p. 3466.
28. *Puṟapporuḷveṇpāmālai* 3, 3. Cited in *TL*, pp. 976 and 3586.
29. *Tolkāppiyam: Poruḷatikāram* 63. Cited in *TL*, pp. 2874–75.
30. *Puṟapporuḷveṇpāmālai* 6, 5. Cited in *TL*, p. 1167.
31. *Puṟapporuḷveṇpāmālai* 7, 4. Cited in *TL*, p. 1862.
32. *Akanāṉūṟu* 13. Cited in *TL*, p. 3842.
33. *Puṟapporuḷveṇpāmālai* 8, 26. Cited in *TL*, p. 2900.
34. *Puṟanāṉūṟu* 373; *Puṟapporuḷveṇpāmālai* 8, 5. Cited in *TL*, p. 3117.
35. *Tolkāppiyam: Poruḷatikāram* 76. Cited in *TL*, p. 3304.
36. *Tolkāppiyam: Poruḷatikāram* 76. Cited in *TL*, p. 2725.
37. *Puṟapporuḷveṇpāmālai* 8, 2. Cited in *TL*, p. 3575.
38. *Piṅkalanikaṇṭu*. Cited in *TL*, p. 847.
39. *Tolkāppiyam: Poruḷatikāram* 79, commentary. Cited in *Tl*, p. 2871.
40. *Puṟapporuḷveṇpāmālai* 10, *kāñci* 1. Cited in *TL*, pp. 3266–67.
41. *Puṟanāṉūṟu* 372. Cited in *TL*, p. 3117.
42. *Puṟanāṉūṟu* 2, colophon. Cited in *TL*, p. 3620.
43. Heidel, *Gilgamesh Epic*, p. 70.
44. See Lopez, "The Crossroads Within the Wall," pp. 17–43. Cited in Ramanujan, "Toward an Anthology of City Images," pp. 239–40.
45. I thank A. K. Ramanujan for this information offered in a seminar on the *Cilappatikāram* at Harvard University, November 10, 1987.
46. Zimmer, *Myths and Symbols*, p. 186.
47. van Gennep, *The Rites of Passage*, p. 21.
48. McLuhan, "Tennyson and Picturesque Poetry," p. 280.
49. O'Flaherty, tr., *The Rig Veda*, p. 43.
50. *Cilappatikāram*, "The Prologue" 74.
51. *iyal-icai-nāṭakap-poruḷ-toṭar-nilaic-ceyyuḷ*. Quoted in Cāminātaiyar, ed., *Cilappatikāram*, p. 6. Te. Pō. Mīṉāṭcicuntaraṉ interprets the term *nāṭakam* as dance (*kūttu*) and his interpretation is followed here. See his *Kuṭimakkaḷ kāppiyam*, p. 77.
52. *Tolkāppiyam: Poruḷatikāram* 549.
53. Quoted in Winternitz, *Some Problems of Indian Literature*, p. 44.
54. Vaiyāpurip Piḷḷai, *Tamiḻ ilakkiya caritattil kāviya kālam*, p. 269.
55. Quoted in Cāminātaiyar, ed. *Cilappatikāram*, p. 5.
56. Vaiyāpurip Piḷḷai, *Tamiḻ ilakkiya caritattil kāviya kālam*, p. 272.
57. Mayilainātar (14th c. C.E.), in his commentary (*cūttiram* 387) on the *Naṉṉūl* (The Good Book, 13th c. C.E.), a medieval grammar, refers for the first time to the five great narrative poems (*aimperuṅkāppiyam*) without however naming them. It is Kantappa Tēcikar (19th c.) who mentions them by name: *Cīvakacintāmaṇi*, *Cilappatikāram*, *Maṇimēkalai*, *Vaḷaiyāpati*, and *Kuṇṭalakēci*. Mu. Aruṇācalam, however, considers this untenable and surmises that Mayilainātar had probably in mind, besides the first three, the *Peruṅkatai* and *Cūḷāmaṇi*, instead of the *Vaḷai-*

yāpati and *Kuṇṭalakēci*. See Aruṇācalam, *"Mutarkāppiyaṅkaḷ"* 1:93–135. The *Cilappatikāram* is also referred to in the Tamil tradition as a narrative poem of threefold Tamil, that is, poetry, music, and dance (*muttamiḻ-kāppiyam*), and a narrative poem with dance (*nāṭakak-kāppiyam*).

58. Mīṉāṭcicuntaraṉ, *Kuṭimakkaḷ kāppiyam*, pp. 27–43.

59. Rosenthal & Gall, *The Modern Poetic Sequence.*

60. Poe, "The Philosophy of Composition," p. 15. Quoted in Rosenthal & Gall, *The Modern Poetic Sequence*, p. 6.

61. Rosenthal & Gall, *The Modern Poetic Sequence*, pp. 6–7.

62. Brough, "Poetry in Classical Sanskrit," p. 95.

63. *Taṇṭiyalaṅkāram*, ed. Irāmaliṅkat Tampirāṉ.

64. See Pērāciriyar, commentary on *Tolkāppiyam: Poruḷatikāram* 419.

65. *avaiyaṭakkam, Tolkāppiyam: Poruḷatikāram* 419.

66. See *The Rāmāyaṇa of Vālmīki: An Epic of Ancient India. Vol. 1: Bālakāṇḍa*, tr. Goldman.

67. *Cilappatikāram*, "The Prologue" 101–102.

68. Quoted in Kane, *The History of Dharmaśāstra*, 2.1:567–68.

69. See Thurston, *Omens and Superstitions*, p. 71. Robert Graves also refers to this belief and writes that the punishment for looking at snakes coupling is to be turned into a homosexual. See his *Greek Myths*, 2:14.

70. *Tolkāppiyam: Poruḷatikāram* 492.

71. Cāminātaiyar, *Caṅkattamiḻum pirkālattamiḻum*, p. 45.

72. Pōntaip Pacalaiyār, *Akanāṉūṟu* 110, in Hart, tr., *Poets of the Tamil Anthologies*, p. 120.

73. Noble, "Narrative, Image, and Song in the *Cilappatikāram*," p. 45.

74. Ōrēruḻavaṉār, *Kuṟuntokai* 131, in Ramanujan, tr., *The Interior Landscape*, p. 59. A revised translation appears in Ramanujan, *Poems of Love and War*, p. 75.

75. Ōta Ñāni, *Kuṟuntokai* 227, in Ramanujan, tr., *The Interior Landscape*, p. 73.

76. Winternitz, *A History of Indian Literature*, 1:33–34.

77. *Der Rig-Veda aus dem Sanskrit ins Deutsche Übersetzt*, 2:258.

78. Heidegger, "The Nature of Language," p. 63.

79. Heidegger, "The Nature of Language," p. 66.

80. *Vyākaraṇa-mahābhāṣya* of Patañjali, ed. Kielhorn & Abhyankar, 3:58.

81. *Vākyapadīya* of Bhartṛhari, ed. Subramania Iyer, p. 201.

82. Ong, *Orality and Literacy*, p. 59.

83. Bakhtin, "Epic and Novel," p. 16.

84. Nilakanta Sastri, for instance, writes, "That poem [the *Cilappatikāram*] is best looked upon as the handling of an old popular saga which, like the *Rāmāyaṇa* of Vālmīki, threw into oblivion earlier versions of the story of Kōvalaṉ and his wife Kaṇṇaki, the model of chastity." See his "Early Tamil Literature," p. 62.

85. Noble, "The Tamil Story of the Anklet."

86. Besides the Tiyākarācacuvāmi temple, Noble mentions three other temples in Tamiḻnāṭu and Kerala that have images of Kaṇṇaki or traditions related to her worship: (1) a stone image in the Cellattamman temple in Maturai; (2) a family temple in Pūmpukār, consecrated in 1972; and (3) a shrine near Idukki, Kerala. See Noble, "The Tamil Story of the Anklet," pp. 113–14, fn. 9.

87. A term in feminist discourse made popular by the poet Adrienne Rich, who defines it as "the act of looking back, of seeing with fresh eyes, of entering an old text from a new critical direction." See her "When We Dead Awaken," p. 35.

88. Noble mentions a 1942 film of the *Cilappatikāram* titled *Kaṇṇaki,* with P. U. Ciṉṉappā as Kōvalaṉ, P. Kaṇṇampā as Kaṇṇaki, and N. S. Kiruṣṇaṉ as the goldsmith. See Noble, "The Tamil Story of the Anklet," p. 271, fn. 48.

89. Ong, "Oral Residue in Tudor Prose Style," p. 146.

90. *TL,* p. 691.

91. *Pañcatantra,* ed. Kielhorn and Bühler, 4&5:40.

92. *The Pañcatantra,* tr. Ryder, p. 432.

93. Frere, "Chandra's Vengeance," pp. 187–202.

94. Schorer, *William Blake,* p. 27–28.

95. A. K. Ramanujan in a seminar on the *Cilappatikāram* at Harvard University, November 10, 1987.

96. Eliade, *Patterns in Comparative Religion,* p. 101.

97. This dogma states that "the Virgin Mary, the Immaculate Mother of God, when the course of her life was finished, was taken up, body and soul, into the glory of heaven." Cited in Unger, *Unger's Bible Dictionary,* p. 702.

98. See Dumézil, *The Destiny of a King,* pp. 70–84.

99. See *The Mahābhārata, Book 5: The Book of the Effort,* tr. and ed. van Buitenen, pp. 395–413.

100. See Beck, "The Study of a Tamil Epic," p. 25.

101. *Akanāṉūṟu* 73, 1:277.

102. Quoted in Zvelebil, *The Smile of Murugan,* p. 216.

103. See Pandian, "The Goddess Kannagi," pp. 177–91.

104. John Milton, *A Mask,* p. 203.

105. Hevawasam, *Pantis kōlmurakavi,* p. 611.

106. Obeyesekere, *The Cult of the Goddess Pattini,* p. 588. I have made a few minor revisions in the translation.

107. Choondal, "The Kaṇṇaki Legend," p. 197.

108. Obeyesekere, *The Cult of the Goddess Pattini,* p. 536.

109. Schomer, "Paradigms for the Kali Yuga," p. 142, fn. 2.

110. See Weideger's selections from Hermann H. Ploss' ethnographic classic *Das Weib* (1885) titled *History's Mistress,* pp. 57–58.

111. Sankara Pillai, *Tōṟṟam pāṭṭukaḷ,* p. 188 & p. 201, fnn. 2 and 16.

112. Jaini, *The Jaina Path of Purification,* p. 173.

113. See Govindarajan, *A Flash of Light.*

114. Govindarajan, *A Flash of Light,* p. 6.

115. Jaini, *The Jaina Path of Purification,* p. 229. On sallekhana, see pp. 227–33.

116. Chakravarti, *Jaina Literature in Tamil,* pp. 18–19.

117. *Mahābhārata* XII. 27.23 ff. Cited in Hopkins, "On the Hindu Custom of Dying to Redress a Grievance," p. 153.

118. *Rāmāyaṇa* IV.53.12–13. Cited in Hopkins, "On the Hindu Custom of Dying to Redress a Grievance," p. 151.

119. Hopkins, "On the Hindu Custom of Dying to Redress a Grievance," p. 151, fn. 2.

120. Gonda, "The Indra Festival According to the Atharvavedins," pp. 206–207.

121. Cāminātaiyar, ed., *Cilappatikāram,* p. 278.

122. Chakravarti, *Jaina Literature in Tamil,* pp. 10–11, fn. 2, and Ramaswami Ayyangar & Seshagiri Rao, *Studies in South Indian Jainism,* pp. 19–24.

123. Ramaswami Ayyangar & Seshagiri Rao, *Studies in South Indian Jainism,* p. 52.

124. Nilakanta Sastri, *Foreign Notices of South India,* p. 427. See Hsuan-tsang, *Si-yu-ki: Buddhist Records of the Western World,* tr. Beal.

125. *The Śilappadikāram,* tr. Ramachandra Dikshitar, p. 230, fn. 1.

126. See Hein, "A Revolution in Kṛṣṇaism: The Cult of Gopāla," pp. 296–317.

127. For a discussion of this myth in Tamil literature, see Edholm & Suneson, "The Seven Bulls and Kṛṣṇa's Marriage of Nīlā / Nappi-NNai," pp. 29–53; Hudson, "Piṉṉai, Krishna's Cowherd Wife," pp. 238–61; and Hardy, *Viraha-bhakti,* pp. 170–83.

128. For a recent study of the cult of Cāttaṉ, see Dumont, "A Structural Definition of a Folk Deity of Tamil Nad," pp. 75–87.

129. Mōcikīraṉār, *Puṟanāṉūṟu* 186, p. 342.

130. *Maṇimēkalai* of Cīttalaic Cāttaṉār, ed. Cāminātaiyar, p. 201. The reference is to the Tamil edition.

131. Gonda, *Ancient Indian Kingship,* pp. 79 84.

132. Srinivasa Aiyangar, *History of the Tamils from the Earliest Times to A.D. 600,* p. 600–601.

133. See Raghava Aiyangar, "The Mauryan Invasion," pp. 33–43.

134. Māmūlaṉār, *Akanāṉūṟu* 251, 2:396.

135. See Nilakanta Sastri, *A History of South India,* pp. 88–89.

136. "āriyaṉ allēṉ eṉṉum pōtil/ ettaṉai makiḻcci! ettaṉai makiḻcci!" Pāratitācaṉ [Kaṉaka Cuppurattiṉam], "Iṉappeyar," in *Pāratitācaṉ kavitaikaḷ,* 2:91.

137. *The Iliad of Homer,* tr. Lattimore, p. 488.

138. Cāminātaiyar, *Eṉ carittiram.* An abridgement by Cāminātaiyar's student, Ki. Vā. Jakannātaṉ, was published in 1958 by Tiyākarāja vilācam, Madras. This was translated as *The Story of My Life* by

S. K. Guruswamy, and edited by A. Rama Iyer (Madras: Dr. U. V. Swaminathaiyer Library, 1980). Citations are from this edition, and are indicated in the text parenthetically by page number. *Eṉ carittiram* first appeared serially in 122 chapters in the Tamil weekly *Āṉanta Vikaṭaṉ* from January 1940 to May 1942. It covers the first 44 years of his life from 1855 to 1899.

139. Kaliyāṇacuntaram, *Vāḻkkaik kuṟippukaḷ,* 1:160.

140. Diringer, *The Book Before Printing,* pp. 358–61.

141. Schurhammer and Cottrel, "The First Printing in Indic Characters," p. 154.

142. Ellis, *Catulli Veronensis Liber,* p. xii. Ellis quotes Benevenuto de Campesanis (d. 1323) of Vicenza who commemorates the discovery in a Latin epigram:

> Ad patriam venio longis de finibus exul,
> causa mei reditus compatriota fuit.
> Scilicet a calamis tribuit cui Francia nomen,
> quique notat turbae praetereuntis iter.
> Quo licet ingenio vestrum celebrate Catullum,
> cuius sub modio clausa papyrus erat.

143. Thomas Traherne (1637–74), the English Metaphysical poet, languished in obscurity for over two hundred years till a London book collector, William T. Brooke, discovered two manuscripts in 1895, one a folio and the other an octavo, in one of the city's used bookstalls on Farringdon Street in the East End. The first half of the folio contained Traherne's poems, which were published in 1903 by Bertram Dobell. See Wade, ed., *The Poetical Works of Thomas Traherne,* pp. lxxxvi–xcii.

144. "At the time of his death, he was able to bequeath to the world of Tamil scholarship a treasure of immeasurable value, about 3,067 manuscripts (on palm leaf and paper) of literary works of a unique nature." T. V. Viswanatha Aiyar, "Publisher's Note," Cāminātaiyar, *The Story of My Life,* p. v.

145. See Witt, "Toward a Biography of Coluccio Salutati," *Rinascimento* 16: 19–34.

146. The earliest translation of the *Cilappatikāram* to appear in any language was in French. Julien Vinson, Professor of Modern Oriental Languages at the National and Special School, Paris, translated the prologue and three of the cantos (16 through 18) and included them in his *Légendes bouddhistes et djainas,* published in 1900 in Paris by G. P. Maisonneuve and Larose. Since then, translations have appeared in the following languages:

English	V. R. Ramachandra Dikshitar	Madras, 1939
French	Alain Daniélou and R. S. Desikan	Paris, 1961
Hindi	M. G. Venkatesan	Calcutta, 1965

Czech	Kamil V. Zvelebil	Prague, 1965
Russian	I͡Uriĭ I͡Akovlevich Glazov	Moscow, 1966
English	Alain Daniélou	London, 1967
Malayalam	Nenmāṟa P. Viśvanāthannāyar	Trichur, 1975
English	Ka. Naa. Subramanyam	Delhi, 1977

Daniélou's English translation, with line drawings by K. K. Hebbar, was first published in *The Illustrated Weekly of India,* 27 September 1964–17 February 1965. There are, again, a few retellings in English, notably, A. S. Panchapakesa Ayyar, *Kōvalaṉ and Kaṇṇaki: The Story of the "Cilappatikāram"* (Madras, 1947); R. K. Narayan, "The Mispaired Anklet," in *Gods, Demons, and Others* (Mysore, 1964), and Lakshmi Holmström, *Kannagi* (Bombay, 1980).

147. Tennyson, *The Princess,* p. 158.

148. Pārati, *Kaṇṇaṉ pāṭṭu,* p. 269.

149. Shakespeare, "Sonnet 29," p. 28.

150. Brooke, "The Old Vicarage, Grantchester," p. 149.

151. Landor, "Dying Speech of an Old Philosopher," 2:223.

152. Whitman, "When Lilacs Last in the Dooryard Bloom'd," p. 459.

153. Stella Benson, "Five Smooth Stones," *Modern British Poetry,* pp. 664–65.

154. In my discussion of Tamil prosody, I follow Zvelebil, *Classical Tamil Prosody,* and Marr, "Prosody in the 'Eight Anthologies'," pp. 390–452.

155. Hart, *The Poems of Ancient Tamil,* pp. 144–45.

156. Pēreyiṉ Muṟuvalār, *Kuṟuntokai* 17.

157. Quoted in Wood, *Poet's Handbook,* pp. 235–36.

158. For instance, Vladimir Nabokov remarks: "I want translations with copious footnotes, footnotes reaching up like skyscrapers to the top of this or that page so as to leave only the gleam of one textual line between commentary and eternity." See his "Problems of Translation," *Partisan Review* 12:496–512. For an ironic account of the translator, see Zbigniew Herbert's poem, "Translating Poetry," *Polish Writing Today,* pp. 38–39.

159. Picard, *The World of Silence,* p. 43.

Glossary

References are to canto and line (26.40), or to canto and section (29:16). No references are provided for words that appear in the introduction and postscript.

acai a metrical unit
āciriyam one of the four standard Tamil meters, also known as akaval
Ādiśeṣa a mythological thousand-headed serpent who supports the earth on his hoods and on whom Viṣṇu reclines, 26.40
Āgama Jaina scripture; canonical literature, 10.257
Agastya a Vedic seer, 3.1; the star Canopus
Agni the god of fire, 21.63
Aiyai Durgā, 11.254; daughter of the herdswoman Mātari, 16.12
Ājīvika (the living) an ascetic and deterministic sect, founded in the 6th c. B.C.E. by Gośāla Maskarīputra, 27.113
akam the inner world; the erotic
akanilai a class of primary melody-types, 8.49
akaval one of the four standard Tamil meters, also known as āciriyam; the rhythm peculiar to this meter
Ālamarcelvaṉ son of the brahman Vārttikaṉ, 23.98
Aḻumpilvēḷ a chieftain, 25.180
Amarāvatī the city of the gods, 6.22
Amari Durgā as the goddess of war, 12.89
ammāṉai a song sung by girls while playing with wooden balls, each

stanza of which has "ammāṉai" as its refrain, 29:16; a class of poems, each verse of which has "ammāṉai" as its refrain, 29:16

aṇaṅku sacred power; *cap.* Durgā, 12.54

aṅgāgama one of the three classes of Jaina scriptures, 10.254; the others are pūrva and aṅgabāhya

Āṉporunai a river near Karūr, 27.251

Āṇṭāḷ a Tamil devotional poet of the 9th c. C.E.

āṇṭalai a fabulous bird of prey with a head like a man's, 15.232

Antarī Durgā, 12:21

appam a round cake of rice flour and sugar fried in ghee, 5.29

Araṅkam Śrīraṅkam, a holy city on the river Kāviri, 10.212

ārapaṭi a kind of drama having for its theme the acquisition of wealth, and centering round the achievements of great warriors as heroes, 23.223

Araṭṭaṉ Ceṭṭi a merchant prince of Vañci, 30.49

arhat a Jaina sage, 10.25

ārppu excessive pitch of a lute string, 8.36

āṟṟuvari a river song

arukiyal a class of primary melody-types, 8.49

arum a primary melody-type of the pālai class, 3.84

Arundhatī wife of the seer Vasiṣṭha, and renowned for her chastity, 1.29; the star Alcor, 1.60

Ārya an Aryan, 25.167

aśoka the tree *Saraca indica,* 8.154; *cap.* Mauryan emperor

āṭakam a kind of gold believed to be greenish in color, 14.244

Āṭakamāṭam (the golden temple) a Viṣṇu temple in the suburbs of Vañci, 26.71

āṭal dance, 3.31

aṭi a line

Āṭi the fourth month of the year in the Tamil lunar calendar, corresponding to July–August, 23.141

aṭikal a venerable ascetic

Ātimanti the daughter of the Cōḻa king, Karikālaṉ, 21.16

atirvu tremolo, 8.36

Aṭiyārkkunallār a commentator of the *Cilappatikāram* of the12th–13th c. C.E.

ātti common mountain ebony, prol. 16

Avanti Ujjayinī, a city on the river Śiprā in central India, 5.127

āyarpāṭi a village of cowherds

Ayirai a river in Coimbatore district, 28.151

Ayodhyā the capital of the Kosala kingdom, 13.83

Bālakumāra the father of Kanaka and Vijaya, kings of northern India, 26.166

Balarāma the elder brother of Kṛṣṇa, 5.210

Bāṇa the son of Bali and Koṭarī, and a demon with a thousand arms, 6.54

Bhairava a king of northern India, 26.188

Bharata the name of Kōvalaṉ in a former birth, 23.160

bo the tree *Ficus religiosa* under which the Buddha attained enlightenment, 10.17

Brahmā the creator; priest of the gods, often called the Grandfather, 5.216

cadamba Indian oak; the tree *Nauclea cadamba,* 11.88

Caitra the first month of the year in the Hindu lunar calendar, corresponding to March–April, 5.72

Cākkaiyaṉ a class of men whose profession in ancient times was to sing and dance in temples and palaces, 28.69

Cakravāla a mythical range of mountains surrounding the orb of the earth, 7:52

cakravartin a universal emperor

cāmpūnata a kind of fine gold, 3.115

Caṅkamaṉ a merchant from Ciṅkapuram, one of the capitals of Kaliṅga in eastern India, prol. 54

cāraṇar a Jaina sage

Caravaṇam a lake to bathe in, which was supposed to purify, 11.114

Cāttaṉ a grain dealer of Maturai, and author of *Maṇimēkalai,* prol. 13; also Aiyaṉār, a village god learned in texts on heretical religions, 9.38

cāttuvaṭi a variety of drama that has a semidivine being for a hero and treats of virtue, 23.223

cē the tree *Alangium lamarckii,* 12:2

Cedi the city, according to Jaina tradition, of the Vidyādharas, 6.3

Ceḻiyaṉ a title of the Pāṇṭiya king, 20.43

cempakai the harsh note of a lute string, 8.35

cempālai a melody-type of the pālai class, 3.81

Cempiyaṉ an epithet of the Cōḻa king, 1.81

Ceṅkōṭu a shrine of Murukaṉ in Salem district, 24:8

Ceṅkuṭṭuvaṉ a Cēral king, prol. 9

centamiḻ standard Tamil

Centil a shrine of Murukaṉ at Tiruccentūr in Tirunelvēli district, 24:8

Cēralātaṉ a title of the Cēral king, 29:1

Cēṭakkuṭumpi the name of a temple priest, 30.49

cētam an element in dancing, epil. 14

cevvaḻi a secondary melody-type of the pālai class, 3.83

champak an orange-yellow flower of the magnolia family, *Michelia champaca,* 2.26

chowry a yaktail whisk; badge of royalty, 10.167
Cilampāṟu a holy river in the Aḻakar hills in Maturai district, Nūpura-Gaṅgā, 11.127
Ciṅkapuram one of the capitals of Kaliṅga in eastern India, prol. 55
cīr a metrical foot
cītēvi a woman's head ornament, 6.123
Citra a king of northern India, 26.189
Citrāpati Mātavi's mother, 30.22
Cittirai a star in the constellation Virgo, 5.74
Cō the city of Bāṇa, 6.70; the name of a fortress, 17:35
Cōḻa the ruler of the Cōḻa kingdom, prol. 15
Damayantī the wife of King Nala, 14.68
Dāruka a demon killed by Durgā, 20.53
Dhanurdhara a king of northern India, 26.189
dharma a system of laws, duties, rites and obligations incumbent on a Hindu according to his or her class and stage of life, 15.10
digvijaya the conquest of the four quarters
Dravidian a language family of India, Pakistan, and Sri Lanka that includes Tamil, Malayalam, Telugu, Kannada, Gondi, and Brahui
Durgā (the inaccessible one) the name of a ferocious aspect of the Goddess, 6.64
eḻuttu a syllable
Ērakam a shrine of Murukaṉ at Cuvāmimalai in Tañcāvūr district, 24:8
Eṭṭi Cāyalaṉ the name of a merchant prince, 15.175
etukai second-syllable rhyme
Eyiṉaṉ a hunter of the Eyiṉ tribe, 12.14
Gajabāhu a king of Laṅkā, 30.156
gamboge the tree *Ochrocarpus longifolius,* 12:2
Gaṅgā the holy river Ganges, 6.32
Gaṅgas the people of Gaṅga, a kingdom adjoining the Tamil country, 25.166
Garuda a giant bird, devotee and mount of Viṣṇu, 17:28
Gaurī (the white one) a beneficent aspect of the Goddess, 12.90
Gokula the village of Kṛṣṇa's youth, 17:29
Gopāla Kōvalaṉ, 15.95
Hara Śiva, 12:9
Hari Viṣṇu-Kṛṣṇa, 12:9
hariali the grass *Cynodon dactylon,* 6.144
Himālaya (the domain of snow) the name of a mountain range in northern India, 1.16
icai music
icaināṭakam a musical play

Iḷaṅkō Vēṇmāḷ Ceṅkuṭṭuvaṉ's queen, 25.6

Indra the king of the gods in the Vedic, Buddhist and Jaina pantheons, prol. 4

Iṭākiṉi a female goblin who feeds on corpses in the cremation ground, 9.34

Iṭṭacitti a lake, to bathe in, which was supposed to purify, 11.114

Iṭumpil a village in Tañcāvūr district, 28.120.

iyaipu final rhyme

iyal poetry

Jaina a follower of Jainism, a Hindu sect believed to be founded by Vardhamāna Mahāvīra (599–527 B.C.E.), 10.20

Jayanta son of Indra, the king of the gods, 3.2

kaikkiḷai unrequited love

Kailāsa a mountain in the Himālaya where Śiva dwells, 6.3

kaḷavu premarital love

kali one of the four standard Tamil meters

Kālī (the black goddess) the name of the Goddess in her destructive aspect, 6.45

Kaliṅga a kingdom on the east coast of India, 23.146

Kaliṅgas the people of Kaliṅga, 25.165

Kāma the god of love; also known as the Formless One, 2.31

Kaṃsa the king of the Bhojas; cousin of Devakī, the mother of Kṛṣṇa, and Kṛṣṇa's deadly enemy, 6.53

Kanaka a king of northern India, 26.165

kāṉalvari the love songs of the seaside grove

kāñci the portia tree; a poetic theme that describes either the defence of a fort by a warrior wearing kāñci flowers, or the impermanence of life as a prelude to achieving salvation

Kāṇḍava a forest sacred to Indra, burned down by Arjuna as an offering to Agni, 22.56

Kaṅkai the river Ganges, 7:2

Kaṇṇaki the daughter of Māṉāykaṉ, a merchant prince of Pukār, and wife of Kōvalaṉ, prol. 19

kaṉṉi a virgin; *cap.* the Kumari river that in ancient times flowed south of Kaṉṉiyākumari, 7:3

kāṇṭam a book

Kapilapuram one of the capitals of Kaliṅga in eastern India, 23.149

Kāppiya the Kāvya gotra, family or lineage, 30.80

kāppiyam a narrative poem

Karikālaṉ a great Cōḻa king, 6.189

karma (act) usually the consequences of acts in one's life that determine one's fate in the next, prol. 29

kaṟpu chastity; marital love

Kārttikai the wife of the brahman Vārttikaṉ, 23.110
karu the native elements that comprise the relationship between humans and nature
Karunāṭaṉs the Kannada-speaking people, 25.165
kātai story-song, canto
Katampaṉ Murukaṉ or Skanda, wearing a garland of cadamba flowers, 24:11
Kaṭṭiyaṉs the people who ruled over the western part of the Tamil country, 25.166
kaṭṭurai a narrative interlude
Kaucikaṉ the name of a young brahman, 13.60
Kaurava the patronymic of the hundred sons of Dhṛtarāṣṭra, 29:24
Kauriyaṉ a title of the Pāṇṭiya king, 15.1
kavalai a rooted creeper, 11.101
Kāvēri, Kāviri a river in southern India, 1.5, 5.204
kāviyam, kāvya a narrative poem
Kavunti the name of a Jaina ascetic, 10.47
kāya bilberry, *Memecylon malabaricum,* 12:12
Kiḷḷivaḷavaṉ Perunaṟkiḷḷi, son of Ceṅkuṭṭuvaṉ's maternal uncle, 27.133
kiṇai a drum used in the farmland, 10.191
Kīrantai the name of a brahman poet, 23.47
Kōcar a warlike Tamil tribe of the Koṅku country
koel Indian cuckoo, 7:26
Kolli a range of hills in Tiruccirāppaḷḷi district, 24:26
Koṅkaṇ the low country of western India between the Ghats and the Arabian Sea, 25.160
Koṅkaṇas the people of the Koṅkaṇ, 25.165
Koṅku the Tamil country comprising the districts of Coimbatore, Salem, and a part of Karnataka, 12.65
kōpālakaṉ a cowherd
Koṟkai an ancient port, formerly at the mouth of the river Tāmiraparuṇi in the Pāṇṭiya kingdom, 14.98
Koṟṟavai Durgā as the goddess of war and victory, 12.86
kōṭi a secondary melody-type of the pālai class, 3.84
koṭṭiccētam Śiva's dance at the burning of Tripura, 28.71
Koṭumpai Koṭumpāḷūr, a village in Putukkōṭṭai district, 11.82
Kōvalaṉ the son of Mācāttuvāṉ, a merchant prince of Pukār, and husband of Kaṇṇaki, prol. 17
kovvai the vine *Coccinia indica,* 8.95
Kṛṣṇa (dark) son of Vasudeva and Devakī; epic hero and avatar of Viṣṇu, 6.52
Kubera the god of wealth, leader of the Yakṣas, residing in the city of Alakā, 1.34

Kumāra a king of Kaliṅga who ruled over the city of Kapilapuram, 23.145

Kumari Durgā, 12.89; the waters of Kaṉṉiyākumari, 8.5; a hill said to have existed near Kaṉṉiyākumari, 11.28

kumiḻ flower of the cashmere tree, 5.256

kumkum red powder used to mark a woman's forehead, 8.24

kuravai a dance, in a circle, of the Kuṟava women featuring a chain formation of interlocked hands and arms, 3.26

Kuṟavas a hill tribe of the Cēral country, prol. 8

kuṟiñci the conehead, *Strobilanthes* (genus), 14.108; the hill, one of the five traditional regions of the Tamil country; a clandestine union of lovers, assigned by poetic convention to the hill; a melody-type associated with the hill, 24:1

Kuruku the Krauñca mountain in the eastern Himālaya split open by Skanda, 24:10

Kuṭaku Coorg, in modern Karnataka, that formed the western boundary of the Tamil country, 10.139

kūṭam dullness of tone in a lute string, 8.36

Kuṭṭuvaṉ Ceṅkuṭṭuvaṉ, 26.72

Kuyilāluvam a temple of Śiva in the Himālaya, 28.109

Lakṣmī the goddess of prosperity and beauty, and consort of Viṣṇu, 1.27

Laṅkā Sri Lanka, 17:35

Mācāttaṉ Aiyaṉār, a village god, 9.20

Mācāttuvāṉ a wealthy merchant prince of Pukār, and Kōvalaṉ's father, 1.30

Magadha a kingdom in northeastern India with Rājagṛha as its capital, 5.125

māhātmya a genre of epic literature that praises the greatness of a deity

Mālati the name of a brahman woman, 9.6

Malaya Potiyil, a mountain in the Pāṇṭiya kingdom famous as the dwelling of the seer Agastya, 13.31

Mālva a kingdom in central India, 30.156

Māṉāykaṉ a wealthy merchant prince of Pukār, and Kaṇṇaki's father, 1.21

Mandara (dense) the mountain that the gods used for churning the ocean

Maṇimēkalai the guardian deity of the sea, and the family deity of Kōvalaṉ, 15.36; daughter of Kōvalaṉ and Mātavi, 15.43

Maṇivaṇṇaṉ (the sapphire-colored one) Viṣṇu, 10.11

Maṅkalatēvi (the auspicious goddess) a reference to Kaṇṇaki, 30.52

Māṅkāṭu a village in the Kuṭaku hills, 11.62

mantāram shoe-flower, *Hibiscus rosasinensis,* 25.143
Māntaraṉ-Cēral a Cēral king, 23.91
mantra a sacred utterance used in ritual worship and meditation; a spell, 11.152
Māraṉ Kāma, the god of love, 8.1
Maṟavaṉ a hunter of the Maṟava tribe, 12.10
marutam the arjuna tree, *Terminalia arjuna,* 12:23; the farmland, one of the five traditional regions of the Tamil country; the lovemaking that follows a time of sulking, assigned by poetic convention to the farmland; a melody-type associated with the farmland
Māṭalaṉ the name of a brahman, 15.11
maṭalūrtal a social custom where a man rides on a horse made of the stems of the palmyra leaves to declare his love for a woman
Mātari the name of a herdswoman, 15.123
mātavi the climbing shrub *Hiptage madablota,* 2.26; *cap.* the name of a courtesan, and Kōvalaṉ's mistress, prol. 18
Maturai the capital of the Pāṇṭiya kingdom on the river Vaiyai, prol. 20
Maturāpati the tutelary goddess of Maturai
Maya the name of a titan who was the architect of the demons, antagonists of the gods, 2.13
māyā illusion; an aspect of the Goddess, 17:32
Māyavaṉ Kṛṣṇa, 17.5
mayilai Tuscan jasmine, 5.237
mērcem a secondary melody-type of the pālai class, 3.85
Meru the central mountain of the earth, and home of the gods, 1.6
mōṉai alliteration
Mucukuntaṉ a king who helped the gods in their wars against the demons, 5.81
mukavai a song sung during the treading of grain on the threshing floor by cattle, 10.185
mullai a variety of jasmine, 4.35; the forest, one of the five traditional regions of the Tamil country; the patient endurance of a woman during the time of separation from her lover, assigned by poetic convention to the forest; a melody-type associated with the forest
Murukaṉ the Dravidian god of youth, beauty, love, and war; also called Caṇmukaṉ, Kārttikeya, Kumāra, and Skanda, 1.41
mutal the first elements, that is, time and place
Nala a king of Niṣadha, 14.61
Nārada a seer who is a frequent intermediary between gods and humans, 6.23
Narasiṃha (man-lion) the name of one of Viṣṇu's avatārs, 17:34

Nārāyaṇa Viṣṇu, especially during the period of dissolution after each aeon, 17:37
nāṭakam dance; drama
nāṭṭuppāṭal a folk ballad
naṭukal a memorial stone over a warrior's grave
Nērivāyil a town to the south of Uṟaiyūr in the Cōḻa kingdom, 28.118
Neṭiyōṉ Viṣṇu, 22.31
Neṭumāl Viṣṇu, 18.4
Neṭuñceḻiyaṉ the name of a Pāṇṭiya king, 23.226
Neṭuvēl Murukaṉ, 23.196
neytal a variety of Indian water lily; the seashore, one of the five traditional regions of the Tamil country; the sorrow of lovers due to separation, assigned by poetic convention to the seashore; a melody-type associated with the seashore
Nīlaṉ an emissary of Ceṅkuṭṭuvaṉ to the Cōḻa and Pāṇṭiya kings, 28.84
Nīli Durgā, 12:21; Caṅkamaṉ's wife, 23.166
Nirgrantha (unattached, without possessions) an old name of the Jainas, 9.21
nīti justice
nōtiram raga a musical mode, 4.99
ōcai rhythm
pā a stanza or verse-form
Pācaṇṭa Cāttaṉ Pācaṇṭaṉ Aiyaṉār, a village god learned in texts on heretical religions, 9.24, 30.67
Pahruli a river near Kaṉṉiyākumari, 11.28
pālai the ironwood tree; the wasteland, one of the five traditional regions of the Tamil country; the temporary separation of lovers from each other or from their parents, assigned by poetic convention to the wasteland; a melody-type associated with the wasteland; a musical scale of seven notes, 3.149
Paḻaiyaṉ the name of a chief of Mōkūr, 27.140
pālikai the nine kinds of grain sown in earthern pots on auspicious occasions, sprouted and then, at the end of the ceremonies, emptied into a pond or river, 1.70
pāṇaṉ a bard
Pañcavaṉ a title of the Pāṇṭiya king, 20.44
Pāṇḍava a patronymic of the five sons of Pāṇḍu, 17:34
Paṅkalaṉs the people of Bengal, 25.166
Pāṇṭiyaṉ a ruler of the Pāṇṭiya kingdom, prol. 26
Paṟaiyūr a village in the Cēra kingdom renowned for brahmans versed in the four Vedas, 28.69
Parāśara the name of a brahman from Pukār, 23.60

pārati-virutti a kind of dramatic presentation in which an actor is the hero and a dance is the theme, 10.349

parattai a harlot

pāṭāṉ a poetic theme that praises a king's fame, power, and generosity

patikam a prologue or an epilogue

pativratā a chaste and devoted wife

Pattiṉi a chaste woman, that is, Kaṇṇaki as an ideal wife, prol. 39; Kaṇṇaki as a goddess, 28.210

Pattiṉikkōṭṭam a temple of the goddess Pattiṉi

pāṭṭu a song; a poem

paṭumalai a secondary melody-type of the pālai class, 3.83

Pavakāraṇi a lake, to bathe in, which was supposed to purify, 11.114.

Periyār a river that rises in the Āṉaimalai hills, 25.23

perukiyal a class of primary melody-types, 8.49

peruṅkāppiyam a great narrative poem

peruntiṇai mismatched love

pial a raised platform along the house wall that faces the street

Piṉṉai one of Kṛṣṇa's consorts, 17:15

pirital love-in-separation

piṭavam the tree *Randia malabarica,* 13.200

Poṉṉi the river Kāviri, 21.11

Poṟaiyaṉ a title of the Cēral king, 23.89

Porunai the river Āṉporunai, 23.90

Potiyil a mountain in the Pāṇṭiya kingdom famous as the dwelling of the seer Agastya, 1.16

potuviyal a dance with heroism as its theme, 3.42

Pukār a seaport, and Cōḻa capital at the mouth of the river Kāviri, prol. 15; also called Pūmpukār, 3.177

pulavaṉ a learned poet

pullakam a woman's ornament for the forehead, 6.124

Pūmpukār Pukār, 3.177

punartal love-in-enjoyment

puṟam the outer world; the heroic

purāṇam legend; myth

puṟanilai a class of primary melody-types, 8.49

puruṣārtha any one of the four ends of human life: duty (Skt. *dharma;* Ta. *aṟam*), wealth (*artha; poruḷ*), desire (*kāma; iṉpam*), and liberation (*mōkṣa; vīṭu*)

puṣparāga topaz, 14.229

raga melodic mode, 3.65

Rāhu a fierce four-armed, dragon-tailed titan; in astronomy the ascending node, 5.251

rājādhirāja a king of kings

rājasūya a royal sacrifice
Rāma a king regarded as an avatar of Viṣṇu, and hero of the epic *Rāmāyaṇa,* 13.80
rasa/ dhvani the suggestion of mood
Rati (sexual pleasure) Kāma's wife, 2.113
Rohiṇī the favorite wife of the Moon, and one of the twenty-seven lunar mansions; Hyades, 1.49
Rudra a king of northern India, 26.188
sal the tree *Shorea robusta,* 12:2
Samarī (the slayer) Durgā as the goddess of war, 12.90
Saṃjaya an emissary of the kings of northern India, 26.147
Śaṃkarī Durgā, 12:21
Śani the planet Saturn, 10.136
Sarasvatī the goddess of speech, and wife of Brahmā, 12.94; a river associated with learning
Sa, Ri, Ga, Ma, Pa, Dha, Ni symbols representing the Sanskrit names of the musical notes *ṣaḍja, ṛṣabha, gāndhāra, madhyama, pañcama, dhaivata,* and *niṣāda.* They correspond to *do, re, mi, fa, sol, la, si* in solmization, 17:13
Sātakarṇi a Śātavāhana king of the Deccan, 26.155
Siṃha a king of northern India, 26.189
sindura red powder, 24:2
sirissa the tree *Albizia chinensis,* 11.90
Śiva (auspicious) the god of ascetics, and destruction, prol. 46
Śiveta a king of northern India, 26.189
śrotriya a brahman learned in the Vedas
Śukra (bright) the planet Venus, 6.134
Sūra a demon killed by Murukaṉ, 6.56
Talaiccheṅkāṉam a village of the Cōḻa kingdom, 15.12
taṉippāṭal a discontinuous stanza
Taṅkāl a village near Civakāci, 23.79
tēcikam a dance indigenous to the region, here the Tamil country; later termed folk dance, 3.33
Teṉṉavaṉ a title of the Pāṇṭiya king, 11.22
terukkūttu a genre of folk play performed in the open as ritual
Tēvanti, Tēvantikai the name of a brahman woman, and wife of the god Cāttaṉ, 9.50, 30.3
Tēvi the Mother Goddess
tilaka a mark affixed between the eyebrows to ward off evil, 4.71
tiṇai region; landscape
tiṟam pentatonic scale, 8.50
Tirumāl Viṣṇu, 12:4
Tirumāvaḷavaṉ the name of a Cōḻa king, 5.109

tonmai an ancient tale in a mixture of verse and prose
Tonti an ancient seaport of the Cōla kingdom, 14.136
toṭai the stringing together of metrical units into feet and lines
toṭar-nilaic-ceyyuḷ a poetic sequence
toyyakam a part of a head ornament, 6.124
tūkku a mode of beating time, 10.349
tumpai white dead nettle; a poetic theme that describes a warrior wearing tumpai flowers and fighting his enemy
tuṇaṅkai a kind of dance in which the arms bent at the elbows are made to strike against the sides, 5.83
Ujjayinī Avanti, a city on the river Śiprā in central India, 6.33
uḻiñai balloon vine; a poetic theme that describes the storming of a fort, or its defense under a siege
uḷḷuṟai uvamam indirect suggestion
Umā the daughter of Himālaya and Menā, and consort of Śiva, 6.44
Uṟaiyūr an ancient capital of the Cōḻa kingdom, 10.330
ūral a water bird, 10. 158
Uṟantai Uṟaiyūr, 8.7
uri the human elements, that is, the phases of love: meeting, waiting, sulking, lamenting, and parting
Urvaśī an apsaras or semicelestial dancing girl of the gods who was temporarily married to the mortal king Purūravas, 3.2
Utaiya a hill near Pukār, 5.5
ūṭal lovers' quarrel, arising from jealousy
Uttara a king of northern India, 26.188
Uttaragautta a king of Vārāṇasī or Banaras, 15.193
Uttarakuru a transhimālayan land of everlasting happiness, invisible to human eyes, 2.11
Vacantamālai, Vayantamālai Mātavi's maid, 6.198, 11.208
Vaikai, Vaiyai a river in Maturai district, 13.218
Vajra a kingdom on the river Śoṇa, 5.122
vākai sirissa tree; a poetic theme that describes a warrior wearing vākai flowers and celebrating his victory over his enemy
Vaḷavaṉ Karikālaṉ, 17:30
vaḷḷai a song in praise of a hero by women husking or hulling grain, 25.33
Vaḷḷi the consort of Murukaṉ, 24:1
Vāṉavaṉ a title of the Cēral king, 27.262
vañci Indian willow; a poetic theme that describes a king crowned with vañci flowers and conquering his enemy's lands; one of the four standard Tamil meters; *cap.* an ancient capital of the Cēral kingdom, 8.7
Vañcikkōṉ the husband of Ātimanti, daughter of King Karikālaṉ, 21.17

vāram a song in medium tempo, 3.154; a song in praise of a deity
vari a masquerade dance typical of each of the five regions (tiṇais) of the Tamil country, 3.26
Varōttamai the name of a mountain nymph, 11.133
Vārttikaṉ the name of a brahman, 23.99
Varuṇa a Vedic god; in later times, the god of ocean and water, 7:24
Vasu a king of Kaliṅga who ruled over the city of Ciṅkapuram, 23.145
Vāsuki the king of the snakes, 17:32
Vayalūr a village near Civakāci, 23.127
Vedas the primary Hindu scriptures organized into four collections called Ṛg, Sāma, Yajur and Atharva, 5.215
Vēḷāvikkō a palace outside Vañci, 28.198
Vēṅkaṭam the Tiruppati hills which formed the northern boundary of the ancient Tamil country, 6.34
Veṇkuṉṟu (the white hill) a hill on which there was a shrine of Murukaṉ, 24:8
Vēṇmāḷ Ceṅkuṭṭuvaṉ's queen, 28.56
veṇpā one of the four standard Tamil meters
Veṉvēlāṉ Murukaṉ, 29:10
Vēṟ-Ceḻiyaṉ a ruler of Koṟkai, 27.142
veṭci scarlet ixora, *Ixora coccinea,* 12:13; a poetic theme that describes a warrior wearing veṭci flowers and raiding the enemy's cattle
vēttiyal a dance with love as its theme, 3.42
Vicitra a king of northern India, 26.188
Vidyādharas (possessing spells) deities inhabiting the regions between the earth and sky, and having magical powers, 6.4
Vijaya a king of northern India, 26.165
viḷari a melody-type of the pālai class, 3.85
Villavaṉ Kōtai Ceṅkuṭṭuvaṉ's minister, 25.157
villuppāṭṭu a bow song
Vindhyā a mountain range in central India, 6.34
Viṣṇu (the pervader) the supreme god closely identified with Kṛṣṇa, 5.212
Viyalūr a town noted for pepper and elephants, 28.115
Yakṣiṇī female Yakṣas, or semidivine chthonic spirits, and guardians of wealth, 15.124
yāḻ a lute
Yama the god of death, 5.270
Yamunā a river, and tributary of the Gaṅgā, 16.53
Yaśodā Kṛṣṇa's foster mother, 16.50
Yavanas Greeks; foreigners, 5.12

Bibliography

Editions and Translations

Cilappatikāram of Iḷaṅkō Aṭikaḷ. Ed., with the *Arumpatavurai* and the commentary of Aṭiyārkkunallār, by U. Vē. Cāminātaiyar. 8th printing. Madras: Śrī Tiyākarāca vilāca veḷiyīṭu, 1968 [1892].

——. Ed. Puliyūrk Kēcikaṉ (Kē. Cokkaliṅkam). Madras: Pāri nilayam, 1958.

——. Ed. Po. Vē Cōmacuntaraṉār. Tirunelveli: Tirunelvēlit teṉṉintiya caivacittānta nūṟpatippuk kaḻakam, 1969.

——. Ed. Na. Mu. Vēṅkaṭacāmi Nāṭṭār (Parañcōti Muṉivar). Paganeri: Pākaṉēri taṉavaiciya iḷaiñar tamiḻccaṅka veḷiyīṭu, 1942.

——. Trans. into French by Alain Daniélou and R. S. Desikan. *Le roman de l'anneau* (*Shilappadikâram*). Paris: Gallimard, 1961.

——. Trans. into English by Alain Daniélou. *Shilappadikaram: The Ankle Bracelet.* London: Allen & Unwin, 1967.

——. Trans. into English by V. R. Ramachandra Dikshitar. *The Śilappadikāram.* Madras: Oxford University Press, 1939.

——. Trans. into Russian by I͡Uriĭ I͡Akovlevich Glazov, and ed. by A. M. Piatigorskiĭ. *Povest' o braslete* (*Śilappadikāram*). Moscow: Nauka, 1966.

——. Trans. into English by Ka. Naa. Subramanyam. *The Anklet Story: Silappadhikaaram of Ilango Adigal.* Delhi: Agam Prakashan, 1977.

——. Trans. into Hindi by M. G. Venkatesan. *Nūpur-gathā* (*Cilappatikāram*). Calcutta: Bharathi Tamil Sangam, 1965.

——. Trans. into Malayalam by Nenmāṟa P. Viśvanāthannāyar. *Iḷaṅkōvaṭikaḷ racicca cilappatikāram.* Trichur: Kerala Sahitya Akademi, 1975.

——. Trans. into Czech by Kamil V. Zvelebil. *Píseň o klenotu* (*Silappaddi-*

gáram). Prague: Státní nakladatelstvi krasné literatury, hudby a umeni, 1965.

Tamil Works

Aiṅkuṟunūṟu. Ed., with an old commentary, by U. Vē Cāminātaiyar. 5th printing. Madras: Śrī Tiyākarāca vilāca veḷiyīṭu, 1957.

Akanāṉūṟu. 2 vols. Ed., with a commentary, by Po. Vē. Cōmacuntaraṉār. Tirunelveli: Tirunelvēlit teṉṉintiya caivacittānta nūṟpatippuk kaḻakam, 1970–77.

Akapporuḷ (The Meaning of Love) of Iṟaiyaṉār. With the commentary ascribed to Nakkīraṉār. Tirunelveli: Tirunelvēlit teṉṉintiya caivacittānta nūṟpatippuk kaḻakam, 1953.

Akapporuḷviḷakkam (Light on the Meaning of Love) of Nāṟkavirācanampi. Madurai: Tamiḻccaṅka muttirā cālai, 1904.

Aruṇācalam, Mu. *"Mutaṟkāppiyaṅkaḷ"* ("The First Narrative Poems"). In *Tamiḻ ilakkiyak koḷkai: ōr aṟimukam* (Tamil Literary Theories: An Introduction). Vol. 1. Ed. by Cā. Vē. Cuppiramaṇiyam and Tā. Vē. Vīracāmi, pp. 93–135. Madras: Ulakat tamiḻārāycci niṟuvaṉam, 1975.

——. *Tamiḻ ilakkiya varalāṟu* (A History of Tamil Literature), 11 vols. Tiruchitrambalam, Thanjavur Dt.: Kānti vittiyālayam, 1969.

Cāminātaiyar, U. Vē. *Caṅkattamiḻum piṟkālattamiḻum* (Classical Tamil and Modern Tamil). 5th printing. Madras: Śri Tiyākarāca vilāca veḷiyīṭu, 1962.

——. *Eṉ carittiram*. Madras: U. Vē. Cāminātaiyar nūl nilayam, 1950.

——. *Eṉ carittiram*. Abr. by Ki. Vā. Jakannātaṉ. Madras: Tiyākarāja vilācam, 1958. Trans. S. K. Guruswamy and ed. A. Rama Iyer. *The Story of My Life*. Madras: Dr. U. V. Swaminathaiyer Library, 1980.

Caṅkaratās Cuvāmi, Ṭi. Ṭi. *Kōvalaṉ carittiram* (The Story of Kōvalaṉ's Life). Madras: Tiruvaḷḷuvar puttaka nilayam, 1969 [1925].

Caṇmukam, Irāma, Irā. Kācirācaṉ, Ca. Cāmpacivaṉ, and Nā. Vēlucāmi. *Neñcai aḷḷum cilampu* (The *Cilappatikāram* That Rends the Hearts). Chidambaram: Maṇivācakar patippakam, 1983.

Cētuppiḷḷai, Rā. Pi. *Cilampiṉ katai amaippu* (Narrative Structure in the *Cilappatikāram*). Chidambaram: Maṇivācakar patippakam, 1980.

Ceyappirakācu, Nā. *Cilappatikāram kāṭṭum tamiḻakac camutāya nilai* (The Social Condition of the Tamil Country as Depicted in the *Cilappatikāram*). Madras: Vaṉmaḻaip patippakam, 1978.

Ceyarāmaṉ, Na. Vi. *Cilappatikāra yāppamaiti* (The Prosodic Structure of the *Cilappatikāram*). Annamalainagar: Aṇṇamalai palkalaik kaḻakam, 1977.

Cuppiramaṇiyam, Ca. Vē. *Aṭiyārkkunallār uraittiṟaṉ* (A Partial Commentary on the *Cilappatikāram* by Aṭiyārkkunallār). Madras: International Institute of Tamil Studies, 1976.

Cuppiramaṇiyaṉ, Pā. Rājakōpāl. *Tamiḻaka nāṭṭup pāṭalkaḷ: oppāri, tālāṭ-*

ṭup pāṭalkaḷiṉ amaippu (Folk Songs of Tamiḻnāṭu: The Structure of Dirges and Lullabies). Madras: Tamiḻp puttakālayam, 1975.

Cūṭāmaṇinikaṇṭu (The Crest-Jeweled Glossary) of Maṇṭalapuruṭaṉ. Madras: Vittiyānulaṉa yantiracālai, n.d.

Ilaṭcumaṇacāmi, Ko. *Cilappatikāram-Maṇimēkalai kāppiya marapu* (Epic Tradition in the *Cilappatikāram* and *Maṇimēkalai*). Annamalainagar: Aṇṇāmalaip palkalaik kaḻakam, 1977.

Irājacēkaraṉ, Irā. *Pattiṉik kōṭṭam* (The Temple of Pattiṉi). Poompuhar: Pattiṉik kōṭṭam aṟanilai, 1973.

Irākavaiyaṅkār, Mu. *Tolkāppiyap poruḷatikāra ārāycci* (A Study of the Tolkāppiyam: Poruḷatikāram). 3d printing. Manamadurai: Mu. Rā. Nārāyaṇaiyaṅkār, 1960.

Irāmanāthaṉ, Es. *Cilappatikārattu āycciyar kuravaip pāṭalkaḷ* (Songs of the Round Dance of the Herdswomen in the *Cilappatikāram*). Madras: Kalaimakaḷ icaik kallūri, 1968.

Jakannātaṉ, Ki. Vā. *Cilampu piṟanta katai* (The Story Born of an Anklet). 3d printing. Madras: Amuta nilayam, 1962.

——. *Tamiḻk kāppiyaṅkaḷ* (Tamil Narrative Poems). 2d ed. Madras: Amuta nilayam, 1970.

Kācirācaṉ, Irā. *Cilappatikāra āyvaṭaṅkaḷ* (The *Cilappatikāram:* An Annotated Bibliography). Trivandrum: Tamiḻt tuṟai, Kēraḷap palkalaikkaḻakam, 1973.

Kailācapati, Ka. *"Cilappatikārac ceytikaḷ"* ("Observations on the *Cilappatikāram*"). In *Aṭiyum muṭiyum: ilakkiyattiṟ karuttukaḷ* (The Beginning and the End: Ideas in Literature). Madras: Pāri nilayam, 1970.

Kalaikhalañciyam (Encyclopaedia). 10 vols. Madras: Tamiḻ vaḷarccik kaḻakam, 1954–68.

Kaliyāṇacuntaram, Tiru. Vi. *Vāḻkkaik kuṟippukaḷ* (Memoirs). 2 vols. Tirunelveli: Tirunelvēlit teṉṉintiya caivacittānta nūṟpatippuk kaḻakam, 1944.

Karuṇāniti, Mu. *Cilappatikāram: nāṭakak kāppiyam* (The *Cilappatikāram:* An Epic Play). Madras: Añcukam veḷiyīṭu, 1967.

——. Trans. T. G. Narayanaswamy. *Tale of the Anklet: Silappathikaram, A Play*. Madras: Higginbothams, 1968.

Kōmatināyakam, Ti. Ci. *Tamiḻ villuppāṭṭukaḷ* (Tamil Bow Songs). Madras: Tamiḻp patippakam, 1979.

Kōvalaṉ katai (The Story of Kōvalaṉ) of Pukaḻēntip Pulavar. Madras: B. Irattiṉa Nāyakkar, 1983 [1873].

Kuḻantaip, Pulavar. *Yāppatikāram* (Chapters on Prosody). 4th printing. Madras: Pāri nilayam, 1972.

Kuṟuntokai. Ed., with a commentary, by U. Vē. Cāminātaiyar. 4th printing. Madras: Śrī Tiyākarāca vilāca veḷiyīṭu, 1962.

Maṇimēkalai of Cīttalaic Cāttaṉār. Ed. U. Vē. Cāminātaiyar. Madras: Śrī Tiyākarāca vilāca veḷiyīṭu, 1965 [1898].

——. Trans. Alain Daniélou and T. V. Gopala Iyer. *Manimekhalai: The Dancer with the Magic Bowl*. New York: New Directions, 1989.

Mīnāṭcicuntaraṉ, Te. Pō. *Kāṉal vari* (The Love Songs of the Seaside Grove). 2d ed. Coimbatore: Kalaikkatir, 1965.

——. *Kuṭimakkaḷ kāppiyam* (A Narrative Poem of the People). 2d printing. Madurai: Miṉāṭci puttaka nilayam, 1971.

——. *Nāṭakak kāppiyaṅkaḷ* (Dramatic Narrative Poems). Madras: Cēkar patippakam, 1966.

Nālāyirativiyappirapantam (The Four Thousand Divine Compositions). 20 vols. Ed., with a commentary, by Kāñcipuram Pirativāti Payaṅkaram Aṇṇaṅkarācāriyar. Kanchipuram: Granthamālā Office, 1949–63.

Naṉṉūl (The Good Book) of Mayilainātar. Ed. U. Vē. Cāminātaiyar. 2d ed. Madras: Śrī Tiyākarāca vilāca veḷiyīṭu, 1946.

Naṟṟiṇai. Ed., with a commentary, by A. Nārāyaṇacāmi Aiyar and Po. Vē. Cōmacuntaraṉār. Rev. ed. Tirunelveli: Tirunelvēlit teṉṉintiya caivacittānta nūṟpatippuk kaḻakam, 1962.

Navanītakiruṭṭiṇam, A. Ka. *Kaṇṇaki katai: villuppāṭṭu* (The Story of Kaṇṇaki: A Bow Song). Tirunelveli: Tirunelvēlit teṉṉintiya caivacittānta ṉūṟpatippuk kaḻakam, 1975.

Pārati, Cuppiramaṇiya. *Kaṇṇaṉ pāṭṭu* (Kaṇṇaṉ's Song). In *Makākavi Pāratiyār kavitaikaḷ* (The Poems of Makākavi Bharati), pp. 253–80. Madurai: Aruṇā patippakam, 1958.

Pāratitācaṉ [Kaṉaka Cuppurattiṉam]. "*Iṉappeyar.*" In *Pāratitācaṉ kavitaikaḷ* (The Poems of Bharatidasan). 3 vols. Madras: Pāri nilayam, 1958.

——. *Kaṇṇaki puraṭcik kāppiyam* (The Epic of Kannaki's Revolt). Madras: Aṉpu nūlakam, 1962.

Pāratiyār, Cuttāṉanta. *Cilampuc celvam* (The Treasures of the *Cilappatikāram*). 5th printing. Karaikudi: Celvi patippakam, 1962.

Patiṟṟuppattu. Ed., with an old commentary, by U. Vē. Cāminātaiyar. 8th printing. Madras: Cāminātaiyar nūl nilayam, 1980 [1904].

Pattuppāṭṭu. Ed., with the commentary of Nacciṉārkkiṉiyar, by U. Vē. Cāminātaiyar. 6th printing. Madras: Śrī Tiyākarāca vilāca veḷiyīṭu, 1961.

——. Tran. J. V. Chelliah. *Pattuppāṭṭu: Ten Tamil Idylls*. Tirunelveli: Tirunelvēlit teṉṉintiya caivacittānta nūṟpatippuk kaḻakam, 1962.

Piṅkalanikaṇṭu (Piṅkalaṉ's Lexicon). Madras: Ripon Printing Works, 1917.

Puṟanāṉūṟu. Ed., with an old commentary, by U. Vē. Cāminātaiyar. 6th printing. Madras: Śrī Tiyākarāca vilāca veḷiyīṭu, 1964.

Puṟapporuḷveṇpāmālai (A Crown of Stanzas on the Meaning of Heroism) of Aiyaṉāritaṉār. Ed., with a commentary, by Puliyūrk Kēcikaṉ. Madras: Pāri nilayam, 1963.

Rakunātaṉ, Rañcitam. *Iḷaṅkōvaṭikaḷ yār?* (Who Is Iḷaṅkō Aṭikaḷ?) Madurai: Miṉāṭci puttaka nilayam, 1984.

Tamiḻtturai āciriyarkaḷ, aṇṇāmalai palkalaik kaḻakam (The Faculty of the Tamil Department, Annamalai University). *Cilappatikārac cinta-*

ṉaikaḷ (Reflections on the *Cilappatikāram*). Annamalainagar: Aṇṇāmalai palkalaik kaḻakam, 1976.

Taṇṭiyalaṅkāram (Taṇṭi's Book on Ornament [in Poetry]). Ed., with the commentary of Cuppiramaṇiya Tēcikar, by Irāmaliṅkat Tampirāṉ. 8th printing. Tirunelveli: Tirunelvēlit teṉṉintiya caivacittānta nūṟpatippuk kaḻakam, 1966.

Tirukkuṟaḷ. Ed. U. Vē. Vai. Mu. Kōpāla Kruṣṇamācāryār. 4th printing. Madras: Narasimmaṉ, 1965.

Tolkāppiyam: Poruḷatikāram. With the commentary of Iḷampūraṇar. Tirunelveli: Tirunelvēlit teṉṉintiya caivacittānta nūṟpatippuk kaḻakam, 1977.

——. With the commentary of Nacciṉārkkiṉiyar. 2 vols. Tirunelveli: Tirunelvēlit teṉṉintiya caivacittānta nūṟpatippuk kaḻakam, 1966.

——. With the commentary of Pērāciriyar. Tirunelveli: Tirunelvēlit teṉṉintiya caivacittānta nūṟpatippuk kaḻakam, 1961.

Turaicāmip Piḷḷai, Auvai Cu. *Cilappatikāra ārāycci* (A Study of the *Cilappatikāram*). Tirunelveli: Tirunelvēlit teṉṉintiya caivacittānta nūṟpatippuk kaḻakam, 1946.

Vaiyāpurip Piḷḷai, Es. *Ilakkiya maṇimālai* (A Garland of Literary Gems). 3d printing. Madras: Tamiḻp puttakālayam, 1964.

——. *Tamiḻ ilakkiya caritattil kāviya kālam* (The Period of the Narrative Poem in the History of Tamil Literature). 2d printing. Madras: Tamiḻp puttakālayam, 1962.

Vēṅkaṭacāmi, Mayilai Cīṉi. *Cēraṉ Ceṅkuṭṭuvaṉ* (The Cēral King Ceṅkuṭṭuvaṉ). Madras: Ceṉṉai palkalaik kaḻakam, 1966.

Vīrapattiraṉ. *Kōvalaṉ Kaṇṇaki nāṭakam* (Kōvalaṉ and Kaṇṇaki: A Play). Madras: B. Irattiṉa Nāyakkar, 1981 [1889].

Yāpparuṅkalam (The Jewel of Prosody) of Amitacākarar. Ed., with an old commentary, by M. V. Vēṇugōpāla Piḷḷai. Madras Government Oriental Manuscripts Series, 66. Madras: Government Oriental Manuscripts Library, 1960.

Other Works

Ananthan Pillai, P. "The Kaṇṇaki Legend and the *tōṭṭam pāṭṭus*." In *Kerala Studies: Professor A. Gopala Menon Commemoration Volume,* ed. P. K. Narayana Pillai, pp. 162–66. Trivandrum: Oriental Manuscripts Library, University of Kerala, 1955.

Apte, Vaman Shivaram. *The Practical Sanskrit-English Dictionary,* 3 parts. Ed. P. K. Gode and C. G. Karve. Rev. and enl. ed. Poona: Prasad Prakashan, 1957.

Arokiyaswami, M. *The Classical Age of the Tamils.* Madras: University of Madras, 1967.

Asher, R. E. *Some Landmarks in the History of Tamil Prose.* Dr. R. P. Sethu Pillai Silver Jubilee Commemoration Endowment Lectures, 1967–68. Madras: University of Madras, 1972.

Bakhtin, M. M. "Epic and Novel." In *The Dialogic Imagination: Four Essays*. Ed. Michael Holquist, and trans. Caryl Emerson and Michael Holquist, pp. 3–40. Austin: University of Texas Press, 1981.

Balasubramanian, C. *A Study of the Literature of the Cera Country (up to the 11th Century A.D.)* Madras: University of Madras, 1980.

Barnett, L. D. "The Early History of South India." In *The Cambridge History of India,* vol. 1., ed. E. J. Rapom, pp. 593–603. Cambridge: Cambridge University Press, 1922.

Basham, A. L. *The Wonder That Was India: A Survey of the History and Culture of the Indian Sub-Continent Before the Coming of the Muslims.* 3d rev. ed. New York: Taplinger, 1968.

Bates, Ernest Sutherland, ed. *The Bible Designed to Be Read as Literature.* New York: Simon & Schuster, 1936.

Beck, Brenda E. F. "The Study of a Tamil Epic: Some Versions of the *Silappadikaram* Compared." *Journal of Tamil Studies* 1 (1972): 23–38.

Benjamin, Walter. "The Task of the Translator." In *Illuminations,* trans. Harry Zohn, and ed. with an introduction by Hannah Arendt, pp. 69–82. New York: Harcourt, Brace & World, 1968.

Benson, Stella. "Five Smooth Stones." In *Modern British Poetry,* 3d rev. ed. Ed. Louis Untermeyer, pp. 664–65. New York: Harcourt, Brace, 1930.

Beschi, C. J. *A Grammar of the High Dialect of the Tamil Language. Termed Shen-Tamil to Which Is Added an Introduction to Tamil Prosody.* Trans. from the Latin by Benjamin Guy Babington. Thanjavur: Sarasvatī Mahāl Library, 1974 [1822].

Blackburn, Stuart H. "Death and Deification: Folk Cults in Hinduism." *History of Religions* 24.3 (1985): 255–74.

——. "Oral Performance: Narrative and Ritual in a Tamil Tradition." *Journal of American Folklore* 94.372 (1981): 207–27.

——. *Singing of Birth and Death: Texts in Performance.* Philadelphia: University of Pennsylvania Press, 1988.

——, and A. K. Ramanujan, eds. *Another Harmony: New Essays on the Folklore of India.* Berkeley: University of California Press, 1986.

—— et al., eds. *Oral Epics in India.* Berkeley: University of California Press, 1989.

Bowra, C. M. *Heroic Poetry.* London: Macmillan, 1952.

Brockington, J. L. *Righteous Rāma: The Evolution of an Epic.* Delhi: Oxford University Press, 1984.

Brodsky, Joseph. "The Child of Civilization." In *Less Than One: Selected Essays,* pp. 123–44. New York: Farrar, Straus, Giroux, 1986.

Brooke, Rupert. "The Old Vicarage, Grantchester." In *The Collected Poems of Rupert Brooke,* ed. George Edward Woodberry, pp. 149–53. New York: Dodd, Mead, 1915.

Brough, John. "Poetry in Classical Sanskrit." *Indologica Taurinensia* 3 and 4, (1975–76): 93–104.

Brubaker, Richard L. "The Ambivalent Mistress: A Study of South

Indian Goddesses and Their Religious Meaning." Ph.D. dissertation, University of Chicago, 1978.

——. "Lustful Woman, Chaste Wife, Ambivalent Goddess: A South Indian Myth." *Anima* 3.2 (1977): 59–62.

Burrow, T. and M. B. Emeneau. *A Dravidian Etymological Dictionary.* Oxford: Clarendon Press, 1961. *Supplement,* 1968.

Chadwick, H. M. and N. K. Chadwick. *The Growth of Literature.* 3 vols. Cambridge: Cambridge University Press, 1932–40.

Chakravarti, A. *Jaina Literature in Tamil.* Jñānapīṭha Mūrtidevi Granthamālā: English Series 3. New Delhi: Bhāratīya Jñānapīṭha, 1974.

Chari, V. K. *Sanskrit Criticism.* Honolulu: University of Hawaii Press, 1990.

Chellappan, K. "Shakespeare and Ilango as Tragedians: A Comparative Study." Ph.D. dissertation, Madurai University, 1975.

Chidambaranatha Chettiar, A. *Advanced Studies in Tamil Prosody: Being a History of Tamil Prosody up to the Tenth Century* A.D. 4th printing. Annamalainagar: Annamalai University, 1977.

Choondal, Chummar. "The Kannagi Legend in Kerala Folklore." *Folklore* 19.7 (1978): 188–201.

Cixous, Hélène. "The Laugh of the Medusa." In *The Signs Reader: Women, Gender, and Scholarship,* eds. Elizabeth Abel and Emily K. Abel, pp. 279–97. Chicago: University of Chicago Press, 1983.

Clothey, Fred W. *The Many Faces of Murugan.* The Hague: Mouton, 1978.

Coomaraswamy, P. "*Chilappatikāram.*" *Journal of the Royal Asiatic Society of Ceylon* 44 (1893): 81–93.

de Vries, Jan. *Heroic Song and Heroic Legend.* Trans. B. J. Timmer. London: Oxford University Press, 1963.

Der Rig-Veda aus dem Sanskrit ins Deutsche Übersetzt. Ed. Karl Friedrich Geldner, 4 vols. Harvard Oriental Series, 33–36. Cambridge, Mass.: Harvard University Press, 1951–57.

Dhvanyāloka of Ānandavardhana with the *Locana* of Abhinavagupta. Trans. Daniel H. H. Ingalls, Jeffrey Mousaieff Masson, and M. V. Patwardhan, and ed. Daniel H. H. Ingalls. Harvard Oriental Series, 49. Cambridge, Mass.: Harvard University Press, 1990.

Dimmitt, Cornelia and J. A. B. van Buitenen, eds. and trans. *Classical Hindu Mythology: A Reader in the Sanskrit Purāṇas.* Philadelphia: Temple University Press, 1978.

Dimock, Edward C. et al. *The Literatures of India: An Introduction.* Chicago: University of Chicago Press, 1974.

Diringer, David. *The Book Before Printing: Ancient, Medieval, and Oriental.* New York: Dover, 1982.

Dirks, Nicholas B. "Political Authority and Structural Change in Early South Indian History." *The Indian Economic and Social History Review* 13.2 (1976): 125–58.

Dowson, John. *A Classical Dictionary of Hindu Mythology and Religion,*

Geography, History, and Literature. 11th ed. London: Routledge & Kegan Paul, 1968 [1879].

Dumézil, Georges. *The Destiny of a King.* Trans. Alf Hiltebeitel. Chicago: University of Chicago Press, 1973.

Dumont, Louis. "A Structural Definition of a Folk Deity of Tamil Nad: Aiyaṉār, the Lord." *Contributions to Indian Sociology* 3 (1959): 75–87. Reprinted in Dumont, *Religion, Politics, and History in India: Collected Papers in Indian Sociology,* pp. 20–32. The Hague: Mouton, 1970.

Edgerton, Franklin. "Indirect Suggestion in Poetry: A Hindu Theory of Literary Aesthetics." *Proceedings of the American Philosophical Society* 76 (1936): 687–706.

Edholm, Erik Af and Carl Suneson. "The Seven Bulls and Kṛṣṇa's Marriage of Nīlā/NappiNNai in Sanskrit and Tamil Literature." *Temenos: Studies in Comparative Religion* 8 (1972): 29–53.

Eliade, Mircea. *Patterns in Comparative Religion.* New York: New American Library, 1974.

Ellis, Robinson, ed. *Catulli Veronensis Liber.* 2d ed. Oxford: Clarendon Press, 1878.

Elmore, Wilber Theodore. *Dravidian Gods in Modern Hinduism: A Study of the Local and Village Deities of Southern India.* University of Nebraska Dissertations, 4. Lincoln: University of Nebraska Press, 1915.

Finnegan, Ruth. *Oral Poetry: Its Nature, Significance, and Social Context.* Cambridge: Cambridge University Press, 1977.

Foley, John Miles. *The Theory of Oral Composition: History and Methodology.* Bloomington: Indiana University Press, 1988.

Frasca, Richard A. *The Theater of the Mahābhārata: Terukkūttu Performances in South India.* Honolulu: University of Hawaii Press, 1990.

Frere, Mary. "Chandra's Vengeance." In *Old Deccan Days, or Hindoo Fairy Legends Current in Southern India,* pp. 187–202. London: John Murray, 1868.

Fürer-Haimondorf, C. von. "The Historical Value of Indian Bardic Literature." In *Historians of India, Pakistan, and Ceylon,* ed. C. H. Philips, pp. 87–93. London: Oxford University Press, 1961.

Gamble, J. S. *Flora of the Presidency of Madras.* 3 vols. Calcutta: Botanical Survey of India, 1967 [1915–35].

Gerow, Edwin. *A Glossary of Indian Figures of Speech.* The Hague: Mouton, 1971.

Gonda, J. *Ancient Indian Kingship from the Religious Point of View.* Leiden: Brill, 1966.

——. "The Indra Festival According to the Atharvavedins." In *Selected Studies, vol. 4: A History of Ancient Indian Religion,* pp. 206–22. Leiden: Brill, 1975.

Gopinatha Rao, T. A. *Elements of Hindu Iconography.* 2 vols. (4 pts.). 2d ed. New York: Paragon Book Reprint, 1968 [1914].

Govindarajan, Cinnaiah. *A Flash of Light on a Hidden Fact: An Important Place at Neduvel Kundram Mentioned in the Tamil Epic "Silappadikāram."* Thanjavur: Paḻam poruḷ eḻuttu nilayam, 1968.

Graves, Robert. *The Greek Myths.* 2 vols. Rev. ed. Harmondsworth, Middlesex: Penguin, 1960.
Hardy, Friedhelm. *Viraha-bhakti: The Early History of Kṛṣṇa Devotion in South India.* Oxford University South Asian Studies Series. Delhi: Oxford University Press, 1983.
Hardy, Thomas. *The Mayor of Casterbridge.* Ed. James K. Robinson. Norton Critical Editions. New York: Norton, 1977.
Hart, George L. III. *The Poems of Ancient Tamil: Their Milieu and Their Sanskrit Counterparts.* Berkeley: University of California Press, 1975.
——, trans. *Poets of the Tamil Anthologies: Ancient Poems of Love and War.* Princeton Library of Asian Translations. Princeton, N.J.: Princeton University Press, 1979.
——. "Some Aspects of Kinship in Ancient Tamil Literature." In *Kinship and History in South Asia,* ed. Thomas Trautmann, pp. 29–60. Michigan Papers on South and Southeast Asia, 7. Ann Arbor: Center for South and Southeastern Asian Studies, University of Michigan, 1974.
——. "Woman and the Sacred in Ancient Tamil Nad." *Journal of Asian Studies* 32 (1973): 233–50.
Heidegger, Martin. "The Nature of Language." In *On the Way to Language,* trans. Peter D. Hertz, pp. 55–108. San Francisco: Harper & Row, 1971.
Heidel, Alexander. *The Gilgamesh Epic and Old Testament Parallels.* 2d ed. Chicago: University of Chicago Press, 1949.
Hein, Norvin. "A Revolution in Kṛṣṇaism: The Cult of Gōpāla." *History of Religions* 25.4 (1986): 296–317.
Herbert, Zbignew. "Translating Poetry." Trans. Jan Darowski. In *Polish Writing Today,* ed. Celina Wieniewska, pp. 38–39. Harmondsworth, Middlesex: Penguin, 1967.
Hevawasam, P. B. G. *Pantis kōlmurakavi* (The Thirty-five Songbooks). Colombo: Pradīpa prakāṣakayō, 1974.
Hiatt, L. S. "The Pattini Cult of Ceylon: A Tamil Perspective." *Social Compass* 20 (1973): 231–50.
Holmström, Lakshmi. *Kannagi: A Modern Version of "Silappadikaram."* Bombay: Orient Longman, 1980.
Homer. *The Iliad.* Trans. Richmond Lattimore. Chicago: University of Chicago Press, 1951.
Hopkins, E. Washburn. "The Divinity of Kings." *Journal of the American Oriental Society* 51 (1931): 309–16.
——. *The Great Epic of India: Its Character and Origin.* New York: Scribner's, 1901.
——. "On the Hindu Custom of Dying to Redress a Grievance." *Journal of the American Oriental Society* 21 (1900): 146–59.
Hsuan-tsang. *Si-yu-ki: Buddhist Records of the Western World.* Trans. Samuel Beal. 2 vols. in one. New York: Paragon Book Reprint, 1968 [1884].
Hudson, Dennis. "Piṉṉai, Krishna's Cowherd Wife." In *The Divine*

Consort: Rādhā and the Goddesses of India, ed. John Stratton Hawley and Donna Marie Wulff, pp. 238–61. Boston: Beacon Press, 1986.

Ilakkuvaṉār, S. *Tholkāppiyam (In English), with Critical Studies.* Madurai: Kuṟaḷ nēṟi, 1963.

Induchudan, V. T. *The Secret Chamber: A Historical, Anthropological, and Philosophical Study of the Kodungallur Temple.* Trichur: Cochin Devaswom Board, 1969.

Ingalls, Danielg H. H. "General Introduction." In *An Anthology of Sanskrit Court Poetry: Vidyākara's "Subhāṣitaratnakośa,"* pp. 1–53. Harvard Oriental Series, 44. Cambridge, Mass.: Harvard University Press, 1965.

Irāmāvatāram of Kampaṉ. *Araṇyakāṇṭam.* Trans. George L. Hart and Hank Heifetz. *The Forest Book of the Rāmāyaṇa of Kampaṉ.* Berkeley: University of California Press, 1988.

Jaini, Padmanabh S. *The Jaina Path of Purification.* Berkeley: University of California Press, 1979.

——. "Karma and the Problem of Rebirth in Jainism." In *Karma and Rebirth in Classical Indian Traditions,* ed. Wendy D. O'Flaherty, pp. 217–38. Berkeley: University of California Press, 1980.

Jesudasan, C. and H. Jesudasan. *A History of Tamil Literature.* Calcutta: Y.M.C.A. Publishing House, 1961.

Kailasapathy, K. *Tamil Heroic Poetry.* Oxford: Clarendon Press, 1968.

Kane, P. V. *The History of Dharmaśāstra.* 5 vols. 2d ed., rev. and enl. Poona: Bhandarkar Oriental Research Institute, 1968.

Kāvyādarśa of Daṇḍin. Ed., with a commentary, by Rangacharya Raddi Shastri. Government Oriental Series, class A, no. 4. Poona: Bhandarkar Oriental Research Institute, 1938.

Keyes, Charles F. and E. Valentine Daniel, eds. *Karma: An Anthropological Inquiry.* Berkeley: University of California Press, 1984.

Krishnaswamy Aiyangar, Sakkottai. *"Manimekhalai" in Its Historical Setting.* London: Luzac, 1928.

Landor, Walter Savage. "Dying Speech of an Old Philosopher." In *Poems, Dialogues in Verse, and Epigrams,* 2 vols., ed. Charles G. Crump, 2:223. New York: AMS Press, 1983.

Levy, Gertrude Rachel. *The Sword from the Rock: An Investigation into the Origins of Epic Literature and the Development of the Hero.* London: Faber & Faber, 1953.

Lipking, Lawrence. *Abandoned Women and Poetic Tradition.* Women in Culture and Society Series. Chicago: University of Chicago Press, 1988.

Liu, James J. Y. *Chinese Theories of Literature.* Chicago: University of Chicago Press, 1975.

Lopez, Robert S. "The Crossroads Within the Wall." In *The Historian and the City,* ed. Oscar Handlin and John Buchard, pp. 17–43. Cambridge, Mass.: M.I.T. Press/Harvard University Press, 1963.

Lord, Albert B. *The Singer of Tales.* Harvard Studies in Comparative Literature, 24. Cambridge, Mass.: Harvard University Press, 1960.

Lukacs, Georg. "The Epic and the Novel." In *The Theory of the Novel: A Historico-Philosophical Essay on the Forms of Great Epic Literature,* trans. Anna Bostock, pp. 56–69. Cambridge, Mass.: M.I.T. Press, 1920.

Mahābhārata. Ed. Vishnu. S. Sukthankar et al. 19 vols. Poona: Bhandarkar Oriental Research Institute,, 1933–66.

——. *Books 1–5.* 3 vols. Trans. and ed. by J. A. B. van Buitenen. Chicago: University of Chicago Press, 1973–78.

Manickam, V. T. "Harlots in Ancient Tamil Literature." *Proceedings of the First International Conference-Seminar of Tamil Studies* 1 (1968): 340–43.

——. *Marutam: An Aspect of Love in Tamil Literature.* Karaikudi: Tēmā, 1982.

Marlowe, Christopher. *Dr. Faustus.* In *The Complete Works,* vol. 2, ed. Fredson Bowers. Cambridge: Cambridge University Press, 1973.

Marr, John Ralston. "Prosody in the 'Eight Anthologies.' " In *The Eight Anthologies: A Study in Early Tamil Literature,* pp. 390–452. Madras: Institute of Asian Studies, 1985.

McLuhan, Marshall. "Tennyson and Picturesque Poetry." *Essays in Criticism* 1 (July 1951): 262–82.

Milton, John. *A Mask Presented at Ludlow-Castle, 1634.* In *Poetical Works,* vol. 2. Ed. Helen Darbishire. Oxford: Clarendon Press, 1955.

Mohan Thampi, G. B. "Rasa as Aesthetic Experience." *Journal of Aesthetics and Art Criticism* 24.1, pt. 1 (1965): 75–80.

Nabokov, Vladimir. "Problems of Translation: *Onegin* in English." *Partisan Review* 12 (1955): 496–512.

Narayan, R. K. "The Mispaired Anklet." In *Gods, Demons, and Others,* pp. 157–67. Mysore: Indian Thought Publications, 1964.

Nāṭyaśāstra of Bharata. Trans. Manmohan Ghosh. Calcutta: Royal Society of Bengal, 1950–61.

Nilakanta Sastri, K. A. *The Cōḻas.* 2d rev. ed. Madras University Historical Series, 9. Madras: University of Madras, 1955.

——. "Early Tamil Literature as a Source of History." In *The Sangham Age,* n.e., pp. 59–65. Calcutta: Bharathi Tamil Sangham, 1968.

——. *Foreign Notices of South India from Megasthenes to Ma Huan.* Madras: University of Madras, 1972.

——. *A History of South India from Prehistoric Times to the Fall of Vijayanagar.* 4th ed. Madras: Oxford University Press, 1976.

——. *The Pāṇḍyan Kingdom: From the Earliest Times to the Sixteenth Century.* Madras: Swathi, 1929.

Noble, Sally A. "Narrative, Image, and Song in the *Cilappatikāram.*" Master's thesis, University of Chicago, 1981.

——. "The Tamil Story of the Anklet: Classical and Contemporary Tellings of *Cilappatikāram.*" Ph.D. dissertation, University of Chicago, 1990.

Obeyesekere, Gananath. *The Cult of the Goddess Pattini.* Chicago: University of Chicago Press, 1984.

——. "The Goddess Pattini: A Jaina-Buddhist Deity." In *Buddhist Stud-*

ies in Honour of Walpola Rahula, ed. Somaratna Balasooriya et al., pp. 185–200. London: Gordon Fraser, 1980.

——. "The Goddess Pattini and the Lord Buddha: Notes on the Myth of the Birth of the Deity." *Social Compass* 20.2 (1973): 217–29.

O'Flaherty, Wendy D., trans. *Hindu Myths.* Harmondsworth, Middlesex: Penguin, 1975.

——, ed. *Karma and Rebirth in Classical Indian Traditions.* Berkeley: University of California Press, 1980.

——, trans. *The Rig Veda: An Anthology.* Harmondsworth, Middlesex: Penguin, 1981.

Ong, Walter J. *Orality and Literacy: The Technologizing of the Word.* New Accents. London: Methuen, 1982.

——. "Oral Residue in Tudor Prose Style." *Publications of the Modern Language Association* 80 (1965): 145–54. Reprinted in Ong, *Rhetoric, Romance, and Technology,* pp. 23–47. Ithaca, N.Y.: Cornell University Press, 1971.

Ostriker, Alicia Suskin. *Stealing the Language: The Emergence of Women's Poetry in America.* Boston: Beacon Press, 1986.

Ovid. *Metamorphoses.* Trans. Mary M. Innes. Harmondsworth, Middlesex: Penguin, 1955.

Pañcatantra. Ed. F. Kielhorn (Part 1), and G. Bühler (Parts 2–5). Bombay Sanskrit Series 1, 3, 4. Bombay: Nirṇaya Sāgar Press, 1868–69.

——. Trans. Arthur W. Ryder. Chicago: University of Chicago Press, 1925.

Panchapakesa Ayyar, A.S. *Kōvalaṉ and Kaṇṇaki: The Story of the "Cilappatikāram."* Madras: C. Coomaraswamy Naidu, 1947.

Pandian, Jacob. "The Goddess Kannagi: A Dominant Symbol of South Indian Tamil Society." In *Mother Worship: Theme and Variations,* ed. James J. Preston, pp. 177–91. Chapel Hill: University of North Carolina Press, 1982.

Parry, Milman. *The Making of Homeric Verse: The Collected Papers of Milman Parry.* Ed. Adam Parry. Oxford: Clarendon Press, 1971.

Pertold, Otakar. "Die ceylonische Göttin Pattinī." *Archív Orientální* 13.3–4 (1942): 201–24.

Picard, Max. *The World of Silence.* Trans. Stanley Godman. London: Harvill Press, 1952.

Poe, Edgar Allan. "The Philosophy of Composition." In *Edgar Allan Poe: Essays and Reviews,* ed. G. R. Thompson. The Library of America. New York: Literary Classics of the United States, 1984.

Rabin, Chaim. "The Song of Songs and Tamil Poetry." *Studies in Religion/ Sciences religienses* 3 (1973): 205–19.

Raghava Aiyangar, M. "The Mauryan Invasion and the Aramboly Pass." In *Some Aspects of Kerala and Tamil Literature,* trans. J. Parthasarathi, pp. 33–43. Trivandrum: University of Kerala, 1973.

Ramachandra Dikshitar, V. R. *Studies in Tamil Literature and History.* 2d printing. Tirunelveli: Tirunelvēlit teṉṉintiya caivacittānta nūṟpatippuk kaḻakam, 1983.

Ramanathan, S. *Music in "Cilappatikaaram."* Madurai: Madurai-Kamaraj University, 1979.

Ramanujan, A. K. "Form in Classical Tamil Prosody." In *Symposium on Dravidian Civilization,* ed. Andre F. Sjoberg, pp. 73–104. Austin, Tex.: Pemberton Press, 1971.

——, trans. *The Interior Landscape: Love Poems from a Classical Tamil Anthology.* Bloomington: Indiana University Press, 1967.

——, trans. *Poems of Love and War from the Eight Anthologies and the Ten Long Poems of Classical Tamil.* Translations from the Oriental Classics. New York: Columbia University Press/ UNESCO, 1985.

——. "A Tamil Epic: *Cilappatikāram,* 'The Lay of the Anklet.' " In *Lectures in Indian Civilization,* ed. Joseph W. Elder, pp. 104–106. Dubuque, Iowa: Kendall/ Hunt, 1972.

——. "Toward an Anthology of City Images." In *Urban India: Society, Space, and Image,* ed. Richard G. Fox, pp. 224–44. Monograph Series. Durham, N.C.: Duke University Press, 1970.

Ramaswami Ayyangar, M. S. and B. Seshagiri Rao. *Studies in South Indian Jainism.* Vizianagram Maharaja's College Publication 1. Madras: Hoe, 1922.

Rāmāyaṇa of Vālmīki. Ed. G. H. Bhatt et al. 7 vols. Baroda: Oriental Institute, 1960–75.

——. *Vol. 1: Bālakāṇḍa,* trans. Robert P. Goldman. *Vol. 2: Ayodhyākāṇḍa* and *Vol. 3: Araṇyakāṇḍa,* trans. Sheldon Pollock. Princeton Library of Asian Translations. Princeton, N.J.: Princeton University Press, 1984–90.

Renou, Louis. "Sur la structure du *kāvya." Journal asiatique* 247 (1959): 1–113.

Rich, Adrienne. "When We Dead Awaken: Writing as Re-Vision." In *Lies, Secrets, and Silence: Selected Prose, 1966–1978,* pp. 33–49. New York: Norton, 1979.

Richman, Paula. *Women, Branch Stories, and Religious Rhetoric in a Tamil Buddhist Text.* Foreign and Comparative Studies/ South Asian Series, 12. Syracuse, N.Y.: Maxwell School of Citizenship and Public Affairs, Syracuse University, 1988.

Rosenthal, M. L. and Sally M. Gall. *The Modern Poetic Sequence: The Genius of Modern Poetry.* New York: Oxford University Press, 1983.

Ryan, James Darrell. "The *Cīvakacintāmaṇi* in Historical Perspective." Ph.D. dissertation, University of California at Berkeley, 1985.

Sankara Pillai, G. *Tōṟṟam pāṭṭukaḷ* (Songs of Origin). Kottayam: National Book Stall, 1958.

Sanskrit-Wörterbuch. Comp. Otto Böhtlingk and Rudolf Roth. 7 vols. St. Petersburg: Kaiserliche Akademie der Wissenschaften, 1855–75.

Schomer, Karine. "Paradigms for the Kali Yuga: The Heroes of the Ālhā Epic and Their Fate." In *Oral Epics in India,* ed. Stuart H. Blackburn et al., pp. 140–54. Berkeley: University of California Press, 1989.

Schorer, Mark. *William Blake: The Politics of Vision.* New York: Holt, 1946.

Schubert, James W. "Death and Destruction in the Tamil *Śilappadikāram:* What Is Really Behind the Flaming Breast of Madurai?" *Literature East & West* 18, 2–4 (1974): 166–70.

Schurhammer, Georg and G. W. Cottrel. "The First Printing in Indic Characters." *Harvard Library Bulletin* 6.2 (1952): 147–60.

Schwartzberg, Joseph E., ed. *A Historical Atlas of South Asia,* 2d imp. Association for Asian Studies Reference Series, 2. New York: Oxford University Press, 1992.

Sen, Nabaneeta. "Comparative Studies in Oral Epic Poetry and the Vālmīki Rāmāyaṇa: A Report on the *Bālakāṇḍa." Journal of the American Oriental Society* 86.4 (1966): 397–409.

Sesha Aiyar, K. G. *Cēra Kings of the Sangam Period.* London: Luzac, 1937.

Shakespeare, William. "Sonnet 29." In *Shakespeare's Sonnets,* ed. Stephen Booth, pp. 27–28. New Haven: Yale University Press, 1977.

Shulman, David Dean. *The King and the Clown in South Indian Myth and Poetry.* Princeton, N.J.: Princeton University Press, 1985.

Sidhanta, N. K. *The Heroic Age of India: A Comparative Study.* London: Paul, Trench, Trubner, 1929.

Singaravelu, S. *Social Life of the Tamils: The Classical Period.* Kuala Lumpur: Department of Indian Studies, University of Malaya, 1966.

Sivaraja Pillai, K. N. *Chronology of the Early Tamils. Based on the Synchronic Tables of Their Kings, Chieftains, and the Poets Appearing in the Sangam Literature.* Madras: University of Madras, 1932.

Smith, David. "Classical Sanskrit Poetry and the Modern Reader." In *Contributions to South Asian Studies* 2, ed. Gopal Krishna, pp. 1–24. Delhi: Oxford University Press, 1982.

Sreedhara Menon, A. *Social and Cultural History of Kerala.* New Delhi: Sterling, 1979.

——. *A Survey of Kerala History.* Kottayam: Sāhitya Pravarthaka Cooperative Society, 1967.

Sreenivasan, Kasthuri. *The Anklet: A Play in Three Acts.* Bombay: Bharatiya Vidya Bhavan, 1982.

Srinivasa, S. A. *Studies in the Rāma Story.* 2 vols. Seminar für Kultur und Geschichte Indiens an der Universität Hamburg No. 25. Wiesbaden: Franz Steiner, 1984.

Srinivasa Aiyangar, P. T. *History of the Tamils from the Earliest Times to A.D. 600.* Madras: C. Coomaraswamy Naidu, 1929.

Stcherbatsky, Th. "Theory of Poetry in India." Trans. from the Russian by Harish C. Gupta. *Indian Studies Past & Present* 10.4 (169): 289–314.

Stevens, Wallace. "The World as Meditation." In *The Collected Poems of Wallace Stevens,* pp. 520–21. New York: Vintage Books, 1990.

Subrahmanian, N. *Pre-Pallavan Tamil Index.* Madras University Historical Series, 23. Madras: University of Madras, 1966.

——. *Sangam Polity: The Administration and Social Life of the Sangam Tamils.* Rev. ed. Madurai: Ennes, 1980.

Subrahmanyan, S. *The Commonness in the Metre of the Dravidian Languages.* Research Project Publication, 22. Trivandrum: Dravidian Linguistics Association, 1977.

Subramaniam, Ka. Naa. "*Silappadikaaram:* An Epic of the Tamils." *Indian Literature* 20, 2 (1977): 66–77.

Subramanian, S. V. *Descriptive Grammar of Cilappatikaaram.* Trivandrum: University of Kerala, 1965.

Subramoniam, V. I. "*Pañcatantra* and *Śilappatikāram.*" *The Mysore Orientalist* 2.1 (1969): 1–5.

Tamil Lexicon. 6 vols. and *Supplement.* Madras: University of Madras, 1924–39.

Tennyson, Alfred Lord. *The Princess: A Medley.* In *The Poetic and Dramatic Works of Alfred Lord Tennyson,* ed. W. J. Rolfe. The Cambridge Poets Series. Boston: Houghton Mifflin, 1898.

Thiagarajah, M. A. "Cēranāṭu During the Caṅkam and the Post-Caṅkam Period." Ph.D. dissertation, University of London, 1963.

Thomas, A. "Tamil Prosody Through the Ages." Ph.D. dissertation, University of Kerala, 1974.

Thurston, Edgar. *Omens and Superstitions of Southern India.* London: Fisher Unwin, 1912.

Traherne, Thomas. *The Poetical Works of Thomas Traherne.* Ed. Gladys I. Wade. London: P. J. & A. E. Dobell, 1932.

Unger, Merrill F. *Unger's Bible Dictionary.* 3d ed. Chicago: Moody Press, 1966.

Untermeyer, Louis, ed. *Modern British Poetry,* 3d rev. ed. New York: Harcourt, Brace, 1930.

Vaidyanathan, S. Review of *Shilappadikaram: The Ankle Bracelet,* trans. Alain Daniélou. *Journal of the American Oriental Society* 87 (1967): 205–8.

Vaiyapuri Pillai, S. *History of Tamil Language and Literature: Beginning to A.D. 1000.* Madras: New Century Book House, 1956.

Vākyapadīya of Bhartṛhari, with the *vṛtti* and the *paddhati* of Vṛṣabhadeva, *kāṇḍa* 1. Ed. K. A. Subramania Iyer. Deccan College Monograph Series, no. 32. Poona: Deccan College Postgraduate and Research Institute, 1966.

Vanamamalai, N. "The Folk Motif in *Silappadikaram.*" In *Studies in Tamil Folk Literature,* pp. 1–48. Madras: New Century Book House, 1969.

——. "Hero Stones and Folk Beliefs." *Journal of Tamil Studies* 2 (1972): 37–44.

van Gennep, Arnold. *The Rites of Passage.* Trans. Monika B. Vizedom and Gabrielle L. Caffee. Chicago: University of Chicago Press, 1960 [1908].

Varadarajan, M. *A History of Tamil Literature.* Trans. E. Sa. Viswanathan. New Delhi: Sahitya Akademi, 1988.

——. *Ilango Adigal.* Makers of Indian Literature Series. New Delhi: Sahitya Akademi, 1967.

——. *The Treatment of Nature in Sangam Literature.* 2d ed. Tirunelveli: Tirunelvēlit teṉṉintiya caivacittānta nūṟpatippuk kaḻakam, 1969.

Vijayalakshmy, R. *A Study of "Cīvakacintāmaṇi."* Lalbhai Dalpatbhai Series 82. Ahmedabad: L. D. Institute of Indology, 1981.

Vinson, Julien. *Légendes bouddhistes et djainas: traduites du tamoul.* 2 vols. Paris: G. P. Maisonneuve & Larose, 1900.

Visvanatha Pillai, V. *A Tamil-English Dictionary.* 8th ed. Madras: Madras School Book and Literature Society, 1972.

Vithiananthan, S. "The *Pattuppāṭṭu:* A Historical, Social, and Linguistic Study." Ph.D. dissertation, University of London, 1956.

Vyākaraṇa-mahābhāṣya of Patañjali. 3 vols. Ed. F. Kielhorn and rev. K. V. Abhyankar. 3d ed. Poona: Bhandarkar Oriental Research Institute, 1962–72.

Wade, Gladys I., ed. *The Poetical Works of Thomas Traherne.* London: Dobell, 1932.

Wadley, Susan S., ed. *The Powers of Tamil Women.* Foreign and Comparative Studies Publications, South Asian Series, 6. Syracuse, N.Y.: Maxwell School of Citizenship and Public Affairs, Syracuse University, 1980.

Waley, Arthur. "Notes on Translation." *The Atlantic Monthly* 202.5 (1958): 107–12.

Walker, Benjamin. *The Hindu World: An Encyclopedic Survey of Hinduism.* 2 vols. New York: Praeger, 1968.

Warder, A. K. *Indian Kāvya Literature.* 3 vols. Delhi: Motilal Banarsidass, 1972–77.

Weideger, Paula. *History's Mistress.* Harmondsworth, Middlesex: Penguin, 1985.

Weil, Simone. "The *Iliad,* Poem of Might." In *Intimations of Christianity Among the Ancient Greeks,* pp. 241–61. London: Routledge & Kegan Paul, 1957.

Whitehead, Henry. *The Village Gods of South India.* Calcutta: Association Press, 1921.

Whitman, Walt. "When Lilacs Last in the Dooryard Bloom'd." In *Walt Whitman: Complete Poetry and Collected Prose,* ed. Justin Kaplan, pp. 459–67. The Library of America. New York: Literary Classics of the United States, 1982.

Winternitz, Moritz. *A History of Indian Literature.* 3 vols. Vol. 1 trans. S. Ketkar. Vol. 2 trans. S. Ketkar and H. Kohn. Vol. 3, fasc. 1 trans. H. Kohn. Calcutta: University of Calcutta, 1927–49. Vol. 3, pts 1 and 2 trans. Subhadra Jha. Delhi: Motilal Banarsidass, 1963–67.

——. *Some Problems of Indian Literature.* Delhi: Bharatiya Book Corporation, 1977 [1924].

Witt, Ronald. "Toward a Biography of Coluccio Salutati." *Rinascimento* 16 (1976): 19–34.

Wood, Clement. *Poet's Handbook.* Garden City, N.Y.: Garden City, 1942.

Yu, Anthony C., ed. *Parnassus Revisited: Modern Critical Essays on the Epic Tradition.* Chicago: American Library Association, 1973.

Zimmer, Heinrich. *Myths and Symbols in Indian Art and Civilization.* Ed. Joseph Campbell. Bollingen Series, 6. Princeton, N.J.: Princeton University Press, 1946.

Zumthor, Paul. *Oral Poetry: An Introduction.* Trans. Kathryn Murphy-Judy. Theory and History of Literature, 70. Minneapolis: University of Minnesota Press, 1990.

Zvelebil, Kamil V. *Classical Tamil Prosody: An Introduction.* Madras: New Era, 1989.

——. "The Lay of the Anklet." *Mahfil: A Quarterly of South Asian Literature* 4.3 and 4 (1968): 5–12.

——. "The Nature of Sacred Power in Old Tamil Texts." *Acta Orientalia* 40 (1979): 157–92.

——. *The Smile of Murugan: On Tamil Literature of South India.* Leiden: Brill, 1973.

——. *Tamil Literature.* Band 2, Abschnitt 1 of *Handbuch der Orientalistik,* Zweite Abteilung, *Indien.* Ed. Jan Gonda. Leiden: Brill, 1975.

——. *Tamil Literature.* Vol. 10, fasc. 1 of *A History of Indian Literature.* Ed. Jan Gonda. 10 vols. Wiesbaden: Harrassowitz, 1974.

Index

Other Works in the Columbia Asian Studies Series

TRANSLATIONS FROM THE ASIAN CLASSICS

Major Plays of Chikamatsu, tr. Donald Keene 1961

Four Major Plays of Chikamatsu, tr. Donald Keene. Paperback ed. only. 1961

Records of the Grand Historian of China, translated from the Shih chi of Ssu-ma Ch'ien, tr. Burton Watson, 2 vols. 1961

Instructions for Practical Living and Other Neo-Confucian Writings by Wang Yang-ming, tr. Wing-tsit Chan 1963

Chuang Tzu: Basic Writings, tr. Burton Watson, paperback ed. only 1964

The Mahābhārata, tr. Chakravarthi V. Narasimhan. Also in paperback ed. 1965

The Manyōshū, Nippon Gakujutsu Shinkōkai edition 1965

Su Tung-p'o: Selections from a Sung Dynasty Poet, tr. Burton Watson. Also in paperback ed. 1965

Bhartrihari: Poems, tr. Barbara Stoler Miller. Also in paperback ed. 1967

Basic Writings of Mo Tzu, Hsün Tzu, and Han Fei Tzu, tr. Burton Watson. Also in separate paperback eds. 1967

The Awakening of Faith, Attributed to Aśvaghosha, tr. Yoshito S. Hakeda. Also in paperback ed. 1967

Reflections on Things at Hand: The Neo-Confucian Anthology, comp. Chu Hsi and Lü Tsu-ch'ien, tr. Wing-tsit Chan 1967

The Platform Sutra of the Sixth Patriarch, tr. Philip B. Yampolsky. Also in paperback ed. 1967

Essays in Idleness: The Tsurezuregusa of Kenkō, tr. Donald Keene. Also in paperback ed. 1967
Two Plays of Ancient India: The Little Clay Cart and the Minister's Seal, tr. J. A. B. van Buitenen 1968
The Complete Works of Chuang Tzu, tr. Burton Watson 1968
The Romance of the Western Chamber (*Hsi Hsiang chi*), tr. S. I. Hsiung. Also in paperback ed. 1968
The Manyōshū, Nippon Gakujutsu Shinkōkai edition. Paperback ed. only. 1969
Records of the Historian: Chapters from the Shih chi of Ssu-ma Ch'ien, tr. Burton Watson. Paperback ed. only. 1969
Cold Mountain: 100 Poems by the T'ang Poet Han-shan, tr. Burton Watson. Also in paperback ed. 1970
Twenty Plays of the Nō Theatre, ed. Donald Keene. Also in paperback ed. 1970
Chūshingura: The Treasury of Loyal Retainers, tr. Donald Keene. Also in paperback ed. 1971
The Zen Master Hakuin: Selected Writings, tr. Philip B. Yampolsky 1971
Chinese Rhyme-Prose: Poems in the Fu Form from the Han and Six Dynasties Periods, tr. Burton Watson. Also in paperback ed. 1971
Kūkai: Major Works, tr. Yoshito S. Hakeda. Also in paperback ed. 1972
The Old Man Who Does as He Pleases: Selections from the Poetry and Prose of Lu Yu, tr. Burton Watson 1973
The Lion's Roar of Queen Srīmālā, tr. Alex and Hideko Wayman 1974
Courtier and Commoner in Ancient China: Selections from the History of the Former Han by Pan Ku, tr. Burton Watson. Also in paperback ed. 1974
Japanese Literature in Chinese, vol. 1: *Poetry and Prose in Chinese by Japanese Writers of the Early Period,* tr. Burton Watson 1975
Japanese Literature in Chinese, vol. 2: *Poetry and Prose in Chinese by Japanese Writers of the Later Period,* tr. Burton Watson 1976
Scripture of the Lotus Blossom of the Fine Dharma, tr. Leon Hurvitz. Also in paperback ed. 1976
Love Song of the Dark Lord: Jayadeva's Gītagovinda, tr. Barbara Stoler Miller. Also in paperback ed. Cloth ed. includes critical text of the Sanskrit. 1977
Ryōkan: Zen Monk-Poet of Japan, tr. Burton Watson 1977
Calming the Mind and Discerning the Real: From the Lam rim chen mo of Tsoṅ-kha-pa, tr. Alex Wayman 1978
The Hermit and the Love-Thief: Sanskrit Poems of Bhartrihari and Bilhaṇa, tr. Barbara Stoler Miller 1978
The Lute: Kao Ming's P'i-p'a chi, tr. Jean Mulligan. Also in paperback ed. 1980
A Chronicle of Gods and Sovereigns: Jinnō Shōtōki of Kitabatake Chikafusa, tr. H. Paul Varley. 1980

Among the Flowers: The Hua-chien chi, tr. Lois Fusek 1982

Grass Hill: Poems and Prose by the Japanese Monk Gensei, tr. Burton Watson 1983

Doctors, Diviners, and Magicians of Ancient China: Biographies of Fang-shih, tr. Kenneth J. DeWoskin. Also in paperback ed. 1983

Theater of Memory: The Plays of Kālidāsa, ed. Barbara Stoler Miller. Also in paperback ed. 1984

The Columbia Book of Chinese Poetry: From Early Times to the Thirteenth Century, ed. and tr. Burton Watson. Also in paperback ed. 1984

Poems of Love and War: From the Eight Anthologies and the Ten Long Poems of Classical Tamil, tr. A. K. Ramanujan. Also in paperback ed. 1985

The Columbia Book of Later Chinese Poetry, ed. and tr. Jonathan Chaves. Also in paperback ed. 1986

The Tso Chuan: Selections from China's Oldest Narrative History, tr. Burton Watson 1989

Selected Writings of Nichiren, ed. Philip B. Yampolsky 1990

Saigyō, Poems of a Mountain Home, tr. Burton Watson 1990

STUDIES IN ASIAN CULTURE

1. *The Ōnin War: History of Its Origins and Background, with a Selective Translation of the Chronicle of Ōnin,* by H. Paul Varley 1967
2. *Chinese Government in Ming Times: Seven Studies,* ed. Charles O. Hucker 1969
3. *The Actors' Analects (Yakusha Rongo),* ed. and tr. by Charles J. Dunn and Bungō Torigoe 1969
4. *Self and Society in Ming Thought,* by Wm. Theodore de Bary and the Conference on Ming Thought. Also in paperback ed. 1970
5. *A History of Islamic Philosophy,* by Majid Fakhry, 2d ed. 1983
6. *Phantasies of a Love Thief: The Caurapañcāśikā Attributed to Bilhaṇa,* by Barbara Stoler Miller 1971
7. *Iqbal: Poet-Philosopher of Pakistan,* ed. Hafeez Malik 1971
8. *The Golden Tradition: An Anthology of Urdu Poetry,* ed. and tr. Ahmed Ali. Also in paperback ed. 1973
9. *Conquerors and Confucians: Aspects of Political Change in Late Yüan China,* by John W. Dardess 1973
10. *The Unfolding of Neo-Confucianism,* by Wm. Theodore de Bary and the Conference on Seventeenth-Century Chinese Thought. Also in paperback ed. 1975
11. *To Acquire Wisdom: The Way of Wang Yang-ming,* by Julia Ching 1976
12. *Gods, Priests, and Warriors: The Bhṛgus of the Mahābhārata,* by Robert P. Goldman 1977

COMPANIONS TO ASIAN STUDIES

INTRODUCTION TO ASIAN CIVILIZATIONS
Wm. Theodore de Bary, Editor

Sources of Japanese Tradition, 1958; paperback ed., 2 vols., 1964
Sources of Indian Tradition, 1958; paperback ed., 2 vols., 1964; 2d ed., 2 vols., 1988
Sources of Chinese Tradition, 1960; paperback ed., 2 vols., 1964

NEO-CONFUCIAN STUDIES

Instructions for Practical Living and Other Neo-Confucian Writings by Wang Yang-ming, tr. Wing-tsit Chan 1963
Reflections on Things at Hand: The Neo-Confucian Anthology, comp. Chu Hsi and Lü Tsu-ch'ien, tr. Wing-tsit Chan 1967
Self and Society in Ming Thought, by Wm. Theodore de Bary and the Conference on Ming Thought. Also in paperback ed. 1970
The Unfolding of Neo-Confucianism, by Wm. Theodore de Bary and the Conference on Seventeenth-Century Chinese Thought. Also in paperback ed. 1975
Principle and Practicality: Essays in Neo-Confucianism and Practical Learning, ed. Wm. Theodore de Bary and Irene Bloom. Also in paperback ed. 1979
The Syncretic Religion of Lin Chao-en, by Judith A. Berling 1980
The Renewal of Buddhism in China: Chu-hung and the Late Ming Synthesis, by Chün-fang Yü 1981
Neo-Confucian Orthodoxy and the Learning of the Mind-and-Heart, by Wm. Theodore de Bary 1981
Yüan Thought: Chinese Thought and Religion Under the Mongols, ed. Hok-lam Chan and Wm. Theodore de Bary 1982
The Liberal Tradition in China, by Wm. Theodore de Bary 1983
The Development and Decline of Chinese Cosmology, by John B. Henderson 1984
The Rise of Neo-Confucianism in Korea, by Wm. Theodore de Bary and JaHyun Kim Haboush 1985
Chiao Hung and the Restructuring of Neo-Confucianism in Late Ming, by Edward T. Ch'ien 1985
Neo-Confucian Terms Explained: Pei-hsi tzu-i, by Ch'en Ch'un, ed. and trans. Wing-tsit Chan 1986
Knowledge Painfully Acquired: K'un-chih chi, by Lo Ch'in-shun, ed. and trans. Irene Bloom 1987
To Become a Sage: The Ten Diagrams on Sage Learning, by Yi T'oegye, ed. and trans. Michael C. Kalton 1988
The Message of the Mind in Neo-Confucian Thought, by Wm. Theodore de Bary 1989

MODERN ASIAN LITERATURE SERIES

Modern Japanese Drama: An Anthology, ed. and tr. Ted Takaya. Also in paperback ed. 1979

Mask and Sword: Two Plays for the Contemporary Japanese Theater, by Yamazaki Masakazu, tr. J. Thomas Rimer 1980

Yokomitsu Riichi, Modernist, Dennis Keene 1980

Nepali Visions, Nepali Dreams: The Poetry of Laxmiprasad Devkota, tr. David Rubin 1980

Literature of the Hundred Flowers, vol. 1: *Criticism and Polemics,* ed. Hualing Nieh 1981

Literature of the Hundred Flowers, vol. 2: *Poetry and Fiction,* ed. Hualing Nieh 1981

Modern Chinese Stories and Novellas, 1919–1949, ed. Joseph S. M. Lau, C. T. Hsia, and Leo Ou-fan Lee. Also in paperback ed. 1984

A View of the Sea, by Yasuoka Shōtarō, tr. Kären Wigen Lewis 1984

Other Worlds; Arishima Takeo and the Bounds of Modern Japanese Fiction, by Paul Anderer 1984

Selected Poems of Sō Chōngju, tr. with intro. by David R. McCann 1989

The Sting of Life: Four Contemporary Japanese Novelists, by Van C. Gessel 1989

Stories of Osaka Life, by Oda Sakunosuke, tr. Burton Watson 1990

The Bodhisattva, or Samantabhadra, by Ishikawa Jun, tr. with intro. by William Jefferson Tyler 1990